Regiment, 96th D[ivision]. [...] ment, 7th Divisi[on...] Infantry, 77th D[ivision...] Division. ★ **M[c...]** *Bache.* ★ **McL[...]** Marine Division[...] Company, 6th Marine Division. [...] [...] am Leader, Company K, 5th Mari[ne...] **Miller, Earl.** Machine Gunner, C[o...] ★ **Minamoto, Yoshiro.** Comma[nder...] Squadron, Japanese Imperial Ar[my...] 7th Marine Regiment, 1st Marin[e...] cations Specialist, 1st Battalion He[adquarters...] ★ **Moroz, Mike.** Squad [...] egiment, 96th Division. ★ **M[...]** 383rd Regiment, 96th Division. [...] t Tank Battalion, USMC. ★ **Ow[ens, Charles.]** [...] ne Regiment, 1st Marine Division. [...] **Parsons, Lloyd.** Pilot, Marine [F]ighter Squadron, UMF (N) 542. [...] **Powers, James.** Communications Specialist, Marine 8th Defense & Anti[aircraft Artillery Battalion.] ★ **Prather, Eugene.** Commanding Officer [Headquarters Compan]y, and Adjutant, [1]st Battalion, 32nd Regiment, 7th I[nfantry Division] ★ **Reeves, Maurice.** 1st Sgt. Co. C, 13th Combat En[gineer Battalion, 7th Division.] ★ **R[...]ogle, Art.** Supply Officer, *USS Luc[...]* **Rice, Earl.** Rifleman, Co. A. 7th Marine Regiment, 1st Marine Divisi[on.] ★ **R[...], B[...].** Radio Operator, 594th Joint Signal Assault Co. 27th Division. ★ **Roddy, Joe.** Deck Officer, *USS Cephus*, U.S. Coast Guard. ★ **Rodman, Gage.** Platoon Leader, Co G. 17th Infantry Regiment, 7th Division. ★ **Rose, Albert.** Radio Technician, Marine Night Fighter Squadron 533. ★ **Schichler, Ernest.** Communications Specialist, 77th Signal Company, 77th Division. ★ **Schweitzer, Leonard.** Rifleman, Company K, 306th Regiment, 77th Division. ★ **Seibert, Donald (Si).** Platoon Leader, Co. F, 382nd Regiment, 96th Division. ★ **Sexton, Martin.** Company Commander, Co. K, 4th Marine Regiment, 6th Marine Division. ★ **Siegel, William.** Executive Officer, 706th Tank Battalion. ★ **Smith, Ed.** Deputy Commander, 17th Regiment, 7th Division. ★ **Spencer, Richard.** Plans and Operations Officer, 1st Battalion, 307th Regiment, 77th Division. ★ **Staley, Ken.** Rifleman, Co. K, 383rd Regiment, 96th Division. ★ **Sturgis, Alanson, Jr.** Forward Observer, 292nd Joint Assault Signal Company, 77th Division. ★ **Thom, Charles R. (Dick).** Plans and Operations Officer, 381st Regiment, 96th Division. ★ **Van Arsdall, C.J.** Commanding Officer, *U.S.S. Anthony.* ★ **Walker, Anthony.** Commanding Officer, Reconnaissance Company, 6th Marine Division. ★ **Westman, Paul.** Rifleman, Co. K, 382nd Regiment, 96th Division.

OPERATION ICEBERG

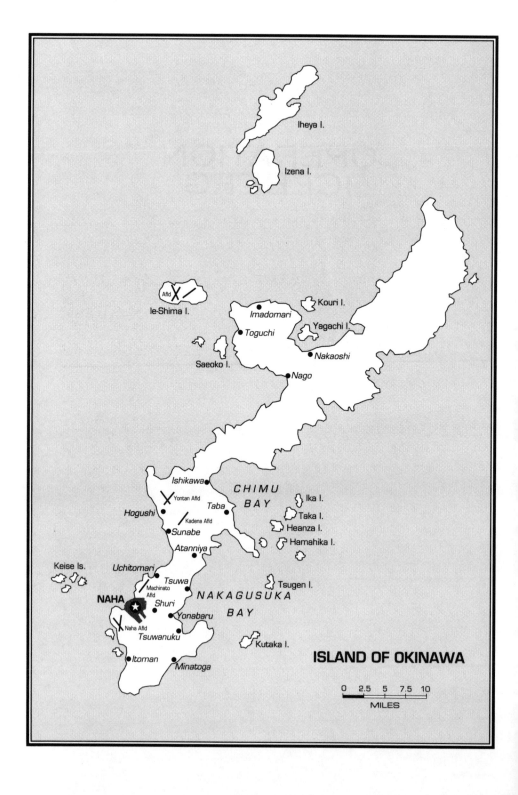

Iheya I.

Izena I.

Afld

Ie-Shima I.

Kouri I.

Imadomari

Yagachi I.

Toguchi

Nakaoshi

Saeoko I.

Nago

Ishikawa

CHIMU BAY

Ika I.

Yontan Afld

Taba

Taka I.

Hogushi

Heanza I.

Kadena Afld

Hamahika I.

Sunabe

Atanniya

Uchitomari

Keise Is.

Tsuwa

Tsugen I.

Machinato Afld

NAKAGUSUKA

NAHA

Shuri

BAY

Naha Afld

Yonabaru

Tsuwanuku

Kutaka I.

Itoman

Minatoga

ISLAND OF OKINAWA

0   2.5   5   7.5   10

MILES

OPERATION ICEBERG

THE INVASION AND CONQUEST OF OKINAWA IN WORLD WAR II

GERALD ASTOR

DONALD I. FINE, INC.

New York

Copyright © 1995 by Gerald Astor

Library of Congress Catalogue Card Number: 94-68093
ISBN: 1-55611-425-7

Manufactured in the United States of America

10 9 8 7 6 5 4 3 2 1

Designed by Irving Perkins Associates, Inc.

Excerpts from Ernie Pyle from Last Chapter *by Ernie Pyle.*
Copyright © 1945 by Scripps Howard Newspaper Alliance.
Copyright © 1946 and © 1974 by Henry Holt and Co., Inc.
Reprinted by permission of Henry Holt and Co., Inc.

To those who were there and stood their ground for their comrades, their country and their faith.

For Sonia, who has stood for me and honored me as my wife.

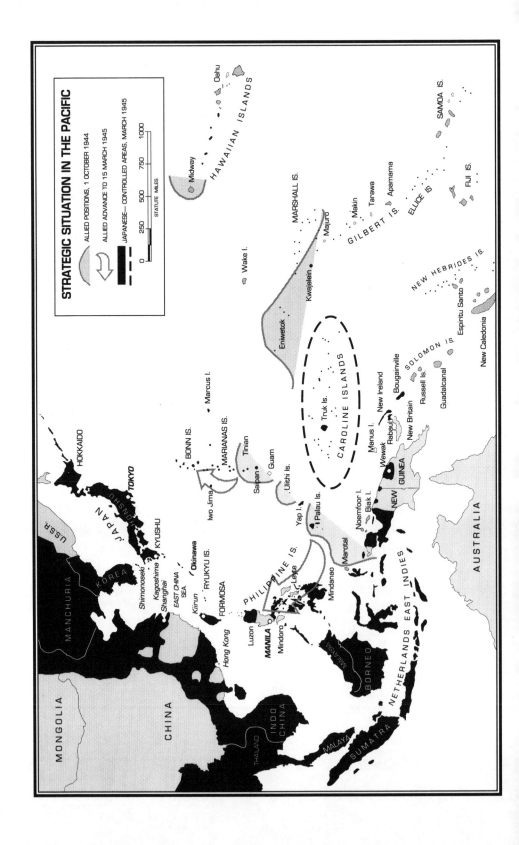

STRATEGIC SITUATION IN THE PACIFIC

ALLIED POSITIONS, 1 OCTOBER 1944

ALLIED ADVANCE TO 15 MARCH 1945

JAPANESE— CONTROLLED AREAS, MARCH 1945

STATUTE MILES

0   250   500   750   1000

CONTENTS

ACKNOWLEDGMENTS

I am indebted first and foremost to all of the individuals listed under Roll Call for their generosity in lending me their private papers, photographs and, most of all, sitting for interviews.

Valuable assistance was rendered by the Archives Branch of the U.S. Military History Institute, Carlisle Barracks, Pennsylvania, under the direction of Dr. Richard J. Sommers and his associate, Dr. David Keough. The U.S. Naval Academy Alumni Association furnished me with names and addresses of several participants. The Naval Institute at Annapolis gave me access to its oral history collection, and through its magazine *Proceedings* I was able to find a number of individuals.

Leatherneck Magazine printed my notice asking for Marine veterans to contact me. The *Liberty Light* publication of the 77th Infantry Division carried a notice of my interest.

The Marine Corps Historical Center in Washington, D.C., and particularly Amy Cantin of the Personal Papers Division, was most helpful. The Naval Historical Center in Washington, D.C., also gave me valuable materials.

Dr. Hisashi Takahashi helped me contact Japanese survivors. Accent on Language, in New York City, translated interviews and documents from the Japanese.

Col. Tom Cross, USA ret. and Col. Walter Moore, USMC ret. located sources for me. George Nelson provided me with research that he had collected. Stub Haggas of USMC Fighter Squadron 542 supplied me with voluminous papers on that outfit's experiences. Gordon "Pete" Boyd, in addition to his own memoirs, armed me with a library of documents and books on destroyers at Okinawa.

The 1st Marine Division Association, Maurice Reeves of the 7th Infantry Division Association, Stephen Behil of the 27th Division Association, Angelo Carbone of the 77th Division Association and Iden Johnson of the 96th Division Association all generously aided me with names and addresses.

My friend Alan Shapiro acted as a sounding board for some of my thoughts and gave me materials relevant to the debate about the use of the atomic bombs.

Finally, I appreciate the faith that Don Fine, my publisher, has shown over the years.

PREFACE

Social scientists, including historians, tend to dismiss anecdotal and personal accounts because by their very nature they may be nothing more than individual experiences rather than expressions of an overall truth. They have good reason to be wary. For years writers working the news and feature beats have sought to dramatize a point of view through what happened to a homemaker, businessman, lawyer, doctor or whomever they could tag as typical. Academicians drawing upon these sources must recognize the perils of deadlines, competitive journalism and books aimed to exploit the interest of the current moment.

On the other hand, restricting the description of what those at orientation sessions for soldiers used to call "the big picture" also depends upon subjective decisions—which official papers, speeches and verified documents does one use? The authors of these have their own biases, agendas and limitations to what is available. In any case, absent for the most part is humanity, and when describing the life and death struggles of war, leaving out that element is just not acceptable. Who were these people who fought, bled and died on a far-off island unknown to most Americans even as it was invaded? What manner of person opposed them? From where did he rise and what fueled his willingness to do battle? How did men feel about themselves, their behavior and that of their comrades in arms? What were their perceptions of one another and of their enemies? What do they think the struggle meant?

For these reasons I've based my four books, including *Operation Iceberg*, largely, but not exclusively, on what those who were there said, wrote and remembered. I don't for a moment claim that mine is the definitive work on an event; anyone who does strikes me as highly suspect. Nor do I claim that my sources are free of error, selfless or able to see beyond their own vantage points.

But I have sought to work with a reasonably large number in order to avoid the curse of the tree being mistaken for the forest. That may result at times in a sense of repetition, but the fact that an experience was replicated many times over tends to lend authenticity to the experience. Some survivors have a near-incredible recall, perhaps bolstered by their transcription of their memories shortly after the events. Others are laconic or hazy on specifics. Some are eloquent; some are cliché-driven.

A big cast, close to a hundred voices, does make it difficult to keep track of individuals. But that is the nature of modern warfare with great aggregations of combatants. Even so, no matter how many are included in an account, some units, some achievements must be omitted for lack of space. To those who may feel snubbed, my apologies but no slight was intended.

The size of the Okinawa story and the number of people defy telling in a straight linear progression. There was a first day, April 1, 1945, but after that Operation Iceberg settled into the confusion of chaos, its beginning lost and its present in a bloody swirl. It is a tale better suited to the image of a mosaic.

It is also a chronicle of the ghastly. A writer friend once questioned me about my use of detail in a book I wrote about the abominations committed by Dr. Josef Mengele. He suggested it might be better to refrain from the explicit and allow a reader's imagination to supply the stuff of horror. He has a point, but imagination can also be used to deny and stifle the unpleasant. I plead that only by spelling out what war does to minds and bodies can we hope to disabuse the armchair warriors and bellicose politicians of the "surgically clean" war they so fondly embrace as an instrument of policy. There have been times when we have found it necessary to take up arms, and perhaps occasions will rise again. But war is ugly, hideous, and those who resort to it should be aware of what they do even in the cause of virtue. I hope this book adds to that understanding.

CHAPTER I

OPERATION ICEBERG

It had been a winter of some discontent for the United States military leaders. The swift advance across France following the D-Day invasion of Normandy on June 6, 1944, had halted at the German border early in December. Then a last spasm blitz of the Third Reich's armies in the cold, snowy forest of the Ardennes had punched a deep salient into the American lines. Not until six weeks later could that bulge be erased at a cost of some 85,000 GIs.

Still, spring brought better weather and the Nazi armies were in ever-quickening retreat. With the collapse of Germany, the Allied forces dealing with World War II's second priority, Japan, could look for an infusion of hundreds of thousands of fighting men with all the fire-power they could muster.

Winter had not been kind in the Pacific either. The Marine assault on a seven-square-mile pile of volcanic ash and rock known as Iwo Jima felled almost 28,000 U.S. Marines before the flag run up on Mount Suribachi flew with impunity. But now there was a base to which long-range bombers could find refuge on their way back from pounding the ultimate target, the home islands of Imperial Japan.

Costly as the tiny chunk of real estate had been for the U.S. Marines, the empire of Japan, that had once stretched to within a few hundred miles of Australia and penetrated deep into China and Southwest Asia, had now shrunk back to its original size. Within a few months of Pearl Harbor, all of the islands south of Japan down to the rim of Australia—

from the Philippines to the Solomon Islands and portions of New Guinea—had fallen to the Imperial Army, backed by a puissant navy and effective air force. The troops of Nippon extended their grasp as far east as the Gilbert and Marshall Islands, threatening Midway, the last U.S. outpost before Hawaii. And even Alaska felt itself in jeopardy as the Japanese installed forces on two of the Aleutian Islands, Attu and Kiska.

But in the years that followed, the Allies mounted a series of painstaking operations that slowly, and at a costly price to both sides, ousted the Japanese from their gains. The strategy, frequently described as "brilliant" by historians was in fact the only course open. Success required the shortest and best protected supply lines. Anyone studying a map could see no alternatives existed, although the tactics employed against each particular site sometimes generated controversy.

The campaign had begun in 1942 as U.S. Marines and the Army units landed on Guadalcanal, part of the Solomon chain. Eventually they forced the Japanese to abandon their plans to seize that jungle-clad territory. From there the Americans pushed through the Gilberts, Marshalls, Marianas and ultimately retook the Philippines. A series of bruising slugfests at sea, most notably in the Midway and the Gulf of Leyte encounters, ravished the Imperial Navy. After the bloody struggle for Saipan and the equally savage win on Iwo, B-29 bombers now struck at the heart of Japan, with a strategy of destroying the ability to produce war materials and the will of the civilians and armed forces to continue the struggle.

West of Iwo Jima and south of Japan a series of flyspecks appear on the map. These are the Ryukyu Islands, about 140 small patches, all that remain from some ancient mountains and volcanoes that thrust themselves through the East China Sea eons ago. Known as the "Loochoo" or "Lew Chew" in Chinese and Japanese dialects, they were in 1945 unremarkable, undeveloped, agrarian islands marked by steep rocky ridges, a northern wilderness and few roads.

Unprepossessing as they may have been, one of the Ryukyus glittered like a pearl in the eyes of the American commanders. The Great Loochoo, Okinawa, by far the biggest of the Ryukyus, lay only 350 miles from Kyushu, southernmost home island, while Iwo was perhaps 1,200 miles away.

During the winter and with the nearing of spring, the Japanese had shown no willingness to bow to unconditional surrender, the avowed policy of the West. Victory depended on an actual invasion of Japan. Okinawa was close enough and large enough to become the warehouse for the assault. Furthermore, the 485 square miles of Okinawa (about sixty miles long and from two to eighteen wide) contained sizable flat areas perfect for big air bases to pound the enemy defenses before and during an invasion. Protected anchorages in the Ryukyus would provide safe harbors for the fleet of ships required to maintain the invasion forces. Planners spoke of Okinawa as the equivalent of England for the Normandy invasion.

The strategists briefly considered using the island of Formosa (Taiwan in today's lexicon) as the staging area for an assault upon Japan. But it was farther away from Japan than Okinawa. It also was heavily garrisoned and U.S. strategists estimated they would need nine combat divisions to overcome the defenders. That much manpower, with its ammunition and supplies, was not available. Okinawa, by an early estimate defended by fewer than 50,000, seemed more manageable.

Planning for the assault on Okinawa started in the fall of 1944. The American Pacific Theater commanders, in consultation with the British, who would play a minor supporting role with naval forces, agreed to invade on April 1, 1945, under the code name, Operation Iceberg. Within six weeks of that date, Adolf Hitler would be dead in his bunker and those who assumed leadership in Germany would submit the Fatherland to the humiliation of unconditional surrender. Little more than four months later, after the devastating blows of the first two atomic bombs, Imperial Japan would accept the same terms in defeat.

On the clock of human history, the time from that April first, and Easter Sunday, until the guns of the world temporarily fell silent is a matter of seconds. But for tens of thousands of young men—soldiers, marines, sailors, airmen—as well as civilians of all ages, it became their eternity.

The decision makers dubbed April 1, 1945, "Love Day" as the opening salvo of Operation Iceberg. It was not only Easter Sunday but also April Fools' Day. The cruelest joke would be the ease with which it began. The code name of Iceberg is another irony, for the campaign resembled the topography of a seagoing glacial mass. While the visible Okinawan real estate seemed fairly benign, the island housed a deadly aspect hundreds of feet beneath its surface.

The bitterest deception of that Easter Sunday, one which nominally celebrates the resurrection of Jesus Christ and all that is implied in the salvation of humankind, is that it began a descent into all of the horrors that war inflicts upon the living. For three and a half years World War II had now ravaged body and mind. Okinawa presented the end stages of this hideous disease.

By the time of Okinawa, both sides, fed a steady diet of real and invented images of atrocities, armed with newer and ever more lethal weaponry, their normal human frailties exacerbated by miserable living conditions, calloused and angered by too much time spent on the front line edge of death and destruction, waged a war without mercy, leavened occasionally by flashes of valor and even nobility. Much of what would happen during Operation Iceberg presaged the kind of war that would be fought a generation later in Vietnam, Cambodia and Laos.

The final terrible consequences of Okinawa might also include the dead and maimed from the nuclear explosions at Hiroshima and Nagasaki. The savagery of the fighting, the determined resistance of the defenders, undoubtedly helped tip the decision to use the ultimate weapons of mass destruction.

CHAPTER II

THE SITE AND
THE SIGHTS

The total land surface of the Ryukyus amounts to only 1,850 square miles, less than the smallest U.S. state, Delaware. Only thirty of the islands housed more than a handful of people. Okinawa as the main site for Operation Iceberg, "The Great Loochoo" in local parlance, covers a quarter of the entire land mass and lies in the middle of the chain. Its closest companions were a clump of much smaller islands known as the Kerama Retto and off its northwestern coast one of sufficient size for a large airfield, Ie Shima.

As a battlefield and a base, Okinawa had its drawbacks. The subtropical climate generated heavy rainfalls, monsoon surges and ferocious typhoons that would lash the islands between May and November. In 1945 the road network was limited and not designed for motorized traffic. Downpours in the rainy season created near impassable quagmires.

Heavily forested with bamboo, banyan, pandanus (a kind of pine), but not junglelike, the land supported pigs, goats, a small number of cattle and horses, a multitude of ravenous insects and a particularly venomous viper known as the habu. Orientation lectures to troops headed for Okinawa warned about the deadly consequences of the reptile's bite.

The indigenous people resemble but do not duplicate the racial stock of the Japanese and the local culture is a mix that includes Chinese influence. Veneration of ancestors, a strong element in the people's religion, stimulated the construction of elaborate concrete burial tombs, which would figure strongly in the fortifications facing the invaders.

The Great Loochoo itself stretched generally north and south for sixty miles, with a narrow girth that ranged from a mere two miles to a modest eighteen. With rough, mountainous terrain covering the northern two-thirds of Okinawa, three quarters of the prewar 435,000 people lived in the more gentle, hilly south. They cultivated almost every square foot of arable ground which lay between a series of steep ridges and deep ravines. The crops included sweet potatoes, bananas, beans, sugar cane and rice. Okinawa's major towns, Naha, Shuri, Itoman and Yonabaru, names that would become familiar to leathernecks and GIs, were in the south, along with the vital Yontan and Kadena airfields.

Coral reefs fringed almost the entire island. Even at high tide the water was not deep enough for shallow draft, small craft to pass safely onto the shores. Cliffs that abutted the sea divided beaches into strips from 100 to 900 yards in length. These strands often measured only ten to forty-five yards wide at low tide. Two major airstrips at Yontan and Kadena sat on plains little more than a mile from the western beaches of southern Okinawa.

In 1853, less than 100 years before the huge, 1,500-vessel invasion Love Day fleet would appear off the coast, Commo. Matthew Perry of the U.S. Navy sailed into the harbor of Okinawa's principal city, Naha. At that time, the people of Okinawa paid tribute to both the Chinese and Japanese in return for an uneasy independence.

Perry then took his six gunboats to what is now Yokohama and convinced the emperor of Japan to sign a trade treaty. Exposed to Western influences, Japan changed rapidly, adopting among other things, a more vigorous imperial stance which led to the annexation of Okinawa in 1879.

Considered a part of Japan, just as Alaska and the Hawaiian Islands are now integrated into the United States, Okinawa received an influx of administrators, officials, professionals, and, above all, military forces from the north. Fully vested citizens of the Imperial Empire, the Okinawans were regarded by those who came to govern, manage and defend the place as rustics and perhaps inferiors. However, the Japanese soldiers stationed on Okinawa never generated the hostility manifested by the peoples of the occupied territories like the Philippines, Solomon Islands or other lands conquered after Pearl Harbor. The native inhabitants may have resented the attitudes of those from Nippon but they considered the Allies their enemies and they were willing to fight for their homeland and Japan. To the 80,000 troops from various parts of Japan hunkering down to defend Okinawa were added 20,000 Okinawan conscripts. Their officers from the Japanese army had no complaints about their performance under fire. Tsuneo Shimura, a captain who had graduated in 1940 from the Imperial Military Academy, remarked, "We had about 100 Okinawans attached to the battalion [24th Division, 32nd Infantry Regiment]. Some were middle school and a few university graduates. They fought well. Their knowledge of the terrain was very useful, especially for night moves."

The war had first come to Okinawa late in 1944. On October 10, 1944, raids from Task Force 58 of the U.S. Navy launched 1,400 sorties and 600 tons of bombs along with thousands of rockets pummeled military installations and Naha's port facilities. Incendiaries ignited uncontrollable fires in buildings constructed of wood and paper. Most of the city, home to 65,000 people, was destroyed almost overnight. About a thousand civilians perished, double the number of military personnel killed.

In succeeding months, attacks continued although the pilots found a dearth of visible targets. Marauding U.S. submarines preyed on shipping in the East China Sea, sinking vessels that bore reinforcements and supplies or evacuated nonessential civilians.

The import to both the Imperial Army command and the chiefs of the Japanese 32nd Army that garrisoned Okinawa was unmistakable. From Tokyo came the word to defend to the death. Order number 82 issued by 32nd Army headquarters declared, "The Empire is determined to fight a showdown battle with an all-out effort for the preservation of additional unity when the enemy advances to the Nansei Shoto [another name for the Ryukyus]. Should we be unable to defend the Nansei Shoto, the mainland and the southern frontier would become isolated . . . a life and death problem for our nation." Those on the island had known for years this would be their destiny and had spent years in preparation.

The preinvasion American figures on Japanese strength on Okinawa and the surrounding islands considerably underestimated the number of troops. Interrogators collected scraps of information from documents and an occasional prisoner taken elsewhere but their knowledge of the Ryukyus was scant. A submarine dispatched from Pearl Harbor to photograph the beaches disappeared. The only real source of intelligence lay in aerial reconnaissance and early in the game the enemy had gone underground. To the prying eyes of the pilots and to the lenses of the cameras, Okinawa began to look as if it were devoid of humans. Photographs indicated defenses around Naha, behind the Hagushi beaches on the western coast about twenty miles from Naha and along a ridge known as the Shuri Line, which centered on an ancient walled city dominated by Shuri Castle and girdled the island.

Subterranean defenses had been an increasingly prominent hallmark of Japanese strategy, as American GIs and leathernecks painfully learned during the island-to-island trek towards Okinawa. In places like Tarawa and Iwo Jima, the Nipponese had burrowed into nearly impregnable coral for their emplacements, rendering themselves all but invulnerable to the usually lethal barrages of heavy naval guns. Flame throwers and satchel charges, demanding close-in work by the attacking troops, became the only means to overcome the inhabitants and stifle their deadly fire. As the Americans improved their techniques, their adversaries honed countermeasures. Snipers with rifles and grenades picked off assault teams toting flame throwers and explosives. Anti-incendiary devices like wet mats or blankets smothered fires. Ventilation systems became well disguised and less susceptible to an attack.

For close to two years, the local Okinawa commanders drove their men to dig, ever deeper. The overseers exhorted the men with the slogan, "Confidence in victory will be born in fortifications." The soldiers willingly embarked on construction of shelter that might preserve them from enemy bombardment. Furthermore, the approach offered a glimmer of hope for survival, if not victory.

Okinawa was not a coral atoll but a veneer of that substance coated much of the land toward the south. Bulldozers were not available. The troops excavated by hand with picks and shovels, often wearing them down to stumps on the coral crust before reaching the dirt below. Then Capt. Koichi Itoh, who had survived a childhood case of tuberculosis and graduated from the Imperial Military Academy, says his men created 10,000 meters of caves using only hand tools. They worked every day including Sundays; the single holiday was New Year's Day.

Tsuneo Shimura noted that officers labored as industriously at these tasks as enlisted men. "Some men refused to show up for roll call. They were not AWOL or deserters but working in the caves. Every moment they felt might make the difference between life and death. They dug with hand tools and by the light of lamps lit by pine resin." Shimura noted that the soldiers never forgot where they dug, and later, wounded men sought refuge where they knew they could find some protection.

The Japanese also incorporated into their defensive emplacements the thick tombs of limestone blocks that the Okinawans had raised to honor their dead. The Japanese intelligence experts had their own blind spots. Someone in the strategy hierarchy counseled, "Take advantage of the American Army's respect for tombs." In a typical human error of projecting one's own beliefs upon others, the advisor saw the enemy as reverential towards ancestors. While Americans might extend piety towards their own departed, they hardly would sacrifice any advantage to honor that of their foes.

That error aside, the result of this industry and ingenuity was a honeycomb of underground bunkers, some as many as five stories below ground. Many of these connected through a web of tunnels that produced as much as sixty miles of subterranean corridors. A single cave could house as many as 1,000 men. Trucks, even tanks, could be parked inside. Intersecting automatic weapons fire forged deadly mutual protection for entrances. Openings from inside the caves allowed positions to be shifted during artillery and air bombardments. Egress to the systems was artfully concealed. Spider holes—small, well-hidden pits—sited near entrances provided sentries clear, surprise fire lanes upon interlopers.

The rooms of the underground hideaway for the 32nd Army headquarters resembled those of a barracks, with desks, chairs and electricity. Kitchens provided good, hot food from a bountiful supply of canned goods and staples. Beer and sake flowed freely. The almost all-male society was cheered by the presence of thirty women clerks from Japan and Okinawa.

Ladders led from one level to another; communications traveled by an internal telephone system, although later the heavy shelling from the invaders destroyed the wiring, making messengers necessary. For some reason, the Imperial Japanese Army never developed an effective means of radio communications.

Life below the earth was not without its unpleasant aspect. The temperature hovered around ninety degrees; the humidity approached 100 percent, making walls constantly damp and causing sacks of rice to ferment and turn sour. The climate induced bothersome skin rashes, and the presence of so many people with few opportunities to practice personal hygiene bred rank aromas.

Concealment was critical, both to deceive the preinvasion sources of intelligence and to fool unwary soldiers once the shooting began. Kitchen smoke vents were carefully screened from observation. The watchwords of those in charge of defense were, "Camouflage is better than concrete."

The U.S. forces focused on three other principal objectives in the Ryukyus: the Kerama Retto, the Keise Shima and Ie Shima. The first of these consisted of eight mounds of steep, rocky slopes that poked 400 to

600 feet out of the water. The largest added up to only a few square miles and provided sustenance for a handful of inhabitants. There were no roads on the Kerama Retto, merely trails for pack animals or humans.

The Kerama Retto offered an irresistible asset. Lying only ten to fifteen miles from Okinawa, these otherwise unprepossessing clumps of hilly land nestled a spacious, well-protected deep anchorage within their waters. Obviously, no enemy troops capable of using small arms, not to mention even small artillery, could be allowed to occupy the surrounding bits and pieces of the Ryukyus.

It apparently never occurred to the Japanese that the enemy would find the natural harbor within the Kerama Retto so attractive, for little effort had been made to install strong points capable of fending off attacks. Instead, they based only about 100 troops there, supplementing them with some 600 Korean laborers. But one additional and potentially dangerous element consisted of several squadrons of plywood motorboats fitted with depth charges.

The sea raider squadron crews were trained to dump their 264-pound explosives as close to the vital areas of a ship as possible. Once the devices rolled off the racks at the back of the speedboat, the pilot had five seconds before they detonated. The thin-hulled, slow-moving and poorly built craft probably would not survive the blast but, strictly speaking, it was not considered suicidal in the same terms as a kamikaze pilot. Altogether there were 350 of these Q-boats concealed around the Kerama Retto. Machine guns, mortars, small arms and ammunition issued to the crews added a further ingredient for resistance to invaders.

At least equally barren and inhospitable as the Kerama Retto, the four tiny coral islets of Keise Shima lay a mere eight miles from where the American forces expected to charge across the Okinawa beaches. Photo reconnaissance indicated defensive gun emplacements behind these areas. From Keise Shima, batteries of 155 mm guns could support the initial assault waves and hurl projectiles at would-be resisters. Conversely, if the defenders were permitted to stay on Keise Shima with heavy weaponry, they could slam both the U.S. fleet and those coming ashore.

The island of Ie Shima, about ten square miles in size, stood less than four miles from the tip of an Okinawan peninsula about twenty miles north of where the initial attack on the Great Loochoo would occur. Flatter than most of its sister islands, Ie Shima boasted a large plateau over much of its interior. Aware of its topographical advantages in an area where flat ground was at a premium, the Japanese had begun construction of no less than three airfields on Ie Shima. Only at the southern end of Ie Shima was the level surface radically broken. Iegusugu Mountain, a 600-foot, sheer outcrop of rock, dubbed "the Pinnacle" by GIs, jutted above the rest of the oval-shaped plateau and the nascent airstrips like the control tower of an aircraft carrier stationed in the East China Sea. South of the Pinnacle, in the town of Ie, many of the 5,000 civilians who remained when the war reached the Ryukyus occupied 300 houses.

Ie Shima, as one more objective in the overall scheme for the conquest of the Ryukyus, also drew the attention of aerial reconnaissance. Just as on Okinawa, the soldiers of Japan, aided by a labor battalion conscripted from Okinawa and the local people, frantically dug in. The eyes in the sky could not discern the maze of pillboxes carved out of homes and tombs, the inevitable caves, three stories high in some cases, hacked into ridges and slopes and tied in by a network of passageways, nor could they pick out the machine gun and mortar positions veiled from view with shrubbery.

CHAPTER III

PLANS AND PLAYERS

Lt. Gen. Mitsura Ushijima commanded the 32nd Army with the roughly 100,000 troops assigned to defend the Ryukyus. Ushijima, according to members of his staff, was a calm, highly capable leader who enjoyed the confidence of his subordinates. His style was to consult with his staff and accept their recommendations.

His chief of staff, Lt. Gen. Isamu Cho, differed sharply in personality. As a young officer, Cho belonged to the extreme right-wing Cherry Society and participated in several failed military coups during the 1930s. His behavior led to his assignment to Manchuria, where he impressed the troops with his physical courage. When liquored up, Cho occasionally performed a dance that featured his samurai sword. "[He] was an impetuous and experienced man. His being impetuous and brave was well known among those in the army," said Col. Hiromichi Yahara, the senior staff officer in charge of operations. "Cho believed in the active strategy but not passive strategy."

Yahara was still another type of officer. Studious, aloof, "sour" to one observer, he preserved his distance from the troops. To Yahara, who had spent ten months at Fort Moultrie, South Carolina, attached to the 8th Infantry during the 1920s, and who bore a reputation as a brilliant, yet conservative and calculating tactician, fell the assignment for drawing up the scheme to thwart the enemy.

The colonel based his plans on the experiences of the Imperial Army in preceding months and upon his best guesses about the Allied moves in the near future. The Japanese strategists now accepted that efforts to prevent the enemy from establishing beachheads were futile. Defenses organized around the shorelines only allowed the opposing navies to bring their huge seaborne guns to bear. Yahara was well aware that on Saipan, where the defenders sought to push the invaders off the beaches with close-in artillery, the American naval and air forces wiped out their big guns.

Although bunker emplacements had been constructed overlooking the coastal areas, Yahara, to the dismay of some junior officers like

General Mitsura Ushijima commanded the Japanese forces defending Okinawa.
(*National Archives*)

General Isamura Cho, Ushijima's second in command, disagreed with the defensive strategy.
(*National Archives*)

Lieutenant General Simon Bolivar Buckner, Tenth Army Commander, Vice Admiral Richmond Kelly Turner and Brigadier General Oliver Smith plan invasion strategy. (*Signal Corps, U.S. National Archives*)

Captain Itoh, abandoned any idea of using them. He argued, "If the U.S. forces should land on Kadena [the airfield near the southwest coast of Okinawa], we'll pursue a strategic drawnout war on the battlefield east-west of Minami-Uebaru [a town along the Shuri Line]. If successful, we'll be able to hold the U.S. force on Okinawa and to give it as much damage as possible, and thus able to hold Okinawa as long as possible. This will later enable us to take advantage over the U.S. force in combat on the mainland of Japan."

It was a purely defensive posture, a war of attrition predicated on the ability of his country to strike at the American ships obligated to stand by in support of the ground forces. It assumed an imminent invasion of mainland Japan.

The 32nd Army included the 62nd Division veterans of combat in China. The 24th Division and the 44th Independent Mixed Brigade were both untested in battle. But all of these men from the Imperial Japanese Army had trained hard. In addition to the 67,000 to 70,000 soldiers from the IJA, General Ushijima also drew on some 9,000 members of the Imperial Japanese Navy. Originally dispatched to Okinawa to build and maintain a series of torpedo boat stations, they had completed their labors and the staff of the 32nd Army transformed most of them into ground troops.

From the local population, 39,000 able-bodied men were conscripted. Of these, 24,000 put on uniforms to become mostly rear-echelon service troops. The remainder, in mufti, worked as labor battalions. An additional 1,500 youths entered the Iron and Blood volunteer units to fight on the front lines. Fortunately for the coming invasion force, the Imperial High Command in the late fall of 1944 withdrew the 9th Division in anticipation of reinforcing the beleagured forces in the Philippines. Suggestions that another organization be dispatched in place of the 9th were eventually rejected; it was decided to keep the proposed unit at home to defend the Japanese islands.

While the Japanese Nambu rifle was markedly inferior to the American M–1, the machine guns of the Nipponese were good weapons. A nasty item known as a knee mortar hurled a 50 mm grenade, and the huge spigot mortar lobbed a monster 320 mm shell (the largest American mortars only fired an 81 mm projectile) which created an enormous explosion when it struck. The trajectory of the knee mortar made it an invaluable component for the Japanese tactic of reverse slope defenses —the arc of the grenades cleared the crest and then wrought havoc on those attempting to scale or hold the forward slope. The spigot's 650-pound load could travel three quarters of a mile but its size prevented the use of sufficient metal to provide devastating fragmentation.

Sorely lacking in the Japanese ordnance was the equivalent of the U.S. bazooka. Although the Germans willingly supplied the plans for their *panzerfaust*, which was more effective than the American version, the Japanese did not bother to manufacture them. They relied on satchel charges carried by individuals and a 47 mm cannon whose high muzzle velocity enabled its projectile to pierce the armorplate of U.S. tanks.

Because of defeats in the Philippines and other islands and with the closure of shipping to those points, Okinawa became a dropping off site for weapons and ammunition. As a consequence, the defenders possessed ample ammunition and firepower, including far more artillery than ordinarily alloted to units. American intelligence badly undercounted the number of heavy guns. The only shortages lay in tanks and eventually in artillery shells.

One severe weakness lay in the Imperial Army's combat theory. At the start of Japan's Greater East Asia War in 1937 and in the first years of World War II, the strategy of infiltration, swift, bold maneuvers and aggressive attacks served well against the lightly armed Chinese and the weakly protected colonial garrisons. However, once the U.S. recovered from the Pearl Harbor attack, it brought to bear tremendous firepower on land, sea and air, and the Japanese never could match it, except to some degree at sea. Furthermore, the style that worked well on the great land mass of China, Burma, and what was then French Indo-China hardly suited the compact islands which isolated garrisons had to defend. And this would hold for Okinawa, even though it was one of the larger islands.

While the propaganda fountains in Tokyo continued to spout optimism, and even with the spectacular achievements through the use of kamikazes, the troops on Okinawa could hardly have failed to realize that the approach of the war to the islands of Japan signaled defeats. Koichi Itoh today claims, "I did not ever suppose, after the start of the war, that we could win it. But after the loss of Saipan I reconciled myself to losing the war."

But however they felt about the future, the soldiers had been inoculated with the vaccine of duty to the emperor. An imperial rescript, issued by the emperor Meiji to soldiers and sailors in 1883, continued to serve as a Bible for Japanese soldiers. Such rescripts were supposed to be the subject of daily study by officers, and military units heard them read several times a year. Every man was expected to devote ten minutes each morning to meditation on the virtues expounded in an imperial rescript.

The code of the warrior, *bushido*, like that of its feudal, samurai predecessor, lists in order of merit: loyalty, obedience, valor, faithfulness, righteousness and simplicity. The soldier was repeatedly instructed to remember that "duty is weightier than a mountain. While death is like a feather . . . When a tiger dies, he leaves behind his skin. When a man dies, he leaves behind his name."

The imperial rescript had also cautioned, "To be incited by mere impetuousity to violent action cannot be called true valor. If you affect valor and act with violence, the world will in the end detest you and look upon you as wild beasts." Enough men in the Japanese forces forgot this admonition to create a hatred which would cost dearly.

In Japanese army barracks they chanted, "Whether I float as a corpse in the waters or sink beneath the grasses of the mountainside, I willingly die for the emperor." Literature named the cherry as first among the flowers, as is the warrior first among men. It concluded, "The life of the warrior is like the life of the cherry blossom but three days old."

Documents later found on Okinawa indicated the indoctrination drumfire on the virtue of a sacrifice fitted neatly with fatalistic religious beliefs. "To have faith in ultimate victory, each of us must kill ten of the enemy. They who perform the highly commendable duties of combat soldiers will become heroes. Each of you must dash forward and accomplish his mission in an aggressive spirit and entrust your life to heaven. Your fate was determined when you were born and becuse you are powerless to do anything about it, dash forward, killing ten. You will be honored for your boldness and bravery. You must prepare yourself for the sake of the emperor." The slogan of the time was, "One plane for one battleship; one boat for one ship; one man for one tank or ten enemy dead."

The Japanese leaders made a special appeal to the native *boetai* who were also called upon for the supreme sacrifice in battle. An epistle specifically for newly inducted Okinawan conscripts declared, "You are within your native land. Each and every one of you serves as a representative of the land. Each of you must shoulder his share of the burden. You are a direct part of the army, assuming a part of its load, charged with a grave responsibility of the empire." The directive concluded, "You must strengthen your belief in the inevitability of victory."

And on Love Day, the 32nd Army issued a proclamation to the civilians, already told that the Americans were barbaric and would rape, torture and murder any noncombatants. "The hated Americans are finally going to land on Okinawa. People of Okinawa, let us vow under the emperor to die protecting our country. All people of Okinawa annihilate the ugly Americans."

To be sure, some of the Japanese soldiers on Okinawa may have been less enthusiastic over the demands of *bushido*. Most of those in the Ryukyus understood that defeat now lapped at the shores of Japan proper. But although morale was surely influenced by the course of the war, training, tradition and the incessant exhortation from Tokyo steered the overwhelming majority toward fealty to actions in accord with *bushido*.

While U.S. civilian leaders stressed patriotism, glory, courage and even sacrifice, no military commander, with the possible exception of a few like the flamboyant general George S. Patton, Jr., declaimed these kinds of abstractions or spiritual values to the troops. American soldiers openly scoffed at any bombastic urgings. The idea of self-sacrifice for the nation was unacceptable (although in actuality some did give up their lives for the sake of others), and even Patton said, "The idea is to make the other guy die for his country." Americans, aware the tide of the war now strongly ran in their favor, carried on at Okinawa because they accepted that the voyage home required passage through Japan.

The division of responsibility among U.S. commanders in the Pacific theater of operations charged Gen. Douglas MacArthur with booting the Japanese out of the Philippine Islands. He naturally relished the opportunity for revenge upon those who had forced him into ignominious retreat early in 1942. Acutely aware of image both for its effect on the enemy as well as individual glory, MacArthur had made good on his boast, "I shall return." And because he and many of the GIs he led had chafed at what they considered the overemphasis upon the achievements of the Marine Corps, to the detriment of the Army, he excluded the leathernecks from the ground forces he brought to the beaches of the Philippines.

The hostility towards Marines by many GIs, from the lowliest private up to a five-star general, and the disdain of much of the Marine Corps for the Army arose from more than the proper apportionment of glory. There were fundamental differences in the missions of the two services and these influenced the ways in which they went about their business.

The Marines generally accepted themselves partners with the outfit that put them ashore and kept them supplied, the Navy. It was clear to the leathernecks that the longer it took to crush enemy resistance, the more vulnerable their associates to naval, air and even shore-based bombardment. Speed of conquest became something of an imperative in order to allow the ships the freedom of movement, the ability to protect themselves. As a consequence, Marine operations stressed quick progress, forging ahead even if that meant leaving behind isolated pockets of Japanese troops to be mopped up later. Haste, which often meant moving out in the face of heavy fire from well-entrenched positions, led to a quick pile-up of dead and wounded. From boot camp on, Marines were imbued with a "see-the-hill; take-the-hill attitude." Certainly not everyone bought the ideal, but even those who rejected the absolute imperative accepted the need to press on quickly.

The style of the Army was usually more deliberate. Infantry school tactics taught officers to wait for support from artillery and tanks. Commanders sought to risk as few men as possible unless the situation favored them. In Europe, Gen. George S. Patton, Jr., had wielded his Third Army along the same principles as the Marines, with armor racing forward, bypassing German strongpoints and leaving these for infantrymen following his advance. But in the Pacific, while armor supported the infantry, the terrain and the absence of good roads eliminated opportunities for sprints led by tanks.

Marine strategists argued that their method incurred no higher total casualties over the long run than the more cautious operations of the

Army which exposed soldiers to shot and shell for a greater period of time and kept the Navy subject to harm's way longer. The virtues of the two theories can still be debated, but on Okinawa, as in several other instances, when Army and Marine units tried to work with one another, the differences sometimes led to serious problems.

While MacArthur busied himself with the Leyte Gulf and Luzon in the Philippines, Adm. Chester Nimitz, as commander in chief, Pacific Ocean area (CINCPOA in navalese), drew the responsibility for the Ryukyus. Until the troops—four Army divisions and two from the Marines—actually splashed ashore, the bulk of the operations would be directed by Navy brass, specifically under the control of one of the Navy's most prominent swashbucklers, Adm. Richmond Kelly Turner. Samuel Eliot Morison, a Harvard professor commissioned by President Franklin D. Roosevelt to produce a history of naval operations with on-site reporting, described Turner in terms of Irish legends. "Turner's long upper lip, bushy black eyebrows and gray hair, steel-gray eyes shooting furious glances when anything went wrong, might have been those of a Celtic chieftain." Justly recognized for adroit maneuvers during a number of Pacifc encounters, he was, however, known to have a fondness for alcohol and rarely accepted the judgments of others.

After the landings, all soldiers would answer to the Army's Lt. Gen. Simon Bolivar Buckner, a stolid, skilled veteran who had graduated from West Point thirty-seven years before and was decorated for "exceptionally distinguished and meritorious service" in leading the campaign that rousted the Japanese from their toeholds in the Aleutian Islands. He was respected by his troops, not considered arrogant by any means but a man fully aware of his exalted status.

Operation Iceberg was a vast undertaking that coordinated a wide range of forces. Air Corps bombers based in China and the Mariana Islands dropped loads on Formosa, Kyushu and Okinawa during the month that preceded the landings. Nine separate seaborne task forces, including one from the British, were marshalled. Some with aircraft carriers steamed north to cut off any effort by the Japanese to reinforce or supply the defenders. They hunted submarines that might interfere with the mission, and planes prowled the skies to ward off aerial attacks against Iceberg.

The ground-troop manpower chosen for the Ryukyu conquest added up to the 7th, 27th, 77th and 96th Infantry Divisions of the Army and the 1st and 6th Marine Divisions. Every outfit had seen considerable combat as a unit, although the ranks for Okinawa would contain a good number of untested replacements. Except for the 27th, which had been hurt badly in the fight for Saipan, all of the army divisions were classified as "reinforced" with extra combat engineer battalions, armor and artillery. Instead of the usual slightly fewer than 15,000 soldiers, these enlarged organizations would come to the Ryukyus with nearly 22,000 apiece, although there were shortages of the basic elements in an infantry division, riflemen. The 27th, which was supposed to serve in reserve, was seriously understrength in this category although it listed 16,000 as its complement. The two Marine divisions numbered 24,000 apiece.

The first objective in the Ryukyus was the Kerama Retto. The idea for grabbing these small patches originated with Adm. Richmond K. Turner. He delegated the job of getting the troops ashore to Rear Adm. Ingolf N. Kiland.

Admiral Turner's proposal that the Navy seize the Kerama Retto, about a week ahead of the main attack on Okinawa, drew opposition from almost all of his colleagues. They pointed to the threat of land-based air attacks, since between Okinawa and Ie Shima, as many as five airfields within fifty miles of Kerama Retto could dispatch planes to hammer the ships and troops engaged in occupying the islands. Some predicted that the losses to the fleet could endanger the entire Okinawa operation since the ships might well be driven far out to sea. But the Iwo Jima operation [February 10 to March 10, 1945], convinced Turner he needed sheltered anchorage for Iceberg to succeed. He disregarded the naysayers and ordered Kiland to proceed.

Turner's plan plotted an island-by-island operation employing a relatively small force. Kiland persuaded his superior that a simultaneous landing on five of the six largest islands on Love Day minus six, would eliminate the enemy more quickly and prevent survival of fanatical bands that could interfere with the use of the harbor.

Kiland and his staff, sailed aboard the U.S.S. *Mount McKinley,* an Amphibious Force Command Ship (AGC–7). With his task force stocked and resupplied at Ulithi Atoll, Kiland moved to Leyte, from where his attack was planned and it would be launched.

For the Kerama Retto operations, only a group of inexperienced landing craft crews was available. In the early light of dawn, amid the rocky shoals and reefs off the coasts, failure to hit the right beach on the right island could be disastrous. Fortunately, Hinunangan Bay on Leyte and the Cabugan Islands offered reasonable facsimiles. Three days of practice runs and an illustrated guidebook on the target beaches, produced by Lt. Comdr. Ellery Sedgwick, Kiland's intelligence officer, provided the seamen with sufficient information for them to accomplish their missions.

The Tenth Army nominated the 77th Infantry Division under Maj. Gen. Andrew Bruce to deal with the scattering of enemy in residence. Elements of the 77th Division, with the Statue of Liberty the central ornament of its shoulder patch, had joined the American Expeditionary Force in France during World War I to participate in the bitter fighting of the Argonne Forest. In March 1942, after more than twenty years on the shelf, the 77th was reborn at Fort Jackson, South Carolina.

South Carolina native Frank Barron was present at the inception as a member of the officer cadre expected to mold 15,000 recruits into a combat-effective infantry division. A 1913 Charleston baby, Barron started out life comfortably. "My father was a bookkeeper or accountant and we enjoyed an upper middle-class standard until the Depression of 1929 when my father lost his savings and, almost, our house.

"One cold winter night during the Depression, my father arrived home in company with a neighboring gentleman. They had both been out all day trying to find a job, any kind of honest work, but to no avail. When they came in, my father told my mother they were going down to the basement to divide the coal and asked her to divide everything in the pantry into halves. Half of everything we had in the way of food and fuel went to the neighbors that night."

Barron grew up with parents whom he says lived the life their Christian religion taught. "We believed in church participation, community service, very strict honesty and integrity, and close family relationships."

An avid high school athlete, Barron played on the Clemson freshman team his first year of college. He describes himself, however, as a "sorry student." Nevertheless, he graduated from Clemson, where he studied textile engineering, in 1936. He also held a reserve commission.

"I was quite concerned about world affairs prior to Pearl Harbor, but I did not think that the U.S. would go to war. The rape of China by the Japanese infuriated me. I was upset about Mussolini's exploitation of Ethiopia and ashamed of the cowardly sellout of Czechoslovakia by Great Britain and the U.S.

"To me, and the people I knew, the Japanese were a treacherous, brutal, unoriginal and vulgar people; about as abominable as supposedly civilized people could be. Later, by their treatment of American prisoners, they proved me to be correct. I had friends who died as Jap prisoners—from mistreatment and starvation. I and my men believed as Bull [Adm. William] Halsey said, the only good Jap was a dead one."

Called to duty in January 1942, Barron reported to Fort Jackson on March 3, the activation date for the 77th. "We started with a cadre of officers and noncoms and received thousands of raw recruits from induction centers. A large number of our men were from New York, New Jersey and Pennsylvania. After a few months training, we sent out cadre to form another division. We then received a number of Southern boys."

The draft number for Henry Lopez, born in St. Louis in 1914, but then a resident of New York City, brought him to Fort Jackson just as the 77th's 307th Infantry Regiment began to form. A high school drop-out who went to work "to supplement the family's meager income," Lopez had never thought about world affairs or politics. "It was the happy, happy time of my life and I was dumbfounded by the news of Pearl Harbor. The sneak attack by the Japanese changed my attitude towards them to one of hatred."

Ernest Schlichter, another 1914 baby, could have obtained a defer-ment because of his work with the optical manufacturer Bausch and Lomb in Rochester. "I quit my job with several of my fellow workers to join the army and do our part of the fighting. We thought if we volun-

After the fight for Ie Shima, (left to right) Sgt. Leonard Pierce, Pfc. Lewis Nesko, Lt. Donald W. Flower, a KIA subsequently, and Captain Frank Barron of the 77th Division awaited shipment to Okinawa itself.

Sgt. Henry Lopez of the 77th Division joined the outfit at its formation in the U.S. and fought through the Guam, Leyte and Okinawa campaigns, where he was wounded. *(Henry Lopez)*

teered, we would have to stay for a full enlistment, whereas if we took early induction, we would be out at the end of the war, earlier. At Fort Jackson they gave us old World War I equipment, helmets, leg wrappings and Enfield rifles. They even put saltpeter in our coffee and soup [a potion to kill sexual drive, according to a constant rumor among World War II soldiers]."

Ed Fitzgerald, a twenty-two-year-old newspaperman in the New York City suburb of Yonkers, appeared to be making some progress in his chosen vocation. "I had a girl and I paid attention to the news in Europe mainly in terms of what was going to happen to me. I was hostile to the whole idea of Hitler, and what he was doing to the Jews. But I didn't have any personal sense of those who would become our enemies.

"I was having a beer early at a ginmill in Yonkers and eating when the radio started to make announcements. The bartender yelled out, 'All you military people are supposed to return.' That was probably as close an awareness as I had of what was about to happen. To us the war was Hitler, and the Japs were those funny little people." But recognizing the inevitable, Fitgerald decided to see if he couldn't have some choice in his future. He enlisted and in March 1942 reported to Camp Upton, New York. "They satisfied themselves that my heart was beating, made sure my genitals were intact, and halfheartedly asked me to testify that all of my sexual desires were directed towards women."

Offered a chance to apply for the Army Air Corps flight training,

Fitzgerald passed the written exam but failed the physical because of his slight stature. After another abortive attempt to obtain a special assignment through a blowhard acquaintance, Fitzgerald resigned himself to accepting the disposition of the Army. He too surfaced at Fort Jackson.

There were, of course, men from other areas of the country who joined the 77th. Dick Forse, a twenty-one-year-old Ohio State student heard about the Pearl Harbor bombing when the Jack Benny show was interrupted on the night of December 7 for an announcement. "I was astounded. I thought the Japanese were insane to attack us." Out of patriotism, he felt obligated to enlist as soon as possible.

Another original with the 77th was Virginian private Desmond Doss, assigned to Company C as a rifleman. Three weeks after he arrived, Doss, a Seventh-Day Adventist received a transfer to a medical battalion because he refused to bear a rifle, saying it conflicted with his religious beliefs.

Iowa farmboy Leonard Schweitzer, drafted upon graduation from high school, says he thought, "The Japanese were a lower class, less educated. The men in my unit [Company K, 306th Regiment] did not respect them." Schweitzer was made a rifleman and after a year received a stripe as a private first class.

As Schlichter indicated, basic training had begun with World War I vintage, bolt action British Lee Enfield and American Springfield 1903 rifles. But within weeks, the fledgling infantrymen received the M–1, Garand, a semiautomatic weapon bearing an eight-round .30 caliber clip; the leg wrappings were replaced with leggings and the old-style soup-plate helmet was discarded in favor of the new model.

By design or by happenstance, the average age of the GI in the 77th was more advanced than in other units. Frank Barron, for example, was approaching thirty when called up. One of the youngest in the outfit, however, was a lieutenant with an extended military heritage. Buckner M. Creel III was born in an Army hospital at Fort H. G. Wright, Fishers Island, New York, in 1923. "My father, a regular Army captain of cavalry was the instructor with the Connecticut National Guard and stationed in Hartford. My maternal grandfather, Maj. Gen. George Hamilton Cameron, USMA, 1883, a replacement with the 7th Cavalry after the massacre and who took the 4th Infantry Division into combat in World War I, was retired and his summer home was on Fishers Island.

"My father had been commissioned from Officers Training School in World War I, served in France with the field artillery. My maternal great-grandfather, USMA, 1851, fought in the Civil War." Indeed Creel could trace forefathers back to the French and Indian wars before the American Revolution.

Learning came easy to Creel and he admits not extending himself. "Born into a horse cavalry family, my earliest days, up to the time I enlisted in the army, were spent on horseback. I also swam, boxed, fenced and played various team sports. I spent several years of my youth on a ranch in Colorado and the nearest friends were miles away. I spent a lot of time with horses, dogs and guns. This was during the Depression; we learned to make do with what we had and keep it in working order. It was great training for the Army's property accountability and maintenance.

"Because of the family's involvement in the military and my father, grandfather and two uncles had served in France during World War I, we were familiar but not entranced with world affairs. My grandfather Cameron spent a great deal of his time writing letters to the editors of the New York *Times*, so he 'instructed us' on the proper positions. Naturally, he disliked Mr. Roosevelt. Granddad was an extremely brilliant individual who had taught at West Point, the War College and the

Captain Buckner M. Creel, III, 77th Division Company Commander, receives a Silver Star from Division CO Gen. Andrew Bruce. *(Buckner M. Creel, III)*

Cavalry School. He was a very knowledgeable student of military history and was impressed with the buildup of the German war machine. My father had been in the occupation of Germany after World War I. He had a great respect for their industry and tenacity. The Japanese, on the other hand, got short shrift until Pearl Harbor and then the 'Yellow Peril' kicked in. We all laughed at the Italians and did not take them seriously.

"I had completed high school and was in a postgraduate situation at Staunton Military Academy. I had been first alternate for appointment to the USMA in 1941 and had a good chance of being admitted in 1942. As an alternative I was scheduled to attend Virginia Polytechnic Institute but when the war came, I enlisted in March 1942."

Like Ed Fitzgerald, Creel believed enlistment conferred upon him the right to choose the kind of Army service he wanted. "I requested cavalry, in the family tradition and because of my background, and I listed it for choices one, two and three. I assume some clerk looked at this and said, 'We have a smartass here' because I was assigned to the coast artillery, which was doubly insulting because our family always looked down on that branch as the 'Concrete Artillery.' "

Less than three months later, Creel qualified for OCS and managed to transfer to the infantry school at Fort Benning, Georgia. Upon graduation and with a commission as a second lieutenant, he reported to an infantry replacement center. Still shy of his nineteenth birthday, he faced a platoon of newly drafted men, ranging from twenty-seven to thirty-five years old. "My first morning I was greeted by a remark from the rear rank, 'And a little child shall lead them.' I agreed that was correct and I then led them on a ten-mile speed hike. After that I broke the rifle stocks of two '03 Springfields while demonstrating the vertical and horizontal butt strokes on the bayonet assault course. I had no more trouble and heard no more remarks."

In December 1943, Creel received assignment to G Company of the 306th Regiment in the 77th Division. His post was as executive officer but the company commander preferred to concentrate on the administrative duties himself and allowed Creel to take the outfit into the field and run the training. "I gained invaluable experience in commanding, maneuvering and handling the troops. I also got to know the individual members of the company, their strengths and weaknesses. As a result, when we went into combat, I knew the company very well, both its capabilities and its limitations."

Creel believes he learned what those soldiers closest to him would be able to handle in battle, but no amount of training prepares a man for the violent bloodletting of war. For the 77th the baptism of fire would begin at Guam.

William Siegel, who would be at Guam with the division, came to the 77th by a somewhat circuitous route. Born in 1920, with a father who operated an auto body shop, Siegel attended Temple University, where he majored in accounting. "I was aware of world affairs. My friends and I, as young people, considered the Japanese a military air threat, not someone we'd have to fight on the ground."

The draft seized Siegel just before his final semester. Perhaps because of the auto body background, he was shipped to Fort Knox, Kentucky, to become a tanker. After an appointment to OCS, Siegel was assigned to the 706th Tank Battalion, which was designated as the armor for the 77th.

The manufacturers of raw civilian material into an effective fighting organization coped with glitches along the production line. Like so many of the outfits hastily mustered in the months after the U.S. entered the war, the 77th as a citizen-soldier organization had only a handful of professionals at the top, and not necessarily the cream.

"In my opinion," says Barron, "the general who commanded the division from June 1, 1942, to the end of May 1943, was either spineless or stupid." The problem at the top, however, was solved with the installation of Gen. Andrew Bruce as division CO. Bruce's commission in 1916 had come through a program at Texas A & M. His subsequent efforts in France earned him a Distinguished Service Cross.

Bruce was an odd mixture of attitudes—the aggressive commander, solicitous at least for those whom he knew, unswerving in his dedication to the destruction of the enemy but so prissy that he objected to the language in the mildly risqué play *The Voice of the Turtle*.

Joseph Budge, who served as a sergeant under Bruce, described him as "a good man for the job. He was harddriving and ambitious, maybe egotistical, but he was responsible for the creation of a very good division. The lads mostly agreed about Bruce. I did ask an oldtimer his opinion and got the reply, 'The only good words the son of a bitch ever said were 'Indiantown Gap.'" He was referring to the transfer of the division for rest and leave in the East, where most of the men came from. after the Arizona desert.

While engaged in training on the East Coast, a shakeout occurred, part of which Barron says he helped engineer. "The colonel who had commanded the 305th Infantry [Barron's regiment] almost from activation was a man devoid of personality with no talent for leadership. He was undoubtedly a man of strong character, probably knew every regulation by heart, a learned West Pointer, but unable to attract loyalty or instill inspiration and enthusiasm. He was succeeded by an alcoholic, political hangover from the National Guard. What held the outfit together was a great bunch of company officers, but we needed more than this."

According to Barron, some relief came in the form of Lt. Col. Arthur Tanzola to take over the 305th. But he and two other company commanders from the 1st Battalion, Captains Arthur Curtin and Hugh A. Plowden, feared for their lives if Lieutenant Colonel M———, their battalion commander, continued in his post. "He was National Guard, a coroner in private life and a disaster in military life. He wanted everybody to like him but he was two-faced and unreliable. We couldn't go over his head to Colonel Tanzola, as he had only recently joined us and knew nothing about us."

Over a bottle of brandy in their quarters, Barron, Curtin and Plowden agreed that, during the coming full-scale combat-team landing maneuvers scheduled in the Chesapeake Bay area, they would do everything Colonel M——— said to do, exactly as he ordered it. "Afterwards, we thought we would talk to Lt. Col. Gordon Kimbrell, a battalion CO in the 306th who had commanded us briefly and whom we thought had a good opinion of us.

"Once we were ashore, I, as reserve company commander, joined the battalion CO at his observation post. It was easy to find him, as I knew he would follow a road to keep from getting lost. Enroute, my runner, Pvt. Lewis Nesko, and I passed the battalion wire team looking for M———. At the observation post, M———, his intelligence officer and an umpire were standing around with a radio that wouldn't work. Here was a battalion commander with no communications to anyone and no knowledge about the attack. I could have said, 'Nesko, go bring the wire team here' and we'd have had communications in five minutes. Instead, I let him sweat and he got clobbered for it. Other similar things happened.

"On the various umpire reports, Companies A, B and C (mine), all looked good but the battalion caught hell. M——— went over things with Curtin, Plowden and me, individually, trying to get alibis but without success.

"The three of us then went to see Colonel Kimbrell. He received us graciously and we proceeded to tell him why it would be tragic for our battalion in the 305th to go overseas, into battle under M———. He interrupted us to say, 'Don't you know you could be court-martialed for this?' We assured him we were aware of this and would prefer a court-martial to going into battle with M———.

"A West Pointer, a great athlete and graduate of British commando training who participated upon raids on Germans, Kimbrell picked up his British trench knife, smiled and said, 'If you ever tell anyone that you talked to me about this, I'll cut your throat. Get out of here—I do talk to the general occasionally.'"

Two days later, M——— announced to his junior officers that, as a result of an old football injury to his knee, he would be entering the post hospital and did not expect to return to the regiment.

"Every officer and every enlisted man rejoiced. Our new battalion commander was Lt. Col. James E. Landrum, a West Pointer, a man of integrity, a great soldier and commander. Another West Pointer, Lt. Col. Edward Chalgren, Jr., also a splendid person and an oustanding leader, took over the 3rd Battalion."

General Bruce improved the 77th's morale and discipline with the creation of the "Bull Dog School," under the direction of Colonel Kimbrell. All officers underwent the course, which included the most realistic conditions possible, lavish use of live ammunition and explosives, practice in small-unit tactics, hand-to-hand exercises and a battery of activities designed to harden bodies and bolster confidence. Under Bruce, beer appeared in the post exchanges, a swimming pool opened, the division newspaper reappeared and movies became more frequent.

According to Barron, the amenities did not distract from intensive training in every possible phase of combat. He believes no outfit ever had more complete or throrough preparation for what it was now about to face.

CHAPTER IV

TRIALS BY FIRE

Along with all of its other schooling, the 77th had practiced in amphibious landings at various locales in the United States. Combat for the troops of the Liberty Division would begin with that aspect, the invasion of the island of Guam on July 21, 1944.

The 305th Regiment went in behind the 1st Provisional Marine Brigade near Agat. One disquieting rumor said the defenders had the option to use poison gas if they felt it necessary.

"We went ashore in the late afternoon," says Frank Barron, CO of C Company. "Half of my company followed me inland but the beachmaster stopped the others and they remained on the beach. We tied in with A Company and I recall discussing the situation with Arthur Curtin. He remarked that we were standing atop a Jap pillbox or gun position and said, 'Glad there are no Japs in it now.' But there were and they came out shooting and throwing grenades during the night. There were Japs behind us and others trying to slip into our area all night. One group charged our command post and another blew up a Marine tank about 200 yards behind us, so there was Marine gunfire coming into our area from our rear as well as Jap fire from all directions—quite a lot of confusion that first night.

"The next morning we dropped our gas masks. Our battalion attacked with A Company leading, followed by us. When A stopped moving, I went up to find out why and was told that Curtin and a few men had moved out to destroy a Jap position. I heard a loud explosion and a sort of greenish-yellow cloud with an irritating odor started drifting towards us. Several men started to retreat and I yelled, 'Get down and put on your gas masks.' Someone hollered, 'Captain, we ain't got any gas masks.' Then I remembered and yelled, 'Stay where you are, anyway!'

"A few minutes later the cloud dissipated. Curtin had blown up a large quantity of Japanese explosives and the picric acid they used had caused the 'gas' cloud.

"That night, our second in combat, we were better organized and better dug in. Despite this, our troops threw dozens if not hundreds of grenades, but there were few, if any, Jap bodies to show for it. Colonel Landrum passed the word that if this ever happened again, we would take up all ammo at dark and leave nothing but bayonets for protection at night. It never happened again!"

Several days later, as the U.S. forces were rapidly advancing with the hope of securing strategic positions before the enemy could regroup, Barron and his troops spearheaded the advance. A machine gun bullet ripped into the C Company commander's upper left thigh. He left Guam for three months of hospitalization and recuperation in the Russell Islands.

Dick Forse, who'd attended radio school, was attached to Cannon Company and part of a crew on an M–8, an armored, self-propelled 75 mm that the men called a tank, even though its protection was limited to high steel sides. "I felt apprehension going into combat but was super alert. My insides jumped at fire in our direction or any sustained fire. Sometimes I started to sweat. I had a small feeling of security surrounded by the steel side of an M–8. I hoped the Japanese didn't have anything larger than machine guns.

"That first afternoon, the platoon sergeant and I were digging our slit trench. It was halfway completed when two artillery shells, incoming, exploded about seventy-five yards away. Both of us dove to the ground. The platoon sergeant was closer to the slit trench, so he jumped in there. I was headed there also but there wasn't room for both of us, so I just hit the ground where I was. My cartridge belt twisted when I hit the ground and my canteen was in the front. I landed so hard, the canteen knocked the breath out of me. As I tried to recover, the platoon sergeant was yelling, 'Oh, God, oh, God!' We remained prone and when there were no more shells, we got up to finish the trench.

"A few minutes later, two more shells exploded. I thought they were close and we both hit the ground in the same places. This time I was the one yelling, 'Oh, God, oh, God!' The sergeant looked at me with eyes big as cups. He thought I'd been hit. When it quieted down and the trench was completed, we went back to the company. We'd been digging sort of an outpost and when we returned, we found the lieutenant had changed his mind. The slit trench wasn't even used.

"We were usually up soon after daybreak. I was seldom the first out because, if there were snipers, I wanted them to use up their ammo at someone else. It seems hardhearted now, but that was how I felt then.

"After breakfast rations we'd start the M–8 and work, usually in support of the 1st Battalion of the 305th. Most days were spent attacking, which meant walking towards the Japanese positions. It meant going forward, sometimes in a skirmish line, sometimes in columns, depending upon the terrain.

"When they hit resistance, we were committed, depending on whether we were close by if they needed the tanks. Usually we fired machine guns unless the resistance was tough. Then if we had a good field of fire, we'd use the 75. After that spot was cleared, we'd continue on the attack.

"In the late afternoon, we would eat when we could. When we stopped for the day, we'd all dig in as part of the battalion defensive perimeter. Our driver slept under the tank with one other man from Cannon Company. The other three of the crew either slept in the tank or pulled guard, one hour on, two off. If the situation was considered dangerous at night, the driver stayed in the tank with guards on either side of the turret. There was seldom any combat at night.

"We acted like a tank infantry team. One infantry spotter on each side of the M–8 as it moved forward. The squad followed and surrounded us at times. They used us as an outpost, ahead of the line at night. We had a machine gun or a BAR [Browning Automatic Rifle] section with us, plus three of four riflemen dug in nearby. Our artillery fire was very good and fierce, although sometimes the impact was too close for comfort.

"Air support looked and sounded very good. Generally, it consisted of bombing and strafing Japanese positions several times by eight or more planes. Mostly it was naval aircraft used to break up Jap resistance. We seldom had naval gunfire after the first day of combat. On Guam we were never under attack by Japanese planes."

The former sportswriter, Ed Fitzgerald, wore the six stripes of a first sergeant in Service Company, 307th Infantry Regiment. He achieved this status he says, "because I could write and I could type." From the beginning his superiors had discerned Fitzgerald's ability to organize and administer, and from the moment he joined the 307th, he had been a staff person. "I got to be a marksman on the range," says Fitzgerald, "but I never had to clean my rifle. It was always turned over to our armorer artificer, who would take it apart and clean it."

But on July 21, 1944, a nervous Fitzgerald joined the other GIs in "endless, queasy hours circling offshore before we were sent in. When they finally told us to move up topside, we watched the shelling and the bombing in awe. They told us there were four battleships and three heavy cruisers out there where we couldn't see them, relentlessly firing broadsides of shells ranging from five to sixteen inches. We could see a long line of slender, graceful, quick-turning destroyers patrolling a steady beat to protect the big ships and turning spitefully every once in a while to fire their own guns at the island. Agat Bay and Agat Village stood in plain view. Clouds of black smoke and leaping sheets of red flame showed the ferocity of the attack. 'There won't be anything left alive on that island by the time you guys get there,' said a sailor standing near me. That's what *he* thought. It was our first lesson in the exaggerated confidence the Navy had in the effectiveness of offshore shelling. What we found out was that when it started, the Japanese went into their elaborate caves, and when it stopped, they came out and started shooting. They fired their rifles and lobbed their mortars down on us from high ground and even opened up with artillery pieces that they had made room for in the same caves they hid in.

"But before we learned this hard lesson, we had to go over what is generally considered the greatest barrier reef in the Pacific. Our landing craft couldn't go over it, so we had to walk over it. We lost a lot of men before we ever got close enough for the Japanese to shoot at us. Everybody was carrying a helluva lot of weight. It was a helluva long distance from the boats to the beach. Some of the men were too seasick to keep themselves upright, some of them stepped into holes in the reef and just disappeared from sight.

"The first worry we had, in the boats and after we got out of them, was that our own planes would aim short and hit us. They were coming in right over our heads. But when we saw the first guys go down in the water without a sound, and we reached for them and they weren't there, we realized that our biggest worry was just making it to the beach without drowning."

Following orders, Fitzgerald and his associates settled in about 500 feet beyond the beach line. They dug in for the night. "I learned another lesson that first night," says Fitzgerald. "Some people could stay in their holes, but some of us had to move around the company area and deliver messages and the orders that the colonel gave the captain to give the lieutenants and me. That's what Charlie Bauer's two silver bars and the bars our lieutenants, Morris Shulman, Rickey Del Mar and Tex Wood, wore, and my six stripes were for. I 'volunteered' a lot of people to do things during the war. I made up my mind that was what I was there for. I thought we in Service Company were lucky we weren't in a rifle outfit like Company C, so we'd better take care of those people in C Company.

"Guam was our high school. Everything before that was kindergarten or grammar school, or if you want to give weight to things like the obstacle course and the infiltration course and amphibious training, junior high school. On Guam we learned the big thing wasn't getting mail or something hot to eat, but staying alive.

"Charlie Bauer and I stood on a hill above Agat on the second day ashore, talking to a warrant officer, Warren Pepple, when the first Japanese planes hit us. They were the first we'd ever seen and suddenly they were right over our heads. Machine gun bullets came first and then shells, digging deep, angry holes in the dirt around us. We threw ourselves down. Pepple got hit in his behind by a shell burst.

" 'Don't worry,' I told him. 'You're only bleeding on the side of your ass.' Charlie called for an aid man while I gave Pepple a drink of water and rubbed some of it on his sweaty face. 'He needs help,' Charlie said to the medic. 'No, he doesn't,' the medic said after a minute of working on him. 'He's dead.' "

"Our regiment [the 306th]," recalls Buckner Creel, the youthful platoon leader, "landed on the second day on Guam. Our first night on Mount Alifan was a disaster. Much panic and indiscriminate firing of individual weapons. No enemy could be seen, just shadows and strange noises in the jungle. In our own company headquarters, Pvt. John Loughead was killed by his own foxhole mate when Loughead stuck his head up and was silhouetted above the foxhole. This was quite a personal loss to me. In the States, Loughead had been a trifler and was always in trouble. But during training in Hawaii he had developed into a good soldier. He and I, being the same size and build, had joined up to pass the Expert Infantryman's Test. Although there was the officer-enlisted man relationship, we had developed a closeness and he was slated to become my radio operator.

"I believe training took over and allowed me to cope with my normal fear as I reacted automatically to situations. In addition, I had added responsibilities. I was not only exec for the company but also had taken command of the 1st platoon. One cannot show trepidation and lead troops in combat. The soldiers will willingly follow an assured, confident leader, so any fear had to be 'cooped' up.

"In our first action, my carbine had jammed. I got rid of it and started to carry an M–1. The additional firepower gave me more confidence when actively leading the platoon on our many combat patrols. And my leading gave the troops more confidence in my ability to lead, react and get the tasks done most expeditiously.

"In my first two contacts with the Japanese on Guam, I found that I did react immediately and with the proper action. First, while on patrol we located a group of enemy soldiers in a defilade position. I responded with a hand grenade. It had the desired effect, killing five of them with no losses to us.

"On the second occasion, I rounded a bend in a jungle trail. I came face to face, at a distance of perhaps ten to fifteen paces, with an enemy soldier. We both dropped to our knees and fired. Apparently, I was the more accurate, since I am still here and he isn't. Both times instinctive reactions took over and governed the situation. One doesn't have time to think out a solution in such cases."

Three days after the first Marines went ashore at Guam, Henry Lopez, now a sergeant with the rifle company that Ed Fitzgerald mentioned (Company C), was well beyond his thirtieth birthday when he and his colleagues landed. Bearing gas masks, light combat packs, Bangalore torpedoes, satchel charges, pole charges and five-gallon cans of flame-thrower fuel, they waded through water three to five feet deep onto the black sand beach. "Huge craters, partly filled with water; debris; uprooted, riddled and shredded coconut trees; some destroyed landing craft, and abandoned marine equipment strewn about the area testified to the intensity of the invasion. The indescribable stench of death contaminated the air, stinging and offending the nostrils."

Company C hiked a mile and a half to spend its first night on the island. "Out of sheer curiosity," says Lopez, "men left their holes to see what a dead Jap looked like. In a large shell crater three corpses lay sprawled upwards, their bloated, blackened bodies blown up like gruesome balloons. Hundreds of small, slimy white maggots squirmed on top of one another and ate their way in and out of this stinking, rotten mess. This disgusting sight, as well as the stench, made many men sick and caused them to throw up their recently eaten rations."

The outfit pressed on, engaging in desultory small skirmishes with the enemy. "I am not ashamed to say that when I first came under fire, I was scared to death. The only way I could cope with the fear was to think of the platoon, keep busy and not let anyone know my feelings."

Lopez and his company were pushing north after the Americans had broken out from the vicinity of the beaches. "We moved in a skirmish line with visual contact on one side with a Marine unit, and on our other side was another company from the battalion. Entering very dense woods with heavy undergrowth, the skirmish line became a single-file column and we lost all contact with those both on our left and right sides. We found ourselves past our objective. There was some firing from our left flank and rear.

"Suddenly, we heard a voice demanding, 'Who the hell is firing at us!' I replied, 'Not us.' The voice then asked, 'Who the hell are you?' 'Americans, who the hell are *you*?'

"Without answering my question, he said, 'If you are Americans, throw up your helmet or come towards me.' I threw up my helmet so he could see it. Whereupon, we were greeted with a heavy volume of fire. I didn't have to think twice. We also opened fire and at the same time took off in the opposite direction. We didn't locate the rest of the platoon or the company that day but did come under mortar fire. We ended up with K Company of the Marines just before dusk and dug in with them. There was Jap equipment in the area where we had been and I believe that the man was a Jap who spoke perfect English and pretended to be a Marine.

"We had been told that the Japs would not surrender, which very few did, and to kill them before they killed you; that they would rather die than surrender, so long as they could take you along with them. During our jungle-training course in Hawaii, a large sign read, IF THEY DON'T STINK, STICK THEM. The civilians we encountered on Guam were treated with kindness and respect, along with medical care and food."

For some members of the 77th, the initial experience of Guam gave them a false sense of the war. Lou De Matteis, a twenty-five-year-old from the Bronx, another original with the division, was with the 304th Artillery Battalion. "When we got off the LCIs at Guam, we started to walk up a hill. We saw a couple of Japs in the distance but we strolled along like we were walking down Broadway. If this is combat, I said to myself, I can't believe it. We just weren't streetwise. But a day or so later we encountered fire and then the overpowering, nauseating stench of dead bodies, all Japanese."

Richard E. Spencer, a thirty-one-year-old OCS graduate, drafted even before Pearl Harbor, had originally come to the 77th as a platoon leader but his ability with paper work and organization brought a shift to liaison officer for the 307th Regiment.

After coming ashore on the fourth day, Spencer learned he should find a foxhole at division headquarters. "The chief of staff, Col. Douglas McNair, found me a hole and a piece of tin to put over it. After dark we were shelled and one man was hit. Colonel McNair was walking around, calming everyone down, like a protective father. My admiration for him was reinforced by later contacts.

"Just after the regiment took Mount Barrigada, Colonel McNair and I hiked across country to visit the 307th. He was unusual because he carried typical officer's equipment—a map case, musette bag, etc. To avoid becoming targets for snipers, most of us tried to look from a distance as much like GIs as possible.

"We spent most of the day finding the regiment and arrived too late for dinner. The colonel invited me to his tent to join him in a small meal prepared by his orderly. It was a small matter that showed his consideration for others.

"I learned to hate the flies. With all the unburied dead Japanese around, these pests were thick. It was difficult to eat from your mess kit without swallowing one. This resulted in almost universal dysentery. Luckily, sulpha pills were effective against this ailment."

Like Spencer, Henry Lopez was pained by the scourge of mosquitoes and flies. "They tormented the men, and dengue fever, with symptoms resembling the flu, spread rapidly throughout the company. Hungry flies resisted all swatting during the daytime, while thirsty mosquitoes that nourished on Scat, the insect repellent found in the jungle kit, and which everyone poured on all exposed parts of the body, dominated the night. They were so vicious that they even bit right through fatigue jackets and pants.

Ernest Schlichter, who passed up a deferment because of a job in a war industry, landed on Guam as a member of a Signal Company in the 77th two days after the initial landings. He slept near the beach that first night, discovering several unexploded sixteen-inch shells, one of which he thought was only a buried stone under his blanket.

"The meager rations we carrried ran out and when we inquired for more, were told there were none. We found that the Navy considered the attack on Guam was an Army operation and the Army considered it a naval operation and neither ordered supplies for the 77th Division. Major McKithen, our Signal Company commander, traded jeeps and generators for Navy emergency supplies of rations. One meal had to do us all day.

"It was the rainy season, making it hard for vehicles, and by this time nearly all our jeeps were traded for food from the Navy. We had to carry all our equipment and walking was hard, as much of Guam was hilly, torn up, and the red clay turned into slippery mud.

"McKithen gave orders to shoot to kill anyone that came in after dark because everyone was ordered to stay on or behind the perimeter at night. McKithen didn't realize that many of our men who were assigned to set up radio, telephone and message centers to and from the regiments would travel back at night, especially from in front of our lines. This was the shortest, quickest and easiest way to our camp during the day but dangerous, especially at night.

"A boy from the message center came in with a report one night. Some of our men saw him and couldn't recognize him in the dark and thought he was a Jap. They had been ordered to shoot to kill anyone coming at night and they riddled him with bullets.

"The next night, Major McKithen went to a meeting that lasted longer than expected. The major came back and must have remembered the orders he gave to shoot to kill anyone outside our perimeter at night. He kept hollering, 'This is Major McKithen,' and if I remember right, 'Let me in.' My new slit-trench companion this night had been a close friend of the boy killed the previous evening. When he saw and heard the major, he started crying and cursing. He kept on saying, 'He killed my buddy, kill the bastard!' He raised his M–1. I tried to calm him, shake him to his senses, prevent him from raising his gun but he got away. The major was now within fifty feet and silhouetted in the clearing. I knew he couldn't miss. He was about to pull the trigger when I hit the rifle out of his hands and sent it flying.

"He sat down and cried and said I was sticking up for the SOB. I told him I couldn't blame him for the way he felt but I was trying to keep him from being court-martialed, maybe shot, for killing an officer. I said I wouldn't report him if he wouldn't try it again. He was worn out by then and the next morning promised he wouldn't after I explained the reason for the orders and the circumstances by which his buddy had been killed."

From the start of the war in the Pacific, the Japanese had owned the night. Trained to infiltrate after dark, small numbers of soldiers would sift through positions to catch the Americans off guard in foxholes. After a long day trying to advance against Japanese defenses, hunkered down in holes often muddy or even half full of water, the GIs and leathernecks, their reflexes slowed, their vision restricted and sometimes dozing when they should have been on guard, were the targets of stealthy assassins who wielded knives and bayonets to maintain silence. As the men of the 77th, like Ernie Schlichter, learned, the only defense lay in a policy of shoot to kill for anything that moved after the sun went down.

When the 706th Tank Battalion trundled ashore on Guam, William Siegel, as a staff officer for the unit, acted as liaison from the division advance command post. "It was there that I attended all of General Bruce's briefings with his staff and the regimental COs. Also, I was able to observe the few Japanese prisoners that arrived. When captured, they were very polite, docile and humble, as a rule. We in our unit never considered the Japanese as demons, but rather as sly and treacherous. Furthermore, our instructions were that if we captured any of the enemy, we, as officers, would be held responsible for their well-being, as provided by the Geneva Convention."

Like all Army divisions, the 77th had attached to it special units. Among these was the 292nd Joint Assault Signal Company, 504 officers and men with the mission to furnish communications among troops on the beach, their naval and air support. Alanson Sturgis, Jr. served as a captain with the outfit.

Son of a New York architect, Sturgis graduated from Harvard in 1941 with a reserve commission in the field artillery. "I thought it would be useful to know what it was like to serve as an enlisted man, and so I had joined the Massachussetts National Gaurd and went on 1st Army maneuvers in 1940. There I saw the results of a less than bare-bones military budget. The infantrymen did not have blanks for their rifles. They ran around yelling 'bang!' Our antitank guns were gas pipes mounted on bicycle wheels. Any bombing was done, not with shells, but bags of flour to mark the explosions."

By the time the 77th reached Guam, however, Sturgis and his 292nd JASCO group were fully operational. "On Guam, I was normally with a rifle company at their observation post. We used naval gunfire, mainly for illumination at night. Through the use of star shells it was continuous, because the Japs were the only people who moved at night."

On August 6, after most of Guam had been secured, Dick Spencer's benefactor, Col. Douglas McNair, incautiously entered what was supposed to be a deserted hut. Japanese stragglers, hiding there, shot and killed him. For the division chief, General Bruce, it was a severe blow. He had served under Leslie McNair, Douglas's father, and to his sorrow had heard that the elder McNair had been killed by friendly fire in Europe two weeks before. Now Bruce mourned the death of the son.

With the last of the Japanese subdued, the 77th remained on Guam in a garrison status, recovering from the first exposure to battle and training for what lay ahead. Recalls Siegel, "Living conditions were

terrible. Rain and mud were serious hardships for men and equipment.
Our unit was overcome at one point by dengue fever. The only way we
could dispense any nourishment for the sick was to acquire food and
juices through midnight raids on the supply dumps along the beaches.
When we bivouacked at Orote, our pup tents were still in the mud. Our
camp adjoined a Seabee unit which was housed and fed in comparative
luxury. Our rations were meager—all canned or dried. Our best Sunday
dinner was fried Spam and powdered potatoes."

In November, three months after the first men of the division hit the
beaches, the troops boarded ships seemingly bound for New Caledonia
and a period of rehabilitation and rest. But while at sea, orders from
MacArthur abruptly reversed their course. The 77th now was to join an
amphibious operation on Leyte, the southernmost island of the
Philipines.

Buckner Creel observes that the experience on Guam was invaluable
for the new ordeal by fire. "Since our unit was not involved in heavy
action on Guam, we were 'blooded' gently. As a result, we had a chance
in a combat situation to learn our trade and practice it so that we were a
much more efficient, confident and cohesive unit when we landed on
Leyte. We now *knew* how to live and survive in a combat situation. And
had conquered our initial fear of the Japanese soldier, who had been
touted as the master of the jungle and warfare in general. We had
discovered that they were just as disturbed in a combat zone as we
were, and, additionally, our equipment was far superior to theirs. Our
confidence grew."

The 77th's participation at Leyte involved a masterstroke, a surprise
landing at Ormoc Beach behind the Japanese lines. Although U.S.
forces were battering the enemy from three sides on Leyte, the defenders continued to hold out, sustained by fresh troops and supplies fun-
neled through Ormoc. Says Ed Fitzgerald, with Service Company of
the 307th, "They had been pouring reinforcements ashore there, more
than 100,000 landed [in spite of repeated attacks from the air and the
loss of thousands of men aboard transports that were sunk] and were
moving rapidly to back up the reduced armies facing the Americans
pushing inland from the east. MacArthur decided to hit them from
behind.

"The end run was mounted so quickly we didn't even take all of our
people with us. We took only those who were essential. We left personnel people, mail people and all kinds of support people behind. Those
of us who went got on a shiny new LST. Eating in the mess hall was like
eating in Horn & Hardart's [a now-extinct chain of cafeteria and vend-

ing-machine restaurants]. One day, the captain, who was a young lieutenant who looked barely twenty-one, dropped the ramp and let us
jump off and swim in the beaufiful blue water, and after that we
thought *he* was great.

"He was no Mister Roberts, though," Fitzgerald said. "When we got
to the beach at Ormoc, the morning of December 7 and he shoved that
ramp onto the shore and let us off, a flight of Japanese airplanes raced
in like a swarm of angry bees trying to get even with us for poking a
stick in their nest. We were just beginning to lug off our ammunition
and food when he began to back off the beach.

" 'Where the hell are you going?' a bunch of us screamed at him.

" 'Listen, you dumb bastards,' he yelled back, opening up the water
between us and our stuff and leaving us standing up to our asses in the
water, 'don't you know these fucking things cost five million bucks?' "

Watching the goings-on from the air were Piper Cubs, observation
planes for the 77th Division artillery. With the men pouring ashore,
General Bruce sent a message by Cub to Gen. John Hodge, XXIV
Corps commander, "The 77th has landed; 7 Come 11." He meant that,
with his forces in place, the 7th Infantry Division could head up the
coast from the south while the 11th Airborne could proceed down the
valley north of Ormoc City.

Fitzgerald and his comrades dug in only fifty or sixty yards from the
beach for the night when an astonishing confrontation occurred. "We
were wriggling uneasily in our slit trenches, trying to duck the madden-
ingly random mortar fire coming from just a few hundred yards ahead
of us, when suddenly a Japanese version of an LST plowed up on the
beach behind us and dropped its ramp just about where Captain Courageous had abandoned us."

Apparently, the Japanese had not realized that the Americans now
occupied that stretch of shore. "Don't let them get ashore," Fitzgerald
heard Capt. Charlie Bauer holler. "This was the most aggressively 'military' I'd ever seen my gentle Philadelphia friend. 'Get them on the
ramp! Watch the side of the ship! Get them if they jump!' "

In the space of a single hour, 749 of the 750 Japanese soldiers were
dead. The single survivor was found a week later, curled up in the
crow's nest of the shambles that remained of the transport.

John Kriegsman, a former Peoria, Illinois, youth, whose thirty-five-
dollar-a-semester tuition fee was covered by his Reserve Officers' Training Corps pay while at the University of Illinois, flew Piper Cub observation planes for the 77th's artillery. "Flying in the South Pacific had
lots of advantages over the European theater with the Germans and

their .88 gun. Intelligence told us the Japanese would not fire on the little planes with the big wings for fear of retaliation. If we did receive fire, we could fly out over the ocean for protection. But as a result of stories about the treatment of pilots when forced down in enemy territory, we did not wear parachutes. We preferred death to capture.

"During these first days on Leyte, the Cub surveillance was constant. Initially, beaches were used as airstrips. As the infantry occupied an area, the flat fields and roadways were established as landing strips. The Cubs were constantly in the air, directing artillery fire, dropping rifle grenades to flush Japs out of buildings, hauling white stove gasoline to infantry units mired in mud, hauling out the wounded and dead, delivering blood plasma and even mail."

In the succeeding days, the Japanese air arm continued to hit the beach area. Dick Forse jumped into watery slit trenches in what had been a rice paddy. A bulldozer had just tugged his M–8 out of the muck when "eight to ten Val dive bombers attacked the beach. I fired the .50 caliber machine gun at three or four of them as they pulled out and climbed to the clouds. I tried to arch the fire above the planes and with a good lead on each one but I don't think I hit any. Just then four P–38s from the 5th Air Force zoomed up and shot down three or four.

"We were attacked by two dive bombers the next day. All but the M–8s had moved out when the Japs came. They didn't dive on us but flew towards us. Both M–8s fired at the planes until they each released two bombs. I felt I was really accurate, it was like a hose and I was sure the plane I was firing on had to run into the rounds. We didn't shoot either down, but I think we must have hit them because they dropped their bombs too early, and they exploded in a field about 100 yards away."

Henry Lopez with Company C was among those initially concerned with the enemy aircraft but little opposition from enemy ground troops greeted the Americans and they quickly penetrated inland. The convoy that had carried them and which was vital for supply and evacuation of wounded remained under prolonged attack, losing two ships and three more being severely damaged. While the Liberty Division soldiers initially had surprised the enemy, the opposition soon stiffened.

Company C led the attack that took the village of Ipil and the pace of advance began to be measured in yards. Says Lopez, "Dark, moonless and starless nights were occasionally filled with imagined terrors. Darkness and fear, more often than not, played weird tricks on the eyes. The shape of a bush, a log, or a waving palm frond would at times resemble a watching, waiting, or a slinking Jap; even the pattern of moonlight with its soft shadows was confusing. For this very reason the men had been taught during jungle training that to better distinguish an object at night, it was best not to look at it squarely but to view it from the corner of the eye instead. With the coming of each night, with its many hidden terrors, the men silently prayed for clear skies and a moonlit night filled with bright stars.

"While on Leyte, a patrol from my company was sent out to try and locate and contact a unit from the 306th to tell them our 1st Battalion was advancing north on Highway 2 to the road junction, the prime target. The squad had advanced some distance when they were fired on by a patrol from the 306th which did not know who they were. Three were wounded, including Sgt. Alfred Junkin.

"Less seriously injured than the others, Junkin decided to return to 1st Battalion HQ and have litter bearers help evacuate the wounded. When Junkin returned with the aidmen, they found no one there. As a result, I was sent with others to locate the 306th and find out if their men had picked up our wounded.

"During this mission we came under mortar fire from the Japanese on a high ridge. One soldier came to me and said, 'Sergeant, let's go back and report we were not able to find the 306th.' I replied, 'If you want to go back, go ahead.' I knew he couldn't go alone without having to explain what happened. When we got to Okinawa, I would have another incident with this same soldier."

Lou De Matteis with the 304th Artillery Battalion was at sea when the Japanese aircraft hit the flotilla. "We could see two or three ships smoking; they were on fire all night, like beacons. One plane roared overhead, low enough so we could see the scarf of the neck of the pilot. His wingtip hit the top of our mast and then hit a destroyer. It split in two and within ninety seconds sailors were in the burning water, helmets bobbing there like coconuts." For the men of the 77th this was their first sight of the kamikaze, a tactic adopted during the battle at sea off Leyte and Samar, another Philippine island.

"It was getting dark when we finally started in," says De Matteis. "Nobody seemed to know where we'd land. We headed for a bright light on shore. When we got close, a machine gun from a Japanese emplacement opened up. We backed off and then moved to an area marked with flashlights. We were told to unload. The Navy wanted no part of it; they left us with our LCIs barely loaded. We were completely surrounded on the Yamashita Line. There was no sleep at night with action going on all around us.

"A couple of days later we were guarding the trail leading inland, and a couple of sailors came ashore. They were looking for souvenirs and started to go up the trail. I warned them there were still some enemy around. They insisted nobody was there and went off, like they, too, were heading down Broadway. A couple of hours later, they brought both of them in, dead. The sailors were always hungry for souvenirs. If you picked up a Nambu pistol from a pile of weapons collected after an action, you could sell it for maybe fifty bucks. But if you were a good story teller, and you described to a sailor how you took this bloody pistol off a Jap officer after a hand-to-hand fight, you could get as much as $500 for it."

Ed Fitzgerald, endeavoring to maintain his career as a writer, had begun to write articles about his experiences and send them to his wife Liby, who acted as the agent. "The first piece was on the ferocity with which the American soldier hunted souvenirs. Any piece of Japanese military equipment would do, but flags were precious and the ultimate souvenir was a samurai sword. No Japanese was ever buried still wearing or carrying anything that an American GI thought was worth something as a souvenir. Even if you already had one just like it, you could trade it to a sailor or a Seabee for something really useful, like a few cold beers."

The collection of enemy artifacts cost more than a few casualties, due to incautious searches that exposed relic hunters to enemy fire (the sailors cited by De Matteis) or booby traps for the unwary who picked up what seemed to be a discarded piece of equipment. By the time they would hit Okinawa, the men of the 77th had learned from experiences on Guam and Leyte of the danger of gathering souvenirs.

One week after the 77th first surprised the enemy with the Ormoc maneuver, the stage was set for an all-out attack against the hard kernel of Japanese resistance. "I had developed a reputation as a successful leader of reconnaissance and combat patrols," notes Buckner Creel. "When the decision was made to attempt a flanking movement out of Ormoc, I was selected to lead one of the patrols to determine if the planned route was feasible. We went out December 14 and did not get very far because there was a lot of Japanese activity. I took out a patrol the following day, and passed through the lines of the 307th Regiment [the outfit to which Ed Fitzgerald and Henry Lopez belonged]. I arranged recognition signals to allow us back in. We waded a river and managed to make our way down the proposed route. We started to pick up enemy patrols, groups and miscellaneous activities.

"After considering the alternatives, I sent the rest of the patrol back to a rendezvous point and arranged that they should wait there for me. I continued on alone, through rice paddies, across streams into bamboo thickets. I discovered a possible route for our coming attack.

"Meanwhile, back at the rendezvous spot, Sgt. Bill Barrett, my assistant patrol leader, came upon a Japanese group setting up an ambush. Our men destroyed the enemy and then hightailed it for the lines of the 307th. I believe Barrett earned a Bronze Star for what he did.

"Having gone as far as I could," says Creel, "I had already started back when I heard the sound of the gunfire. Although worried and concerned for the safety of my men, I figured things were probably under control. But I still had the problem of getting myself back with the information I had obtained.

"Since it was getting late in the day, I opted for speed and boldness rather than stealth. I left the paddies and streams and brazenly started walking back, standing erect, across country. We didn't wear our steel pots on these missions, so I had tied a khaki handkerchief around my head. I noted that I had apparently come into a sector where the Japanese soldiers seemed to act as if it were a rest area. The troops moved around with their rifles at 'sling arms.' I quickly slung my M–1 over my shoulder and took off at a rapid pace.

"At least twice, I ran across small groups of Japanese, several hundred yards off. When they seemed to notice me, I would wave at them and proceed determinedly on. It was a good thing darkness was falling. At six feet, one inch, I am not a typical Japanese soldier. My fatigue uniform, after I crawled through the rice paddies and underbrush, was a dirty, nondescript color, so it did not give me away.

"When I reached the prearranged rendezvous site," continues Creel, "I found no patrol, but some newly dead enemy scattered about. Realizing what had happened, I hurried to the river, crossed it and reached the lines of the 307th. The signal we'd agreed upon was a series of three shots from my M–1. But it was so clogged with mud from the rice paddies that it wouldn't fire semiautomatic. I got off the rounds by ejecting and reloading manually. The GIs yelled, 'All right! All right! We hear you. Come on in.'

"When I got to their positions, they asked me if I was the lieutenant who was lost. I denied ever being lost, and after finding out my patrol was safe, I headed for the 306th debriefing area, pulling leeches off my lower body. Some of these were quite large and full of my blood, since they'd been there most of the day. I am not really fond of leeches since that day. I was informed that I had been recommended for the Distinguished Service Cross but that the XXIV Corps Headquarters had downgraded the request and approved a Silver Star instead."

Recalls liaison pilot John Kriegsman, "On Leyte, the week after that ship with 750 men was destroyed, the fighting turned into a slaughter of the enemy. It took six days for two bulldozers to bury the dead. On Christmas Eve, another Combat Team loaded on a landing craft for an all-night 'cruise' to Palompon on the west coast for a surprise landing Christmas Day to prevent the escape of the remainder of the enemy. The main street became a landing strip for the Cubs. They were the only link to Ormoc City, since the road was still under control of the Japs."

Buckner Creel and his men often tried to supplement the drab K- and C-ration diets. "We supplemented the food with bananas, plantains, peppers and coconuts. Invariably, diarrhea followed. Although we had been taught at the jungle-training center on Oahu that one could drink the coconut milk from green coconuts but not eat the meat; conversely, one could eat the meat of the ripe coconuts, but the milk from them would give you the runs, we usually forgot and suffered the consequences. On Leyte, because we were 'liberating' the people, quite frequently we were able to add rice, chicken and, even once, the fatted hog."

Following Guam, while G Company stayed in a rest area, the unit's cooks approached Creel to complain that they had not qualified for the Combat Infantryman's Badge, an honored trophy that also increased a soldier's pay ten dollars a month. "They expressed a desire to earn the CIB," says Creel. "In the Leyte campaign, I assigned all the cooks and their helpers to the 4th platoon, as ammo bearers and assistant gunners. One of them was wounded. When they had served the required time to qualify for the CIB, I released them back to the battalion trains [rear echelon] and informed them that they should now have an appreciation of how important hot food was for the combat soldier. From then on, for the rest of the war, G Company got hot chow if it was humanly possible. Our CIB cooks would get to us with heated C rations and hot coffee. Other units wondered how we did it. When I explained our technique, several others adopted it. Our combat cooks also qualified for the bronze arrowhead device for their Asiatic-Pacific campaign medal because they landed with the first wave in the assault landing at Ormoc on Leyte."

On Christmas Day, 1944, General MacArthur officially announced that the campaign for Leyte had ended. The men of the 77th feasted on turkey, dressing, gravy, asparagus, mashed potatoes, fruit cocktail and Coca-Cola. Some of the GIs in Henry Lopez's C Company suffered ptomaine poisoning from tainted turkeys.

The division busied itself with the dangerous task of mopping up, cleaning out holdouts from the Japanese forces while coping with booby traps and unexploded shells. There were enough of the enemy still shooting, in spite of MacArthur's proclamation, to create savage firefights and cost a number of lives. The resistance petered out and there came a time for the troops to shift to rest areas for a few weeks before heading for the Ryukyus.

While in this phase, the 77th began to integrate replacements. Among them was a twenty-two-year-old from Fairfield, California, Larry Gerevas. "I worried about world affairs and having to go to war while I was still a kid. All through grammar school I had friends that were Japanese and Chinese. The Japanese were demonized by the movies prior to the war. The Army continued this propaganda to the inductees with films such as the *Why We Fight* series. The whole point of this brainwashing was to make one angry enough to kill them and think of the Japs as subhuman. After months of talks and films, I felt I was justified in killing Japs. When I came to the 77th Division, the men in my unit really hated Japs. Many of them had been wounded or had buddies killed.

"As a replacement, I felt like the new kid on the block. All the old-timers had been through a couple of campaigns together and shared a lot of experiences and lost many friends. The replacements felt more comfortable being with each other but we were assigned to different platoons.

"The veterans seemed to love to talk about their combat experiences. They would talk about how this guy got hit or how they killed some Japs, but they would talk to each other, not to the replacements. I remember listening to every word and becoming more frightened than ever.

"A few days after joining Company K, the supply sergeant was stacking some machine guns and somehow one fired into his chest. He died as he was carried out of the supply tent. The old timers took this in stride, not too concerned. This coldness was frightening to me. Now as I look back, I don't think any of them thought they would go home alive. These were tired and demoralized men that were bitter about being used up in the meat grinder of combat."

CHAPTER V

LOVE DAY FOREPLAY

With the four Army and two Marine divisions to be committed, the entire Ryukyu operation was expected to involve 172,000 combatant forces supported by another 115,000 troops. Hauling this enormous number of people with all of their equipment required eight transport squadrons from the Navy, flotillas which totaled more than 450 ships. Of necessity, these would be supported by warships for screening and attack purposes. The total amphibious forces added up to more than 1,200 vessels. The number does not include ships from the Royal Navy, Adm. Marc Mitscher's Fast Carrier (Aircraft) Force, some units from other groups. At least 1,500 Allied craft would participate in Operation Iceberg.

To keep the enemy back on its heels, in mid-March, the Allied navies punched away at Japanese ships and installations on Kyushu. The foe counterattacked mainly with kamikazes and conventional bombing raids. Over a period of days, they scored hits on a number of aircraft carriers—*Enterprise, Intrepid, Yorktown, Wasp* and, most devastatingly, on *Franklin*. A series of explosions and fires rocked the huge ship and the final count showed 724 of the crew killed or missing and another 265 wounded. Another 1,700 owed their lives to rescue efforts by nearby cruisers and destroyers which plucked them from the water after all but key personnel received the abandon-ship order. Eventually, the fires aboard "Big Ben" were extinguished. The shattered remains, a mass of twisted, charred metal with a temporarily patched hull, managed to stay afloat under its own power as it traveled 12,000 miles to New York for repairs.

A critical decision in the design of U.S. carriers had specified wooden flight decks rather than steel ones. The use of a lighter-weight material enabled U.S. carriers to bear a greater number of planes compared to the complement aboard British ships which lay down steel. But Japanese bombs penetrated the thin, flammable wood and crashed through to explode amid hangar decks, munitions magazines and power plants. (The *Wasp* also had a missile smash down into the ship's interior before going off between the second and third decks but the crew quickly extinguished the blaze.)

The tradeoff, additional firepower and speed in place of safety—the weightier decks introduced a top-heavy quality and slowed the British carriers—was partly adjusted by intensive instruction in firefighting instituted by the Navy earlier. Experts who had served with the New York City and Boston fire departments convinced the Bureau of Ships to issue new fog nozzles that produced a fine spray and snuffed out flames more quickly than the usual heavy stream of water. Big ships received additional fire mains, ones that worked independently of a vessel's power plant, which often shut down after a big hit.

As Love Day approached, the extensive casualties for the Navy continued because of the need to sweep the waters off the Ryukyus clear of mines. During the sanitation of 2,500 square miles of ocean, the fire-support destroyer *Halligan* struck a mine that set off her two forward magazines. Smoke and debris rose 200 feet in the air and the ship was abandoned with a loss of 153 and thirty-nine wounded, well over half her complement. Other minesweepers suffered through attacks by the increasing forays of kamikazes.

While the Navy coped with its problems, the 77th Division readied itself for Kerama Retto. Frank Barron missed all of the fighting on Leyte while recovering from the bullet wound incurred on Guam. When he returned to the 305th Regiment in the Philippines, as it prepared for its next campaign, he was assigned as the CO of Company A, a post formerly held by his friend Arthur Curtin, hurt so badly on Guam that he never came back to the division.

"All of the rifle and heavy weapons companies went to Kerama Retto on LSTs. Regimental headquarters and other units were on the *Henrico*. I believe I had about 150 to 160 enlisted men and five officers [20 to 25 percent below the normal complement]. This also included recent replacements.

"Our battalion was to take the island of Zamami. We were to clean up

Six days before Love Day, troops attend church services aboard an LST at Aka Shima in Kerama Retto. (*Jack Lewis*)

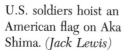

U.S. soldiers hoist an American flag on Aka Shima. (*Jack Lewis*)

On Aka Shima, civilians palaver with interpreter Max Dorthy, Specialist, 2nd/class. (*Jack Lewis*)

these islands in three days, reloading combat ready and then prepared to execute any one of seven possibilities. From the map it looked like there were two possible beaches on Zamami. The one selected appeared to me to be a death trap—right in the main harbor with a peninsula flanking each side. The Japs could have had grazing crossfire covering the entire approach. While I thought it was suicidal, somebody knew something I didn't; this was not the beach the Japs defended.

"It was a very strange feeling to be in a line of amtracs winding their way between strange little islands to form in waves headed for Zamami Harbor. There were geysers all around, but I think they were mostly Navy shorts with a few Jap mortars interspersed. As soon as we hit the beach, we were out of the amtracs and then over a pair of four-foot seawalls. Now we were in the streets and rubble of Zamami town.

"Within thirty minutes or less, two of my men brought in an Okinawan civilian. As they came upon him in a cave, he cut his own throat; he had just killed his wife and two children to spare them the treatment they had been told would be their fate at the hands of the Americans."

Barron and his troops encountered very little resistance during their first day and occupied the town area easily. His former outfit, C Company, pushed onto the high ground and during the night repulsed several attacks. "First the Japs would start firing mortars into the C positions. The intensity of this fire would gradually increase in order to keep the GIs down in their slit trenches. Suddenly the fire would lift and immediately a line of charging, screaming Japs would appear almost on top of them. Some would penetrate the position before they were killed or withdrew. Machine guns cut down the bulk of the attacking Japanese."

On their second day on Zamami, Barron's A Company explored one of the 350–450-foot high, double-humped peninsulas. "On the eastern side, the ground sloped off rather sharply," recalls Barron, "but on the western ridge there was a sheer drop down to the beach. Because of the narrow frontage, I deployed about eight or ten men in a semicircle. As we moved forward, I took a position within this semicircle, following closely behind the point man. The remainder of the platoon was strung out behind, and others in the company back of them.

"As we reached the top of the first hump, I realized the riflemen around me had frozen. Simultaneously, I focused on a little group of civilians. Right on the edge of the precipice a young woman held a baby in her arms with another young woman beside her and a two- or three-year-old child just in front. They were about thirty or forty feet away from me, all staring at us like little frightened animals.

"At that moment, a man's head appeared from behind the woman's shoulder. I could only see his head and neck but he had on a uniform collar. If this man had a weapon, say a grenade, we were in real trouble, unless we opened fire and shot the whole crowd off the hill. I beckoned to the man to approach me, while at the same time taking a couple of steps that I thought might position me to see whether he had anything in his hands. In a second they were all gone. A few steps and I was able to look down the side of the cliff to see their bodies bouncing off the side of the walls on the way down.

"I could have shot the woman and eliminated the threat of the man behind her with the same shot. Obviously, we all took a chance with the idea of saving these innocent people, but to no avail. I did, however, jeopardize the safety of my men and myself."

Within a few hours, Barron and his troops returned to their LST. There had been a rumor that they would be aboard the far more comfortable *Henrico*. But in that hope they were disappointed. They could not know at the time how fortuitous their ship assignment was.

Elements of the 304th FA Battalion had been assigned to come ashore via DUKWs, amphibious trucks, once the beaches were secured. The terrain of Kerama Retto denied even minimal landing strips for the 77th's air section, eleven Piper Cubs that spotted for the big guns. "While on Leyte, we found out we were going to leave a week before the main task force for Okinawa," recalls John Kriegsman, who headed the unit. "About the same time we were issued two of the craziest-looking hooks we had ever seen on any aircraft. Along with the hooks were instructions on how and where they were to be mounted on our Cubs. Mystery was the order of the day! We figured we were to hook something but we didn't know what!

"Word circulated that we were to operate off an LST ship. A naval commander was to arrive on a transport and explain how the hooks were to be used. He came and was extremely vague. He was unable to supply a photograph or even a sketch to show how the LST was fitted to handle a Cub. He did tell us that at Iwo Jima, an LST was used for the Marines' L–5 Stinson, a much heavier plane than ours. The Navy commander left without any further information.

"The day before we were schduled to depart, LST 776 with what was called a Brodie Device mounted on its deck showed up. Several of us from the air section, including Lieutenant Montgomery and myself, went on board. The crew explained how the device worked and what we would need to do to use it. The convoy got underway with our LST as a part of it. We had no chance to practice landings or takeoffs. But Lieutenant Montgomery and I were expected to put down on that ship which could only accommodate two Cubs.

"With the convoy underway, we were the show of the day. All eyes and field glasses from nearby ships were on us as we gingerly flew around the LST, valiantly trying to hook the loop. Lieutenant Montgomery was the first to succeed after only three passes. I managed in five. Thanks be to God, we did not damage the precious-looking planes.

"The Brodie Device gave LST 776 a strange look. Forward was a steel pole about thirty feet high. An arm protruded over the port side of the ship for about thirty feet in a ten-o'clock position. The same setup existed on aft part of the ship with that arm in an eight-o'clock position. From one arm to the other ran a wire like a trolley cable. Atop both ends of the arms was a sort of receiving platform for the crew to stand on and manipulate the trolley.

"When a plane was to land, a nylon rectangle about three feet wide and four feet long would drop from the trolley device and roll aft. Meanwhile, the LST would turn into the wind at full speed, and since the vessel had little or no keel, it rolled gently. The arms sticking over the side described an arc of perhaps thirty feet. The pilot approached the loop in sort of a porpoise fashion, trying to get the rhythm of the ship as he came in so that when he hooked or, worse, missed the loop, the arm wouldn't come crashing down on him.

"Cubs ordinarily were tail-draggers. For a three-point landing, you pulled the joy stick into your belly. It was as natural as pulling on your trousers. Not so when you hook the loop. You had to remember to jam the stick ahead at the slightest tug when you hooked in order to keep the nose down and the prop from going up into the cable, where it would be chewed to pieces.

"Perhaps the worse thing that could happen was to believe you were hooked when you weren't and jam the stick forward. Diving thirty feet straight down on the deck could make a big problem. The maneuvers required extreme concentration, particularly since we had no practice or formal instruction.

"Securely hooked, the trolley would roll along the cable. The ship's crew would halt it and at the forward end, the sailors would transfer the plane to a cable leading down to the deck.

"For takeoff, they installed a twelve-inch nylon loop in a small eye atop the hook. Pilot, passenger and Cub would then be lifted, connected to the trolley and transferred to the larger cable. The crew would pull the trolley as far aft as possible. The plane would be held there while the LST headed at full power into the wind. The Cub pilot applied maximum rpms and then signaled when ready. The crew would release him.

"The length of the cable was about 250 feet. When the pilot figured he was about three quarters along, he pulled the 'chain,' much like flushing an old-fashioned toilet with an overhead tank. The plane might still not have enough airspeed to fly but it was free of the trolley. Using the thirty feet of altitude, the pilot nosed down to pick up enough airspeed just before hitting the water. From there on, it was normal flying.

"We didn't feel it was risky except we were concerned about our lack of opportunity to practice. We were the only two Cubs available for observing the initial Kerama Retto landings."

On Palm Sunday, U.S. warships began a bombardment of Kerama Retto. Under the cover of this fire, teams of frogmen swam in toward the beaches to map the reefs and mark spots where coral threatened landing craft. Unlike the shores of Normandy, France, some ten months earlier, where the invaders could use the Higgins smooth-bottomed powerboats that carried twenty-four soldiers, the reefs girdling the Ryukyus as well as many other Pacific targets, could only be crossed with amphtracs (known to some GIs as amtracs) or LVTs, in naval argot. These were track-borne, water-going, gasoline-engine-powered craft that could crawl over the roughest surfaces bearing a load of twenty troops.

Four battalion landing teams of the 77th Division clambered out of their amphtracs in the early morning of March 26 on the beaches of four islands in the Kerama Retto group. Thanks to the preparations and practices carried out in the Philippines, the troops landed at the right places and almost all on schedule. The covering fire had been so effective that not a single man or amphtrac was lost.

"As the 77th Division convoy approached the Kerma Retto, on March 26," recalls Kriegsman, "we took off from our LST to observe what we could. The radio asked us if we noticed anything unusual. We reported a funny thing. All the islands had these railroad tracks leading from the water to caves. There were dozens of them with nothing else visible. We couldn't figure out what that meant.

"The information was probably the greatest observation we made. Those caves contained the small fast boats with depth charges. While the Japanese had figured an American task force might attack Okinawa, they apparently did not believe anyone would bother to look at Kerama

Retto. Otherwise they might have done a better job of camouflaging the tracks."

Until the discovery by Kriegsman and his fellow pilot, the Navy was unaware of the Q-boat menace. On March 28, two days after Kriegsman radioed his findings, one of the suicide boat pilots "chickened out," dumping his depth charge forty to sixty feet way from his target. The same evening, three boats out looking for prey were destroyed, and the following morning another trio lost an engagement with a U.S. vessel. Not until March 31 did a Tenth Army Operations Summary officially note that suicide boats might threaten the invasion of Okinawa.

Official accounts declare that the ragtag defenders, a small complement of soldiers bolstered by the Q-boat pilots and Korean laborers, offered only sporadic resistance with minimal effect. However, in several instances where the U.S. forces headed into the hills, the Japanese and some of their Korean conscripts fought hard. On the island of Zamami hand-to-hand combat brought out Japanese wielding rifles, pistols and sabers.

"The GIs did not think it was so easy," remarks, Kriegsman. "The only way to snuff out the Japs was to walk over the rock mountains. The boat crews did not give up easily. Navy destroyers poured five-inch shells into the caves to neutralize them.

"Second in command of the division artillery, Col. Royal Gervais and combat team commander Lt. Col. Edward Lever, along with several other officers and men, decided to investigate one of the nearby caves, maybe get a boat. As they approached the cave, they saw a couple of Japs run inside. With drawn pistols they all ran to catch them, bent on taking them alive for questioning. As they reached the cave, a terrific explosion occurred. The cave erupted like it was a huge cannon barrel. Colonel Lever was the first to arrive, with several others right behind them. They caught the full blast. For perhaps six of them, the war was over."

Among the defenders in Kerama Retto was Yoshihiro Minamoto, a farmer's son from Kumamoto-ken on Kyushu, who entered the Army Officers School as a nineteen-year-old in 1941. "We felt threatened by the United States for its failure to understand the survival of Japan with its limited resources," says Minamoto. "We believed that a war of self-defense was necessary in order to break out of the ABCD (America, Britain, China, Dutch) economic confinement.

"As it [the bombing of Pearl Harbor] resulted, although it became a sneak attack, it was caused by the dereliction (or procrastination) of the

Japanese ambassador in Washington. When the war broke out, we believed that a declaration of war had been made and announced.

"We were aware of America's national power, especially its superior economic might and its naval power, the latter being the strongest in the world but we had almost no information on its army. I had a lot of confidence when hostilities first broke out, but I began to have doubts from about 1943 on, and had lost all confidence by the time of my participation in the Okinawa battle. From about 1944 on, the reporting of the war effort in Japan, particularly that of the Navy, was deliberately aimed at lifting morale."

Minamoto, who graduated from the Army Officers School in April 1944, received the assignment of commander of the 3rd Company, 3rd Army Marine Advance Squadron on Tokashiki Island in Kerama Retto. When the U.S. forces began operations against his positions, he had had no previous combat experience.

"We were subjected to fierce air attacks and naval bombardment. The effect was overwhelming. The land attack by the American 77th Division was unbelievable and we marveled at the barrage. When the American forces landed, we subjected the landing fleet to a surprise attack by suicide boats—*tokkotei*. We thought they had a 40 percent chance of being effective." The U.S. Navy records report the *tokkotei* as 100 percent ineffective. Minamoto, with a number of men, retreated into the hills of Tokashiki.

Just as Frank Barron found, the men of the 304th FA Battalion, occupying the island of Geruma Shima, discovered among the indigenous residents, a pattern of mass suicide that would mark much of the battle for the Ryukyus. Then Sgt. Lansing Gilbert of Headquarters Battery pieced together the stories of self-destruction on Geruma Shima. "A sergeant who led a patrol came back and told us that they came upon a cave and on entering they found a man who had killed himself with a crude spear. Farther in the cave they found twelve women and one small boy, all of whom had been strangled with twisted rope. One woman had attempted to strangle herself and her baby with the same piece of rope but the rope slid, failing to kill the child, which was still alive when the patrol arrived." Having rescued the toddler, the Americans handed the girl to some local women who had survived.

Later, 1st Sgt. Francis Wood, questioned a fifteen-year-old boy through a Chinese-American soldier who could write a language the Okinawans understood. The youth said those on the island knew that Tokyo had been bombed but were unaware of events in the Philippines. Asked why the citizens committed suicide, he insisted the Japanese soldiers had not told them to kill themselves. Instead, he said the "people were just scared."

Wood continued to probe for explanations and from another civilian captive he got the reply, "They were scared. When the Americans invaded Saipan, some wounded soldiers were brought to this island and put in the school building. I talked to them and they told me that the Americans were killing all the women and children. I told the village people about it and from this and other stories, the people became extremely scared of the Americans."

"About the fifth day of the Kerama Retto operation," says Kriegsman, "a landing strip was established on the island of Zamami. It was mostly deep sand. However, it had a flat area about the size of a city lot, with some sort of grass growing on it. We could make our takeoff roll on the hard surface. By the time we got to the really deep sand, we would be light enough to pick up speed, and almost roll out over the water.

"The big trouble was landing. Because of the rough mountains being so close, we had to make our approach over the water in spite of a prevailing but slight tailwind. When we landed, we almost stopped dead in the sand. While that saved us from going into the hills, it presented a problem. With the stick in our belly, we couldn't move. If we released the stick a bit too much, the wind would blow our tail up in the air. That happened once. Luckily, the prop stopped crosswise, and did not break as the plane nosed over.

"That strip served as our base for the remainder of the week. And two days before the invasion of Okinawa itself, Long Tom artillery [155 mm howitzers] were placed on two very small atolls about two miles off the point of Naha [Okinawa's principal city and port]. We were called on to observe the firings of the Long Toms as they zeroed in on prepared targets in preparation for landings the following day."

When the Kerama Retto operation ended, the Americans listed 530 of the enemy killed, 121 prisoners and almost 1,200 civilians rounded up. The 77th Division mourned seventy-eight dead and 177 wounded. Close to 250 suicide boats were seized and eventually rendered harmless, although one officer who attempted to joyride in one lost his life to a booby trap.

As many as 300 Japanese soldiers and Korean laborers hid out in the back-country hills of the rugged islands and they would not actually surrender until after V-E Day. Kerama Retto remained a dangerous place to venture. Tom Hamilton, flag secretary to Admiral Kiland aboard the invasion flagship, remembers, "We had strict orders not to go ashore. One officer, however, decided to look for souvenirs. They found his dead body. I had the problem of accounting for his death. Under the circumstances, since he had disobeyed orders, his family was not entitled to benefits. But I decided to treat his case as a killed in action."

CHAPTER VI

THE OLD BREED

The island-to-island drive in the Pacific, a series of sledgehammer blows against the bedrock of Japanese resistance, had exacted a terrible toll. The Marines, starting with the first 1942 strike on Guadalcanal in the Solomons, bore much of the brunt, particularly during the early going. The 1st Marine Division, the original expeditionary force on the "Canal," then participated in the onslaught at Peleliu. Many military historians consider the latter invasion strategically unnecessary, but the losses among the Marines from many different units in the series of campaigns had been severe. Among the harder hit organizations was the 1st Marine Division, the "Old Breed," so named because it entered World War II with mostly career leathernecks, some of whose service dated back to World War I.

By the spring of 1945, Marines who saw combat as early as 1942 had become scarce and the listed 26,274 men available for Operation Iceberg included thousands who had yet to hear a shot fired in anger and many who had only put on the uniform within the past six months. In particularly short supply were the junior officers and upper-echelon noncoms, the ranks usually charged with leading movement forward.

Jim Moll, son of a New Jersey milkman, attempted to join the Marines at ages sixteen and seventeen but his mother refused to sign the papers. "I don't know why I was so interested in becoming a Marine. Maybe for the adventure—I used to read everything I possibly could about the Marines from the day I learned to read."

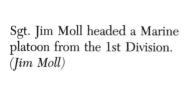

Sgt. Jim Moll headed a Marine
platoon from the 1st Division.
(Jim Moll)

By the time he was old enough to enlist without parental consent,
Moll stood 6'3" and weighed a muscular 200 pounds. "I was always in
pretty good shape. My older brother and I lifted weights, worked out on
the parallel and horizontal bars, jogged in the evenings.

"From the first day with the Marines I loved the life. We had great
drill instructors, Smith and Bailey, both of them had been in for many
years before Pearl Harbor. The first thing they do to a boot is strip him
of all forms of identity. They shave his head, give him Marine fatigues
and then teach him discipline, teamwork and plenty of hard training.

"Much to my disappointment, after three weeks of boot camp I was
told I was going to be a drill instructor myself. I told them I wasn't
going to be a DI and wouldn't drill the platoon the next day. I wanted to
ship out and see combat. That night a dozen guys said they would like to
become DIs. I confronted my drill instructors the next day and again I
got blasted. So I drilled the platoon on what was the lowest day of my
life. But I got lots of support from the DIs and the guys. Still, it was a
sad day when I had to say goodbye to all my buddies. From that day on
I believed what the Marines tried to teach; in the Corps you only make
acquaintances, not friends.

"Later Smith and Bailey told me they didn't care for the assignment either. Shortly after, Smitty went into the Marine Air Force and Bailey went to sea; both were killed."

As a DI, Moll attended a series of special courses—chemical warfare school, rubber-boat instruction for night raids, jujitsu and others. He volunteered for every duty that might liberate him from Parris Island. A temporary assignment with a training program at the University of North Carolina brought an opportunity to escape overseas via a replacement battalion.

"I wound up on Pavuvu [in the Solomon Islands] early in 1944, where, as a buck sergeant, I joined A-1-7, Able Company, 1st Battalion, 7th Marine Regiment. I became platoon guide, sort of the assistant to the platoon sergeant. Most of our time was spent learning warfare tactics, making practice landings, setting up defensive positions, going on night patrols and working with our weapons.

"My first taste of combat was Peleliu. We went in on a Higgins boat, which meant we had to climb over the sides—later models of landing craft had ramps that were lowered. It was an unbelievable experience. There were about fifteen men in our boat. Nobody was talking because there was so much noise you couldn't hear. As you passed between all the big battlewagons, cruisers, etc., they were all blasting away with all their big guns. The noise was deafening. As you looked toward the island, all you could see was explosions, smoke, fire, and overhead planes were diving to drop bombs, fire rockets. You wondered how the hell anybody could be alive on the island when you hit the beach.

"You looked at the men on the landing craft and everyone was solemn. Some were staring in awe at all the fireworks. Some had their eyes closed. Some were talking to themselves; you could see their lips moving, probably praying. I said a few prayers myself.

"As we got closer to the beach, we could see the enemy's shells dropping and some of our landing craft being hit. I could hear machine gun bullets hitting the armor plate in front of me. As we got closer, my heart was beating like a jackhammer. I was sweating profusely and I was waiting for the boat to hit the beach, as I was to be the first one out on the right side. There was so much anxiety, anticipation, hope and other things whirling around in my brain, I don't think there was room for fear. One of my thoughts that consoled me was that this is what I had asked for and if I died, I wanted to go like a good Marine. I knew every guy in that boat felt the same way.

"Fortunately, most of the men in my craft made the beach. Other boats carrying men from our platoon weren't so lucky. When we hit the beach, my legging caught on something as I was climbing over the side. I fell headfirst into the water. I quickly got up and waded onto the beach. About fifteen feet off to my right a Jap machine gunner located in a shallow pillbox was firing on some Marines wading through the water. I crawled over to the pillbox and aimed my tommy gun into it. The damn thing wouldn't fire because sand got into the mechanism when I fell into the water. I pushed a hand grenade in the hole and eliminated him.

"About two minutes later, I was hit in the upper arm by shrapnel, about one inch square. It went through my sleeve and lodged an inch from where it punctured the skin. It didn't even hit the bone, as it traveled almost parallel to it. The shrapnel was red hot and burned like the devil, so maybe it cauterized itself. I was able to dig the piece out with my K-bar knife, so I never turned into sick bay with it. My only regret is that I never will receive a Purple Heart for being wounded.

"It doesn't take long for a man to learn how to survive in combat but sometimes you're in a position where survival is strictly how lucky you are. If you're standing up or in a foxhole with a buddy, you never know

Charles Owens, only 15 years old, completed Marine boot camp in 1942. *(Charles Owens)*

who the sniper is going to aim at and there is no way to fully protect yourself from being ambushed while on a patrol.

"Near the end of the battle for Peleliu, I had my 'bells rung' pretty good. Late on one afternoon, Baker Company attacked up a hill but got pinned down with very intense fire. They sent our company (Able) up so Baker could withdraw. By the time Baker left and we started back, it was getting dark. The Japs were laying down some of their big mortar shells.

"As I was coming down the slope, one of these came down near me. All I can remember is that I was airborne. When I came to, it was pitch dark. Fortunately, I wound up in our own lines. My whole brain seemed numb and everything ached, from my toenails to the hair on top of my head. I wasn't able to shake off some of the effects of that concussion until we got back to Pavuvu. To add to the misery, the few of us left from our platoon all had bad cases of dysentery. We couldn't eat or drink without squatting by the numbers—maybe this was the origin of what they call 'the raggedy-ass Marines.' "

"In March 1942, I turned fourteen," says Georgian Charles Owens, "and in October, I enlisted in the Marine Corps. When the Japs had bombed Pearl Harbor, people in the South got angry but I didn't know whether they'd be easy to beat. As a kid I read all I could about World War I because my father had been in France. I was the only son, with one sister, the Depression was on and I looked for any way to earn money. I managed to join the Civilian Conservation Corps, just before they disbanded it. I used my discharge from the CCC in place of a birth certificate to get into the Marines. My mother thought the recruiting sergeant was just playing games with me when I brought home the papers and she signed them. But they needed warm bodies in 1942 and the next thing she knew, I was at Parris Island.

"I was not prepared for the shock of boot camp. The other recruits weren't either. The drill instructors went about snapping us out of our civilian shit, just as I did seventeen years later as a gunnery sergeant serving as a DI. There was a very large recruit who had played football for Holy Cross. He took me under his wing. If anyone my size picked on me, he'd make me fight them. But beyond that, although they all knew my age, I was protected as long as I held my end of the job up."

To get out of duty at the guard barracks in Norfolk, Owens volunteered for sea duty and drew the Marine detachment aboard the battleship *New York*, then serenely steaming up and down Chesapeake Bay on training maneuvers. Still unhappy with his assignment, Owens heeded the advice of a veteran sergeant who counseled him to take an unauthorized absence for a day, which drew a captain's mast. "I told the captain of the ship that I did not join the Marine Corps to go up and down Chesapeake Bay. He like to have had a heart attack. The next week I was sent to a replacement battalion in Camp Lejeune, North Carolina.

"I joined A Company, 1st Battalion, 7th Marine Regiment in May 1944, and I saw my first combat September 15, of that year [at Peleliu]. I was in the first wave; I was terrified at what I saw on the beach—dead Marines and parts of bodies. I knew this was no game and I wished I was back on the *New York*.

"I had been told and found out fast that the Japanese soldier was a tough SOB and was willing to die. I was wounded that first night on Peleliu by enemy mortar-shell fragments in my neck. I was put on a hospital ship. I had trouble speaking at first but then a doctor asked me if I wanted to go back to my company if I could. I knew if I did not, I might end up in another company and in the Marine Corps; a rifle company with 235 men was like a family. You knew the people and felt safer being with them. So I chose to go back ashore to find my outfit and join them. They were just going up to take the place of the 1st Marine Regiment, led by Col. Chesty Puller.

"In A Company, 1st Battalion, 7th Marines I was a member of the 60 mm section. Besides being mortar crewmen, sometimes we were put on the lines or used as stretcher bearers. That is a hell of a job in combat. Sometimes, everyone is in a foxhole and you have to get out and get the wounded to a safe place where they can be taken to the rear.

"Many of my buddies in A-1-7 were killed on Peleliu. I made new friends."

Another A-1-7 replacement, Philadelphian Earl "Rags" Rice, followed a different route to Peleliu. "I didn't know my father, who died when I was a few weeks old in 1926," says Rice. "I dimly remember being held up to kiss my mother as she lay in her coffin when I was three. Relatives raised me but I was a kid who got into a lotta trouble. I played hooky from school and finally left after the eighth grade. Twice, they sent me to a Protectory [a Catholic institution that harbored problem children]. Nowadays they couldn't hit you but back then the brothers hit me often.

"I didn't know or care anything about world affairs. I only wanted to make money for myself. When Pearl Harbor came, all it meant to me was that I sold out all of my newspapers, kept going back and getting more of them and selling them. But when I was seventeen I enlisted, mainly becase I wanted to get out of where I was and do something with my life. I signed up with the marines. Why, I guess it may have had something to do with the movies of the time.

"Boot camp was very tough. I was very small, maybe weighed about 112 pounds and I had a baby face. I looked like I was about fourteen. I had never even shaved. One day, the corporal came up to me in ranks and I had just a little fuzz on my cheeks. He grabbed me by the collar and started shouting at me. I had just failed to qualify on the rifle range and I felt so bad, I think tears came to my eyes. Guys were always picking on me.

"Over time I added some weight, built myself up to a solid 145 pounds and I felt ready to take people on. I even tried to fight one of those guys who'd made it tough for me but he wouldn't come out of his tent. Eventually, I even qualified as a sharpshooter with a rifle."

As a member of a replacement battalion, Rice shipped out to the Pacific and to the island of Pavuvu for permanent assignment. "I came down with ptomaine poisoning and malaria. One day I went to the toilet thirty-nine times. It got so bad, I spent hours just sitting there with water all around me; it rained so hard. A couple of guys saw how bad I was and took me to Lieutenant Gravit. He sent me to sick bay. They took my temperature; it was 106. But they said they were full up and shipped me back to the battalion. Lieutenant Gravit told the guys to bring me to the hospital and if they didn't take me in, he'd see that some of them had to go to the hospital.

"I spent a week there and by the time I was discharged, I was down to within a few pounds of 100. Gunnery Sergeant Clark informed me which tent I was in, so I hauled my cot and seabag down the company street. While I was walking to the tent, I could see guys looking at me and hear them say, 'What the hell are they sending us, the scrapings from the bottom of the barrel?'

"By the time I reached the tent I was determined to make them eat their words. But as I started to put my cot together, a fellow named Cat Allen told me to move to another tent. Allen was six foot, lean, mean, tough, from Georgia. I insisted the sergeant had assigned me here. He said, 'Out, or else . . .'

"I took that piece of wood that fits into the cot, about eighteen-inches long, half an inch thick. I said, 'I know you can lick me, but before you nail me, I am going to get in one shot across the mouth with this stick. I am quick and I know I can do it and you're going to lose all your teeth.' Allen let me stay that night but I moved to another tent the next day.

"Cat Allen became my group leader and he never let up on me. My squad leader, Joe Gallant, didn't care for me either. He'd had two brothers killed in the Pacific, one more on the way over and still another in boot camp. No matter how hard I worked, they weren't satisfied. One day, I was called in and told that my group leader and squad leader had decided I couldn't make it as a rifleman. I was to be a stretcher bearer. That made me mad as hell. I yelled at Allen, 'You're going to be the first one I pick up.'

"The night before we left for Peleliu we had a big drinking party, home-brewed stuff. Everybody got drunk. A fellow named Boland, a big, good-looking sergeant, talked to me about what I was going to do after the war. I said I thought I'd travel and just see the rest of the world. He couldn't believe that I wasn't going to get more education. He'd already been to college and was a very smart guy.

"When we went in to the beach at Peleliu, it was terrible. I had never seen dead bodies like this, lying on the beach, floating in the water, mangled. Cat Allen was in a hole with another Marine who saw a Jap soldier but he froze and couldn't fire. He told Cat there was one out there. Cat stuck up his head to look and took a bullet right through his skull. They called me as a stretcher bearer to get him. I carried him back and dropped him off at a collection place. There wasn't anything to do for him. It had happened like I said it would—he was the first one I picked up."

After depositing Allen's body, Rice returned to the outfit's position and as night fell was directed to occupy a vacant foxhole. Only after he settled in did Rice realize that he was alone. There would be no one who would stand watch if he slept. "It was a most terrifying night. I was dead tired from the day and I couldn't stay awake. I started to doze off and then I could hear them out there crawling towards me on my right and left. I tried to peek out but I couldn't see a thing; all I knew is that they were coming towards me. Around 5:00 A.M. it finally became light enough to see, and when I looked out, what I had heard were land crabs, crawling all over the place.

"It became very hot and with not having slept and with all that heat while I carried men on stretchers, around midday I just went down. That hurt my pride. They took me to the hospital ship, stayed overnight. I thought about what I had said to Cat Allen and I decided one thing. My days as a stretcher bearer were over. I was going back to my outfit as a rifleman, come what may.

"I missed two days, the only two days I missed combat while I was in the war. When I got back, a guy told me I had missed the biggest day there, when a lot of guys got killed. Boland, who talked to me about getting educated, had been sick and they told him to get behind some trees until he felt better. But he wouldn't do it. He came forward and was killed. MacDonald, a weight lifter, who wrote letters to his wife regularly and who'd been so good to me, had his whole chest blown out. My squad leader, Joe Gallant, stood on top of a tank blasting away with his submachine gun when he was killed. I felt very bad about the way I had spoken to Allen and Gallant out of anger at Pavuvu. They were both brave men who will live in my memory until I die."

Rice, to his joy, was relieved of his litter-bearer role and returned to A-1-7 as a rifleman. He sailed back to the base established on Pavuvu. "Things were good for me until I came down with jaundice, impetigo, an ear fungus and another attack of malaria. I couldn't open my mouth to eat without severe pain and I did a lot of bad things, which earned me a court-martial." Still, he continued to serve with Company A as it boarded a ship destined for the April first landings.

One of the officers for A-1-7 at Okinawa, Don Farquahar, replaced a machine gun platoon leader lost at Peleliu. A native of Hollywood, California, Farquahar enjoyed a tranquil youth, active in his church, the local YMCA and serving as student body president in his high school.

"I entered the University of Redlands in the fall of 1940. I was at a fraternity rush party when we heard over the radio that the Japs had bombed Pearl Harbor. You can imagine what a pall that cast on our party. We were all the right age for service and none of us knew how long it would be before we were gone. We didn't expect the Japs to have the power and tenacity they did. But as they began to take over all of the Pacific, we began to wonder how long the war would last.

"All of the services sent recruiters to the campus and offered various programs that led to a commission. Our entire fraternity joined the Marine Corps. I don't know if it was the glamour of being tough or fearless or the very best. I enlisted in the V–12 program [a Navy and Marine Corps operation that enrolled young people before they actually went on active duty] and I had one semester in the Redlands V–12 unit before going to Parris Island in September 1943.

"Boot camp was about what I expected. I was in a platoon with my friends from Redlands and among other V–12ers from USC, Oregon, Cal Poly, University of the Pacific and other West Coast schools. We had all-American football and basketball players. Some of the guys were NCAA champs in the 100- and 440-yard dashes. We were smarter than the average DI and quicker and in better shape than the average recruit. Some of the DIs were in awe of our platoons and some were really tough. But they managed to get through to us that being Marines was something special. I learned it then and still believe it."

Farquahar passed through the required phases of training until he picked up his commission. "I had finished high in my class and I became company commander for a troop train of 600 men traveling across the country. We ran out of food in Meridian, Mississippi, but stocked up in New Orleans. I stopped the train and exercised the troops in the wilds of New Mexico before we reached Camp Pendleton. Aboard the transport for the Russell Islands I was more scared of the ocean and its big waves than a Jap torpedo.

"They asked us in the Russells if anyone wanted to join the division immediately. Three of us still together from Redlands went over to the 1st Division at Pavuvu. This was probably the best move we had made in the Corps. I was given the machine gun platoon in A Company, 1st Battalion, 7th Marines. The company commander, Lt. Robert Romo, was also from Redlands, so we got along well.

"The machine gun platoon consisted of three squads of thirteen men. There were three machine gun sections to each squad, a gunner, a loader and two ammo carriers, all commanded by a sergeant. A gunnery sergeant and one officer were in overall charge. When we went into battle, each machine gun was attached to one of the rifle platoons.

"The opportunity to join the division before Okinawa was a real plus. I knew the machine gunners, most of the ranking NCOs in the company and, of course, all of the other officers. I'm convinced that you fight for the guys on your left and right, and not for the glory of the Corps."

Nolen Marbrey, born in Huntsville, Alabama, was also a replacement in the 1st Division. "I was a little on the lazy side," remembers Marbrey, known as "Bama" after he entered the service. "I spent a lot of time with my friend Richard, who lived next door. We hunted, fished and stole watermelons. Both of us were from large families that weren't rich. We wore patches on our overalls and went barefoot in the summertime to save our shoes for the winter.

"One day, I told Richard, 'What are we going to do about the war?' He said, 'Nolen, I've been thinking about the Army. How about you?' I said I didn't like the brown uniform. After we talked about it a couple of times, I finally decided on being a Marine. Richard said, 'Nolen, I think you made a mistake.' I've thought about his words a few times since then.

"Yes, I was sorry I volunteered. I was sent to San Diego for boot camp and then to the Marine paratroops in Camp Gillespie. I was hurt on my second jump and informed I'd be kicked out of the paratroops after my leg (a chipped bone and pulled muscles) healed. My next stop was Camp Elliot, California, for infantry training. All this was hard for ole Nolen to comprehend. This Marine Corps was hell, especially Camp Gillespie.

"After Camp Elliot, I boarded a ship in San Diego for a 30- to 35-day trip across the Pacific to join the 1st Division in Melbourne, Australia. I was one of the replacements for the Marines killed on Guadalcanal and I joined K Company, 3rd Battalion, 5th Regiment in the 1st Division. Okinawa would be my fourth beachhead."

Bob Craig, in contrast to Marbrey, grew up in fairly affluent circumstances. "My father was a mining engineer, my uncle was the superintendent and my grandfather, the general manager of the company. The latter two had come to the U.S. from the coal fields of Scotland in 1884, when the first coal fields of Western Pennsylvania were first opening and being developed."

Craig was born in 1923 in Yatesboro, Pennsylvania [a small mining town about fifty miles northwest of Pittsburgh]. The family moved to Indiana, Pennsylvania, as a result of a coal company consolidation and Craig attended grade and high schools there.

"In attempting to describe myself as a young boy and then a teenager, I wish I could rely on poet Robert Burns, whose verse translated into regular speaking English from the Scotch vernacular is, 'Oh, Lord, what a gift you would give us to see ourselves as others see us.' The point is, my wife, with whom I grew up, went through public school, occasionally dated, laughed when I described myself as 'athletic, not feisty, very studious, not really outgoing but from time to time somewhat daring, although admittedly leaning toward the cautious—the better part of valor is discretion.'

"Hitler had taken over Germany, Mussolini was entrenched in Italy, Franco was on his way in Spain and the Red Revolution that started in Russia was spilling out into the rest of the world. We were very much aware of what was going on, but not certain as to where this uncontrolled revolution was headed. We had daily discussions of current events on the pros and cons of almost everything that happened. Italy's war with the Ethiopians gained no defenders. But there was discussion about the support the Fascists gave Franco and the support the Communists gave the Loyalists. There was an incongruity that could not logically be explained. One of our classmate's parents belonged to the Communist Party and we belittled her no end when she tried to convince us that theirs was the only way to lead us out of the Depression, while at the same time destroy the 'evils' of the capitalistic system that caused the Depression.

"Prior to the beginning of World War II, I think it's fair to say that, among our friends, we had no bad feelings re: Germans, Italians, or Japanese as people. We heartily disagreed with their leaders but we had too many of our friends (with the exception of the Japanese, none of whom lived in our community) with these ethnic backgrounds.

"We were not happy with Germany and Italy and what they were doing to our former allies in Europe, but until Czechoslovakia, Belgium, Holland and France were overrun, we all hoped we would not become directly involved and that England and Russia would ultimately prevail.

"Our differences with Japan were presumably being worked out in diplomatic meetings, but the attack on Pearl Harbor and the Philippines showed we had been duped. After the initial confusion as to why and how such a catastrophe could happen, outrage, anger and hatred for the Japs became the bywords. No one thought the Japs would be a pushover, especially since the main body of our fleet was at the bottom of Pearl Harbor. The initial fear was that the Japs would return to finish off Hawaii as a base, and then maybe make an attack or landing on our West Coast."

After graduation from high school, Craig had entered the University of Virginia in 1940, where he majored in American history with an ultimate goal of law school. In October 1942, as an eighteen-year-old soon to be subject to the draft, Craig enlisted in the Marine Corps Reserve and became part of a program designed to produce platoon leaders.

Called up in 1943, he started the process of being a Marine officer in the V–12 program at Princeton University. "Basically, it continued our college education along with courses in military matters—map reading, military courtesy and discipline, weaponry. It was not a substitute for basic training but rather, a supplement. Because we were nineteen- and twenty-year-olds, under the rules of the day, we could not be commissioned until we became twenty-one."

After his stint at Princeton in V–12, Craig reported to the Parris Island installation. "Boot camp was not a shock to me. Oh, some of the cute tricks the DIs pulled seemed like 'chickenshit' at the time but most of us 'college boys,' as they liked to call us, knew what they were up to and we weren't going to let them get away with it. As part of the training discipline, they were trying to break us, and if they did, we'd be busted out of the OCS program. After basic training was over, several DIs congratulated us on our ability to pass the test.

"My Boy Scout background was a tremendous help in getting through boot camp. All the long hikes, camping out, working on merit badges and being away from home during the formative teens were learning experiences for which there is no substitute."

Upon completion of this phase, the Corps dispatched Craig and 1,200 other officer candidates to Camp Lejeune to await openings in the OCS program at Quantico, then the only facility for churning out commissioned personnel. The extraordinary losses of junior officers at Tarawa, Guam, Saipan and Peleliu brought a change. A special school to fill the junior-officer ranks opened right at Lejeune, and Craig, along with 400 colleagues, matriculated.

"It was a very, very rigorous program. The average weekday started with reveille at either 4:00 or 4:30 A.M. and ended as late as 9:00 P.M. Since we were not permitted to leave the base at any time, they usually gave us a 'field party' on Saturday afternoon. It was like a picnic with Cokes, beer and candy, all *verboten* items during the week.

"Our instructors, officers and noncoms, were all combat-seasoned veterans from the Guadalcanal and Cape Gloucester campaigns. They were the best, since they had experience from assault landings and jungle warfare. Of course we had a lot of grousing, bitching, griping because we were not used to the type of life and treatment, but our resiliency and determination came to the fore any time someone made a derisive remark about 'college boys.' If that was intentional, it worked.

"The course lasted eight weeks and then we were commissioned as 2nd lieutenants. The doctors who examined us in the required physicals said that as a group we were the worst specimens they had seen. We were all physically run-down, and especially underweight, because we basically lived on K and C rations as part of the program."

Following a five-week orientation course and after a two-week leave, Craig joined a contingent that met up with the 1st Division at its base on Pavuvu, an island in the Russells, which are part of the entire Solomon Islands chain. The 1st Division casualties from Peleliu totaled more than 6,000 and Craig took over a rifle platoon in G Company, 2nd Battalion of the 1st Regiment. The outfit had lasted only two weeks at Peleliu before losing 70 percent of its complement. Deemed no longer effective as a fighting force, the 1st Regiment withdrew to Pavuvu for replacements.

Says Craig, "We had no problem of acceptance with either the NCOs or the officers. They were only too glad to find that restaffing could be

Lt. Bob Craig led a platoon for the 1st Marine Division.

accomplished so quickly. I never felt that the men might not like the idea of a 'rookie' as their leader." With the influx of thousands, including Craig, the 1st Marine Division was now actually overstrength as it prepared to strike the Okinawa beaches.

Another recruit from the Keystone State, Elmer Johnson, also restocked the 1st Division manpower. The eldest of five kids, and born in 1921, Johnson escaped the worst of the Depression as a result of his father's job in the Tyrone, Pennsylvania, post office.

"I played in the high school band and the director made an offhand remark that if a war came, he and I would get in a military band and toot our way through it. All through high school I planned on joining the Navy but that remark started me in motion. I applied to the Naval School of Music in Washington, D.C. Meanwhile, as a senior, I also enlisted for thirty days in the Army's Citizen Military Training Camp at Fort Meade, Maryland, in 1939. If you attended for four years, you could receive a commission in the Army reserve. But when I came home from the CMTC, I found the Navy had rejected me, so I joined the Marines.

"My father had warned me for several years that war was coming and we'd be in it. That was one reason I volunteered. My mother, however, hated the idea of me in the military. Her brother was killed in World

War I and my dad's grandfather had been lost during the Civil War. My father did not object to my decision because he remembered he had been turned down in World War I.

"Boot camp was a snap for me, since I had just been through the CMTC course. I got into the band at Parris Island and later transferred to Quantico. After Pearl Harbor, I decided I wanted out of the band and was accepted for the armorer school in Philadelphia. I spent three years there, got married, fathered a child and became, eventually, the senior NCO at the school.

"Some time in 1944, the Marine Corps issued an order that any Marine who had not been overseas would go, with no exceptions—or at least that's what I was told. Since I had five years in and hadn't been overseas, one of the most exciting times of my life was to begin.

"My wife and child returned to Tyrone while I left Philadelphia for Camp Lejeune and was placed in the 29th Replacement Draft. This was my first experience in a line outfit and as a gunnery sergeant—the field first sergeant for which there is no army equivalent—I was surprised to find I could do the job. As a former bandsman, I was familiar with all of the military formations, and as an expert in the use and repair of small arms, I stood out.

"The training at Lejeune was brief and was followed by about two weeks at Camp Pendleton, California. No one in the military would tell us where we were going or what outfit we'd be attatched to. But in the bars of Oceanside, they said we were headed for the Solomon Islands, the 1st Marine Division and would make a landing on Hokkaido in northern Japan. They were wrong about only the last item; it would be Okinawa.

"On Banika in the Russell Islands, there was no time for training either. There was a supply depot there and I knew everyone in the armory. That brought me a recommendation for commission as a warrant officer and a threat of a court-martial. With one of the warrant officers, I discovered an abandoned rifle range. We received permission to fix it up so our entire replacement draft could use it. I obtained the ammunition and the equipment needed from friends at the supply depot. Our colonel was ecstatic. He nominated me for warrant officer.

"Meanwhile, many of our officers wanted .45 pistols. I found out there was a pile of small arms from several operations with the weapons just rusting away. I could get them and for the price of twenty-five dollars each. I didn't take a cent for myself and supplied about thirty officers with the pistols. The colonel became furious when he learned the officers were getting pistols. He figured I must be the source and he called me in for questioning and threatened a court-martial. But he made a mistake; he told me he was going to have a shakedown inspection of the officers' quarters. I passed the information on and the officers had me lock up all of the .45s in a chest in my shack. The colonel was heartbroken when he couldn't find the pistols during his inspection. He came to see me in the small armory I ran and talked about his frustration, all the while sitting on that chest.

"The colonel would not let the enlisted men have their beer rations. Men then offered to do guard duty over the beer, and of course they all got drunk. But we covered for them. I liked whiskey and to get it, I would substitute for officers scheduled to give lectures to the troops in return for their liquor. One time a lieutenant failed to come across. I tied him up in an outdoor shithouse with his laundry line. Of course I was drunk, and shortly thereafter, he and his buddies showed up at one of our parties and beat hell out of me.

"No hard feelings on either side. That's the way it was. I knew these officers were a special group. I was twenty-four, most of them were about twenty-two and they respected me and I admired them. They were mostly from around New York City and places like Dartmouth, Columbia, Yale, from fine families. Most of them died on Okinawa."

CHAPTER VII

RAIDERS AND RECRUITS

The second large Marine Corps body to participate in the Okinawa campaign was the 6th Division that was assembled in the South Pacific. It was the only Marine division activated outside of the United States. The core of the outfit were four Marine Raider Battalions organized into the 4th Marine Regiment. The Marine Raiders resembled both the British commandos and the Army Rangers. President Franklin D. Roosevelt, like his British counterpart Winston Churchill, favored derring-do, and the creation of elite, hard-hitting, fast-moving units struck his fancy. One source of his enthusiasm for a Marine version was Evans Carlson, who, as a young Marine officer in 1937–39, had accompanied the Chinese 8th Route Army on part of its 2,000-mile trek and was greatly impressed by the spirit and guerrilla tactics directed against the Japanese. Previously, Carlson had served on the Little White House honor guard at Warm Springs, Georgia. His report on the tactics and techniques of the Chinese communist armies against the Japanese went to Naval Intelligence and to President Roosevelt, whom he knew from his tour with the honor guard.

Carlson had given up his commission to lecture on the dangers of the Japanese and for support of the Chinese. He donned his uniform early in 1941 and traveled to England to study the methods of the British commandos. Carlson was one of several founding fathers of what would become the Marine Raiders. Captains Samuel B. Griffith II, and Wallace M. Greene, Jr., also surveyed the British guerrilla units. Career

Marine Merritt A. Edson, who learned to survive and fight in the jungle while in pursuit of Nicaraguan rebels during the late 1920s, and Carlson took command of the first two Marine Raider Battalions.

Out of Carlson's time with the Chinese came the expression *gung-ho*, originally meaning to work together but later interpreted as eager to the point of excess. The brass found Carlson's political slant less attractive, but as one general remarked, "He may think red but he doesn't fight yellow."

In addition to surprise strikes and serving as shock troops, the Raiders also learned how to live off the land, self-sufficient units even in the jungles when behind enemy lines. Transported usually on elderly World War I, four-stack destroyers or occasionally on submarines, the Raiders paddled ashore on rubber boats. Carlson's Raiders slipped onto Makin Atoll in the Gilberts in 1942 and wiped out the occupying garrison before escaping to a submarine. Unfortunately, a handful of Marines unable to make it to the beach were left behind. Captured by a newly debarked enemy force, they were beheaded. It was one more atrocity which Marines would remember and for which Japanese soldiers would later pay.

Edson's 1st Raider Battalion crew fought on Guadalcanal and their exploits helped their commander win the Marine Medal of Honor.

By 1944, the time for small-unit attacks behind enemy lines had passed, just as the commandos and Rangers had also lost their original purposes. Furthermore, the ingrained prejudice against elite outfits inevitably handed them the short end of the stick. Harry Manion, as a veteran of the Raiders, remarks, "Many senior officers were totally opposed to the concept of Raiders. [That held for commandos and Rangers also.] We knew we were a breed apart from other Marines. They had artillery, naval gun-fire support, air support, heavy mortars and good resupply, or at least better than ours. Their medical support was much greater. Most of our beans, bullets and bandages were personal items."

The plans for Okinawa specified that the Raider components, already merged into the 4th Marine Regiment along with the 22nd and 29th Regiments, would form the newly created 6th Division. (Because it was created expressly for Okinawa, Naval historian Samuel Eliot Morison erroneously describes the outfit as without combat experience, but in fact, many of the leathernecks had previously seen action.)

Martin "Stormy" Sexton finished his fourth year at the University of Maryland in June 1941. "I and most of my friends were closely follow-

Martin "Stormy" Sexton commanded
a company in the 6th Marine
Division. *(Martin Sexton)*

ing international events. All of the Axis countries [Germany, Italy and
Japan] were viewed with deep and sincere antagonism." Sexton chose
to take up arms even before the U.S. officially entered the war. "I
enlisted because all of my friends had made a decision to do so. The
lines at the enlistment offices were around the block, and no one was
heading for Canada. I chose the Marine Corps because I was convinced
that they were the elite. This impression was gathered by the personal
appearance of individual Marines as well as by reading about their
exploits. I didn't personally know anyone in the Corps.

"I never met anyone who was not shocked by boot camp. At the same
time, I was fortunate in that the majority of my boot platoon were
college men. That exemplified the tenor of the times. Virtually every
able-bodied person was volunteering.

"My drill instructor was a fourteen-year veteran who was fair, firm
and dedicated. The process was to break the individual down and then
rebuild him as a U.S. Marine. In those days, the only officer that was
seen by a recruit was the pay officer when we were paid. The noncoms
were a power unto themselves.

"I was awaiting assignment as an assistant drill instructor at Parris
Island, South Carolina, on December 7, 1941. I was walking past a mess
hall building when a radio blared out the announcement that Pearl
Harbor was under attack. The gunnery sergeant I was walking with,
who was an old China hand, said, 'We will clean those little people up in
two weeks.' Three years later, I was wishing that I could run into that

gunnery sergeant. I had been overseas in two combat operations and was preparing for Okinawa."

Sexton shipped out to American Samoa as a member of a replacement draft. When the 3rd Raider Battalion, stationed on the island, asked for volunteers, Sexton, along with his entire platoon, signed up. All of the newcomers immediately started a crash course in jungle tactics, night navigation, weapons, rubber-boat maneuvers, hand-to-hand combat, forced marches and mock hit-and-run raids.

"The 3rd Raider Battalion," recalls Sexton, "was commanded by Col. Harry (the Horse) Liversedge. He was a huge man who had participated in the Olympic Games [as a shot putter] and more or less typified the type of officer I met in the Raiders. My L Company Commander was Capt. Joe McFadden, who had been an all-American quarterback at Georgetown University. The officers were almost equally divided between outstanding athletes and mustangs [officers who had worked their way up from enlisted status]. Almost a third had been commissioned either in the field or en route to an overseas assignment. It was a great asset, providing extremely competitive leaders who were imbued with a drive to win."

Sexton came under enemy fire for the first time on Bougainville Island in the Northern Solomons in November 1943. "As a rifle platoon commander, I learned how truly difficult it was to control forty-four men under dense jungle conditions. In such terrain it is impossible to maintain visual contact for more than a few feet. Voice commands and rehearsed signals are mandatory.

"I also became vividly aware of the requirement to read the terrain. The Japanese consistently sited their Nambu automatic weapons along prearranged fire lanes. The foliage would be carefully cut to create a firing lane approximately one foot square from ground level. By intently screening the ground in front of you, the firing lanes could sometimes be recognized. Fortunately, on November 2, 1943, I did perceive one, hit the ground and rolled away. Verification came immediately. My runner, Joe Quintana, who was to my left rear, was slightly wounded by a round that creased his right ear.

"Once a person has experienced actual combat and survived, the initial reaction is relief. But the soldier must avoid the trap of being too careful. An offensive can only be successful if it is conducted in an aggressive, unrelenting mode. In many situations such an attack results in saving lives overall.

"I always had great faith in the Marine Corps basic tactical ground combat unit, the four-man fire team. The motivation for this structure is that in many situations, the maximum number of men that one person can control is three. A fire team leader, thus, has three men to control; a squad leader has three fire team leaders to control; and a platoon commander has three squad leaders to control."

With his Raider Battalion now folded into the 4th Marine Regiment, Stormy Sexton, as CO of Company K, fought on Guam in the summer of 1944. Initially in reserve, by the evening of July 21, 1944, Sexton and the troops dug in on Hill 40. At 3:00 A.M. the Japanese attacked, hurling explosives, firing rifles and sticking the wounded in foxholes with their bayonets. Marine ammunition ran low and a few enemy soldiers penetrated the lines, but when daylight came, Sexton's crew still held their position against an estimated 750 attackers. Casualties for both sides ran high.

"Col. Alan Shapley, the regimental commander, a former quarterback at the Naval Academy, personally spoke to me. I vividly recall the colonel congratulating K Company and stating that if we had not held, the 4th Marines would have been kicked off the beach."

One of the veteran Marine graduates of the Raiders was Maj. Anthony Walker. The son of a Baltimore lawyer, Walker was born in 1917.

Tony Walker, who led the 6th Marine Division Recon Company, won a second Silver Star, awarded at Quantico, VA after the War. *(Tony Walker)*

While he was still an infant, his mother volunteered to go to France to take care of French and American wounded. "As a youth," says Walker, "I was athletic and always willing to fight. I was aware of world affairs and knew about the aggression of the Germans, Japanese and Italians, none of whom I admired at all. I graduated from Yale University, then enlisted in the Marines. My mother had told me that the only wounded men who wanted to go back to the front and fight were U.S. Marines.

"Boot camp was no shock to me. My platoon was lucky to have an old veteran corporal, broken from sergeant, as our drill instructor. He treated us fairly. They taught us how to drill, how to shoot, and I thought the training was excellent.

"When Pearl Harbor came, I was an officer, teaching officer candidates at Quantico. Pearl Harbor simply meant that we were going to fight, which was an opportunity we all had been looking for. Friends of mine in the Raiders recommended I join them. Also, I wanted to go overseas and my outfit, the 9th Marines, did not seem to be going anywhere. Lt. Col. Jimmy Roosevelt, the President's son, was the commander of the 4th Raider Battalion, formed in late summer of 1942, and he said we would leave for the fighting front as soon as we were trained. After several months of training at Camp Pendleton, we sailed across the Pacific to Espíritu Santo in the French-controlled New Hebrides. There we learned to live in the jungle. After two months on Guadalcanal, in June 1943, we were ordered into action on New Georgia Island. Colonel Roosevelt had been evacuated to the United States, for illness, and was replaced by Lt. Col. Michael Currin."

As a captain, Walker led a company of the 4th Raider Battalion in a series of battles on New Georgia, north of Guadalcanal. The first landing at Segi Point introduced Walker and his colleagues to one of the ragtag outfits that provided some aid and comfort to the first Americans, "Coastwatcher Kennedy and his Army," a band of natives and a European settler carrying out guerrilla resistance to the Japanese. From Segi, rubber boats ferried Walker and his company to their debut under fire. At the Choi River, recalls Walker, "A magnificent performance by the 3rd platoon under D.V. Brown—driving a strong enemy force off a ridge line. Our first casualties happened here, five KIA and Steve Klos, WIA."

The enemy fought harder at Viru Harbor and the climax of New Georgia occurred at Bairoko Harbor. "We started the attack with a rebel yell [others insist it was an Indian war whoop] that scared hell out of both friend and foe. We broke the enemy outpost line and held up in front of his main line. We could see where he had cut away trees and brush for fields of fire. Other companies of the 4th Raiders passed through us but were not able to break the enemy line. I was wounded by enemy shrapnel. We suffered numerous casualties from enemy mortar and artillery fire falling along the ridge line. Raiders were light infantry with no weapon larger than a 60 mm mortar. We needed heavy fire support, artillery or naval gunfire or close air support to take the fortified enemy position at Bairoko.

"Partly because of our failure at Bairoko, higher authority decided early in 1944 to reorganize the four Raider battalions as the 4th Marines, a regular infantry regiment. There had been no active 4th Marine Regiment since it was lost at Corregidor."

Walker served as operations officer for the 3rd Battalion of the recreated 4th Regiment on Guam. "Spent the night of D-Day at Hill 40 with Stormy Sexton and his K Company. We had an interesting night fighting off a battalion of counterattacking Japs." For Operation Iceberg, Walker now drew command of the Reconnaissance Company of the 6th Marine Division.

Sgt. Harry Manion, one of Walker's subordinates in the Reconnaissance Company, says, "We were glad to get him as our commanding officer. A former Raider company commander with much combat action, he was no stranger to patrol work [the basic task for the Recon outfit]. He got the nickname 'Cold Steel Walker,' I think, at Bairoko Harbor, New Georgia. He was always up front, constantly unaware of enemy fire, a leader of men in the true meaning." Some embellished the valor of Walker with a tale that traced his nickname to a bayonet wound to his posterior during hand-to-hand combat. (In fact, Walker points out that his nickname derived from his tenure as the head of a school for bayonet training. And rather than a Japanese bayonet poked into his backside, it was a fragment from a mortar explosion while he lay face down. The legend reflects the common desire to magnify the exploits of a leader.)

Manion adds, "If a leader's personality can inspire men to go that one extra step, Major Walker is the man to emulate. Sometimes he would get a person so mad at him, you would forget your own problem. For many years after knowing this giant among giants, I would use the same ploy to get men to do more."

Walker recalls the formation of the Recon Company as including both former Raiders and other survivors of South Pacific battles. "Our new men," he adds, "we selected from incoming replacement drafts for their physical toughness and willingness to fight, first-class material for the difficult and dangerous missions assigned Recon Company by our division commander, Maj. Gen. Lemuel C. Shepherd. We spent six months in organizing and training on the Canal. Then on March 15, 1945, we loaded aboard ship and set sail for Okinawa."

As one of these reconnaissance experts, Manion notes that the Marines had always stressed the value of his trade. "Before World War II, scouting and patroling was part of a Marine's boot camp training and subsequent promotion exams. Entire field manuals were devoted to the subject and the landing party manual had a chapter on it. During the war we had 'scouts out' in almost every field movement. Point, flanks and rear guard covered the party. The scout was a trained, patient, buddy-team Marine. He and his buddy were ahead of the point man.

"Reconnaissance, the eyes and ears of a larger unit, must be taught. Not every Marine can be a good scout or reconnaissance man. Poor eyesight, lack of patience and other physical and mental qualities may be missing. This goes for officers as well as for enlisted men."

Manion himself started an extended military career before the initial Japanese attack on the United States. As an eighteen-year-old high school graduate enrolled in the Ford Motor Company Trade School, aspiring to an engineering degree from the University of Michigan, Manion's formal learning ended when the union struck the auto manufacturer.

"I sought an education elsewhere. Since the war had started September 1, 1939, and my relatives were in the Canadian Royal Essex Scottish Highlanders, I thought I'd try to join a military service and go for a degree in engineering. I learned too late that officers were the only ones who could pursue an education in a degree direction. An officer had to be at least five feet, six inches tall. I never grew over five feet, four. The Coast Guard was my choice, since I had an able-bodied seaman's rating for the Great Lakes. But they weren't taking applications. The only recruiting station open was the Marine Corps.

"Parris Island, South Carolina, was an unforgettable experience. Growing up in a poor section of Detroit geared me for the 'tough' drill instructors. The first corporal DI to deck me, I gave a vertical butt stroke with my '03 rifle and almost got kicked out of the Marine Corps. Street fighting wasn't unacceptable; just the Marines had an idea of who could hit who.

"Our equipment was mostly from the First World War. The most modern item was the coveralls. Sizes were big and bigger. Mine fit me quite big. The boots were of excellent leather and needed neat's-foot oil to waterproof them. They were the best boots I was ever issued.

"Each recruit learned infantry drill, rifle and automatic rifle, submachine gun and pistol, hand grenade, pack equipment and clothing, combat signals, combat principles, scouting and patroling, field sanitation, personal hygiene, first aid, among other subjects. Most of us directly from schools had a better shot at the book material. Most in our platoon were over twenty-five and not up to the schooling.

"When any of the recruits would cause a problem, the DIs had a solution: Scrub the shower room with a toothbrush; settle your differences with the lads from the South in the boxing ring; run around the parade ground with your rifle over your head until ordered to stop.

"I was a special guard at the U.S. Navy Yard in Washington, D.C., when the Japanese attacked Pearl Harbor. I was asked to become a member of a naval intelligence team slated for South America. Then, suddenly, German-descent personnel like myself were told our services were no longer needed.

"Shortly after, the Marine Raider and parachute officers showed up and asked for physically fit men who were not afraid to fight. I grew up in the back alleys of Detroit and was a captain of my high school track team. The line for the paras was long; the one for the Raiders short, so I joined it.

"The Marine Raiders were formed with ten men to a squad, a squad leader and three fire teams. The teams could have two submachine guns and one M–1 rifle; a Browning automatic rifle and two M–1s, or two BARs and one rifle. BAR men also carried a .45 caliber pistol and two magazines.

"I was a BAR man, and in the Raiders you always had a buddy. We did almost everything together. You must protect and help your buddy at all times. We became almost as one. Sometimes a nod of a head would suffice for many words. This could mean the difference to our lives.

"War in the Pacific seemed to have a time schedule. Fight in the daylight and dig in at night. The Raiders went around the clock. Whenever the enemy was most relaxed, we liked to hit him. On patrol we could lay within a foot or so of the enemy and breathe normally. Weapons ready if needed. Knives, rifles, etc., but never used unless absolutely necessary. This 'trick' is not easy to learn."

Manion learned his craft as a point leader from Marine Raiders who had fought the Japanese on Guadalcanal. By 1944, reconnaissance platoons were integral units in Marine regiments. The Army fielded intelligence and reconnaissance platoons and likewise attached them to infantry regiments.

In the Marines, these specialized platoons enjoyed a certain amount of independence, says Manion. "A couple of dozen Marines and one corpsman—we lived away from the rest of the battalions and headquarters." His experience was not unique. William Manchester in his autobiographical account of his Marine service describes a similar style for his recon platoon.

On the eve of the 4th Marine Regiment strike at Emirau, notes Manion, "I came down with another bout of malaria. After two days of home-cooked Cs and a few horse pills, I was ready to go. The doctor said I would miss the operation. Baloney! On the day the regiment was to sail, I took my gear, which I had buried in a poncho on the beach, and got on an early liaison LCVP. I told a chief petty officer I was part of the advance party."

Once at the Emirau beach, Manion reported to an officer, who dispatched him to scout for a rifle company. However, there were no enemy troops on Emirau and after a few days, Manion soon returned to Guadalcanal. His commanding officer chewed him out for being over the hill from the medics but allowed him to rejoin the platoon.

Guam, his next port of call, was a different affair. "Col. Alan Shapley had us in his cabin and gave us our first-day orders. Push inland as fast and as far as possible. Stay in contact. Get some prisoners.

"Recon platoon, full of steak and eggs, climbed down into a LCVP and made for the beach and Mount Alifan. Transferred to an LVY [amphibious tractor] for the final run over the coral to the beach. We took a hit from a small gun on our right flank. Into the water and made the beach. Moved past the infantry. Up a draw, moving a few shell-shocked Japanese out of the way. Moved into a graveyard on a hill. Got fired on by some of our flyboys."

Manion and colleagues pulled back under orders and then were sent forward to tie in between the 22nd Marine Regiment and the 4th. "Picked up some ammo and grenades and moved back to the designated draw. By this time it was very dark. At regiment, we had picked up a young 2nd lieutenant who was to take over as platoon leader [previously a gunnery sergeant occupied the post].

"Recon formed a Vee facing the enemy. Three of us were at the apex. Two Johnson light machine guns handled by Pfc. Roy Ownes and Pfc. James Ware. I had a Thompson submachine gun. We were getting settled when we heard some conversation to our right. The men were from a naval gunfire team. The U.S.S. *Salt Lake City* was about to send up some rounds. Overhead came a star shell.

"In the light we could see an entire Japanese army about a grenade-throw ahead of us. I went back and found the lieutenant. He thought we shouldn't get excited. Pulled his poncho over his head. He was either crying or praying, maybe both. The cruiser started firing some heavy explosives. That really shook us up. The Japanese were yelling and running toward us. Recon moved up to the near flank of the 4th Regiment. The Japanese came though. We could see them very clearly and threw grenades and fired ammo until our barrels were too hot to touch. Next morning there were many bodies in the draw. No doubt many of the cruiser's shells did a yeoman's job. Gunnery Sergeant Cutting took the lieutenant back with a few men to get ammo and water. It's amazing how much water a person can drink in a firefight. We never saw that lieutenant again.

"Coming down from the top of Mount Alifan, we passed through an artillery battery and obtained some Cs from them. Since recon are on the move and do not have a supply man, we were forced to bum beans, bullets and bandages where we could find them. In battle we would never take anything without asking.

"The only man we lost to action on Guam was a fellow who went back down a hill to get water. We found him tied to a tree, stabbed to death."

It was on the return from Guam to Guadalcanal that the recon platoons from the 22nd and 29th Regiments merged with Manion's 4th to form the company under Tony Walker. "There was a natural rivalry among the platoons," says Manion, "and some lack of rapport could be expected." But the influx of newcomers placed a premium on training, reducing internecine competition.

"We tried to teach them: Training saves lives, so pay attention. Instant obedience to orders. Don't have time to explain things in the field. Learn Japanese weapons, language and tactics. Learn all of our weapons. Learn patrols in brush, roads, trails and jungle, night and day. Learning is a constant necessity.

"Physical training was almost always going on," says Manion. "Night work was practiced over and over. If men can do our work at night, they can do it easy in the daylight. The infantry shoot, move and communicate. Almost all their movement is done in the daylight hours. They normally have batteries of artillery, naval gun fire and close air support at their disposal. They have hospitals, mess hall and supply support. Armored vehicles are part of the tank, infantry and artillery package. Recon have normal small arms—nothing else.

"Our officers were solid. They wanted to learn. They didn't take their ranks too seriously. Major Walker ordered me to instruct a group of officers who were going to become the civilian affairs personnel. They were mostly Marine and Navy reserves, just in from the States. I exposed them to the psychology of the enemy soldier and the Marine in the field. Theft in the field is not unusual. Shell-shocked men can do crazy things. Indigenous people are not necessarily agreeable. Don't wander about by yourself. Keep your weapons handy. Trust your hunches. Don't hunt for souvenirs. Stay out of caves unless the MPs say okay. Don't wander around at night. They had many questions, hypothetic ones about enemy shelling, snakes, foxholes, food, bathing.

"We got the word we were going north again. A long ship ride on an APA [Navy troop carrier]. Big transport meant long, monotonous days and nights. Stock up on many paperbacks. Cards for cribbage and hearts games, chess set, pens and paper, Japanese-language paperback, cleaning gear for weapons, saltwater soap to wash clothes, cigars and other tobacco, lighter/matches, and any other material that would help pass the time. Relax; excitement coming up."

Merrill McLane, a graduate of high school in Rockport, Massachusetts, in 1934, enlisted in the Marines for four years at that time. When he completed his hitch, he entered Dartmouth, one of the few American institutions of higher learning that offered a Marine Corps reserve program before World War II. Upon receiving his diploma in 1942, McLane now pinned on the gold bars of a second lieutenant. His letters home recorded much of his journey through the South Pacific to the shores of Okinawa.

When he sailed from San Diego to New Caledonia in October 1943, although the American situation in the Pacific remained precarious, McLane enjoyed an idyllic voyage. "Officers eat in a pleasant dining room. The bulkheads or walls are of walnut, the deck is polished, chairs are upholstered, and the lighting is indirect. Breakfast begins with fruit —we have had honeydew melon. Then there is hot and cold cereal followed by ham or bacon and eggs, hot cakes. This is one place where butter is not rationed. We have all we can eat. Noon chow is the big meal with soup, meat or fish, dessert and the ever present coffee or tea and of course vegetables. Supper is about like the noon meal, perhaps a bit lighter. The one we had tonight included chicken giblets, rice, gravy, potatoes, peaches and devil's food cake."

The crew of shellbacks—those who had previously been inducted for crossing the equator—initiated pollywogs like McLane into the kingdom of Neptune. The ceremonies mimicked a college fraternity hazing, dousing with colored but allegedly harmless concoctions, electric shocks to the backside, whacks with paddles, bizarre haircuts, all carried out by costumed veterans of such activities.

"Life at sea for passengers on troopships becomes monotonous after the first few days," wrote McLane. "Reading is the chief occupation. The Red Cross provided every person on the ship with a book. The most popular are detective stories like Ellery Queen and Perry Mason. Westerns are also popular, along with magazines such as *Life,* the *Reader's Digest, Coronet* and *Esquire.* The doctors have medical books and some marine officers read technical manuals about weapons and tactics." McLane himself went through James Hilton's *Lost Horizon,* Thoreau's *Walden,* a book of short stories and *H.M.S. Corvette,* an account of sea duty in the North Atlantic.

"Sleeping is a time killer aboard ship. Everyone sleeps eight to ten hours a night, along with naps during the day. We don't get much exercise. Officers and men spend a lot of time gambling. Although prohibited by Naval regulations, no effort is made to stop it. The favorite games are poker, blackjack, crap shooting and pinochle."

On New Caledonia, McLane became a member of the 4th Raider Battalion, which had already received its baptism of fire on New Georgia, an island north of Guadalcanal. McLane became a platoon leader in a rifle company. For months his outfit underwent training and the integration of replacements such as himself. In his off-duty hours, McLane investigated the lives of the indigenous Melanesian people and the Polynesian stock imported by the French.

The 4th Marine Regiment soon inhabited Guadalcanal itself, now secured from the enemy, and built an encampment. The tranquility that now pervaded the site of one of the fiercest campaigns in the Pacific was not an unmixed blessing. "For the first months, perhaps a year, we could go naked for swimming or bathing. But this all ended when the Red Cross came to the island. Just because a dozen or so nurses were at the site of the headquarters about twenty or thirty miles away, we were forbidden to go naked anymore."

McLane's first anticipated operation against the enemy on April 5, 1944, six months after leaving the States, brought him to Emirau, a tiny island northeast of Guadalcanal. "The original plan was to attack Kavieng (a Japanese outpost in New Guinea) but it was strongly defended and we would have had high casualties. By taking Emirau, which had no Japanese on it, and establishing an air base, we neutralized Kavieng without the loss of troops."

For two weeks, McLane and his platoon guarded a lagoon, alert to any effort by the enemy to land there. None showed up and the Marines indulged themselves in simple pleasures—swimming, walking barefoot and in their skivvies, using hand grenades for catching fish.

McLane again seized the opportunity to study the local forms of human and animal life before returning to the encampment on Guadalcanal.

McLane entered the shooting war on the beaches of Guam, along with the Army's 77th Infantry Division. "From Guadalcanal to Guam was about 3,000 miles and the [trip] was to take about a month. But the campaign on Saipan, north of Guam was a more difficult operation than had been anticipated. Since we could not land until Saipan was secured, we had to wait at sea. The result was that we were aboard the vessel for fifty-five days. The food was adequate but all we had was our combat uniforms, one pair of extra socks in our packs along with a change of skivvies." A brief stopover in the Marshall Islands allowed McLane to delve into another culture and ethnic strain, the Micronesian people.

"We landed on Guam on July 21, 1944. The landing on the beaches was not difficult, and there was little resistance. Our Naval gunfire had destroyed their telephone lines and most of their big guns. It was hot and humid, so I let my men discard their gas masks. I threw away mine too. Two or three men collapsed from the heat, and the weight of the hand grenades, ammunition, packs, weapons they were carrying.

"My platoon met resistance at the top of a little hill. The Japanese threw grenades and we threw grenades back. They came over the hill, killing one of my men before we disposed of them. War correspondents who had come ashore with us were close to our fight and wrote it up. In Boston they carried headlines such as, ROCKPORT LIEUTENANT LEADS FIGHT FOR IMPORTANT RIDGE."

He wrote home: "A few days after our landing, a tragic event occurred in the platoon. At night, when in combat, we remain in our foxholes which we dig before dark. Two men sleep in a hole, taking turns staying awake. No one leaves the hole until daybreak. If someone has to go to the bathroom, he has to do it in his helmet and then scatter it with his arm outside the hole. Anyone observed crawling, walking, standing or running is considered to be a Japanese, and is to be shot at without warning. This is because the Japanese favor nights for their fighting, and they are very skillful at using darkness, much more than we are. As a result, we do our advancing in daylight and the Japanese do theirs at night. It can be an infiltration by one or two soldiers who throw hand grenades into foxholes, or it can be a wild charge of hundreds to a few thousand.

"That night we were all in our foxholes by dark and I had made my rounds of each one, chatting with all of the platoon. In the foxhole with me was Sergeant McCain. Everyone was expecting a counterattack to try to push us back into the sea, or at least to the beach. Nothing developed early in the evening, and I had dozed off while McCain remained awake.

"Sometime around midnight, I was awakened by a rifle shot near our foxhole. No other sound followed. McCain, a veteran of the New Georgia campaign, whispered to me that he was worried and would like to crawl to where the shot had come from. My concern was that he would be fired at by other members of the platoon. We discussed it and I gave permission. Before he crawled away, I passed the word around in a low voice what McCain was doing. He wasn't long in returning. He told me that ———— had got out of his foxhole and been shot and killed by ————. What a shock!

"There was nothing further to do except to stay alert for an attack and wait until morning. When it was light, the body was removed for eventual burial in the cemetery opened on Guam for Marines and Army soldiers.

"I talked with the platoon member who had done the shooting. He was experienced and well liked by the other Marines. I had two problems. First, should the man who had fired be punished? Second, what kind of a letter should I write to the parents of the lost Marine? I solved this at once. It would be the same as I wrote to the parents of other platoon members killed on Guam, that he'd been lost in combat and no mention of the incident that caused his death.

"I needed guidance as to what I should do about the other problem. I talked to the company commander who informed the battalion commander, who called back with word that the situation should be handled at company level. The company commander talked it over with me, exploring different approaches, finally saying the decision was mine. There was no time to give a lot of thought to the matter. The company would soon be moving out to another position. I shuffled about headquarters for a few minutes and reached my decision. No official action would be taken nor would what happened appear in written reports. The man who had done the shooting would remain in the platoon in his old position.

"After McCain and I informed him of this and reassured him that what he had done could have been duplicated by any one of us, I added there would be no further discussion of the subject. McCain passed the word around the platoon. That ended the incident. It was one of the most difficult decisions I ever had to make and I'm pleased to say it was correct. Although the Marine we lost that night was not forgotten, the platoon operated smoothly during the remainder of the campaign."

Continuing to satisfy his curiosity about people, McLane found time to investigate the natives of Guam. "They are called Chamorros. They look like American Indians, only darker. They are a good-looking people, fairly short, and with black hair. It's hard to know how they looked originally. The Spanish colonized the island more than 300 years ago, so there has been plenty of time for intermarriage to change their appearance. They still know Spanish, at least some words such as *buenos días* and they count in Spanish. But because the U.S. has had the island since the Spanish-American War, a lot of them speak English."

The reception of McLane's company—the first to encounter them in substantial numbers—by the Chamorros bespeaks the hostility evoked by the Japanese who stoutly insisted they liberated the Pacific and Asia from the overbearing attitudes of the West. Says McLane of the meeting with a huge group, "They had probably heard us when we were still in the jungle, and had spread the news around. There were at least a thousand of them. They surrounded us, cheering, laughing and singing. The men ran up to shake our hands. The women were rather bashful but they came close in groups of four or five. They all gave out with organized cheers like 'Hip! Hip! Hooray!' Then, while singing "America" and other national songs, they walked amongst us talking and laughing.

"No wonder they were delighted on our arrival. They had been waiting over two years for us. The men said the Japanese told them the Americans would never be able to land on Guam because their ships all had sunk. The Chamorros said they did not believe this and other stories of the Japanese, although twice a week they had to cheer at mass meetings when they were told of the loss of American ships. During the months preceeding our landing, the Japanese forced them to work from 6:00 A.M. to dusk digging trenches to defend the island. The only food they received was a handful of rice and if they failed to work they were beaten."

A German shepherd and his handler were assigned to McLane's platoon while he was on Guam. McLane was not impressed. "I placed them in the first squad, at the head of the platoon but not leading the patrol because the handler, with one hand holding the leash, could not defend himself in the event of an attack. Three or four riflemen were in front of them. The dog was supposed to smell out any Japanese hiding in the jungle around the trail.

"It was a typical day on Guam, hot and humid, too much for the dog. After an hour or so I had to shift the dog and handler to the rear, not by themselves but with riflemen around them. But the dog could not maintain our pace. I had to slow the platoon down or lose the dog."

Since they did not encounter any of the enemy, the shepherd would not have been a help anyway.

The Japanese also employed animals to hunt their foes. "We were on a company patrol and in the middle of the morning came to a clearing about the size of a football field. The company halted for a break and as we looked across the field, out came two or three big dogs. We had never seen anything like them on Guam, so we whistled to get their attention and called them over. Right in the middle of our whistling, from behind the dogs came a group of Japanese soldiers. They were war dogs.

"The platoon that had advanced into the clearing farther than mine began firing and the Japs returned the fire. It didn't last long and my platoon did not get into it. As we passed by the clearing and entered the forest, we saw a number of dogs that had been shot along with their masters.

"They were Akitas. We knew nothing about them because our intelligence officer had never been briefed on Japanese war dogs. It didn't matter because dogs on either side did not play a critical role in the war."

In the late summer of 1944, McLane and the 4th Raider Battalion, now thoroughly blooded, settled in at Guadalcanal for the third time. This would be his longest stint on the island and from it he would sail nearly 4,500 miles to take part in the Okinawa invasion.

The artillery component destined for Okinawa included the 8th Anti-Aircraft Artillery Battalion with 90 mm guns. One of the 8th's members was James Powers, son of a foreign affairs specialist working at the Boston *Globe*. A graduate of Browne and Nichols School (a day prep institution), Powers was probably far more aware of world affairs than most of his generation. "Mother, a superb cook and hostess, put on many a dinner to host colleagues of our dad, other figures in the newspaper business, American and foreign diplomats and intelligence people, foreign press and political figures.

"Our family was fully supportive of democratic forces abroad and opposed to isolationism and appeasement of the Axis powers. My parents, both Democrats, were products of the Progressive and Wilsonian era of American politics.

"As our family has a long military tradition, we did not disdain these enemies. One of Dad's biggest problems in the prewar years was with American naval types who grossly underestimated the fighting capacity of the Japanese and the significance of their air power. One admiral told him, 'Why, if those little yellow bastards start anything, we will finish them off in six months!' Racism blinded our military to the danger.

"We were under no illusions that the Japanese would be any sort of pushover. We had a tenacious, disciplined foe on our hands. When Europeans were running about wearing bull's horns in their hats and sacking monasteries, the Chinese and Japanese were writing sophisticated military texts and treatises. When Dad had told the admiral that, and warned of the capabilities of the Zero [Japanese fighter plane], the officer laughed at him. [During the first years of World War II, the Zero was superior to U.S. aircraft.]

"We reacted with anger but not wholly with surprise at the attack on Pearl Harbor. Dad had predicted an attack ten days before, although he expected it to fall first on the Philippines. He told me that surprise attacks of this nature have been characteristic of Japanese history over many centuries."

While a freshman at Harvard in August 1942, Powers tried to enlist in the Marine Corps. "Partway through processing my papers, President Roosevelt, mindful of the British experience with entire college classes enlisting together in World War I [with subsequent massive losses], directed that college students be taken in by the draft at a controlled rate. The Marine Corps advised me of this rule and put my enlistment on hold until I received my draft notice. I was sworn in March 19, 1944."

As a boot at Parris Island, Powers says he had his problems with the DIs but, having spent summers working on farms and competing as a long-distance runner, he had the endurance to keep up. "I reported to New River, North Carolina, with assignment to the Surveyors School. A sergeant major, about the size of King Kong, with a fat cigar in his mouth, crossed out 'Surveyors School,' saying, 'Hell, we got enough of those jerks,' and reassigned me to the 90 mm AAA school."

Powers qualified as a cannoneer and served on a gun crew, preparing for infantry support in the Pacific until someone noticed his Harvard background and posted him to the Fire Direction Center, which computed field artillery missions for the four batteries of the 8th. "My protestations that I was one of the worst math students in college brought no reprieve. The lieutenant in charge said, 'If you're smart enough to get into Harvard, you are smart enough to handle what the Marine Corps has in mind.' "

While his duties focused principally on fire control, Powers would find that, as a Marine on Okinawa, he would be expected to fill other, more dangerous slots.

CHAPTER VIII

THE 7TH AND 96TH INFANTRY DIVISIONS

Among the U.S. Army divisions that would engage the Japanese on Okinawa, the 7th claimed the dubious honor of longest time overseas and earliest commitment to combat. In retrospect, ill-advised strategy had led the Japanese to strike at the Aleutian Islands, specifically Attu, 650 miles west of the Nipponese supply base in the Kuriles, and Kiska, another 378 miles farther east of Attu. A strike at Alaska via this route was not part of the Japanese high command's script but only a precaution to protect the northernmost flank of the Imperial Empire. However, the U.S. reacted as if this were a challenge it could not dismiss. For both sides the effort required perseverance under the frigid conditions amidst almost perpetual snow and mist. Maintenance of their presence in the Aleutians cost the Japanese useful troops, equipment and ships that could have strengthened them in the Solomon Islands. Similarly, the American input pulled away resources that might have bolstered the forces struggling on Guadalcanal.

The campaign to drive out the Japanese who seized the sparsely populated subarctic wastes in June 1942, had begun with aerial raids that same month. The two sides traded punches through the air and at sea throughout the summer and into the winter of 1942–43. In the spring of 1943, two years before they would wade ashore at Okinawa, troops from the 7th Division were scheduled to push the enemy from Attu.

Until January, the men of the 7th, nicknamed the "Hour Glass" because of the shoulder patch design and originally designated a "motorized division," had been maneuvering about the Nevada desert as a prelude to joining the Allied armies fighting the Afrika Korps in North Africa. But decision to hit in the Aleutians forced a change to amphibious work, albeit at Fort Ord near Monterey, California, a terrain and climate with no relevance to the bleak shores of Attu.

Ed Smith, son of a Boston firefighter, attended the Boston Latin School before admission to West Point. He graduated in 1939 and his first assignment included security at the Panama Canal. "I didn't think much about either the Germans or the Japanese in those days. But while handling security on all the ships that went through the canal, we all talked about the way the Japanese always flew about the ships taking pictures with their cameras."

Ordered to Fort Ord, Smith started with the 7th Division as lieutenant in the 2nd Battalion of the 17th Infantry Regiment. In three months he worked up to the Battalion S–3, the officer in charge of plans and operations, and held the rank of captain. "I became a major and then battalion commander while we went to the desert from September '42 to February '43. We were a good unit and so was the whole division. Maj. Gen. A. E. Brown was excellent, a really fine commander who did a wonderful job training us for desert warfare. But when we returned to Fort Ord, we were issued northern equipment and headed for Attu."

Among the 7th Division originals was Eugene C. Prather, a Gooding, Idaho, farmboy born in 1919. "I was a better than average student, easygoing but not athletic—just couldn't run well. I didn't have time for after-school practice sessions because during the Depression I had to be home to help on the farm.

"World affairs from 1937 to 1940 were not uppermost in our minds. We were too busy trying to make money for college and working for grades that brought scholarship consideration or master classes. Girls, of course, also took time, money and precedence. But in 1940, several of our friends in the National Guard were mobilized and recent ROTC graduates were ordered to duty. These events brought world affairs to our attention.

" 'Demonizing' of the Germans had begun but was more among the veterans of World War I. The anti-Japanese propaganda did not start with great intensity until Pearl Harbor. But after that there seemed to be a progressive increase in anti-Japanese feeling. [As the war deepened] the Japanese were taking few prisoners and surrendered only if unconscious or otherwise unable to resist. It is difficult to say how much individuals *hated* the Japanese soldiers and officers versus believing that it was a matter of killing first or being killed.

"We had no Orientals in our units after Pearl Harbor. Few of our officers and enlisted men had ever met a Japanese (or other Oriental). Probably most of us saw them in the field as people who were trained and ordered to do a job, the same as we were." [Stationed in California, the 7th Division took in about 500 Nisei draftees from the West. But after the bombing of Pearl Harbor all Nisei were disarmed and given labor positions with medical or engineering units. Ultimately most were transferred out to all-Nisei outfits.]

In 1941, Prather completed four years of study in agriculture and entomology for a Bachelor of Science degree from the University of Idaho. "Our ROTC class, June 1941, crossed the stage at graduation and received a sheepskin [diploma], reserve commission and orders to report to active duty. Our ROTC training was mostly devoted toward parade-ground discipline, military history and small unit tactics.

"We checked in at Ford Ord in July 1941, and were welcomed by Col. Frank Culin, who said he was glad to see us and that officers' school was in the officers' mess at 7:00 P.M. We were still having officers' school enroute to Attu. Many of us owed our lives to Colonel Culin, although that man was never real popular.

"By happy circumstance, I had very good instruction. When I reported to A Company, 32nd Regiment, I was assigned as platoon leader for the 2nd Platoon. Staff Sergeant Eaves, the platoon sergeant escorted me to the barracks and we did a regular Saturday a.m. inspection of the men and the barracks. When we finished, Eaves took me into his room, closed the door and after some remarks about the inspection asked, 'Well, do you want to take full command right now or sort of watch and see how things are done?' Fortunately, God gave me the wisdom to answer. I said I would take command but I would need and appreciate any pointers and advice he could give me. Eaves was thirty-three, had a sixth-grade education, sixteen years' service, a wealth of horse-sense and army know-how, which he was willing to share with me.

"By the time we left for Attu, I was named 1st Battalion S–1 [executive officer] and Headquarters Company Commander."

Solomon Berger, whose parents emigrated from Lithuania in 1917 after the Russian Revolution, was born in Baltimore in 1924. "I was a good student in school, liked athletics and loved history. I was quite aware of world affairs, keenly interested in what was happening in the Spanish Civil War of 1936, Fascist Germany and Italy. Also, since I am of Jewish ancestry and religion, I followed what was happening to the Jews in Germany. I hated the Nazis when they started the restrictions and expulsions of the Jews in the early 1930s. I knew when I graduated from high school, that I would try to stop the Nazis and Japanese. I had only revulsion for these countries.

"I graduated from Baltimore City College in June 1942. In January 1943, I went to the draft board to tell them to take me ahead of married men. They sent me to Fort Sill, Oklahoma, for basic training on the 105 mm howitzer and the .50 caliber Browning machine gun. On the army IQ test I did real well and was called before a board of colonels for an interview about OCS. I declined the offer to attend, so I could stay an enlisted man. I loved the army life and always tried to be the best soldier I could be."

Berger became a member of the 7th Division while it was going through its amphibious paces at Fort Ord. His background brought him a spot with the .50 caliber machine gun squad for division artillery.

Like every infantry division, the 7th included a combat engineer battalion. Among the 13th Engineer Combat Battlion officers was Bob MacArthur, a native of Wisconsin who spent his teens living in the New Haven, Connecticut, area. A fair high school student with an avid interest in sports, MacArthur matriculated at the University of Wisconsin looking for a degree in mechanical engineering.

"I didn't think much about world affairs. I was suspicious of the Japs, considered their warlords like Tojo and company in the same slime as Hitler." His ROTC at Wisconsin landed him in the 13th Engineers when called up.

The first men from the U.S. expeditionary force had clambered onto Attu's small sandy beaches on May 11, and altogether 11,000 from the 7th Division participated in the capture of the rocky, mountainous tundra. The spring thaw turned the ground into thick mud that defied the efforts of trucks and tractors.

"Somebody in supply fell in love with the Blucher boot. It was all wrong for the climate in the Aleutians and many men wound up with sore or frozen feet," recalls MacArthur.

"Attu was an amazing situation for us," says Ed Smith, who led his 2nd Battalion in the opening assault. "We had trained for the desert and had no experience in northern climates or living. The equipment was unsuitable. It was particularly bad for the feet. I had close to 1,000 people in the battalion when we started the assault. At the end of a week we were down to the size of a company, little more than 200 men. Men kept being taken out because of their feet, from trying to live on

Attu and from being shot by the Japanese. They were always above us. Wherever the fogline was, we knew the Japanese were behind it. And it was foggy most of the time. It got dark at about 2:00 A.M. and cleared by 5:00 A.M. We knew they could see us to fire but we could not see them to fire back."

The Americans progressed very slowly against the well-dug-in defenders who took full advantage of the natural features—steep ridges, sharp ravines—to shield themselves from the supporting U.S. naval bombardments. As movement of the invaders bogged down, Rear Adm. Thomas Kinkaid, commander of the North Pacific Force, fearful of a counterattack by the Japanese fleet, relieved the 7th Division leader, Maj. Gen. A. E. Brown.

The decision typified the concerns of naval strategists versus those of Army commanders intent on overcoming the foe with the least expenditure of men and materials. Putting the prerogative to judge the leadership of ground combat in the hands of an admiral was as absurd as if General Brown had been given control of the fleet. Ed Smith, more than fifty years later, criticizes the relief of a man he considers "an outstanding commander."

The change of leadership had little to do with the final outcome. The defenders numbered 2,379 and could not expect either reinforcements or evacuation. Squeezed into an ever smaller piece of territory, on May 29, about a thousand of the survivors erupted into one of the biggest banzai charges of the war.

The 13th Engineers, according to Bob MacArthur, "back-packed rations and ammo to the infantry, built roads and water points. Attu was the first place I got shot at," adds MacArthur, "and I didn't like it. The Japs had these 77 mm pack howitzers and I dived into a hole. They would sit on the edge of a ridge at the fog line, where we couldn't see them, and lob mortars at us. On the night before their big attack, we'd been up for something like thirty-six hours. It must have been about 4:00 A.M. and we were in our tents playing poker, having a great time, when suddenly these guys come streaming back, yelling, 'The Japs are coming.' The battalion commander, Lt. Col. James Green, a West Pointer, drew his pistol and told them, 'This is as far as you go.'

"Grenades were being thrown back and forth, a lot of rifle, carbine and pistols firing." In fact, MacArthur, according to the 7th Division history by Edmund Love, "was able to improvise a firing line that drove off at least one large group of enemy." Then MacArthur gradually withdrew his men until a sound defensive position could be created and the scattered Americans could be organized into a cohesive force.

MacArthur's immediate superior, Capt. George Cookson, whose feet were in wretched shape, played a major role in mounting the GI defense. Cookson himself describes what happened as "initially complete chaos, a barroom brawl. One didn't know who was whom, where or what was going on."

"It went on for most of the next day," says MacArthur. "They penetrated as far as the tents for the medics and field artillery. I put Cookson in for a Silver Star but many years later I learned they knocked it down to a Bronze Star."

The captain was equally appreciative of MacArthur's role. "He was a major factor in the action, a real leader, a soldier's soldier, and never received the recognition he deserved."

Reporter Robert Sherrod, an on-scene chronicler of numerous Marine engagements during World War II, says some of the onrushing Japanese soldiers shouted such imprecations as "Japanese drink blood like wine!" And they came on with every form of small arms and bayonets, overrunning some positions before they were finally cut down.

Later, MacArthur saw the remnants of the Japanese troops commit suicide. "It was the damndest thing. I watched them up on a ridge, taking their grenades—they had a button that detonated them—bang them on their helmets and hold them to their chest while they went off. I couldn't fathom it. I heard that they had been told that if they surrendered, we'd run over them with bulldozers."

As a machine gunner charged with protecting the artillery, Solomon Berger occupied positions well behind the infantry and never came under fire.

The body count for Attu added up to 2,351 dead Japanese and twenty-eight prisoners against about 600 Americans killed and 1,200 wounded. These statistics do not include men disabled, in some instances permanently, by the brutal conditions. In his evaluation of the operation, Samuel Eliot Morison, noting this was only the third U.S. amphibious operation of the war, said, "The operation succeeded although clumsily executed. The loading and unloading of transports was badly done, naval bombardments were delivered from unnecessarily long ranges, and the 7th Division, owing to initial training for desert warfare and poor top leadership showed little dash or initiative." Armchair historians always enjoy the last word.

Kiska, the second objective in the Aleutians received intensive hostile attention of U.S. forces on July 22. Naval forces and army bombers banged away at the enemy while army fighter planes strafed positions. But the Japanese had embedded themselves so well that not a single soldier was killed. Then, unknown to the Americans, the enemy had decided to flee. Under the cover of a thick fog, a flotilla of destroyers and cruisers slipped into a harbor. Within less than an hour, the well-disciplined sailors and soldiers carried out the evacuation of more than 5,000 people.

For several days, U.S. ships continued to hammer at the now deserted island. Photo reconnaissance, when the mist and clouds broke, showed massive destruction; no one realized that much of it had been engineered by the departing Japanese. Ignored were the parked trucks near the shore, the failure of coastal defense guns to respond or the lack of antiaircraft fire, all signs of abandonment.

On August 15, the first of the 7th Division GIs arrived in Kiska. For nearly a week, as thousands came ashore and fanned out, the troops hunted for defenders. They found none, and only the deserted emplacements and booby traps indicated the Japanese had once occupied Kiska.

Berger recalls, "Even though the Japanese had pulled out two weeks earlier, we had casualties from trigger-happy men in my unit who shot up a bulldozer and the GI driver." In fact, the army counted twenty-five dead and another thirty-one wounded in such mishaps. Nor were those at sea immune as an enemy mine exploded against the stern of a patrol vessel, leaving seventy dead or missing.

The next combat mission for the battle-tested veterans of the 7th Infantry was Kwajalein Island, part of the world's biggest coral atoll in the Marshalls. Following the Aleutian campaign and with the disappearance of any threat to Alaska from that region, the 7th had sailed to the far more pleasant clime of Oahu. "We had come down the gangplank in Honolulu," says Ed Smith, "wearing our parkas."

While the 4th Marine Division struggled to conquer the northern parts of Kwajalein—Roi and Namur—the 7th Division, after a thorough course in amphibious warfare, landed January 31, 1944, following the customary heavy shelling from the sea.

At Kwajalein, Morison praised the improvement over Attu as the battleship *Pennsylvania* closed to within one mile of shore to blast targets while "the 7th Division, under a resolute commanding officer proved itself second to none as an amphibious force."

"The assault on Kwajalein," says Bob MacArthur, "was a classic assault on fortified positions. I went in on the third wave and there was no opposition at first. We worked with small teams of infantry. They kept the ports covered with small-arms fire and we had these seven-second fuses on the fifty-pound satchel charges—dynamite. We'd blow the doors open and then the flame throwers would come in through the smoke and dust. It was all over in six days."

Like Prather and Berger, Maurice Reeves, a native of Conway, Arkansas, became a member of the 7th Division at Fort Ord. He gave up life on a farm to enlist in 1940, when he was twenty-one. Reeves drew the 13th Engineer Battalion, where he learned the role of a combat engineer, which included infantry tactics, bridge building, demolition work, laying out and detecting mine fields, construction of obstacles like tank traps. By the time of Pearl Harbor, he had advanced to staff sergeant and when the outfit sailed for Attu, he was first sergeant.

His company was not at the scene during the banzai charge on Attu but Reeves received his indoctrination in the imperatives of combat his second night on Kwajalein. "The company commander instructed me to have the men dig two-man foxholes into a defensive area for the night. Somewhere around midnight, the Japs attacked, with some moving through our area. We lost one soldier in this engagement, a T/5 who left his foxhole. I had given specific orders that no one was to get out of his foxhole."

Unlike the 7th Division, whose activation predated Pearl Harbor, the 96th Division did not come to life until August 1942. Until then, it had existed as a reserve outfit with headquarters in Portland, Oregon. The names of graduates of ROTC from the state universities of Oregon and Washington went into filing cabinets in the post offices of the Northwest. Even as a sense of increasing urgency crept over the military establishment in 1940, the 96th languished. Its members, when called up for duty, received assignments to other organizations now flesh and blood rather than paper rosters.

Not until August 1942, did the 96th set up formal shop at Camp Adair, Oregon, with much of the enlisted cadre drawn from the 7th Infantry Division, with whom it would eventually share two invasions. (Ed Fitzgerald of the 77th had almost been transferred to the 96th when his boss realized he would lose his master of paperwork and quashed the orders.)

Brig. Gen. James L. Bradley, a West Pointer, assumed command and soon pinned on a second star. Early on, Brig. Claudius Easely, who had competed in marksmanship internationally, became assistant commander. Easley supervised rifle instruction and emphasized target practice with an almost fanatic passion. One fruit of his labors was a nickname, "the Deadeyes," for the 96th.

Among the first officers assigned to the 96th was Charles "Dick" Thom, a lawyer who grew up in what was then rural Long Island, New

York, at Port Jefferson. Married, and having passed the bar, Thom undertook the ROTC course at college six years before he was summoned to duty in March 1942. After a tour at the Fort Benning Infantry School, Thom reported to the 96th Division in its newly erected camp. He notes, "I had a ten-day layover in California while they installed the toilets."

Thom, one of the older, better educated officers, attended both a cannon course, the use and maintenance of the M–7, self-propelled 105 howitzer, and one for battalion commanders. In between, he suffered with the troops during maneuvers in the Cascade Mountains and enthusiastically participated in amphibious training at San Diego. "We worked with the Marines and it was very good instruction. The next thing we knew, we were in Honolulu learning jungle combat tactics."

Just as other organizations had been drained of some of their veterans to contribute a cadre to the 96th, it too had lost some of its more veteran members. The coming invasion of Europe required trained infantry, and the ranks of the 96th supplied many. To fill in the gaps, the Army had now shut down its Army Specialized Training Program (ASTP), which put hundreds of thousands of GIs on college campuses for study of subjects that in many cases bore no direct relevance to military requirements. The educational institutions' grounds allowed for close-order drill, but even those that had formerly offered ROTC courses lacked the ranges and open land where men could develop proficiency with weapons and learn tactics. The shoulder patch, designed to symbolize the lamp of knowledge but often referred to as "the flaming pisspot," got no respect from those undergoing the rigors of army camps.

Many former ASTP enrollees reported to the 96th at the port of embarkation, San Francisco, as the division prepared to sail for the Pacific war. Dick Thom initially feared the infusion of such untutored soldiers would lessen the efficiency of the organization. "They turned out to be smart kids, quick to learn, good riflemen, good shooters, solid killers and thoroughly reliable. On the other hand, some of the men who had let you know how tough they were, folded faster."

Another early entry into the ranks of the Deadeyes was Bob Jackson. A 1919 baby in Bakersfield, California, he recalls, "I was not deeply interested in international events but had a penchant for history. I remember thinking that the lieutenant governor at the time was a jerk to be picketing the Japanese ships picking up scrap in San Francisco. My motivations were completely driven by that which hung between my legs.

"I was very influenced in high school by the excellent but rather 'pinko' teachers—it was *that* time and most young intellectuals were quite left—so my world view was rather leftish. I recall an argument with my father in my senior year at University of California in which he demolished me by saying, 'If that's the way you think, why don't you go to Russia?' Having lived in Hawaii from 1927 to 1932, I didn't demonize the Japanese. I think my attitude would be more like someone from a border state and his attitude toward the then 'Negro,' or like my father's remark, 'I have some great Jewish friends but I hate kikes.' Later, in my command, the men looked upon the Japanese as less than human and they committed some acts that today would be called atrocities."

Equipped with a degree in agricultural economics, Jackson could not find a job in California. His stepfather arranged placement with DuPont Plastics in New Jersey. Drafted for one year, it soon became obvious to Jackson that he was not to become a civilian for a long time. Assigned to the 7th Division, he began his career as an infantryman, but parlayed his skill as a typist into the less arduous job of company clerk.

Don Dencker was a member of Company L, 382nd Regiment, 96th Division. *(Don Dencker)*

Jackson's fears that his military service would last more than a year were confirmed with the bombs at Pearl Harbor. He tried to attend OCS for quartermasters but the quota was filled. He then applied for infantry OCS. "They felt me and found I was warm, so I went to the Benning School for Boys. I found the teaching method the most effective I have ever seen."

With freshly minted gold bars on his shoulders, Lieutenant Jackson presented himself to the 1st Battalion commander of the 382nd Regiment in the 96th Division at Camp Adair. "He was 'old Army' and wore pink jodhpurs and highly shined boots. I did not envy his batman under the circumstances. We were up to here in mud.

"The colonel twitched his pretentious mustache and asked me what I'd done badly at OCS. I answered that the .37 mm antitank gun was a complete mystery to me. He was a capricious old bastard so he assigned me to the antitank platoon."

Jackson discovered that he and his fellow draftee officers benefitted from the noncoms assigned to the 96th. "Many of them were not draftees or even early volunteers, but men, who in the severe depression of the late thirties, found a home in the Army. While not highly sophisticated, they had learned 'the system.' It seemed to me that most were from the South. They weren't, thank goodness, the typical 'old Army' boozer but were closer to being like us, the recently called-up."

Aided by some of the professional soldiers, Jackson stumbled through the process of converting raw recruits inducted through Selective Service into combat soldiers. Along the way, experience matured him. "On one of the night maneuvers I received my first reaming from our new battalion commander, Colonel M.; it was not my last. One of my recently appointed squad leaders took a short snooze. Unfortunately, Colonel M. stepped on him in the dark. I received an early lesson in the responsibilities of a platoon leader. Colonel M. fined me twenty-five dollars under Article of War 104. I don't think I took it very well because I felt it was not my fault. I was later to understand the basics of authority and responsibility; it has helped me throughout my life.

"Colonel M. was a fine leader. We hated his guts. A former school principal, he was rather prim, 'followed the book out the window,' as we used to say. For example, newsreels of GIs showed them with their helmet straps hanging loose (how romantic looking!). We wanted to emulate them. 'Not regulation,' said Colonel M.. 'Chin straps will be buckled at all times.' It was frequently pointed out by my argumentative, young civilian soldiers that 'everyone was doing it,' even the regimental commander. Colonel M., ever the teacher, resisted because he knew that learning the basics was more important than fashion; the straps served a purpose keeping heavy helmets from falling off. Colonel M. changed his requirement when battle experience showed that troops, under artillery fire, were concussed by the pull of the strap on the chin."

Like Thom, Jackson greeted the initial appearance of former ASTP men with dismay. "They had no military training to speak of. A barracks was set aside and we were charged with making soldiers of these men. They were very bright—they must have had very high IQs because they'd been accepted at prestigious universities. But they knew nothing about soldiering. We were given about six weeks to bring them up to speed, so we worked them hard and long. Discipline was the greatest problem; they were not used to the restraints on their individuality that the Army required. Most turned out to be superior soldiers in combat, though they were never happy in the pettiness and routine of garrison living."

As weapons platoon leader for Company A, Jackson sailed to Hawaii with the 96th. "My old outfit, the 7th Division, was already camped near us. We were the two main divisions of the XXIV Corps. The 7th had just returned from their battles at Kwajalein and Eniwetok. I visited my old company in the 17th Infantry, saw the holes left by casualties, admired their battle-stained fatigues but could find little personal contact. I was now an *Officer* and they only remembered me as the goof-off private I had been. It was hard for them and hard for me. I never returned." Back with the 96th, Jackson concentrated on practice for amphibious action.

Leonard Lazarick's parents, both born in Poland, emigrated to the United States in the early 1900s. When the Pennsylvania native was born in 1923, the family supported itself with a dry goods store but in 1928, his father began to build a moving picture theater. The crash of 1929 almost bankrupted the family and only the partnership of a local bootlegger allowed the enterprise to continue.

"Times were hard," says Lazarick. "We had a large vegetable garden and I don't remember ever being hungry. Men, down on their luck, often stopped by the house and my mother always gave them something to eat. No one was turned away. The whole family worked in the movie house. My father was the manager, mother sold tickets, my sisters were usherettes, my brother was the parking lot attendant and doubled as stage manager when they had vaudeville. I was assigned lesser jobs like picking up candy wrappers, polishing brass handles and washing windows.

"I was an intractable child and resented authority. It is not a trait that stood me in good stead in the military or in the work world. I did well in school academically but my behavior left something to be desired. I was a buffoon and got a kick out of making people laugh, even at inappropriate times. I loved sports but was not a gifted athlete. Coaches never had difficulty cutting me from the ranks of aspiring athletes, although I played basketball while at a small college where not too many tried to make the team."

When World War II began, Lazarick was a student at the Philadelphia College of Pharmacy and Science, majoring in chemistry. Several months shy of completing his sophomore year, he entered the service early in April 1943, and became a member of Company K, 382nd Regiment.

"During our training on Oahu," says Lazrick, "I was assigned to a demolition training group for about two weeks. We were instructed by 96th Division engineers in how to make a fuze, set a charge and effective techniques of tamping. We also learned about shaped charges, Bangalore torpedoes, flame throwers and underwater demolitions. The course included ways to disarm several different types of Jap land mines. When I finished the training, I became the platoon demolition specialist but I was hardly an expert. Still, the little knowledge I gained came in handy."

Among the ASTP contingent, whom Dick Thom praised for their killer quality, was Ellis O. Moore, son of a musician and teacher, reared amid the affluence of a New York City suburb, Pelham Manor. As an eighteen-year-old at Washington and Lee University in Lexington, Virginia, Moore enlisted in an army reserve program in 1942, writing to his Aunt Janie, "This will not do me much good if they lower the draft age but it is the only thing my eyes are good enough for." Early the following year he noted "a gloomy atmosphere has settled over the fraternity house" after ten men were lost to graduation or to the army. And in February 1943, Moore received his orders to Camp Cumberland, Pennsylvania.

Ellis Moore had begun to court Peggy Sorrells before he donned a uniform. During a stopover in Fort Worth while en route to Camp Hood, Texas, Moore managed to arrange a brief meeting with Peggy Sorrells. Her father, executive editor for the Scripps-Howard newspaper chain in Fort Worth, witnessed their brief encounter and filed a story for the local newspaper.

". . . They stood together, this boy and girl, but they were far apart —separated by that poignant ten minutes pregnant with the heartache of all eternity. They said nothing, just stood there. The weird, harsh illumination of the railroad yard picked up the silver threads of tracks and switches, and etched these two in sharp lines. Nearby was a line of shuffling, restless soldiers watching intently, gazing as though fascinated, but silent with that curious intuitive stillness with which people watch the sufferings of others . . .

"Ten minutes—and the line of shuffling soldiers moved on, and the boy with them, into a darkened coach, which will roll them to their destiny, whatever and wherever it may be. She stood there as they rolled away, thinking what thoughts nobody will ever know. He will come back, not as an 18-year-old, but a man—or not at all . . ."

Moore mailed a series of chatty letters home describing his basic training for assignment to a tank destroyer unit. He boasted, "I really surprised myself on the rifle range. I shot 169 out of a possible 200. It was the fifth highest in the platoon . . . In our .30 caliber machine

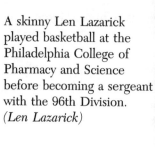

A skinny Len Lazarick played basketball at the Philadelphia College of Pharmacy and Science before becoming a sergeant with the 96th Division. (*Len Lazarick*)

gun firing I got second in our platoon with 19 bulls out of 21 shots." He advised his parents he expected to attend the tank destroyer communications school for six weeks. Moore sent home most of his fifty dollar a month pay, telling his folks to use the funds for a maid or dental repairs.

The cheery tone of his notes turned to gloom. "There's a line of officers, noncoms and privates, up at Battalion HQ trying to get transferred out of here into the Paratroopers. Enlisted men are always complaining but when officers start griping publicly before their men, you know something is wrong. Our 2nd Lt. said he had never seen as punk an outfit as this. Our sergeant, who's been in for five years, compared this to a concentration camp. This place is really a dump. No order. I could run this battalion better than the majors do. We go one place for work and when we get there, we're told we don't belong there and are sent off to another place. Conflicting orders are always sent out. Our 2nd Lt. told us today that's the reason we didn't go to radio school—two colonels sent down conflicting orders. Billy [his brother] is smart to get in the navy." Like so many newcomers to the services, the civilian-oriented Moore could not comprehend the thrashings of huge military bureaucracy.

Eventually, Moore entered a radio course but quit tank destroyers when accepted to ASTP at Illinois Institute of Technology (IIT) in Chicago in July 1943. "Boy, this Chicago is really a serviceman's paradise. In the last 24 hours, I've seen a baseball doubleheader, roller skated and ate three meals in addition to riding about ten miles on street cars, all at Chicago's expense. Also last night I saw a wonderful colored jazz band. Only six pieces but they could really beat it out. Had Red Allen and J.C. Higgenbotham on trumpet and trombone, respectively and they're just about the best."

Moore coped easily with the liberal arts subjects but physics and, subsequently, analytical geometry baffled him. An announcement that after two terms of basic engineering, those with satisfactory marks could transfer to medical or foreign language study buoyed him. "It's a cinch I'll never be an engineer." Both the academicians and the military had begun to realize that their dream of creating a huge pool of well-educated soldiers with adaptable skills for the Army was unrealistic. Course and performance requirements dropped.

In November 1943, as he began a second semester, Moore naively wrote, "A lot of people think that by the time this twelve weeks is up, Germany will be knocked out completely, or close to it." He continued to savor Chicago's cultural scene, enthusiastically reporting on a visit to the local opera house. But shortly before Christmas, rumors about the demise of the ASTP started to circulate. Moore searched for a way to transfer to the Air Corps. But in April 1944, the crunch for foot soldiers squeezed him off the college campus and to Camp White, Oregon, as a member of the 383rd Regiment in the 96th.

The mainly long-distance relationship with Peggy Sorrells culminated in a wartime wedding at the Pelham Manor home of her parents. Moore's brief furlough allowed a weekend honeymoon at the New Jersey shore, then the couple rode a train bound for Camp Beale, California, the temporary home of the 96th Division.

Peggy Sorrells Moore kept her new in-laws informed of their adventures. "The train trip was a lot of fun. We sat with two V–12 [Navy college reservists] boys all the way out. Naturally we pulled our wedding pictures out at every opportunity and passed them around. We were amazed at the lack of waiting to get into the dining car. There seemed to be plenty of food for everyone. At one place in Nevada they had a USO at the station and served coffee, milk, sandwiches, cake, cookies, candy, ice cream, chicken to all of the servicemen and their wives."

Ellis Moore, communications specialist for the 96th Division, flourished a captured Japanese rifle. *(Ellis Moore)*

While she remained in Sacramento at a hotel, Moore checked in at Camp Beale. "He called me about 11 o'clock of the night he left to say that he was lonesome and things out at the camp were lousy and in a mess. He didn't know whether he'd be able to call again. Rumors out there say they'll be leaving Beale at the end of next week. I'm just praying he'll get in this weekend and I can go back with him until he does leave."

The next letter from Moore said, "Peggy and I had a wonderful twenty-two days of married life together." His address now was an Army post office number as he sailed for Hawaii.

Like Moore, Don Dencker followed the route of the ASTP to the 96th Division. "Virtually 100 percent of the boys from the Roosevelt High School [Minneapolis] class of June 1942, went into the armed forces," remembers Dencker. "At the time, I thought the leaders of Germany were evil but the people generally good. The object should be to get rid of Hitler and his henchmen. The Japanese were not to be trusted and eventually had to be stopped from further expansion in Southeast Asia. My attitude didn't change much except for the slinky Japs. After Pearl Harbor they became the 'dirty Japs.'

"While on a streetcar headed for a homing pigeon club meeting—I had raised them since I was sixteen and donated some to the U.S. Army Signal Corps—I heard about Pearl Harbor from someone who got on and shouted the news. That night my best friend and I took our girl-friends horseback riding in spite of a developing blizzard. What the hell, we were going to war.

"I was a draftee but since I had prequalified for the ASTP, I waited until June 1943, before I was called up while a student at the University of Minnesota."

Again, like Moore, Dencker shipped to Camp Hood, Texas, to learn the arts of a tank destroyer while awaiting his transfer to the ASTP. He too was enrolled at the Illinois Institute of Technology. When the Army began to wipe out its ASTP units, Dencker received assignment to Company L of the 383rd Infantry.

"It was a great decision," says Dencker, "as it provided a great infu-sion of virile young men with superior intelligence into many infantry divisions, but it was really a letdown for the ASTP men. Almost all took it in stride.

"About 2,000 came to the 96th Divsion, replacing many older men and some misfits. I am convinced the ASTP people proved a significant factor in the superior performance of the 96th. Those who survived became an increasingly high percentage of the sergeant leaders. [In fact, survival over time in infantry combat almost guaranteed promotion.]"

Whatever their intelligence and virility, life on a college campus had not prepared the likes of Dencker for the demands upon a foot soldier. "Two days after joining Company L, I made a thirteen-mile forced march with full field equipment. I made it, but my feet almost didn't. Blisters galore. Amphibious maneuvers followed and then we left for Hawaii. All ASTP men were well integrated into the division prior to the jungle training in Oahu. I'd say we were well accepted into the division."

George Brooks, a third ASTP student dispatched to the 96th, found his reception somewhat different. Raised in Stony Point, a hamlet about fifty miles north of New York City, Brooks, a good student, built model airplanes as a kid. "I think I was perhaps a little more interested in world affairs than my contemporaries. I knew about the Germans because my father was wounded in World War I (Meuse-Argonne), and I used to read magazines such as *Flying Aces* about the air battles (dogfights). I was less familiar with the Japanese but from high school history I knew of Admiral Perry and his mission to open Japan to the West. My attitude toward Japan turned very negative after Pearl Harbor.

"I had finished high school and was working and realized I would have to enlist or be drafted. I enlisted in the Army Air Corps. My basic training was minimal. It consisted of close-order drill and learning a few basics about the military. We had no weapons training. Within a few months I passed some tests for the ASTP and was sent to IIT.

"We had been assured by captains and colonels that if the program was terminated, or if we flunked out, we would be returned to the service branch from which we came. Naturally, when we were told we were all going to the infantry, we were disappointed and more than a little bitter. We had been lied to or at least badly misinformed.

"The basic infantry training I received in the 96th amounted to a total of three weeks. We had rifle training, we threw grenades, we crawled in the mud under machine gun fire, got in foxholes while they ran over us with a tank and we had close-order drill. Altogether I would say the training was very inadequate. However, subsequent amphibious instruction was very good because the entire 96th participated.

"When we in the ASTP joined the 96th at Camp White, we were so busy with basic training, we didn't have much time to become acquainted with the regular members of the division. The noncoms who trained us were very civil and very helpful. We even received a visit from General Easley [Assitant Division Commander] one day on the rifle range.

"When we completed our basic and were assigned to various companies [for Brooks, Company K, 382nd Regiment], it was not long before some of the enlisted men began to show their resentment. Many of them had very little education and were wary of college boys. Some of them couldn't read or write. Personally, I had little trouble but that wasn't true for everyone. We from the ASTP were all buck privates and all the ratings were already filled. The attitudes changed slowly for the better and, once in combat, the friction all but disappeared, or at least became dormant."

Melvin Coobs also traveled the circuitous route of Air Corps to ASTP to infantry. A small-town Iowa kid whose father had served in World War I, Coobs remembers he was out hunting rabbits when his parents informed him of the December 7, 1941, events. "Because of my lack of knowledge, I was overconfident, felt there would be an easy victory." He entered the service in 1943 as an eighteen-year-old with a background in radio and radar from courses at a school sponsored by the Signal Corps.

Because of his technical knowledge, Coobs was consigned to Keesler Field in Mississippi for basic training. "I had worn glasses since third grade and was initially assigned to learn to be a radio technician in the ground crew. But a couple of weeks after another quick physical at Keesler, I was informed I was being reassigned as a radio gunner. I was happy for the change but I didn't see how I could serve in such a position. I couldn't see well without my glasses even though they claimed my eyes tested out at 20/40—on induction they were 20/200. Apparently, the need for radio gunners was so great, they were willing to take a chance. I always wondered what would have happened the first time I got in a plane and tried to fit goggles over my glasses.

"The interviewer mentioned that my Army intelligence test score qualified me for the ASTP. When I found it involved attending college, I applied and went to Lake Forest College in Illinois. After the breakup of the program, I came to the 96th Division. I had a one-month concentrated refresher course and then joined the division for its amphibious exercises.

"The noncoms in our outfit [Company I, 383rd Regiment] were the older and more mature men. Some were getting by on the strength of seniority. Several were real disasters when we got into combat. Not a single ASTP man received any stripes before we went into combat. I found out that the 1st sergeant had called the company together before we arrived. He made a big point of the fact that we had been sitting in classrooms while they were out in the mud and snow on maneuvers. He was determined to keep any of these 'schoolboys' from making any rank. He had been a bartender in prewar days and his intelligence was limited. When we did go into combat, he faked blindness to get himself out."

Like George Brooks, New York City boy Mike Moroz knew precious little about the job of an infantryman when he left the ASTP for the Deadeyes. "I was at New York University when I was drafted and shipped to Camp Grant, Illinois, for six weeks of basic training in the medical corps. When they shot down the ASTP in March 1944, I left the University of Illinois for Camp White. That's where I was first introduced to the rifle and there was only time for a few weeks of training before we left for Catalina and amphibious work. In Hawaii, I had about a month of jungle-warfare schooling, learning things like how to shoot from the hip. Then we boarded ships, headed for combat."

CHAPTER IX

LEYTE LANDINGS

Early in August 1944, the Deadeyes had disembarked for a brief stay on Oahu. While the highest echelons plotted their future, the troops prepared for what lay ahead with a week of jungle warfare practice in the wilderness of the Hawaiian island. The mission for the 96th was disclosed, Yap, a Japanese outpost which lay between two other enemy-held islands, Ulithi to the east and Peleliu to its west. For six weeks, the brass and strategists huddled over maps, aerial photos and diagrams of Yap.

On the very day that the 96th weighed anchor, September 15, U.S. Marines attempted to crack the very hard nut of Peleliu defenders. More than a month passed before the leathernecks finally overcame organized resistance. Men of the Army's 81st Division received the assignment to capture Ulithi with its fine harbor. After heavy bombardments from the sea and air, the Japanese decided to pull out the Ulithi garrison, along with most of the civilians, and when the combat team from the 81st waded ashore September 21, their visit was unopposed. Quickly, military construction personnel transformed the atoll into a prime staging area for other operations.

And aboard the division flagship, the *Rocky Mount,* as soon as the ship dropped her pilot and headed out from Pearl Harbor, General Bradley, CO of the 96th, announced a change in plans. Instead of Yap, the 96th was on its way to the Philippines, specifically the island of Leyte.

The decision makers had picked up the pace for liberation of the Philippines. Gen. Douglas MacArthur, supreme commander for the Southwest Pacific area, had always focused on the Philippines. Not only did they have a strategic value in carrying the war to Japan, but MacArthur passionately wished to fulfill his promise, 'I shall return,' uttered after he had been forced to flee to Australia in 1942. [MacArthur's command covered all ground forces, some air forces and the Seventh Fleet. Adm. Chester Nimitz, commander in chief, Pacific fleet and Pacific Ocean areas, ruled over Adm. Bull Halsey's Third Fleet and the VII Army Air Force. Gen. H. H. Arnold headed the XX Army Air Force, which included the B–29s under his deputy, Gen. Curtis E. LeMay. The fourth top command belonged to Gen. Joseph Stilwell, who directed the China-Burma-India operations which covered the XIV Army Air Force.]

Originally the grand design envisioned a methodical move up the Philippine chain beginning with the large, southern island of Mindanao, which would provide landing fields for support of the ground troops. Adm. Bull Halsey reported that naval forces hitting the Philippines noticed that the Japanese airpower seemed less formidible. Plans were reappraised. The development of the fast carrier forces suggested a shortcut. The Navy could furnish tactical air power and, instead of slowly stepping from stone to stone, the American forces could strike first in the middle of the archipelago, at Leyte. The change pushed up the target date for Leyte by two months, and further study of the maps and disposition of the opposing forces indicated that Yap could be bypassed. As a consequence, even as the Deadeyes weighed anchor, the convoy bearing the troops altered course and headed for Leyte.

Similarly, the 7th Division, which had expected to strike at Yap, wound up instead as part of Leyte's southern attack force. The XXIV Corps, composed of the 7th and 96th, beached along a 5,000-yard stretch of black sand around Dulag. The overall assault plan called for the XXIV Corps to link up with the X Corps (24th and 1st Cavalry Divisions) coming ashore to the north.

"At first," says Bob MacArthur, with the 13th Engineers, "it seemed very pretty with the volcanic black sand and the palm trees." But the engineers soon encountered big problems as the torrential tropical rains made dirt roads into quagmires that sucked down the wheels of heavy equipment. It was a harbinger of what lay ahead on Okinawa. Disease rampaged through the 13th; schistosomiasis, a liver-seeking parasite, infected a fifth of the battalion and eventually forced the evacuation of Col. George Cookson, who was now the CO.

Among those with the 7th Division, seeing the enemy up close and personal for the first time, was a young second lieutenant from Utah, Gage Rodman, a former student at Weber College. "My reaction to the attack on Pearl Harbor was that the Japs were insane. I was twenty when I enlisted in 1942 and I joined the service to beat the draft. My initial reaction to military service was that it would be just another job but more serious."

He started with the Air Corps, learning the mechanics of the bombsight at Lowry Field, Colorado. The work apparently bored Rodman because he sought the challenge of OCS and was quickly accepted on the basis of a score of 140 on the AGCT examination, where 110 was sufficient to qualify.

Upon completion of the course, Rodman became the leader of the 3rd platoon, G Company, 17th Infantry Regiment. The veterans in his unit accepted him "easily." The voyage from Hawaii to Leyte lasted thirty days as the massive armada circled about until a proper convoy could be organized.

On D-Day by the beaches near Dulag, Rodman supervised the unloading of supplies. He chafed at his noncombatant role and sought out

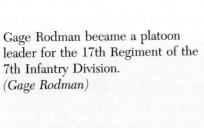

Gage Rodman became a platoon leader for the 17th Regiment of the 7th Infantry Division.
(Gage Rodman)

his colonel. "I told him that since I had trained with my platoon, I should be with them. The colonel said he wished he had more men like me. I found my outfit shortly thereafter, took over my platoon and told the lieutenant who had temporarily replaced me to report back to the company CP [command post]. He was happy to do so.

"My baptism of fire came October 28, 1944. We advanced along a line towards the Marabang River. We ran into heavy small-arms fire. We took no casualties but we found three dead Japanese when we reached the river. We stopped there for the night. I was a little shaky but didn't show it, as my men were mostly veterans from Attu, the landing and subsequent push inland."

Rodman was a faithful correspondent to his family and a V-mail letter early in November described one of his adventures. "I was in a little mixup the other day and thought the kids might enjoy an account. I was ordered to flank a Jap position late in the afternoon. It had held us up all day. We got up in some Kunai grass about eight feet tall. I left the platoon while I went to have a look where we were going. The grass ended at a clearing with coconut trees on the edge. I knelt by a tree to look across the opening and a machine gun cut loose at me from the jungle on the other side. Three bullets hit the tree a foot above my head. I ducked and crawled back to the platoon, led them around through the jungle on our side. When we were 100 yards past the Japs, we turned to come up at their rear. I saw a Jap stick his head up, about 300 yards away. I knelt down and fired. He went one way and his hat the other. Later we found him with a hole at the bridge of his nose. When I shot, about ten more Japs jumped and ran. We all fired and got most of them.

"We crossed the field and came up behind a lot of trenches and three pillboxes. We took one pillbox just by shooting the man inside. Then we split up and jumped the other two. My half took the box on our left. The Japs turned their guns around and began firing out the rear but couldn't hit us. We cleaned out the trenches and began throwing grenades. Finally someone just put a phosphorus grenade in and three Japs ran out in the smoke, firing right at us with pistols. I shot one four times from six-foot range. Others were doing the same. We captured their machine gun and counted twenty-five dead Japs."

Rodman concluded with a note of concern for his brother Walt in Europe, who, as a member of a cavalry recon squadron, had arrived on the beaches of Normandy at D plus three. The incident described by Gage Rodman won him a Bronze Star.

On the basis of Leyte and, subsequently, Okinawa, Rodman comments on the quality of veterans and replacments. "Our unit was out-standing. Many of my men had fought on Attu. The first thing you learn from veterans is that if you are the platoon leader, you must lead and prove you can lead. You accept and ask for advice from veterans, espe-cially squad leaders and the platoon sergeant. You give each other confidence. That makes a team. You are mutually dependent on each other, confident, but not overconfident, and observant. You see how the veterans look ahead, not down. One learns to look up also [throughout the war in the Pacific, the Japanese made extensive use of snipers who tied themselves into treetops]. One quickly learns which shells are close and which are not. Veterans are aware of what is going on. Replace-ments can expose themselves needlessly. They have to learn to stay alert to the situation and to depend on their comrades.

"Replacements, who were made to feel they were joining a gilt vet-eran outfit, seemed to be less effective, as they were at first too jumpy, and that can be contagious. They were less inclined to look beyond themselves. They were less aggressive due to inexperience. It only took a few patrols and up all night with infiltrators to make them veterans, but a higher percentage of replacements were hit than the veterans. Their lack of confidence in themselves and their fellow soldiers seemed to make them more vulnerable.

"A lack of realistic basic training was probably a big factor but experi-ence is the only real teacher. There are so many little things that one learns without knowing it, so if they survive the first day, these little things help them. They did seem to know what to expect or what was expected of them. It was too late to try and teach them what to do when you had to go out on patrol or when lying in the dark listening to every strange sound."

Rodman remarks, "It is amazing how little sleep one can get by with when you're keyed up. It's after going into reserve that exhaustion sets in. That's where the 'thousand-yard stare' is seen. The brain is now numb. Someone says, 'Halt! Fall out!' and one is instantly asleep, more like unconscious. A half-hour later, one is somewhat refreshed. The brain starts to function."

Although Maurice Reeves with the 13th Combat Engineers had es-caped the threat of enemy guns in the Aleutians, he had come under fire at Kwajalein his second night ashore.

"On Leyte, danger was more frequent with shellfire and small arms peppering places where the engineers tried to construct bridges, clear minefields or retrieve supplies after an area started to burn when an ammunition dump exploded."

Recalls Bob Jackson, the heavy weapons platoon leader for A Company of the 96th Division, "When we landed on Leyte, our battalion was the middle one of the three that landed abreast. Though we were all in the first wave, we all became mixed together on the beach and no one seemed to know what was going on. I surely didn't and went into a sort of numbness. I was able to gather up most of the weapons platoon, along with a platoon from B Co., and get the mortars and machine guns aimed inland. We didn't know whether we were under fire or not but there was a great deal of banging away at something. It was noisy as hell.

"We dug in on the beach. That night we set up a fear-filled perimeter. It was to be the first of a long series of wet foxholes. When frightened, my motto was to eat. I ate much of the bag of hard candy we were given as part of our landing rations. I rather doubt any of us fired *at* anything. We had not seen a Japanese or anything else moving. Star shells from the mortars and from the destroyers off shore kept the night bright. I suspect that we were in no danger from anything but our own wild firing."

"We moved out through the swamps and wild undergrowth. A rice paddy was almost a blessing and a path was heaven. We were constantly wet and, in spite of the admonition about hanging onto gear, we were soon down to web belts, ponchos and goodies—cigarettes, issue chocolate and maybe a part of a K ration—kept in the waterproof landing bag.

"The mosquitoes and other animals were awful. This swampy land was home to leeches and we had all been frightened by the medicos about the liver fluke for which this animal was the host. Our feet were a mess because we dared not take off our boots; we might not get them on again. Most of us had developed fungus which the medicos had warned us about, but we were unable to take the proper precautions of changing socks. I took off my boots about the fourth day and was shocked at the huge ringworm-type lesions all over my feet and up my legs. The carefully-husbanded foot powder was about as useful as an invocation to the gods.

"Resupply, we were told, was out of the question. This was while the Battle of Leyte Gulf [a huge naval encounter that shattered the last effective, aggressive units of the Japanese Navy] was in progress. We had little news, most of it was bad. There seemed a good chance we'd be stranded. With our immediate problems looming so large, we seemed to shuck this off. When you're miserable the big problems don't gain so much attention. By this time, we'd had little action; the enemy were environment and fear, not the Japanese."

Jackson and his troops entered into what military historians call "small-unit actions," firefights of short duration by handfuls of soldiers against largely unseen enemy. "Each of us developed a wariness, a perpetual crouch and a fear of what lay just ahead. It was quite similar to our childhood fears of what was in the closet. What we knew or had experienced of the Japanese fighting man to this point was that he was suicidally devoted—as an individual—to killing Americans. He was incomprehensible to the American mind. In our minds, his devotion kept each of us fearful and alert to his seemingly haphazard actions."

During one skirmish the battalion commander was killed. In another, seasoned enemy soldiers set up ambushes and exploited strong pillbox defenses against the 96th Division advance. In support of the attack, which included Jackson and Company A, 81 mm mortars laid down a barrage. "It was closer support than we had used before, so those not moving, like me and my runner, took very flat positions. A short round landed directly at the junction of two companies. Among those mortally wounded was my runner, with whom I lay almost helmet to helmet and whose severed head looked at me. I didn't have a scratch."

After a series of other limited but deadly encounters, the Leyte campaign for Jackson and his closest associates petered out. "Looking back, I see what a well-trained unit we were. There was little panic and jobs were done to the best of our abilities under terrible circumstances. This was not the stuff of awards but competent soldierly activity under the great stress of fear."

There were, however, moments of exceptional valor. Pvt. Ova A. Kelley, of Company A, a soldier previously not recognized by Jackson as out of the ordinary, who, when his outfit became pinned down, "got mad and went charging at the enemy, throwing grenades and firing his M–1. It threw the enemy off and the rest of A Company charged, cleaning out the Japanese company." A posthumous Medal of Honor citation for Kelley noted that the entire enemy force of thirty-six men was wiped out.

When the fighting was limited to patrols in search of men hiding out in caves, an epidemic of hepatitis swept through the outfit. With all other officers either wounded or sick, Jackson temporarily became company commander. Eventually the disease struck Jackson, who persevered until he could turn over the organization to the first recovered officer. He then entered a hospital.

"After a couple of weeks I felt pretty well but the doctors would not release me. Not that I was pushing all that hard, until I heard our battalion was embarking. As at other times, the prospect of being a replacement officer in another outfit scared me more than the Okinawa campaign. I talked my way out of the hospital and got a ride out to our troopship the night before we sailed. I was back with my own."

Dick Thom, of the 381st Regiment, arrived at Leyte in a critical position. "My battalion commander was unique, a reserve officer activated in 1939. He had been a supply officer and never been to infantry school and had been made battalion CO just before desert maneuvers. He was a CPA, and he wanted an educated man as his S–3 [plans and operations for a battalion]. He chose me and relied on me to give the orders. He would receive instructions from regiment but never issued a tactical order up to the time he was wounded, shot in the shoulder, and evacuated."

Thom contends that with all he had to do, there was not time to be frightened, at least on Leyte. And it was on Leyte that the erstwhile lawyer on a reconnaissance mission killed his first enemy. "I had become disoriented and suddenly this officer appeared, about ten feet away. I shot and killed him; he had a saber, which I guess I wanted more than he did. I used it to whack at the jungle.

"My regiment never turned in a prisoner on Leyte. You couldn't get your own wounded back from the jungle there, and we sure as hell wouldn't waste time on one of their wounded."

Buck private George Brooks of Company K, 382nd Regiment was in the first wave at Leyte, October 20, and he recalls the searing heat, ninety-eight degrees at 10:00 A.M. "The normal reaction when we first came under fire was fear, an anticipation of the unknown. Everyone doesn't handle it the same way. Our battalion commander in fact blew his cork that first day and had to be shipped back. Most of us were sustained by our religion and the closeness and mutual support of our buddies.

"While we were in the amtrac heading for shore, one of the guys was so nervous he kept fiddling with the safety on his rifle. He had the barrel close to his cheek. All of a sudden we heard a loud bang and when we looked over at this guy, he had black powder up the side of his face and a bullet hole in his helmet. It's funny now, but not then."

Don Dencker, Company L of the 382nd, went in at Blue Beach as part of an assault company at 10:00 A.M. "We made it safe for Doug to go ashore that afternoon, as did many thousands of other dogfaces." MacArthur, wearing well-pressed suntans, his trademark cap atop his sparse hair, the scowling visage either a statement of his pride or a rebuke to the landing-barge coxswain who halted the boat short of the beach, actually stepped in the shallow waters of Red Beach where the

1st Cavalry to the north secured the area.   "We were about as ready psychologically as any outfit could be for combat after so long on ships," points out Dencker. "I spent fifty days on LST 745. But that much time at sea meant we weren't in as good shape physically as we should have been. We became exposed to very high temperature and humidity—we had twenty inches of rain in our first thirty days on Leyte. Our fatigues rotted away.

"Companys L and K took Hill 120, 600 yards inland, in forty-two minutes. Three minutes later, the U.S. Navy shelled Hill 120. Initially, I didn't have much fear as I was so excited. Later, fear sank in but almost everyone managed to live with it. We had twenty battle casualties on the landing day, including five or six from that naval shelling of Hill 120 after we captured it.

"On Leyte, the only one who didn't measure up was our first sergeant, who was demoted to private for malingering at a field hospital after being slightly wounded by the naval bombardment on Hill 120. Our company commander was wounded by a Jap 75 mm shell. The executive officer and Lieutenant [Cledith] Bourneau were also hit. Both were patched up and returned to the company to continue to lead. Two of our platoon sergeants received battlefield commissions; one was well deserved and the other not.

"Almost all other promotions were from the ranks to replace casualties, the sick and the evacuated. Leyte was a hellhole with yellow jaundice, hepatitis, jungle rot and other diseases."

Confusion governed the beach where Mike Moroz, Company L, 382nd, touched down in the second wave. "We landed alongside of the troops who were supposed to be in front of us. There was enemy fire on the beach. A fellow took two or three steps and got a bullet in his head. He and I had switched positions because I was supposed to be the assistant to the flame thrower, Ed Johnson, and wanted to be closer to Johnson. The safety valve on Johnson's flame thrower went out and he threw the whole thing down.

"Tanks were shooting at our own tanks. Later, though we sent a Sherman medium tank out front, all buttoned up. A few hundred yards behind we had a light tank. As fast as the Japs would climb on the Sherman, the light tank would open up with its 37 mm using buckshot to knock them off and then we'd shoot them. They were the enemy, not people. They were the reason we were there.

"We got into a swampy area and the trucks couldn't pass through it. For seven days, all we had in the way of food and ammunition was what we had carried originally. One night the sergeant ordered us to dig in for the night. We were in the middle of a rice paddy, two inches of water covering layers of clay. We built like a dam site around us."

Melvin Coobs counts himself as having spent eighty-eight days in combat on Leyte, beginning with the October 20, initial landing, which went well. "We were all concerned about being hurt or killed but we were also afraid we wouldn't be able to hold up our end of the unit's responsibilities in a combat action. We took our initial objective rather easily but then when we dug in for the night, we found ourselves under enemy artillery fire. We did just what we had been taught for months not to do. We marched out in the dark about a mile to find a new location for our perimeter.

"We had landed during the rainy season, so a lot of our attention was directed toward keeping the rain from hampering other activities. Many nights we would dig foxholes and have them fill with water. The terrain, the mountainous jungle made travel difficult, impossible on many occasions. All resupply came up on another soldier's back. It was always a problem of fighting the weather as well as the Japanese."

For Len Lazarick, the Leyte campaign was a short one. "I landed with the first wave, managed to get about 100 yards inland and was wounded. I was returned to a troopship which had surgical facilities on board. After two days, dozens of noncombatant vessels like mine hastily weighed anchor and left Leyte. The second battle of the Philippine Seas was getting underway so all nonfighting ships were ordered out."

Returned to duty and to the island after the worst of the fighting was over, Lazarick worked a detail assigned to unloading fifty-five gallon drums of fuel oil and gasoline. "We were on call around the clock and had tents right on the beach. I developed a fungus infection in both ears and was unable to open my mouth and chew solid foods. The medics sent me off to the hospital, where I was treated and put on a liquid diet. That lasted until it was time to depart for Okinawa. All soldiers able to walk were discharged from the hospital and put aboard troop transports. I was given a bottle of alcohol and an eyedropper for my ears."

Newlywed Pvt. Ellis Moore, assigned to communications, by V-mail to his wife, a week after reaching the shores of the Philippines announced, "Yep, it's me, safe and sound and at the moment." He reassured her, "as far away from action as I can be and still be on the same island with it. We were on a ship for five weeks after leaving Pearl Harbor and I was plenty sick of it. First of all we stopped at [censored] where we got mail. Then we went to [censored]. The next stop after the [censored] was this island which we can only identify by saying it's one of the Philippines.

"I'll never forget the naval bombardment this island got for a few hours before we landed. It was terrific and to us who were waiting to land, it inspired confidence, as I honestly couldn't see how anything could live through that barrage. As a matter of fact, we didn't get much opposition on the beach and it wasn't until we pushed inland that we hit trouble. I landed with the second wave of assault troops, three minutes after the first troops touched the shore, and I must admit I was plenty scared when we were ordered to jump out of our landing boats. I think I was lucky being in an early wave because the Japs trained their mortars on the later ones and gave them trouble . . .

"From the newspapers you all undoubtedly know more about the overall Philippine campaign than we do. All we get are rumors about how other outfits are doing. However, I do know about the war that concerned our outfit, and it is hell, even though I don't think we got a strong dose of it. We were up there for six days with the infantry troops but there is a big difference between us and the infantry. Their job is to probe ahead looking for Japs to kill and in doing so exposing themselves to be killed by the Japs. Our job was strictly keeping a radio set going and while we were always within a couple hundred yards of the front line, we still had the security of a few riflemen in front of us. Aside from the obvious dangers of rifle and mortar fire, the worst thing about the fighting is the fatigue. Some of the guys had fifty to seventy-five pounds of radio equipment on their backs. This is bad enough ordinarily but when you have to walk through swamps up to your neck, it's almost too much. A couple of times, I felt like just stopping right in the middle of one of those swamps."

Several paragraphs later, Moore noted, "I'm afraid I failed Bobby [Peggy's younger brother] so far concerning any Jap equipment he would like. I saw plenty of stuff up front, but couldn't lug a lot of junk besides the radio equipment we had. I did pick up a few Jap papers, postcards, etc. Perhaps later on I'll be able to get a helmet or something like that.

"The natives are very friendly and seem to be happy that we have come. The Japs must have treated them miserably. Most of them are wearing the rags they wore when the Japs came. They said the Japs took their food leaving them hardly enough to live on. Many of the men and boys are at the front now fighting without rifles and their own knives which are wicked and will take off a head with one swipe. They are very useful as guides and the first days, when supplies were scarce they got us coconuts and sugar cane."

Subsequently, Moore wrote home about the hospitality extended to him and some fellow GIs by a slightly more affluent local family with six children that shared their four rooms and food with the eight soldiers. "The father said that most of the Filipinos hate the Japs. The Nips took all the good homes, demanded the pigs, chickens and food and if the natives refused they cut their heads off. I think that is one reason the natives seem to relish chopping off Jap heads now. The boys and girls were put into forced labor units to work on the airfields at 2½ pesos a day in Jap invasion money—with which you could buy a pair of pants for 200 pesos. This family had three close relatives killed a week before we came."

By mid-November, Moore had settled into a garrison-style life on Leyte. To his Aunt Janie, he wrote, "We get a big kick out of listening to Tokyo Rose as she tells us how we are cut off, how our navy is at the bottom of the sea and how we can never expect reinforcements to reach us and so must look forward to the terrible fate of being slaughtered by the victorious Nips, aided by the whole native population."

In fact, broadcasts from Tokyo provided the troops with more than just propaganda and false stories about how well American prisoners were treated. Moore advised his parents, "From it, [an editorial from the newspaper *Nichi-Nichi*] I gather that the Japs aren't as confident about the war as they once were. The main gist was that although resources and materials may run low for the Japs, the 'divine winds' will eventually blow for the Nips and bring them victory." At this point in the war, neither the civilian public nor the lesser ranks of soldiers had been officially informed on the phenomenon of the kamikaze, sometimes referred to as the 'divine wind.' Moore continued, "[The announcer] said the Jap flyers all had great spirit of 'self-sacrifice' instilled in them and that when they took off on their flights they were prepared not to come back again. Illustrating this, he read the latest Imperial War Communique which said that many Jap flyers had given their lives over the Philippines but in so doing had sunk thirty-nine American vessels, including nineteen carriers, two battleships, six cruisers and other smaller ships and had taken the lives of thousands of U.S. sailors." The Japanese continually exaggerated the damage inflicted by kamikazes.

"Next came a discussion of the Dumbarton Oaks Conference going on in Washington and the World Security Council with special emphasis on the proposed international police force. The announcer said the Japanese people felt an international police force was the best way to insure World War III. The Japanese he said, had another plan which he thought would interest all peace-loving countries, disarmament of all countries!"

Moore reported that the program ended with the Tokyo Symphony under the direction of a German, playing Tchaikovsky's Piano Concerto no. 1. "From the sound of the orchestra one gathers the impression that most of His Highness's best musicians are off serving the Imperial cause. However, it was music and provided entertainment. I don't know how we'd manage on these rainy afternoons if we didn't have Radio Tokyo."

As the men of the 96th recovered from their adventures on Leyte, the openings in their ranks due to casualties filled with a stream of replacements. Among the newcomers was an almost twenty-four-year-old draftee and former farmer in Colorado, Paul Westman. "I had an agricultural deferment, which was automatically issued by the draft board since someone had to manage the family farm for my widowed mother while my younger brother was still in high school. We didn't have a radio and didn't hear about the attack on Pearl Harbor until three days later when a neighbor told us. My reaction was to go to another neighbor and ask him what was likely to happen.

"When my brother finished his education, I was reclassified 1-A. I went through the seventeen-week basic training cycle at Camp Joseph Robinson in Arkansas. My MOS [Military Occupation Specialty] was 745, rifleman. We saw the film series *Why We Fight* [propaganda movies aimed at explaining how the United States had become involved and what the troops could expect from the enemy. A production called *Kill or Be Killed* attempted to dramatize the nature of combat.]. These were graphic and a violent preview to what would shortly be the real thing. It was upsetting to say the least."

When he reached Leyte, Westman spent several days in the replacement depot at Tacloban. "While I was in the chow line at Tacloban, I saw a number of American prisoners who had been liberated from the Cabanatuan Camp [a POW installation run by the Japanese for those captured during the early days of the war]. These people were not much more than living skeletons. Right then, I made up my mind that if ever I was in danger of being taken prisoner, I would shoot myself. And after seeing the condition of these men, I could only think of the Japanese as inhuman."

Westman received assignment to Company K of the 96th Division's 382nd Regiment. "The jungle-training and combat patrols in secured areas of Leyte were plenty realistic. All rifle squads had live ammunition and combat-experienced NCOs watched us replacements. There weren't many healthy bodies in the company when I joined it. The medics on Leyte didn't seem to be able to do anything for the many

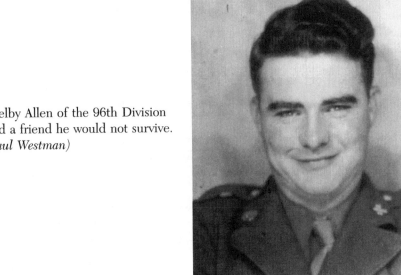

Shelby Allen of the 96th Division
told a friend he would not survive.
(*Paul Westman*)

cases of jungle rot, dengue fever and the parasitical diseases of the
stomach. Not that they didn't care but they had no knowledge.

"I was fortunate in being assigned to a unit that had just been pulled
off the line and was guarding rear areas. I got valuable training experience. The veterans of the outfit treated us with considerable reserve at
first. It was about a month before most began to act as if I belonged. On
my part, I tried to be pleasant and, above all, not to goof up."

On his first night of guard duty with the 1st Squad of the 1st Platoon,
Westman made a close friend, whom he would never forget. "Shelby
Allen, of Cincinnati, with black curly hair, an engaging personality and
not one to be intimidated by rank to the extent that I was. I felt drawn
to him the instant we met.

"When we were set up on the beach in March, preparatory to embarking on the Okinawa operation, we spent some time training with
life rafts. At one point I became separated from the life raft and was
being carried seaward by what I presume was the undertow. Shelby was
the only one to notice and come to the rescue. I was nearly done in but
he finally got me back to the raft. Quite likely, he saved my life."

With the last of their training done, the additions integrated into the
ranks, the 96th left Leyte bound for Okinawa.

CHAPTER X

LOVE DAY FOR
THE ARMY

The American strategists had selected the Hagushi beaches on the west side of Okinawa, near its middle, as the optimum site for the initial entry. Another possible port of call, the Minatoga beaches on the southeast coast, struck observers as the kind of terrain that provided natural defensive areas that had been so costly for invaders at Tarawa and Iwo Jima. A further attraction of the Hagushi option lay in the proximity of the airfields of Yontan and Kadena. The order of battle named the 1st and 6th Marine Divisions and the 7th and 96th Divisions to be the first combat organizations for the assault. The 77th, fresh from its chores in the Kerama Retto, and the 27th Infantry Division would be in ready reserve, aboard nearby transports. The 81st Infantry Division was designated as the area reserve. The 2nd Marine Division would execute a feint toward the east coast of Okinawa to freeze Japanese forces there.

Beginning on March 25, hundreds of ships, including ten battleships and eleven cruisers, stood off the Hagushi area of Okinawa and in the seven days of preparation for Operation Iceberg heaved more than 13,000 large-caliber shells—from six to sixteen inches—at the shore. Minesweeping operations cleansed the waters. Overhead, carrier planes dumped tons of explosives, wiping out ground-based enemy aircraft, and fended off Japanese air attacks, which scored an occasional hit on the armada.

Underwater demolition teams swam in the shallows for two days before the scheduled appearance of the first amphtracs to blow away

A U.S. Navy LCM launches a flame tipped salvo of rockets at the Okinawa beaches. *(Signal Corps, U.S. National Archives)*

Amphtracs—amphibious tractors—rendezvous before heading for the beach on Love Day while a battleship blasts the shoreline. *(Signal Corps, U.S. National Archives)*

Landing craft ferry GIs from the 96th Division to the Okinawa beaches on Love Day. *(National Archives)*

obstacles. Unlike the formidable steel doors, bottom-ripping hedgehogs and tetrahedrons, wire and mines that menaced the assault force on D-Day in Normandy, the Japanese planted only wooden posts driven into the coral. The UDT experts destroyed the obstacles without a single rifle shot from any shore defenders. For that matter, no coastal guns spewed fire at the fleet, to the puzzlement of the Americans.

L-Day dawned cool and slightly overcast. At 6:20 A.M. the sun broke through as if it were a rocket signaling the fire support ships to open up. Adm. Richmond Kelly Turner ordered, "Land the landing force!"

For Lt. Bob Jackson, with the 96th Division, the trip from Leyte to Okinawa had significantly improved the quality of his life. "Coming under Admiral Nimitz's command, the shipboard treatment was a remarkable contrast to Army troop life. We ate three good meals a day; we were, in spite of crowding, relatively comfortable. We even had ice cream! This was but a foretaste of the way the Navy ran an operation as compared with General MacArthur's neglect of his ground troops.

"The religious had attended services at 3:00 A.M. It was a gorgeous Easter/April Fool's Day. We embarked into the landing craft and spent the usual two hours boating around in circles, under an azure sky—I can't help the cliché. There was no shore activity except that of our shore parties, so we rode in basking in the cool but sunny weather, which reminded me of San Francisco on such a day. The landing, with those expert seamen, was dry footed, unlike most of our previous experiences with Army boat commanders. We came ashore, got into columns of companies and moved inland as if it were a school exercise.

"We landed at the waist of Okinawa abreast of the 7th Division. The mission was to cross the island, capture an airfield and then turn south while the Marine units, arriving above us, turned north. Since my battalion was in Corps reserve, we landed in the third wave."

Pfc. Ellis Moore, aboard LST 789, had left the Gulf of Leyte on March 24 for the 350-mile trip to Okinawa. "They said this would be a hell of a lot rougher than Leyte and this was easy to believe after our briefings. There was an estimated garrison of 60,000 Jap troops, plus 20,000 Okinawans and Koreans [an undercount by at least 20,000 enemy]. We were landing at the neck about one-third up from the southern tip on the west coast. With the 7th Division on our left, we were to cut across the island, about three miles wide at that point and then drive two divisions abreast down the slopes to the southern tip. Two Marine divisions were to land north of us, cut across and then swing up north. The main opposition was expected to be in the Marine sector where the Japs could retreat slowly into the rugged mountainous terrain of northern Okinawa. [It was a totally erroneous understanding of where the enemy intended to make his stand, due either to faulty information or poor communication between the intelligence sections and the line troops.]

"There were hundreds of maps and aerial photos of every sector of our objective, but those things are for colonels and generals to pore over, not privates. One thing we did think about plenty was the ten-foot sea wall that was said [by intelligence specialists] to run all the way around the island. The Navy promised to knock that wall full of holes during their preliminary bombardment, but if they didn't, it was easy to picture us being picked off one by one by the Japs as we crawled over the top.

"The trip was a rough one, and sometimes I wondered if that rolling, creaking LST would last through it. We spent most of the time on our cots or down below, reading, shooting the bull, speculating about the operation. Our S–3 [Plans and Operations officer], Captain Young, estimated it would take twenty days to secure the island. The most pessimistic guess was that it would take thirty days. I did not work up into a nervous frenzy, though Lord knows why.

"L-Day, April 1, began for us about three-forty-five in the morning. Reveille, then breakfast, as the the LSTs slowly crept forward. Last-minute checks on equipment, ammunition, weapons. As gray dawn broke, you could see huge hulks of battleships way ahead, belching occasional balls of fire, with the roar of the guns reaching us seconds later.

"H-hour was set for 0830 and as it grew lighter, we went below and piled into our landing craft, LVTs (Landing Vehicle Tanks). One of the most uncomfortable moments of making an invasion is when they turn on the motors of all fifteen or sixteen LVTs in the tank deck of an LST. There is no outlet down there until they open the front and release the smaller craft. When all LVT motors are on, the fumes are unbearable.

"We were soon out in the water, however, bobbing up and down around the mother LSTs. The sun was coming up by this time and it was a huge red mass as it appeared from behind the hazy Okinawa hills. I couldn't help but think at the time, 'Well, here we go, straight into the rising sun.'

"As 0830 drew nearer, the naval bombardment grew in intensity. Just about every ship in the bay, about 1,500 of them, was pouring lead into the Okinawa beach and the hills beyond. LCIs (Landing Craft Infantry) with their weird rockets, LSTs and their 20 and 40 mm guns, destroyers, cruisers and battleships with their five, eight, ten and sixteen-inch guns. Overhead, wave after wave of planes droned over the island, dropped their eggs, and then reformed to start it all over again. It was a thrilling sight that took our minds off what was just ahead. From 0800 to 0830, the roar of the guns was continuous, with no time elapsing between great blasts. How could anyone stay alive within half a mile of the beach? We were soon to see that no one could.

"I was in the Zero boat that hit the beach between the second and third waves. We scrambled over the shattered sea wall and soon were looking for cover in the open potato, tomato and cabbage fields. There was no opposition on the beach—no mortars or artillery even. However, if the Japs had chosen to defend the beach and had lived through the naval bombardment, they could have made life miserable for us. We had landed on the wrong beach, a half mile from the correct one, and it took two hours for the battalion to reassemble. With any opposition at all, we would have been slaughtered."

For S–3 Dick Thom, with the 1st Battalion of the 96th Division's 381st Regiment, which fielded assault troops for the initial waves, conditions before the operation stirred anxiety. "When we finished our work on Leyte, we were short on everything. We couldn't replace the machine gun sights—anything optical had gone bad in the jungle. We couldn't draw ammunition. We scavenged all the M–1 ammunition we could find and laid it out on ponchos. I wound up with one and a half magazines for my carbine. The men had only a single bandolier. We made satchel charges with short and long fuses out of dynamite.

"We knew nothing about Okinawa until we were already at sea. It was supposed to be non-jungle, but since it was closer to Japan, it would be tougher than Leyte. We didn't really expect resistance on the beach. The Japs had learned they couldn't stop us there. We went in on amphtracs. No one sat down, everyone had his head over the rail, looking. There was only a little light firing from a wooded area after we first moved off the beach."

Shortly after the landing parties had begun to clear the undefended beaches, small craft started to dump massive numbers of pallets piled high with supplies. "We sent back people to pick up stuff," says Thom, "but they were strafed by the Navy. We used red smoke grenades and these bright red iridescent panels to mark our positions. They should have known that we were between these two indicators. There was an air liaison officer with every battalion, a Navy gunfire team, and everyone had their own radios. It was all confusion, you couldn't get any information through at all. There was a constant stream of messages, so you couldn't get emergency ones through. The only place an operation is surgically clean is on an island not occupied by the enemy."

Unlike Thom, Don Dencker, with Company L in the 382rd Regiment, also marked for the opening round, had been led to believe there would be heavy opposition at the shore. The lack of resistance initially was "a great surprise."

Len Lazarick, of Company K in the 96th Division's 382nd Regiment, had recovered from his fungal infection during the trip from Leyte to Okinawa. "We sailed through a typhoon for several days. Soldiers and sailors alike became seasick. We were not allowed on the outer decks and our sleeping quarters below reeked of vomit and body odor. Our ship, the U.S.S. *Banner* (APA 60), shuddered and pounded along. From time to time we could see other ships in the convoy and it gave me an appreciation for 'Tin Can' sailors. Their destroyers listed to and fro at such an amplitude that I wondered how they stayed afloat. Oil tankers were awash with water over the decks and no one could be seen above deck.

"When we were close to Okinawa, the seas calmed down mercifully. Early in the morning of April 1, we were served a sumptuous breakfast of steak and eggs, bread and coffee. It gave new meaning to the expression that the 'condemned ate a hearty meal.' However, the 382nd was in reserve, so we didn't get ashore until late morning. We had to transfer from landing craft to amphibious tractors to get over the coral reef protecting the beaches.

"The usual softening up process was in full swing during our waiting period, but the knot in the belly and the tightness in the throat still came up despite the distance, about two miles from the shore. Our trip to the beach was uneventful and we landed near the Yontan airstrip and were deployed on flat farmland overlooking the beaches. It was midafternoon and we were ordered to dig in about 500 yards off the beach. News from the assault troops was encouraging because the resistance was light and they were making great progress. Jim Peters, my buddy in the 1st squad, proudly announced that his dysentery was under control. He insisted the entire squad visit the platoon slit trench and observe [that he was cured]. Peters, a 6'3", 190-pounder, normally, was down to 155 but at that moment he was a very happy soldier."

For Paul Westman, the rifleman replacement in Company K, Okinawa promised his baptism of fire. "Off the invasion beach, we loaded in the amtracs and formed up for the run in. The air attacks on the ships were beginning and ships were being hit. When the amtrac ran up on the beach, we bailed out and ran like striped apes for the sea wall."

Don Dencker remarks, "Company L had 168 men who landed on Okinawa, although the table of organization specifies 193 for a rifle company. Many intended replacements went to Europe to replace casualties from the Battle of the Bulge [December 1944–January 1945]." The total number of members for the infantry divisions hitting the beaches at Okinawa was about one and a half times the usual complement, but the excess came from attached units such as amphibious tractor battalions, extra engineer outfits, quartermaster companies, medical personnel and others.

But even as the 96th sailed from Leyte, reinforcements were already in the pipeline. Herman Buffington, who had entered the army the previous summer, completed his seventeen weeks of basic training at Fort McClellan, Alabama, near his Rome, Georgia, home. After a brief furlough, he was on his way west to a port of embarkation. "With a band playing, we shoved off. After days and days at sea, we reached Saipan in the Mariana Islands. The island was green and there were Jap bodies all about. The island had only recently been wrested from the enemy."

Buffington and his fellow replacements occupied a tent camp and pulled patrol, daytime searches for hold-out Japanese. At night, armed guards accompanied those who headed for the latrines. The encampment grew huge and they began to show movies in an outdoor theater. Occasionally, someone discovered extra spectators, fugitive Japanese soldiers who sneaked peeks at the entertainment.

"We loaded on a ship," recalls Buffington, "and we were certain it was to Formosa. During a month on board we were taught about Japanese living habits and their currency. Some fifteen days out, we were told our destination—Okinawa. Most of us had never heard of it. Finally anchoring off the island, shortly before Easter, our convoy was large after being assembled in midocean. One night we were told to be ready about dawn. There was a big breakfast and, since the day was Easter Sunday, the tune "Easter Parade" was being played over the speakers. It made you plenty homesick. The chaplain told us, 'Some of you will never return.' I wished then I had joined the Navy. But I found out later those guys didn't have it easy either.

"We carried guns, knives and bayonets as we left the ship. It was just dawn when we went overside and filled the LSM boats. It took nine hours to get in. The sun was shining. It was a pretty day, weatherwise. Our ships put up smoke screens to protect us from air raids.

"The actual landing wasn't too rough. And then six or eight of us got on a truck and we rode about a quarter of a mile down the beach and inland about another quarter of a mile. I was assigned to K Company, 383rd Regiment, 96th Division. I was surprised not to have encountered Japs. We all were. I still wished I had joined the Navy, though."

Members of the 7th Infantry Division, like Lt. Gage Rodman, a platoon leader with G Company, of the 17th Infantry Regiment, Pfc. Solomon Berger, with division artillery, Capt. Gene Prather, a staff officer with the 32nd Regiment, like everyone in the division, were pleasantly surprised by the absence of Japanese along the waterfront.

Maurice Reeves, first sergeant of Company C with the 13th Engineers of the 7th Division, says, "I came ashore with company headquarters, several waves back of the line platoons, who came in with the infantry. The ship-to-shore bombardment had leveled all buildings. I picked up a small wooden box which rattled. I pried open one end and found a postcard with Japanese printing on one side. On the other side, written in English, was THERE COULD HAVE BEEN A BOOBY TRAP IN HERE. Under the circumstances, someone had prepared this before our landing."

From a mountaintop on Tokashiki Island, Japan's Yoshihiro Minamoto watched Love Day unfold. "As I observed the landing operations, I was convinced this was a complete defeat. The soldiers felt the same way. But we thought it was our destiny to share the fate of the island, and so held onto our pride. [And to continue not to surrender.]"

CHAPTER XI

TURKEY WINGS
AND ORANGES

On Love Day, Operation Iceberg dispatched the 1st and 6th Marine Divisions, which composed the III Amphibious Corps, commanded by Maj. Gen. Roy S. Geiger, toward the northern stretches of the Hagushi beaches.

"I was aboard a troop transport and it was the the evening before we stormed onto Okinawa," wrote Ernie Pyle, the most celebrated war correspondent of World War II. "We were carrying Marines. Some of them were going into combat for the first time; others were veterans from as far back as Guadalcanal. They were a rough, unshaven, competent bunch of Americans. I was landing with them and I felt I was in good hands . . . We were nervous. Anybody with any sense is nervous on the night before D-Day . . . We would take Okinawa—nobody had any doubt about that. But we would have to pay for it. Some on the ship would not be alive in twenty-four hours."

Pyle shared a cabin with a Marine major and awoke early for a predawn breakfast of ham and eggs. "Our assault transport carried many landing craft on deck. A derrick swung them over the side, we piled into them as they hung even with the rail, and then the winch lowered them into the water. I went on the first boat to leave our ship. It was just breaking dawn when we left and still more than two hours before H-hour. Our long ocean trip was over. Our time had run out. This was it.

"All around us hundreds of other boats were putting off and churning

135

Supplies pile up on Hagushi Beach after the landings. (*National Archives*)

From the air, the Hagushi beaches, where the Americans landed on Love Day, revealed no indication of the defenses that lay beyond. (*Signal Corps, U.S. National Archives*)

the water, but there was no organization to it. They weren't yet forming into waves. These early boats carried mainly the control crews who would manage the colossal traffic of shore-bound invasionists in the next few hours . . .

"An hour and a half before H-hour at Okinawa, our vast fleet began its final, mighty bombardment of the shore with its big guns. They had been at it for a week, but this was a concentration whose fury had not been approached before. The power of the thing was ghastly. Great sheets of flame flashed out from a battery of guns, gray-brownish smoke puffed up in a huge cloud, then the crash of sound and concussion carried across the water and hit you. Multiply that by hundreds and you had bedlam. Now and then the smoke from a battlewagon would come out in a smoke ring, an enormous one, twenty or thirty feet across, and float upward with perfect symmetry.

"Then came our carrier planes, diving on the beaches and torpedo planes, carrying heavy bombs and incendiaries that spread deep-red flame. Smoke and dust rose up from the shore, thousands of feet high, until finally the land was completely veiled. Bombs and strafing machine guns and roaring engines mingled with the crash of naval bombardment and seemed to drown out all existence . . .

"The water was a turmoil of movement: dispatch and control boats running about, LSMs and LSTs moving slowly forward to their unloading areas, motor torpedo boats dashing around as guides. Even the destroyers moved majestically across the fleet as they closed up for the bombardment of the shore . . .

"H-hour was set for 8:30. By 8:00 A.M. directions were being radioed and a voice boomed out to sea to form up waves one and two, to hurry up, to get things moving. Our first wave consisted solely of heavy guns on amphibious tanks which were to get ashore and blast out the pillboxes on the beaches. One minute behind them came the second wave —the first of our foot troops. After that waves came at about ten-minute intervals. Wave six was on its way before wave one ever hit the beach. Wave fifteen was moving up before wave six got to the beach."

Pyle, a veteran eyewitness to the abattoir-quality of such adventures, felt so miserable and fearful of what lay ahead, he could not talk. He excused himself "to use a civilized toilet for the last time in many days. I got a drink of water, though I wasn't thirsty." Back on deck, however, after a sailor introduced himself and said he read Pyle's columns, the correspondent was able to chat with a knot of seamen who gathered around him.

"Word came by radio that waves one and two were ashore without much opposition and there were no mines on the beaches. So far, so good. We looked at the shore through binoculars. We could see tanks moving across the fields and the men of the second wave walking inland, standing upright. There were a few splashes in the water at the beach but we couldn't make out any real fire coming from the shore.

"It was all very indefinite and yet it was indicative. The weight began to lift. I wasn't really conscious of it, but I found myself talking more easily with the sailors and somehow the feeling gradually took hold of me that we were to be spared."

With the seventh wave, Pyle chugged towards the now less ominous shore, transferring to an amphtrac to cross the reef. "I had dreaded the sight of the beach littered with my mangled bodies, and my first look up and down the beach was a reluctant one. Then like a man in the movies who looks away and then suddenly looks back unbelieving, I realized there were no bodies anywhere—and no wounded. What a wonderful feeling.

"Our entire regiment came ashore with only two casualties: one was a Marine who hurt his foot getting out of an amphibious truck; the other was, of all things, a case of heat prostration! And to add to the picnic atmosphere, they had fixed me up with a big sack of turkey wings, bread, oranges and apples. So instead of grabbing a hasty bit of K rations for our first meal ashore, we sat and lunched on turkey wings and oranges."

Platoon leader Bob Craig, as part of the 1st Division reserve, headed for the shore with his men in midafternoon and scribbled a few notes at the time. "We were in division reserve and went over the side about 2:30 P.M. We passed a battleship, cruiser and a couple of destroyers. They tossed shells inland, intermittently. Our LCVP [Landing Craft Vehicle Personnel] stuck on a coral reef about 200 yards out. Waded ashore, and moved inland about 200 yards and started to dig in. Lost one squad leader, Corporal Boris. Dropped a rifle on his foot and hurt it. He should be back.

"About dusk (6:30 P.M.) we moved up the hill toward Yontan Airfield. Were halfway up when a Jap plane came over. All the ships opened up with their AA. While we dodged falling shrapnel, the Jap landed on the airfield and got out of his plane. When he tried to run, some boys in an amtrac got him.

"We moved across a corner of the airfield, past a motorless Jap plane. Made first contact with the enemy. A sniper. I dived into a shellhole as two shots zipped through the grass near me. Too dark to do anything, so moved another 100 yards and dug in for the night, just east of the village of Sobe.

"Awake most of the night—partly in fear and partly because the fleas in the grass really bothered me. The only activity of the night, aside from the regular naval bombardment, was the appearance of another Jap plane on the Pacific side of the island. We saw a little 20 mm AA but with no results." This was the start of what Craig later would label "the beginning of a journey into hell."

Company A of the 7th Marine Regiment, with Don Farquahar, in command of the machine gun platoon, drew the assignment of reserve for the assault battalion. "We were in the third wave," says Farquahar. "I wasn't scared; the feeling is just like playing football in college, nervous as can be until you get in the game, then the jitters are gone. It was a great relief to find the beaches not defended and a real surprise. We had been trained in kill or be killed, and I had taken some special training in bayonet fighting, so I was rather looking forward to being able to use my special training."

Jim Moll remembers, "They told us Okinawa would not be easy because we were getting closer to Japan proper. There were some larger cities we would have to take, more occasions when we would be up against larger concentrations of enemy troops than what we had met in the past and also more concentrations of civilians.

"It was a blessing to land on the beach without a single casualty. I don't think anybody, including the highest brass, expected this, but whoever planned the operation deserves the highest medal."

Elmer Johnson, as a gunnery sergeant with the 2,000-man 29th Replacement draft consigned to the Marine 1st Division, watched the preassault bombardment in awe. "I still remember how surprised I was at how calmly everyone seemed to go about his business that day," says Johnson. "During the morning, the ship's loudspeaker had kept us informed as though they were watching a ballgame. Anything they could pick up on their radios, they would point out on the loudspeakers."

Then at noontime, he and his mates went ashore. "As we came in, I stepped off the landing craft into a shellhole and almost drowned. Most of our casualties in the division for the day were from accidents like that. Just after I landed, two Jap biplanes flew over us very low; the pilots even waved at us. Then they landed at Yontan and were promptly shot." Johnson and others speak of two misguided enemy pilots who thought the troops below were friendlies and the airport still in Japanese hands. Those on the scene agree that at least one enemy plane did set down on Yontan, and when the flier realized his error, sought to flee but was shot down.

Sgt. Harry Manion, with the Recon Company for the 6th Marine Division, who developed his expertise at scouting and patroling while mopping up on Guadalcanal and then applied his skills on Guam, recalls the trip to Okinawa began with "a brief look at a recreational area —Mog Mog [an island set up for rest and recreation] and then off to the war. Many map exercises on our forthcoming island of Okinawa. Order given for the first day. Cleaned out the brig [minor or even some major infractions did not relieve troops from combat duty] and test-fired some weapons.

"Recon Company went ashore and moved directly inland. Came across some caves, with civilians and perhaps some military. Called out in Japanese for the people to come out. Reply was one shot. In goes WP [white phosphorous grenade]. Out come some civilians. No soldiers. We left them for the civil affairs people.

"Still plenty of daylight. Moved off the left flank of the division. Dug holes, put out security and flaked out. Later, after dark, we heard firing coming from Yontan Airfield area. We learned that a Japanese pilot landed his fighter on the field. Always some who don't get the word."

As a corporal, Bama Marbrey led a four-man fire team when his company boarded their landing craft. "I carried a tommy gun; my assistant had an M–1 rifle, the third man had an automatic rifle or BAR, and the fourth in the group had an M–1. In the Higgins boat, I searched for them and found all three together, waiting for me. We checked our ammunition and gear as well as possible in the crowded boat, then as the side dropped, we tumbled toward the beach.

"Reaching the shore, we hit the ground and ran inland, searching for cover. I realized then that I still hadn't heard any gunfire or shells exploding. We waited, then got to our feet and ran a few yards to the next cover, but still no fire of any kind. Hill, close behind me, whispered, 'What's going on?' I had no answer.

"We waited, tension building up until the roar of my heartbeat ringing in my ears and my nerves stretched taut brought me to my feet. I fired a few rounds at the silence, then sank back to the ground, self-conscious but relieved. I felt better when I heard spatterings of rifle fire on down the line. Others easing their pressure.

"Still nothing happened, so we began to move inland carefully, fearing that all hell would break loose at any moment. I casually noted the pine trees and the red dirt, feeling a small surge of homesickness. I turned thoughts to the possibility of snipers in the friendly looking pines.

"We walked on, soon coming into the open, and found gardens that had been well tended. Cabbages were beginning to cup, and tomatoes hung, blood red, from the vines. We swarmed over the rows, grabbing a tomato in one hand, a cabbage in the other. I bit into a large ripe tomato and my salivary glands went wild with the almost-forgotten flavor. Belatedly, I wondered whether the garden had been salted with land mines.

"With our bounty loaded in one arm, we continued on our way, trying to hold our weapons in a firing position, yet still munching on cabbages. We began to hear shots fired once in a while. Still small arms, no artillery. About a mile past the gardens, we began to see a dead Japanese soldier or two. It was hard to tell how long they had been dead, but from odor, at least a day had passed with them lying in the hot sun.

"The order came down to take ten. I sat back, taking first a bite of a slightly squashed tomato, then a bite of cabbage. I ate until my stomach protested but my taste buds wanted more.

" 'Get your gear on, we're moving out in a scrimmage line,' the lieutenant called out. We had gone about 500 yards when the lead scout sent back a message that a village was just ahead. We skirted the edge of the village and drew no fire, so we came in closer. A few civilians stood close to one building, waving white flags.

"The lieutenant finally persuaded the leader to come closer, talked to him for a minute and then sent the small group behind our lines out of danger. Some of our guys scouted through the village, checking buildings and houses, while the rest of us dug foxholes 200 yards beyond." Marbrey and the other leathernecks settled in for their first night on Okinawa. They were still close enough to the beach to hear the first of what would be a series of raids by Japanese planes intent upon destroying the fleet off shore and in the anchorage at Kerama Retto.

The reactions of Craig, Farquahar, Johnson and Marbrey were replicated by the other Marines who went ashore that first day. Merrill McLane, a lieutenant with the former 4th Raider Battalion, wrote home, "The landing was unopposed, which took us by surprise, because in our other landings, the Japanese have shelled us and counterattacked at night. We don't know what they're up to."

Charles Owens, with the 1st Marine Division, says he fully expected the same sort of fierce give-and-take that he had gone through at Peleliu.

Earl Rice, who belonged to the same company as Owens and Don

Farquahar, came close to participating as a soldier in the 6th Marine Division. While at the Pavuvu encampment, he continued to run afoul of his immediate superiors, mouthing off, refusing assignments and falling asleep while on guard duty (Pavuvu was free of Japanese). Added dirty details such as KP and extra tours walking posts failed to improve his attitude or performance. In the tradition of private and public enterprise, the word of a new entity—in this case the formation of the 6th Division on Guadalcanal—spurred local commanders to attempt to transfer malcontents, misfits and troublemakers, or "shitbirds" in military parlance. Advised of his imminent separation from Company A in the 1st Marine Division, Rice swore to mend his ways and it was with this outfit that he headed for the beach.

"There were so many boats out there," says Rice, "it was like land rather than water. Before we got on the Higgins boat, they gave us only a piece of fruit and some water. Those Higgins boats went up and down, up and down, so the idea was to keep us from getting sick. I puked over the side and then I felt fine after that.

"The guy says, 'fix bayonets.' You don't know who the hell is on that beach, what you're heading into. I remembered what I saw at Peleliu."

Accompanying the Marines on Okinawa, correspondent Ernie Pyle chats with his jeep driver, Pfc. J. P. Murray. (*Signal Corps, U.S. National Archives*)

You fix that bayonet and see everybody doing the same. Then you hit the ground, the boat touches the shore, you can hear it. You know you're going to be getting off. Then you see everybody, myself included, blessing their selves, everyone's full of religion.

"We got off the boat, took off on the beach, waiting to see all the bang, bang, bang. Nothing happened. I got all this gear on me. I got the gas mask. I got the great big pack. I got my poncho, the shovel, my cartridge belt, I've got my M–1, ammo, grenades. I'm weighed down like this and they got me running and running across the beach. All of a sudden we stop and get down on the ground. Twenty seconds and we're up again. Running again. But there's no Japs there. We encountered nothing, absolutely nothing on the beach. We went on up and started climbing these damn hills. You figure when you get to the top of the hill you got it made. But when you got there, there was another one. You had to go down and then climb another. It was supposed to take us fifteen days to get where we got that first day. I was so tired from all that walking; I just wanted to lay down."

In the southwest, the 2nd Marine Division loaded men from troop transports into landing craft and seven waves consisting of 168 LCVPs set course for the Minatoga beaches. At 0830, as the first GIs and leathernecks stepped onto the Hagushi beaches, the vessels bearing the 2nd Marines reversed course and returned to the mother ships. The feint drew one salvo of four rounds. But the official communique from Japanese headquarters triumphantly announced that "an enemy landing attempt on the eastern coast of Okinawa on Sunday morning was completely foiled, with heavy losses to the enemy."

By the time darkness fell on L-Day and all of the invaders had burrowed into the ground for the night, the beachhead stretched along more than twelve miles of the Okinawa coastline. In some places the troops had pushed inland for three miles. The 17th Regimental Combat Team of the 7th Division had occupied a now-deserted Kadena airfield shortly before noon. Patrols from the 17th gazed upon the east coast waterfront of Okinawa in midafternoon. The island had been virtually chopped in half in less than twelve hours.

Marines from the 6th Division took over Yontan, the bigger and better developed of the airstrips, without any opposition. The booty included shattered Japanese planes and supplies, destroyed by the preinvasion bombardments. The swiftness of the advance surprised not only the Americans but, obviously, the enemy, which explains the fate of the unfortunate pilot who sought to land at Yontan after it had fallen.

For the operation, the statisticians figured at least 60,000 men were ashore. The bulk of these were foot soldiers backed up by divisional artillery and tanks, plus a generous number of service troops.

The only serious opposition came from the air. A suicide plane crashed the battleship *West Virginia;* another splashed down close enough to damage some transports. And two kamikazes off Minatoga struck an LST, killing twenty-four, injuring twenty-one and a transport, with a loss of sixteen dead and thirty-nine wounded. While these losses, from a strategic viewpoint, were negligible, they signaled the coming challenge to the Navy.

CHAPTER XII

THE DIVINE WINDS BLOW

Suicidal actions were not unique to the Japanese. American patriotic lore is stocked with expressions—"Give me liberty or give me death"; "I only regret I have but one life to lose for my country." But as a code of behavior, self-sacrifice for the United States owes more to rhetoric than reality. Occasionally, during World War II, an American would hurl himself at a defensive position with no real hope to survive, at least in the eyes of onlookers. Men fell on grenades to protect comrades. There is a tale of a wounded pilot who aimed his stricken plane at an enemy ship. In some worst-case scenarios, men took on missions with long odds. But no one seriously expected American fighting men to deliberately lay down their lives to defend their positions. Although some high commanders ordered their subordinates to hold to the last man, surrender was acceptable under the appropriate circumstances; the Alamo was the exception, not the rule. No one criticized the commanders who ran up the white flags at Corregidor or Wake Island.

Under the Japanese military philosphy, to give one's life for the emperor was a highly praised, even recommended, action. The banzai charge on Attu, cut down by the 7th Division, while it might have temporarily succeeded, could not have halted the inevitable. The Japanese soldiers who had occupied the island were doomed, sooner or later. GIs and leathernecks came to expect that sort of mass, high-casualty charge as characteristic when they exerted pressure against defenders.

Following a hit from a kamikaze, fire and smoke erupt from the aircraft carrier *Bunker Hill.* (*Signal Corps, U.S. National Archives*)

Americans also had seen individual Japanese pilots try to crash into them, or strike ships, certainly more frequently than such tactics were employed by American airmen, but until late 1944, it was not recognized that this was now a deliberate strategic weapon.

The series of defeats suffered on land, at sea and in the air after the loss of Guadalcanal convinced some Japanese military theorists that the last hope lay in assaults that would destroy the principal weapon bringing the war to Japan, the aircraft carrier. American land-based bombers could never have hoped to reach the homeland had not the floating airfields provided tactical support for ground forces and destroyed the Japanese navy. The fleet air arms enabled soldiers and marines to conquer islands that now served as bases for the big planes. And with the Imperial Navy vanquished, carrier task forces could bring their short-range bombers to the Japanese doorstep.

The immediate inspiration for the suicide airplane came from Rear Adm. Masbomi Arima, who commanded aircraft squadrons which were being defeated in the Philippine skies. (The Zero no longer was the equivalent of newer American planes.) An ascetic and a descendant of Confucian scholars, who eschewed the luxurious quarters available to him in favor of a tiny shack, Arima ignored the tropical heat of the Philippines, appearing always in full uniform. On October 15, five days before the invasion of Leyte, Admiral Arima aimed his own plane at the carrier *Franklin*. An American combat air patrol, hovering in the vicinity, spotted Arima and shot him down, just short of his target. (Some historians erroneously continue to claim Arima actually smashed into the *Franklin*.)

The grand, if unsuccessful, gesture by Arima, who, oddly enough, was raised in England with a public school education there, confirmed a program already in progress under Adm. Takajiro Ohnishi. He had been encouraging Imperial Navy pilots to take such an initiative as a last resort. Now it would become the basic goal of a corps of fliers. Their acceptance and participation in the program that obligated their deaths during the final nine months of the war indicates the deeply ingrained belief in Imperial Japan and its emperor.

Ohnishi dubbed his group *Kamikaze Tokibetsu Kogetitai*, which roughly translates to "the Divine Wind Special Attack Corps." The word "kamikaze" bore special meaning. Japanese history told of a sixteenth century Mongol emperor who organized a huge amphibious force to conquer the country, but a "divine wind" in the form of a typhoon blew away the Chinese-based fleet.

The Japanese Baka rocket-plane carried 2,000 pounds of explosives and a suicide pilot. (*Signal Corps, U.S. National Archives*)

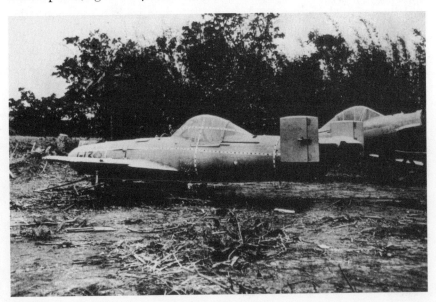

Anything that could fly, from trainers to bombers and fighter planes, eventually even pre-World War II ones with fabric-covered wings, and gliders, were adapted for use by the special attack forces. In addition, engineers designed a 4,700-pound, rocket-propelled flying bomb, the *ohka* or cherry blossom (known to Americans as the *baka,* meaning screwball). The *baka* launched from a Betty-model bomber, when in range of ships, bore a pilot to guide the missile on a one-way trip.

The tactic of suicidal missions expanded to include the kind of suicide motor boats found in Kerama Retto. An even more primitive approach, the *Fukuryu*—Crouching Dragon—called for men with scuba equipment to blast ship bottoms by using mines attached to poles. To Americans all these fell under the label of kamikaze but, strictly speaking, the Japanese applied the term only to the naval air operations. Yoshihiro Minamoto, the defender of Tokashiki Island, says other branches of the service also offered to sacrifice themselves. "I had wartime friends—classmates—in similar kamikaze units of the army. All of them were polite, faithful in their duties, and dedicated people. I was in a marine unit and volunteered for special marine duty *[senpaku tokko]."* But massive use of army personnel in the fashion of the kamikaze did not occur, and volunteers like Minamoto, assigned to Kerama Retto, were denied an opportunity for a suicidal effort.

By no means did every Japanese military man believe duty demanded suicide without thought of a military achievement. According to George Feifer in *Tennozan,* a distinguished naval officer, Capt. Tameichi Hara, told the crew of his cruiser *Yahagi* ". . . hundreds of our comrades have flown bomb-laden planes on one-way missions against the enemy. Thousands more . . . are standing by at every airfield. Hundreds of our comrades are ready in submarines to man one-way torpedoes. Thousands of others will drive explosive torpedo boats or crawl the bottom of the sea to fasten explosive charges against enemy ships. Our job in this mission [the *Yahagi* would participate in a surface sortie against the forces gathered at Okinawa], our mission appears suicidal and it is. But I wish to emphasize that suicide is not the objective. The objective is victory . . . You are not to be slain merely as sacrifices for the nation."

Those who chose the numbered days of a kamikaze required some instruction on tactics. They studied the most efficacious way to hurl their machines at the most desirable enemy ships, the optimum angles of approach, techniques to cope with antiaircraft fire and the opposition's fighter planes, and the choicest hours. Moonlight was undependable illumination for identifying vessels. Daylight provided the foe with better opportunities to shoot them down; dusk and dawn offered the best possibilities. They also waited at bases for the signal to make their final flight, often not knowing which day would be their last until its eve.

Americans, unable to understand the willingness to commit to self-destruction, sometimes insisted the kamikazes must be drunk or on drugs. However, according to one visitor to a group of special attack pilots, the kamikazes refrained from sake whenever there was any possibility that they would be called to take their last flight.

A critical aspect of the special attack force was the 100 percent attrition rate, regardless of mission success or failure. By the time Love Day neared, the ranks of the original corps of kamikaze pilots, drawn solely from naval volunteers, were seriously thinned. As the B–29s pounded the major cities of Japan, the last hope lay in increased kamikaze attacks. The volunteer option no longer provided adequate recruits.

Many of those drafted apparently lacked enthusiasm for their fate. To overcome their reluctance, a form of support groups, not unlike those

The U.S. battleship *Missouri* fends off a kamikaze attack.
(*Signal Corps, U.S. National Archives*)

in the United States today that seek, among other things, to *prevent* suicide, surrounded them. After a brief period of such orientation, most, although not all, yielded their reservations and either accepted or even eagerly looked forward to their role.

The final days of the pilots was spent in the banal routine of life on a military base, with letters to the folks back home to reassure them. Ens. Susumu Kaijitsu, stationed in Korea, had graduated from Nagoya Technical College before becoming a naval aviator. Shortly before he died, he wrote:

"Dear Father, Mother, brothers Hiroshi and Takeshi, and sister Eiko:

"I trust this spring finds you all in fine health. I have never felt better and am now standing by, ready for action.

"The other day I flew over our home and bade a last farewell to our neighbors and to you. Thanks to Mr. Yamakawa I had a chance recently to have a last drink with father, and there now remains nothing but to await our call to duty.

"My daily activities are quite ordinary. My greatest concern is not about death, but rather of how I can be sure of sinking an enemy carrier. Ensigns Miyazaki, Tanaka and Kimura, who will sortie as my

A kamikaze brushes the battleship *Missouri*. *(National Archives)*

wingmen, are calm and composed. Their behavior gives no indication that they were momentarily awaiting orders for their final crash-dive sorties. We spend our time in writing letters, playing cards and reading.

"I am confident that my comrades will lead our divine Japan to victory.

"Words cannot express my gratitude to the loving parents who reared and tended me to manhood that I might in some small manner reciprocate the grace which His Imperial Majesty has bestowed upon us.

"Please watch for results of my meager effort. If they prove good, think kindly of me and consider it my good fortune to have done something that may be praiseworthy. Most important of all, do not weep for me. Though my body departs, I will return home in spirit and remain with you forever . . ."

Imperial Navy ensign Ichizo Hayashi, twenty-three, reared a Christian, counseled his mother, "Please do not grieve for me, mother. It will be glorious to die in action. I am grateful to be able to die in a battle to determine the destiny of our country."

Ens. Teruo Yamaguchi, twenty-two, a university graduate, wrote, "I was selected quite unexpectedly to be a special attack pilot and will be leaving for Okinawa today. Once the order was given for my one-way mission, it became my sincere wish to achieve success in fulfilling this last duty."

Similar sentiments echo and re-echo through the correspondence of the doomed pilots.

One eve of the assault upon the Ryukyus, conventional attacks by bombers scored some major hits against Vice Adm. Marc Mitscher's Task Force 58, pounding the southern Japanese island of Kyushu to prevent any interference with the coming invasions. The carriers *Wasp* and *Franklin* absorbed heavy punishment. The casualties on the *Wasp* totaled 101 killed and another 269 wounded. The damage and losses on the *Franklin* were even worse.

Adm. J.S. Russell was aboard the *Franklin* that morning. "At 7:00 A.M. our first flight deck strike was returning to the ship, and unknown to us, it was being accompanied by a Val [a Japanese dive bomber] who was trailing the flight deck strike back to the ship. He was all by himself and there was a 2,000-foot ceiling and apparently he was stitching in and out of the clouds. He'd duck down just to make sure he was still with the air group and come back up again.

"We were halfway through the launch of the second flight deck strike and suddenly this lone plane started a dive on the *Franklin*. The *Franklin* didn't pick this up. They were a fairly green crew. They'd come back from Bremerton Navy Yard, and this was their first action. [After the near miss by Admiral Arima, the ship had gone to the States and many newcomers manned the vessel.]

"*Hancock* [another carrier], across the formation, came on the voice tactical and said in effect, 'Hey! You're being dived on!' Then a Val came skipping across the flight deck and released two 250-kilo bombs. They didn't miss the centerline of the flight deck by more than ten feet, went into the hangar, and burst at the optimum height to split the light armor on the hangar deck. This meant the ship was exposed down to the second deck . . . The sprinkler system was activated right away and made a tremendous deluge of water.

"The skipper put the ship into the doctrine turn to starboard to list her to port and they started fighting the fires. The captain made a mistake, however, steadying down on a course directly south [with] the wind from the northeast. This put the burning airplanes back aft, those that still remained to be launched, upwind, which enveloped the ship in choking black smoke." Subsequently, the ship shifted its course.

"The air group commander, Commander Parker, and his wingman, who had just been launched, streaked across and knocked [the Val] down.

"I wasn't sure whether the gasoline system of the ship was leaking and causing big fires or whether it was just from the ruptured tanks of the airplanes, because the ordnance on the planes had started to blow up. Later I found the crew had properly secured the gasoline system. The fires were all being fed by the gasoline in the aircraft.

"Various pieces of ordnance were exploded, including 1,000-pound bombs. Also we were using Tiny Tims that day. [These] were twelve-inch diameter rockets with explosive warheads, like 500-pound bombs. As those things cooked off, you'd hear a 'whisht'; a rocket would go by the bridge and you'd see it splash into the sea up ahead. Fortunately, the F4U fighter armed with Tiny Tims, in a three-point attitude, had his nose up a bit, which accounted for the harmless trajectory. However, we had about four of these F4Us with Tiny Tims down in the hangar, and when twelve-inch rockets are ricocheting around the hangars, it's another matter.

Russell continues, "The engine room reported that the ingestion of smoke through the intakes of the machinery spaces was so heavy that they figured they'd have to abandon. The captain told them to set their throttles and abandon the engine room. She burned and exploded for some time.

"The four destroyers which were cut out to screen her joined, and two of them set about rescuing people in various odd places around the ship. One of them put her nose right in against the side of the ship and trapped men would jump aboard from the hangar deck or from the side of the ship, leaving all [the area] behind them enveloped in flames. Many men went over the side. They'd come up from down below, find themselves surrounded by fire, and over the side they'd go. A destroyer was combing the wake, picking them out of the water. The cruiser *Santa Fe* came in with great gallantry, put herself alongside almost like a motor boat, started hoses and began taking the injured across between the two ships."

More than 700 men were listed as killed or missing and 265 were injured. Rescue parties plucked 1,700 from the sea after they abandoned ship. The *Franklin* remained afloat, but barely, as crews from other ships and a few who remained aboard eventually controlled the blazes.

The *Wasp* and *Franklin* hits came from conventional bomb drops. On March 26, the eve of the Kerama Retto operation, Vice Adm. Morton L. Deyo, who had directed the naval bombardments for the Allied invasions of Normandy and southern France in June and August 1944, respectively, now commanded a group of battleships and cruisers that sailed up and down the Okinawa shoreline blasting the coast. His armada also included destroyers and minesweepers.

Like those before and after him, Deyo wondered about the adversary. "Failure of the enemy ashore to react strongly was puzzling. Little had yet been learned of their capabilities or of the location of their strong points. What were they up to anyway? We were here to find out." The first significant information acquired by Deyo and many of the sailors came with their baptism in the kamikaze phenomenon.

"We steamed along the coast all day the 26th [March]," wrote Deyo after the war ended. "My flagship was then the stately old battleship *Tennessee*, slow but ideal for shore bombardment, with her four great turrets, each housing three fourteen-inch guns, her eight, twin five-inch mounts and smaller batteries totalling forty forty-millimeters and perhaps 100 twenty-millimeters, arranged in double or quadruple amounts. Repaired and modernized after Pearl Harbor, she was fitted with all the latest fire control and radar equipment.

"Special night-cruising dispositions had been worked out to counter various forms of attack. They were designed to permit ships to join up or leave at odd hours without confusion or alarm. This night our disposition was a large one of three concentric circles. At the center was placed the *Indianapolis* to give the greatest protection, as she wore the flag of Admiral [Raymond] Spruance [commander of the Fifth Fleet, which was in charge of the Okinawa campaign until the soldiers and marines landed].

"On the inner circle, of 2,000 yards radius, were seven battleships, including *Tennessee.* Fifteen hundred yards beyond was the second circle, upon which were spaced nine cruisers. The outer circle, of radius eight thousand yards, contained twenty-five destroyers, destroyer escorts and destroyer minesweepers. This disposition gave good submarine protection as well as antiaircraft defense. It was expected, at that time, that suicide air attacks would focus chiefly upon the larger and more valuable ships.

"The evening was mild and pleasant, the sea gently rippled. When the full moon rose, we zigzagged rather ponderously, expecting air raids which were threatened but not pushed home. About 3:00 A.M. bogies began to appear on the radar screens, coming from the northward. One plane came close enough to draw fire briefly. Another, scouting low, flew directly over *Porterfield's* [a destroyer] foremast and created much annoyance by toppling one of her radar antennae over the side. The pilot, who must have been equally surprised, staggered off and disappeared. There were no more incidents that night, though snoopers continued to come close enough to keep people awake.

"Soon after daylight we were on course to return to the assault area for the day's shooting, when seven enemy planes were sighted by the outer circle, all approaching us from different directions. Capt. R. W. Bates, who had volunteered to come as my chief of staff for the assault though still suffering from injuries, had seen kamikaze attacks at Lingayen Gulf in the Philippines a few months before, and recognized their tactics. There was something to arouse almost pity as they flew toward us, like lonely, frightened ducks, against so terrible a concentration of artillery. We controlled our pity, however, when we remembered what they had sworn to do.

"If a pilot has really determined to crash his plane into a ship, even a moving one, his chances of success are good unless he or his plane can be shot out of control. Unlike a bomber making a run, he can twist and turn and porpoise to throw off the gunners until the last moment, when he must steady on target. Our AA gunners were good against conventional bombing attacks, but the automatic gear of those days was not as advanced as we could have desired.

"Now the kamikazes were plainly in view in shallow glides and seemed to be picking their targets. They would probably try to reach the inner circles where the more valuable prizes would attract them.

Why be shot down for a lamb when the sheep are just beyond? We sensed that each pilot had steeled himself for the supreme test. His life was now ended, save for a few exalted, terrified moments!

"Our ships are in readiness [Deyo shifts his account to the present tense] and now the destroyers on the outer circle open up with their powerful, long-range, five-inch batteries, firing precisely and rapidly in salvo. Clusters of shell bursts, small white clouds with dirty centers, appear around the oncoming planes, as jagged fragments seek to tear them apart. The bursts close in and move ahead as the ships' gunnery control officers correct their rates. Each pilot seems to choose his own method of approach, some jink and porpoise, others bore in steadily.

"One of the latter now advances, straight into the midst of a tightly bunched salvo. When he emerges, a wing is gone! Futilely, he struggles to survive, but flames creep over the cockpit! Spinning crazily into the water, he splashes and sinks instantly, doomed to die, far from the desperate goal of his sacrifice! One down!

"Now the harsh barking of the forty millimeters comes to our ears and ships in the second circle commence firing right over the outer one, as planes come within range. Soon the inner circle takes it up and so many bursts are in the air that gunnery officers are hard put to identify their own.

"There, as he passes over the destroyers' circle, one falters. The pilot knows that his journey is ended, and that he will never reach the cruiser circle. He has just crossed above the destroyer *Dorsey* and quickly decides to shift his aim to her. He banks steeply, turns back and dives for the destroyer! But the dive is off the mark, the pilot or his controls must be mortally injured. Pulling out feverishly, just clear of the water, he barely saves himself and kicks the rudder to go straight into *Dorsey*'s midship section as she blazes away at point-blank range with everything that will bear. The pilot is a shade too high, and perhaps too close to maneuver. Bravely he noses down, but his hands have lost their touch. Barely skimming the galley deck house, his undercarriage catches some gear, demolishes an icebox, clears the side and crashes into the sea beyond. Two down!

"Five are still coming. Now as they penetrate the inner circles, the sky is filled with bursts, an incessant cacophony reaches the ear from around the compass. The impatient crews of numerous twenty-millimeter guns, last to join the chorus because of their limited range, make up for lost time by spraying their waspish projectiles like hoses into the air. By now friends are not altogether safe from friends, even among our experienced crews. A few casualties will probably result. [But] each plane must be shot out of control before it can reach its mark, or the price exacted from us will be many times greater than just the value of one pilot and one plane.

"Scanning the circle, I see one just beyond the cruisers. Literally smothered in bursts, with no possible escape, he makes a wide change of course to throw off the gunners. Almost at once they are on him again. Out of control, pieces shot out of him, he goes straight into the water. The bomb, or his gas tank, explodes as he hits. A soiled geyser springs up and subsides; with it fall many bits and pieces.

"Almost at once another is reported splashing, well clear of everybody. That will be four down and only one ship—*Dorsey*—barely scratched. This is good shooting!

"The remaining three withdraw and circle to make a new approach. Their commander, not a kamikaze, watching from high above them, must be unhappy over the results. But there is no turning back; their tanks lack fuel to bear them home, even though it might seem futile for them to face such odds again.

"Presently, as we change course and turn, the fifth plane comes in, higher and almost over the inner circle, diving steeply, while the small clouds and dark cotton puffs of our now-confident gunners adjust to meet him.

"Straight he dives for the ponderous old *Nevada,* rugged veteran of World War I, which has survived Pearl Harbor to perform brilliant services at Normandy and now here. Streams of tracers speed from her many guns. The plane is hit, smoke follows him down. The kamikaze staggers, pulls partly out, but then resumes the dive. Just above the ship it bursts into flames! The pilot must now be finished—but so is his work. His burning coffin carries on to its mark and smashes, in livid incandescence, straight into the main deck, just where the great barbette of Number Three, fourteen-inch turret rises and nearly under the guns themselves!"

Both guns of the turret were disabled and required replacement. The conflagration wiped out three 20 mm mounts and demolished one of *Nevada*'s observation planes secured on deck. There was also structural damage to the main deck and to a compartment below. Deyo noted, "There were casualties, mercifully not numerous. The ancestors of that kamikaze must be giving him a hero's welcome." Actually, eleven men died and another forty-nine were hurt.

Deyo's report continues, "Now where is number six? He is further out and in trouble; what hope has he of reaching a target through this relentless flak? Hit and wavering, he loses altitude. He is headed our way but must realize he can never make the inner circle. The cruiser *Biloxi* is just below him; upon her he pins his hope of success. This we can see very clearly; the plane is a Val [dive bomber]. He goes into a shallow dive, aiming for the cruiser's port side. Again the smother of bursting shell; he loses altitude too fast, he cannot make it! No, he keeps on, holding the plane just barely above the water. Very few guns can shoot now for fear of firing into each other. Closer and closer, so slowly now, but the gap is steadily narrowing. There, just alongside, he splashes in. But his momentum actually carries him into the ship's side. His bomb releases and strikes the plating.

"The bomb was an eleven-hundred pounder; it did not explode and was later found, inside the ship. The waterline plating was ruptured for about twenty-six feet. Emergency repairs were made by the crew and *Biloxi* continued without even stopping.

"Now but one lone duck is on the wing. How much he has witnessed of the fate of his comrades will never be known. But what he must know is that a ring of almost impenetrable fire opposes him. He cannot withdraw, he has only the faintest hope of success. Not only death but failure as well must be his fate. It seems that he knows this for he hesitates in an agony of indecision; unable to advance or retire, he draws the fire of so many guns that, in seconds, he flies apart and falls, broken and frustrated, into the sea.

"The attack is finished, everything is silent as we make the turn to return to the beachhead, then release the unit commanders for their day's shooting stations. Suddenly, one hears voices of men, not guns.

"Only seven o'clock? So much has happened, one loses track of time. Cooks and mess people hustle back to the galleys and prepare to feed hungry thousands. Everywhere on deck are empty brass cartridge cases to be stowed for disposal. All are busy cleaning up and getting ship-shape again. A ship is a beehive a good deal of the time, but particularly after an engagement.

"We've been blooded by the kamikazes! They aren't something to laugh at. It is very different from the bomber formations, dropping sticks of bombs which are more than likely to miss. These pilots, though few, make a high percentage of hits. Two hits out of seven. That is about 29 percent, plus a scratch which might easily have been a hit, and that would have raised it to 43 percent. And they have attacked as formidable an assembly of gun power as could be found, perhaps anywhere in the war. It is lucky for us that the whole conception is one of desperation and that they are bound to run out of pilots before long. Furthermore, the blows they deliver are, though serious, seldom mortal."

Deyo was only partly correct. The dreadnoughts with their massive steel shielding could indeed withstand most of the effects of a kamikaze hit. A turret might be smashed and casualties could run into the double figures, but there was little chance that a battleship or heavy cruiser could be sunk. The carriers with their thin decks, however, were highly vulnerable to a crash that would burst through to lower decks, setting off the enemy's bomb load, which in turn detonated the host planes, fuel and ordnance. Thin-hulled destroyers were also seriously at risk.

As the experience of kamikaze raids deepened over the next weeks, tactics for dealing with them evolved, but efforts to disseminate information that might be useful would collide with a wall of naval protocol. Meanwhile, as Love Day had approached, a veil of official silence and censorship continued to hide the kamikazes from the folks back home.

Neither conventional aerial raids nor kamikazes seriously interfered with the Love Day operations. But the fleet absorbed some hard punches that night. A pair of transports, the *Achenar* and the *Alpine,* were struck by kamikazes. One blow fell at twilight, 7:10 P.M., and the other at the seemingly safer hour near midnight. Both ships remained afloat and able to unload their cargo before steaming off for repairs. But another twenty-one sailors died and sixty-eight were injured.

On April 2, the ships in the Kerama Retto anchorage and off the Hagushi beaches reeled from blows inflicted by the divine winds. Mindful of exposure to the enemy, a group of transports carrying soldiers from the 77th Division, after reembarking them from the Kerama Retto operations, headed out to sea to remove themselves from harm's way.

A flock of kamikazes, at least ten planes, bore down on the fifteen-ship convoy. The destroyer *Dickerson* took a direct hit on the bridge. The fifty-three dead included the skipper and the *Dickerson,* unsalvagable, was towed to sea and scuttled. Two other warships escaped with lesser damage from attacks on them.

That night, the bulk of the 77th Division's 305th Infantry Regiment was aboard the *Henrico,* the flagship of Transdiv 50. Dick Forse, the crewman for an M–8, self-propelled, armored 75 mm gun, remembers, "There was no general quarters signal, although there was some firing from other ships. I had noticed that the radar dish on the mast was not going around. I had been sitting on a hatch cover on the main deck, forward. I got up and went on a line for ice cream. We heard the sound of planes coming in. We couldn't see them because the ship's forecastle blocked our view to the front. But I got a glimpse of the tail of a plane as it went by. I dismissed it as the tail of a Hellcat from the U.S. Navy.

"An instant after glimpsing the tail, I heard a 'kerchunk.' I don't remember it as being very loud. The Jap plane, a Frances [two-engine navy bomber], hit the *Henrico*'s superstructure [bridge area] near the spot where I had previously been sitting. One engine broke off and rolled, flaming down a corridor into the wardroom where many officers were writing or just batting the breeze. One of the bombs on the plane also exploded.

"I ran to the side and saw a big hole in the superstructure with showers of sparks and clouds of heavy gray smoke pouring out. The *Henrico*'s steam whistle went off and continued one long shriek for about fifteen minutes before it finally ran out of steam.

"Another guy and I ran inside the forecastle to get out of the way, but we found ourselves in the way of four navy men who were getting into asbestos suits. There were several fires in the superstructure and the ship was dead in the water. There was no power whatsoever and fire hoses couldn't be used. They lowered small water pumps into the sea but most of them stopped working when they hit the water.

"The steam whistle that continued to scream scared us. I must have checked my life preserver fifteen times an hour, hoping it would work if we had to abandon ship. I went below deck to stay out of the way. Battery power lines were being set up everywhere because there was no electricity. There also was no drinking water and no water in the heads. I realized that the ship was listing to starboard, which really concerned me.

"Soon after, all able bodies were called topside and told to stand along the rail on the port side because of the ship's list. A destroyer passed by us up close, trying to hose down fires on our ship. But the sea was too choppy. First the hose would point toward the sky and then down into the ocean. Later they tried to shoot a line to us so we could be towed. They tried four or five times but the line missed. Everytime they fired the line, I jumped a foot.

"The rest of the convoy continued on after the kamikaze attack. Soon we were alone, out in the ocean. I looked out on the horizon and could see two ships burning. Then the moon came up. It was the biggest moon I have ever seen, a full moon that could silhouette the *Henrico* for the Jap subs.

"My morale was not very high at this point. But no subs attacked us and we were later towed by another APA [attack transport] into the Kerama Retto anchorage. It was loaded with ships crippled by kamikazes. Four or five of us slept in the paint locker that night. None of us had any desire to sleep in our quarters, which were two decks below. For breakfast we got an apple and an orange and two cans of beer.

That's the only time I know of when the Navy issued alcoholic drinks to enlisted men in a combat zone.

"The *Henrico* tied up next to another APA, the *Sarasota.* We were to transfer to it. We heard that someone was inside the pitch-black *Henrico* and would not come out. One of the last men taken off it was this soldier. He looked like a teenager, and with great difficulty, some sailors had made their way through equipment below deck, brought him up two sets of stairs to the main deck. He was very distressed, shaking, tears streaming down his face, snuffling, shuffling along rather than walking as he was helped by sailors on each arm across to the *Sarasota.*"

Shortly after the kamikaze blasted the *Henrico,* one of the gun crews on the *Suffolk,* a nearby APA, spotted a man in the water. Joe Taranto, a member of the gun crew, remembers, "We thought he was a Jap pilot. We were ready to shoot him when he yelled, 'I'm an American GI from the 77th Division.' I think that was the greatest day of my life; we were there to save that G.I. from dying."

But aboard the *Henrico* many others were not so fortunate. Transdiv 50's commander and the captain of the ship were killed, along with twenty-one others from the Navy. Among the Army officers in the wardroom were most of the 305th's top command. The dead included the 305th's leader, Col. Arthur Tanzola and his executive officer, as well as eleven more soldiers. Also seriously wounded was the S–3, Maj. Winthrop Rockefeller, later to become governor of Arkansas and a figure of some notoriety.

The *Henrico* was not the only 77th Division transport mauled. Larry Gerevas, a replacement assigned to Company K in the 307th Regiment, sailed from Leyte on the *Telefare.* "Aboard our ship, many of the Army troops were assigned various duties. Some assisted the Navy gunners with the 40 mm antiaircraft guns and others, such as myself, stood guard at various stations on the main deck. The purpose was to prevent any Japs from climbing onto the ship.

"During the air attack on April 2, I was on guard near the bow of the ship. At this location were two landing barges secured to a metal support rack about two feet above the deck. Suddenly, a terrific explosion occurred directly above me. Thinking it was a bomb, I dived under a rack holding the barges. Smoking chunks of metal rained down on the area where I had been standing a moment before. Debris was everywhere.

"Later I learned that a Jap bomber had dived into our ship, sheared off some of the ship's masts, fell on a 40 mm gun mount and then slid

On Leyte, as the 77th
Division prepared to sail for
Okinawa, Larry Gerevas
(right) relaxed with two
buddies. The man at his
right was wounded while his
other companion was KIA.
(*Larry Gerevas*)

into the sea. Three Army men that manned that gun were killed. A few days later, they were buried at sea."

Ed Fitzgerald, the first sergeant of Service Company, was aboard the *Monrovia*. "When the kamikazes started to come in, the captain made me chase guys off the deck. We didn't like it below decks. It wasn't comfortable and we wondered about submarines and if something came busting in there. I was already inside on a ladder going back down when I saw the airplane coming and I knew it would hit. I wasn't that curious that I wanted to stay up there and get a look at the pilot in his white scarf. One sergeant, though, Harry O'Gawa, couldn't resist staying up there. He lost a leg from the explosion." The ship, however, suffered no serious damage.

For the 77th Division Commander, Gen. Andrew Bruce, who regretted the losses, the casualties on the *Henrico* solved what he considered a nagging problem. In a letter to a colleague Bruce spoke of his dissatisfaction with Tanzola and his regiment. He described Tanzola as prone to "ill-considered, impetuous Italian outbursts." The regiment, he recalled, had been described by referees during war games as the "most foul-mouthed, insubordinate, bitching outfit." Bruce recognized Tanzola's devotion to his troops and admitted that he personally liked him. But Bruce nevertheless thought of relieving him because of concerns that he was not an effective combat commander.

"When we heard about the *Henrico* and Tanzola," says Frank Barron, "it was a blow. We liked the *Henrico;* we trained on her in Chesapeake Bay and it was a great ship, great crew. Tanzola was loved and respected. He was one of us and we looked up to him. I think General Bruce was theatrical, while Tanzola was down-to-earth, approachable and dependable."

Barron believes Bruce's distaste for the 305th was a hangover from the period when the general first assumed command, a low period for the troops. They had just suffered through a long stretch of miserable, cold, damp weather in Louisiana maneuvers and then weeks in the desert with severe water limitations. Supply shortages forced some men to go without socks and others coped with worn-out shoes.

Joseph Budge, a Scotsman who emigrated to Hawaii in 1938, had during the course of three years of service, become an infantry replacement assigned to the 77th Division following its Philippine campaign. By a fluke, Budge, originally on the *Henrico*, left the ship shortly before the attack to join another unit in the 77th. Already a staff sergeant and because of headquarters assignments, Budge was able to observe Bruce and Tanzola. "Tanzola's death did hurt morale. He was a warm and human person and I am sure that the lads felt he was a buffer between them and General Bruce, who was a driver. An old-timer told about an argument that the two had on Leyte. Tanzola allegedly told Bruce to go back to headquarters and he [Tanzola] would take the objective in his own good time. He supposedly told Bruce that he should remember that Tanzola was senior to Bruce on the officers' list. What hurt morale more was the poor performance of those promoted in the general shuffle resulting from the *Henrico* mess."

CHAPTER XIII

THE NAVAL WARS

The total number of vessels originally consigned to the Ryukyu conquest added up to 1,457, including 430 troopships. It was the biggest flotilla ever assembled in the Pacific theater. Putting men ashore, supplying them and shelling the enemy jammed the huge fleet in a small area of the sea. The intense concentration presented the Japanese with a grand target. Indeed, the strategy of defense was based upon keeping the enemy ships where they would be vulnerable to attacks emanating from Formosa and Japan.

Manning these ships was the standard mix of professional military men, reservists, enlistees and draftees. Joe Roddy, a native of St. Paul, Minnesota, attended the local Roman Catholic college of St. Thomas and left in 1942, his senior year, for active duty with the Coast Guard. For three summers, prior to Pearl Harbor, Roddy served as a deckhand, pilot and engineer aboard a privately owned seventy-foot motorship, the *Eugeniann.* The owners, a family named McCahill, had used it for cruises on the upper Mississippi, St. Croix and Minnesota Rivers. With the outbreak of war, the McCahill brothers accepted commissions in the Navy and offered the *Eugeniann* to the Coast Guard for patrol purposes. A series of letters between Roddy, the McCahills and various Coast Guard officials climaxed with the assignment of Roddy, as a petty officer, to skipper the *Eugeniann* on the Mississippi.

Six months of this dubious and ultimately boring duty convinced Roddy, like Thomas Heggen's Mister Roberts, to seek a transfer and contribute more directly to the war effort. He obtained a commission and joined the 420-man crew of the *Cepheus,* a 14,000-ton, 460-foot Navy troopship handed over to the Coast Guard for duty.

His tour at sea began with an Atlantic crossing bearing a cargo of food, then a voyage to North Africa to pick up supplies and personnel for unloading at Naples. The *Cepheus* participated in Operation Dragoon, the landings in southern France in August 1944. "There were no Jerry aircraft attacking us," says Roddy. "The invasion was unopposed and the only excitement was a destroyer carrying Churchill which went by."

When the assignment in the Mediterranean ended, the *Cepheus* returned to Norfolk, Virginia, for refitting. At sea again, Roddy and his mates passed through the Panama Canal, bound for the Pacific. "At one of the islands, we were waiting to unload ammunition for a cruiser. It was beastly hot and at 10:00 A.M. they sounded General Quarters. There was no enemy coming but our ship was on fire. Among the crew, myself included, the general reaction was 'Oh shit, I'm dead.' We despaired of

As a deck officer, Lt. Jg. Joe Roddy of the Coast Guard ferried supplies ashore. (*Joe Roddy*)

our existence. There was no place to go if the *Cepheus* blew up. It turned out that the smoke someone saw and believed was from a fire was simply because of the extreme heat vaporizing water on the ship.

"When the *Cepheus* became part of the convoy, a rumor circulated that we were on our way to invade Japan. It struck me as a very unattractive proposition. We didn't know where we were going. The quartermasters on our ship communicated with others at a furious pace like mutes, talking by means of semaphore. Plans were not revealed to us until we were within a couple hundred miles of Okinawa. On L-Day, we saw a remarkable collection of ships. As soon as the light rose, the shelling began, great big ones whizzed overhead. Low-flying planes were strafing the beach.

"We had the impression that everything was going okay, because the great circle of ships around us seemed to be undisturbed. When the kamikazes came, I was not as frightened as I had been when we thought the ship with all that ammunition was on fire. Then you figured there was no possibility of survival. You could see the kamikazes coming, and even when they managed to hit a ship, it wasn't destroyed."

Michael Bak, son of Russian immigrants, and born in Garfield, New Jersey, in 1923, graduated from high school the same year the war with Japan began. He delayed entry into the service for a year, clerking for a local engineering company. A lack of a college degree denied him the opportunity to enlist in the Air Corps for pilot training. "I did have an ambition to go to the Naval Academy," says Bak. "But with my ethnic background and not knowing a lot of people in high places, I never felt I had an opportunity." Before the draft board could accelerate to hot pursuit, Bak volunteered for the Navy.

At the Great Lakes training center, the former major league baseball star and eventual Hall of Fame member, CPO Fred Lindstrom, sought to whip the group that included Bak into shape, instruct them in basic seamanship and the ways of the Navy. [At 18, the youngest man ever to play in the World Series, Lindstrom achieved dubious recognition, after a ball hit by a member of the Washington Senators in the 12th inning of the seventh and deciding game against Lindstrom's New York Giants, struck a pebble. It then bounced over the rookie third baseman's head. The winning run scored, enabling Walter Johnson, on the cusp of closing out his glorious career, to get credit for the victory. Lindstrom's election to the Hall of Fame is based largely on his .311 lifetime batting average, compiled over a thirteen-year period.] "He was a very intelligent man," recalls Bak. "Very efficient, a person you were glad to be associated with. He had a good, positive outlook on life and would try to help you out.

"Boot camp was very strict. They'd get us up in the middle of the night and we'd start trudging through the snow at two o'clock in the morning. Later, when I was at sea and in general quarters situations, I realized they were putting you through the paces to make you feel like you would if aboard ship."

Among Bak's early difficulties was learning to sleep in a hammock. "During our first night, you could hear people falling right out of the hammock onto the floor. I fell one or two times my first night."

From boot camp, Bak, whose membership in the Boy Scouts brought him knowledge of semaphore, attended quartermaster school. He learned how to assist a navigator and the duties for service on the bridge and charthouse. Upon graduation he was assigned to a new destroyer, *Franks,* as it began its shakedown cruise.

"When our ship pulled into Pearl Harbor, we realized the war was on, and I think everybody felt anxious to do what he could to defeat the enemy. It was very quiet when you steamed by and saw the battleship *Arizona* submerged in the water, an awesome sight."

Even more sobering for Bak and his shipmates was an experience shortly after leaving Pearl Harbor. "We were in a formation and the carrier *Liscome Bay* was inside the formation about two or three miles from us. A submarine got her. It was dark out there and as the carrier exploded, we went to general quarters. It was just like putting a candle out. The ball of fire was snuffed out as the ship sank [with the loss of 770 lives]. That's the first time we experienced the horrors of war. It sort of scared everybody. We felt, 'My gosh, this is for real.'"

Bak's ship habitually drew the duty of plane guard. "When the signal of commencing flight operations was hoisted, the *Franks* assumed this role. When the pilots were safely airborne, we returned to our position in the screen. When flight operations were completed and the pilots returned to the carriers, we again assumed our station as a plane guard ship.

"If a plane went into the water, our captain would maneuver as close as possible to the downed pilot, lower our whaleboat and attempt the rescue. Although we rescued a number of pilots using this procedure, our technique was changed when Captain Stephan came aboard. He felt the whaleboat technique was dangerous, especially in very rough weather. Besides, it took too long to get to the pilot.

"Instead, he had three swimmers available to attempt a rescue. They were equipped with leather harness-type belts strapped to their waists.

At the back of each belt a line was fastened to a secured eye ring. The swimmer would dive into the water, and when he got to the pilot, he would grip an arm around him and signal for the men on deck to pull him back to the ship." By both methods, the *Franks* saved twenty-two fliers during the war.

"The tradition was that every time we sent a pilot back via breeches buoy, they would load a fifteen-gallon drum of ice cream on return. It was enough for the entire crew. It was a treat and the high point of the next meal. One of the reasons our crew really went all out to pick up the pilots was to get the ice cream, which was rare for us in the Navy. We had no ice cream making machine aboard our ship."

The *Franks* survived a surface battle with the enemy ships off Samar Island in the Philippines and managed to stay afloat during a typhoon, which rolled the ship so far over that Bak felt certain water would pour down the stacks. The storm, in December 1944, sank three sister destroyers with heavy loss of life.

In mid-March 1945, as part of a task force hammering Kyushu in preparation for Operation Iceberg, Bak witnessed the mounting fury of combined bomber and kamikaze attacks. "We were helpless to do anything. We were sort of like spectators. We had no guns [to fire] since we were quartermasters and signalmen on the bridge. I remember a Jap plane dropped a bomb right smack in the middle of the *Yorktown*. As he was coming up, he came over about fifty to 100 yards from our ship and gave us his hand to his nose. I could see it very clearly. We shot him down."

Unlike Admiral Deyo, Bak never developed any sympathy for the foe. "It was us or them. We thought they were a bunch of bastards. The faster we killed them off, the faster the war would be over. Because of what they did to Pearl Harbor and all those guys who died there, nobody had any compassion for the Japanese."

As Love Day approached, the *Franks* accompanied the battlewagons pounding Okinawa. "That was the most firepower, probably, that we were involved in on a steady basis. *New Jersey, Wisconsin,* and *Missouri,* just sort of lined up off the beach, maybe three, four or five miles maximum . . . All day long they just bombarded away. You'd see those big flames coming out of the guns and the tremendous noise.

"At nighttime, along with three other destroyers, we were in for harassing fire, up and down, one destroyer after another, just firing away every twenty seconds, five-inch salvos. We were told it was to keep the Japs awake."

With the invasion on, the traffic jam in the waters around Okinawa led to the almost inevitable. "It was a very dark night," recalls Bak. "There was a little rain, overcast, and visibility was very poor. We were conducting night fighter flight operations and were screening the carriers. I went off duty at eight o'clock and went down to my bunk.

"About nine-fifteen, we had just finished the night fighter operations and were proceeding back to the screen. I was still below decks when it seemed like we hit something. I didn't know what it was. It was a sudden jolt. I thought maybe we hit a mine in the forward compartment of the ship because I was in the after compartment. All the lights went out; the ship rolled back and forth. I was in my shorts. I quickly jumped out of the sack and made for the deck, figuring that we were going to be going overboard.

"I went topside, and we were rolling about twenty to twenty-five degrees. It was cold as heck but I felt we were okay; we were not sinking. There was a lot of noise, a lot of fellows running and yelling.

Aboard the U.S. battleship *Washington,* crewmen watch kamikazes attack Task Force 58. *(Signal Corps, U.S. National Archives)*

"I made my way up the starboard side of the ship and didn't see any damage. When I got to the bridge, at my station, my God, half the port side of the bridge was sliced away. I was then told that we had a collision with the battleship *New Jersey*.

"The battleship was gone. One of the officers saw me in my shorts and bare feet. He lent me a winter parka with a fur lining. We were told to stay away from the port side of the bridge because the port wing was gone. If you just stuck your head back, you could see part of the stacks; the upper structure of the ship was damaged. Then we heard that the captain was down below and he was hurt and that [Lt. Robert E.] Numbers was hurt. Jack Dillon, a signalman, was also injured.

"[The damage] was just like a knife going through at a forty-five degree angle above the bridge itself. It ripped the entire port side of the ship. The anchor of the *New Jersey* did the damage and, because the anchor was so high up, we weren't hit or damaged below decks.

"From the reports I got from some of my crew members, we missed the *Yorktown* by inches. When we were leaving the formation of plane guard, there must have been a maneuvering board problem error in the direction the ship was supposed to leave for its new location in the screen. We'd been doing this maneuver for a long time and we were an experienced plane guard ship. I don't know what happened or whose fault it was, whether it was the battleship's or ours. It was just an accident at sea.

"The captain was transported [to another ship] for additional medical attention. We knew he was critically injured. He had some ribs broken into his lungs. He died a day or two later. With a lieutenant and two or three other members of the crew, I went to attend the funeral services aboard a tanker. The crew there had a platform extending over the side of the ship. The platform had Captain Stephan's body encased in a canvas bag with a lot of weights attached. Draped over the bag was the American flag. After a brief ceremony, they raised the rear of the platform and the body slid into the water.

"It was an eerie feeling to see a body draped on a slab one moment and next disappearing over the side. I felt sad and helpless to see a man that I admired end his career in this fashion—a collision at sea with one of our own ships instead of dying as a result of enemy action.

"Many of our crew never shed a tear when he died. A good number were glad he was no longer with us. I was personally very fond of him. I also believe that his evasive action to avoid a collision saved the entire crew from either being killed or drowned. No one ever gave him credit for saving the ship from sinking. He remained at his post shouting commands until the time of impact."

The damage to the *New Jersey* was slight, but for Bak and the *Franks*, the Okinawa campaign was over. The *Franks* headed for the naval installation at Ulithi to undergo repairs.

CHAPTER XIV

OPERATION TEN-GO

Based upon the site of a great battle in the sixteenth century, the Japanese used the name *Tennozan* to mark any critical campaign in subsequent history. They considered the fight for Okinawa worthy of *Tennozan,* and code-named their massive onslaught against the enemy amphibious forces Operation TEN-GO.

From April 3 to April 5, the Japanese raids on the U.S. armada amounted to no more than mosquito bites, but on April 6, TEN-GO got off the mark as they swarmed over the targets in the Ryukyus. Endowed with the name of *kikusui*—floating chrysanthemums—ten massed kamikaze blows employing 355 planes concentrated on the Americans hovering in the seas by the islands. About the same number of conventional bombers also struck.

Minesweepers supported by a pair of destroyers, the *Rodman* and the *Emmons,* engaged in the clearance of a channel between Iheya Retto and the main island. In command of the *Emmons* was Lt. Comdr. Eugene Foss. A Harvard graduate (1934), Foss had studied mechanical engineering and with his degree entered the family business, the manufacture of heavy-duty blowers. "I wasn't concerned about what the Germans and the Japanese were doing," says Foss. "I had no strong attitudes about foreign affairs. I wasn't interested in politics.

"I had taken Naval ROTC at Harvard, which offered one of the earliest courses. It included ordnance and seamanship, and there were cruises during the summers. In late May 1941, the Navy called up some of the officers in the reserve. I had an opportunity to get out; the company was heavily involved in defense work, but I chose not to.

"I went to Sonar School in Key West and then received orders for a fitting-out detail at the Bath Iron Works in Maine. It was a new destroyer, the *Emmons,* and I became a 'plank owner,' a member of the original crew. For the moment, it worked out very well, since my wife and child were living in our home in Dedham.

"A destroyer officer had to know everything about everything. I was appointed sonar officer and lieutenant for the deck crew. We were all learning everything about the ship; the chief petty officers were doing the same. I was one of the senior ensigns. There were six or seven Annapolis men but they were not with us long before they got other duties. As soon as reserves were trained, the Annapolis men left. By the end of the war, we had one Academy man in our twenty-two officers.

"The *Emmons* was commissioned right before Pearl Harbor and we were still in Boston Harbor that Sunday. When the news came, they tightened security. You could no longer just walk into the Navy Yard. And they made us tend our five-inch guns as part of the antiaircraft defense of Boston.

"We filled out our crew, got ammunition and immediately went on a shakedown cruise to Chile. After that, we did convoy duty in the Atlantic, did the Murmansk run, participated in the invasion of North Africa, were off Normandy on D-Day, June 6, 1944, and then the landings in southern France along the Riviera, where the word was not to fire on the nice villas because the admirals wanted them. I took command of the *Emmons* in November 1944.

"On New Year's Day 1945, we began our first trip to the Pacific. We'd been converted to a destroyer-minesweeper, which, with added generators and a couple of paravanes for sweeping, added one more duty. On April 6, with a sister ship, the *Rodman,* number 456—our number was 457—we were providing shore gun protection along the northwestern coast for some wooden-hulled minesweepers. When they have their gear out, minesweepers cannot maneuver. Shore gun fire did not materialize.

"But this day, the Japs mounted their first major kamikaze attack. To everybody I knew, this was a totally different philosophy. It was something none of us had any education in. We knew of Marines who would storm anything but nothing of this definitely suicidal action. But we all realized that kamikazes were very dangerous weapons and had heard about them before the Okinawa show. We'd even seen one dive on a light cruiser, coming right out from a combat air patrol.

"There wasn't anything you could do except fire at them. There were no special tactics. We did have the new proximity fuzes on our ammo. These had just been issued to the fleet and we were not sure how well they worked.

"On this fairly mild day, with the weather overcast, around 3:00 P.M. we spotted twenty or thirty of them coming at an altitude of about 3,000 feet. We watched a dozen or so circling overhead, like they were getting their nerve up. We did have a combat air patrol over us also.

"They started to peel off and head for us, one by one. It didn't work. We had all our guns going and our bursts would show the Corsairs where the enemy was. The *Emmons* gunners got as many as six of them and the Marine fighters dropped at least another half dozen." The *Rodman,* however, was in serious trouble. One plane smashed into the forecastle and a close-in explosion by a splashed plane or bomb ruptured a section of the hull. Sheets of flame darted to the height of the bridge and, temporarily, DD 456 lost power.

The *Emmons* moved to assist its stricken partner but soon realized it now faced its own peril. The *Rodman* was in no condition to offer supporting fire nor were the minesweepers, still frantically trying to retrieve their gear. Foss recalls, "They launched simultaneous attacks, four or five at the same time." As many as five kamikazes slashed through the battery of five-inchers, and the spray of 40 and 20 mm cannon fire to smack into the thin aluminum steel of the *Emmons.*

"One landed in the wardroom passge and blew up with its gasoline. Another hit the fantail. We had to shut down the engines because we couldn't steer. We were drifting, like a target. But we still had our antiaircraft guns and five-inchers while they came at us from all sides." A third blow also struck aft as a Val swept away what was still working on the fantail.

"An ensign, assistant gunnery officer Ross Elliot, ordered several people to crouch down on the deck when a plane was coming in for a strafing attack. He draped himself over the men and saved them but lost his own life." Elliot would receive a posthumous Navy Cross.

On the bridge, Foss tried to shift the steering control. But another kamikaze blasted into the superstructure. The impact shattered the bridge and blew Foss overboard. He found himself, badly burned about the face and hands, temporarily blinded, in the water. The final thrust rammed the starboard bow area. Dead in the water, fires out of control, the crew suffering the horrible wounds and burns from molten metal, searing steam and gasoline-fed fires, the *Emmons* suffered the final indignity of an erroneous 'abandon ship' command. Actually, no one gave the order but word spread that the situation was hopeless. A number of sailors jumped into the water, joining others, like Foss, hurled there by explosions or who, because of the fire in their area, had no choice but to take their chances in the sea.

The sweepers, *Recruit* and *Ransom,* started to rescue those in the water. Two more kamikazes appeared, taking aim on the wreckage of the *Emmons* but suddenly shifting their attentions to the pair offering succor. Gunners on the *Recruit* and *Ransom* splashed both planes.

Foss remembers snatches of his ordeal after being blasted overboard. "The chief quartermaster was in the water near me. He had been burned worse than I. We stayed together until they hauled us up on a life raft. We were taken aboard one of the minesweepers but the chief quartermaster died during the night."

Dead and wounded lay scattered throughout the wreckage. Many sailors engaged in tasks below decks knew little of the progress of the battle. The ammunition handlers toiling below heard encouraging reports each time the gunners knocked down an enemy plane, but they also realized the kamikazes had scored a hit. Smoke penetrated their areas, and tongues of flame licked at their powder cans and shells.

E. B. Billingsley, Foss's predecessor as commander of the *Emmons,* collected accounts from some of these individuals:

"Miller and the other men in lower 1 [ammunition handling room] decided it was time to leave. [Joined by others from a different section.] Both crews then climbed up to the forward mess hall expecting to go aft and out through the galley passageway . . . To their consternation they found the galley passageway blocked by fire. Nor could they get forward . . . While they were discussing the problem, they were joined by the first group from the plotting room . . . Altogether twenty-two were now caught in the passageway.

"Apparently, they had not improved their chances of escape by moving up a deck. Behind a watertight door aft of them, the wardroom was a roaring furnace. Behind another one at the forward end of the passageway, No. 1 upper handling room was still afire. The hatch to No. 2 upper handling room couldn't be budged, probably because of the weight of ammunition, or possibly water from the sprinkling system, on top of it. In the meantime the air in the passageway was becoming thinner and the smoke thicker. The temperature was almost unbearable. Some men were beginning to cough and wheeze and to wonder how long they could endure without fresh air. Some relief was found by opening ports in the officers' staterooms. Some tried to squeeze through them but no one was small enough. Mooney got his head through one and got the attention of men on deck, who could offer no help, not even a hose with water pressure. McClure found a .45 automatic in one of the officers' rooms and kept it at hand, determined to kill himself before he could be roasted alive.

"While the trapped men were frantically trying to find a way out, Hudson, one of the plotting room crew, decided to take matters into his own hands, although it involved going up and out through gun 1 at considerable personal risk. Accordingly, he left the group and went forward to the upper handling room. It was still burning but apparently the sprinkler was beginning to have some effect; water on the deck was now ankle deep. Some powder cans and projectiles were still burning, as was the grease on the roller path, but less fiercely than before. He pulled his shirt over his head and started up . . . Hand holds and ladder rungs were so hot they could be grasped only briefly."

On deck, Hudson tried to open a series of hatches to free his shipmates, but failed. He crawled down a hole in the forecastle and sought to open a watertight door that could free the trapped, but the door had buckled and was immovable. Back on deck he and another sailor found a fire extinguisher and sprayed the route he had used. The fires continued but the extinguisher restricted the flames to one side, leaving an opening. Hudson yelled for those below to come up. When the last of the original twenty-two emerged, Hudson stuck his head into the gun mount for a final check on any remaining men. All he could see was a leftover shell spitting and burning. Months later, Hudson was awarded a Silver Star for saving the lives of the others.

Remnants of the *Emmons* crew, led by the gunnery officer, Lt. J.J. Griffin—the skipper was gone, the exec dead and the next in the chain of command badly wounded—struggled to contain the fires and keep the destroyer from sinking. It was a losing effort; she continued to settle ever deeper. Griffin consulted with the few officers still on the *Emmons*. The damage control news relayed to Griffin left no choice. One main engine was inoperable; there was no means to steer her. The fire forward could not be controlled. Except for a pair of 20 mm guns, the ship was bereft of firepower. They were still sinking and faced an imminent explosion of what remained in the magazines and fuel tanks. About 6:00 P.M., some three hours after the first kamikazes appeared, Griffin ordered abandon ship. The last man climbed onto a small mine-disposal vessel, the PGM–11, at 8:00 P.M. Subsequently, Admiral Turner directed another destroyer to sink the burning hulk of the *Emmons*.

Sixty-four died and another seventy-one were injured from a ship's complement of 237. Foss would spend many months in hospitals, undergoing skin grafts and other treatments to repair the effects of the explosion and fire.

Meanwhile, in the area of Kerama Retto, to knock down the enemy aircraft, the besieged constantly scrambled combat air patrols. Around 5:00 P.M. as the foe bore in on the targets, the skies reverberated with the roar and whine of diving, soaring planes spouting cannon and machine gun fire. From down below, every ship brought every gun to bear, scouring the air with almost continuous fiery bursts of gunpowder. The intense shellfire added to the danger posed by the enemy, for jagged fragments fell back to earth, often striking other ships and short or errant rounds landed frighteningly close to friendlies.

Still, the relentless efforts of the kamikazes wreaked havoc in the harbor. LST–447, having unloaded its cargo at Okinawa, and headed for the presumed safety of the Kerama Retto anchorage, spotted a pair skimming in towards that roadstead. The LST commenced firing. Unluckily, the accuracy of the gunners undid the ship. For hits on one Zeke [a Japanese Navy Mitsubishi Zero] persuaded its pilot he could not continue towards his original target. He turned his attentions to LST–447 and, in spite of a stream of machine gun fire that brought black smoke pouring from his tail, flew into the vessel about two feet above the water line. The bomb aboard the Zeke detonated, ripping out the guts of the ship. Within ten minutes the inferno below forced abandon ship.

Meanwhile, the remaining members of the flight zeroed in on the escort carrier *Tulagi* and a trio of merchant marine manned ships— *Logan Victory, Hobbs Victory* and *Las Vegas Victory*—converted to ammunition carriers. *Tulagi* escaped damage but the intense antiaircraft did not prevent bull's-eyes on *Hobbs Victory* and *Logan Victory.*

Tom Hamilton, as flag secretary for Admiral Kiland, was aboard the *Mount McKinley* in the sanctuary of Kerama Retto at the time. "Anytime an ammunition ship was hit, any other time in the war, it blew up just like a bomb and cleaned out the anchorage. One of them had blown up off Sicily and sunk every ship around it, and another one had done the same thing at Seadler Harbor in Manus. This open roadstead we were in was only a mile and a half long and half a mile wide, so we were snuggled up pretty close to these two ammunition ships.

"On this afternoon, when a kamikaze came down and hit one, I was standing on the deck and it obviously didn't blow up, or I would not be telling this story. It just burned like a pile of fireworks for a couple of hours before it sank. Nobody has ever come up with an explanation why it didn't explode. But the most miraculous thing is that about half an hour after that one was hit, another kamikaze came down and hit the other ammunition ship and they were both burning at the same time. We were expecting at any second that either one of them would go up and that would be the end for everybody there. There was no use being inside the ship; you might as well be up where you can see the fun, so we stood there watching those things burn.

Hamilton describes the defenses against kamikazes. "At the battle of Okinawa, they were opposed by nested layers. The first and most effective layer was the Combat Air Patrol [CAP], projected over the area by carriers assigned for that purpose. Navy fighters [and Marine ones as well] would intercept kamikazes as far from their targets as possible. The CAP were guided by the picket screen. These were destroyer-type ships stationed at strategic points around the area perimeter [from fifteen to 100 miles of Okinawa], whose radar would locate incoming attackers and whose air controllers [fighter-director teams] would vector CAP fighters to their targets." When ground troops had secured the airfields at Yontan and Kadena, land-based interceptors became part of the CAP mix.

"Kamikazes which broke through to the ships were engaged at medium range by the next layer, five-inch guns on destroyers and larger screen vessels. By 1945, five-inch antiaircraft shells were equipped with proximity fuzes, which greatly increased their effectiveness. At short range, attackers were engaged by the innermost layer, 40 mm and 20 mm antiaircraft guns, usually in multiple mount 'gun tubs.' These rapidly firing weapons could put up a withering curtain of fire. Each of these layers was effective, and together they defeated a lot of kamikazes.

"We had set up a line of picket ships, most of which were destroyers. We sent out some smaller ones first, but they didn't have a chance against these kamikazes because they didn't have enough guns. So we sent destroyers. Picket Station # 1 was the closest to Japan, and the stations were numbered in order as they got back closer to Okinawa and Kerama Retto. The average life of a destroyer on Picket Station # 1 turned out to be about six hours before getting hit; some of them would sink and others would come limping back. I remember one that had stayed up there and we ordered him back. He sent us a signal that said, 'I have been on Picket Station # 1 for eight hours and am returning. This is better than par for the course.' And he was right."

In midafternoon of April 6, the destroyer *Bush* at Station # 1 and the *Colhoun* at # 2 succumbed to a series of floating chrysanthemums, with more than 100 dead. Both destroyers sank in spite of valiant efforts to keep them afloat. Combat air patrols rushing to aid the pair had run into so many of the enemy some miles off, they could not offer full assistance.

The destruction of *Bush* and *Colhoun* signaled the opening round of kamikaze fury directed at those on picket duty. The first two elements of what Hamilton labeled a 'layered defense'—the destroyer radar screen and its partner, the CAP—had become successful enough to attract the special attack forces. Jumped by interceptors summoned at the behest of the pickets, the minimally fueled Japanese planes discovered they could not evade the enemy aircraft and then fly onto the strategic targets off the Hagushi beaches and at Kerama Retto. Their meager amount of gasoline would only allow them to focus on those closest at hand, the seaborne sentinels. Furthermore, those in command also realized that the advance warning and protection network would need to be destroyed, or at least seriously weakened, if the kamikazes were to penetrate to the bigger targets.

Aside from the damage inflicted, the kamikazes paid off in one other way for the Japanese. The threat of unacceptable losses to the special attack forces caused the American high command to alter its strategy. The almost nightly loads of high explosives and incendiaries incinerating Japanese urban centers and industry were diverted instead to installations and bases from which kamikazes originated.

According to Tom Hamilton, the first official statements about the suicide planes appeared on April 12, by coincidence the date of President Franklin Roosevelt's death. The devastating news of FDR's death kept the sensational news of the deadly Japanese tactic from having great impact. Naval historian Morison, on close terms with the uppermost naval echelons, remarked that until the release of the story, no one was permitted to mention kamikazes, and censors eliminated any words on the subject from letters home. The purpose of the secrecy, says Morison, was to prevent the foe from knowing the effectiveness of the weapon. Like most military organizations, including the American ones, the Japanese habitually overestimated their success. Still, the losses incurred by American ships were heavy, and that may, to some extent, have been a result of the silence on the subject even within the Navy.

Tom Hamilton recalls, "Ellery Sedgwick, the chief intelligence officer on Kiland's staff, decided he ought to go out to each one of those ships that had been under kamikaze attack and had survived and see what he could find out about the assaults. Did they come out of the sun? Did they come in low over the horizon? What time of day? What could he find out that might be useful to those poor guys that were going out on picket duty?

"Sedgwick set up a twenty-page doctrine that he had typed up and I arranged to reproduce it for him. We gave this dope to the skippers of the new division of destroyers as they came in.

"Each item that leaves a flag office or any other Navy-command must have a date and time group on it. Every Navy yeoman is indoctrinated with this procedure into the marrow of his bones. Otherwise, there is no way to identify what goes out."

Copies of Sedgwick's intelligence received its own date and time group identification as they passed to the incoming ship commanders. "They all thought it was great to have," says Hamilton. "Unknown to us, they sent it back upstream to their squadron commander and then he passed it further up until we finally received a request for more copies from the commander of destroyers in the Pacific fleet.

"When Admiral Kiland saw the request, he blew his lid. He wanted to know what it was all about. I told him and he summoned Sedgwick, then lined both of us at attention up against the bulkhead and announced that he was not the senior officer around there, that Admiral Turner was, and he, Kiland, was not authorized to issue any doctrine." Since Sedgwick and Hamilton served on Kiland's staff, the report on kamikazes naturally implied his imprimatur.

"He told us we had no authority to issue anything of this nature and if we did anything like this again, he was going to send us both to Portsmouth—the Naval prison. He ordered us to destroy all copies. We didn't exactly do that. We hid a few. I don't know what our plans were but we wanted to hang on to some of them.

"A few days later, another division of destroyers arrived. The commander of a squadron made a pitch for how important it was that he have the report. Sedgwick joined him and persuaded me to make up another bunch. We swore the commander to secrecy. 'You can give them to your ship captains but don't let anybody else know about it.' He promised.

"Things went along quietly for a couple of days and then, zingo, we got a signal from Admiral Nimitz, commander in chief of the Pacific, wanting more copies. Lo and behold, it had a different date-time-group on it. The admiral [Kiland] almost struck us. I thought he was going to physically hit us, but he didn't, just swore at us, promised us Portsmouth again.

"Sedgwick and I huddled and agreed, we had to knock it off. The old guy meant it. So we decided, no more. One cold and rainy night, a messenger got me out of my sack about midnight. I went down to the flag office, where there was a Navy commander who looked like he had been swimming in his uniform. He was cold, shaking and dripping. He proved to be the commander of a division of destroyers and he was headed for Picket Station # 1. He'd come across the open roadstead in an open boat in the wind and rain because he had talked to skippers of destroyers that had come back from Okinawa. They had told him he simply couldn't take his ships in there without getting the latest version of the doctrine, because it was bad enough anyhow, but suicide without the information.

"I couldn't stand it. Sedgwick had updated the document and I got a copy of it. I swore the yeomen to secrecy and I swore them to use the same old date-time-group on the papers. We made up a bunch and gave them to the commander.

"Everything seemed fine and then after four days, we received a signal from the Chief of Naval Operations, Admiral [Ernest] King, requesting copies. Unfortunately, while the yeomen had been making them up, the watch changed. A new yeoman came on and he didn't know anything about retaining the old date-time identification. I don't know whether Admiral Kiland was going to die of a stroke, a heart attack or shoot both of us, but we had a memorable scene. Fortunately, we were ordered to leave the area before it happened again."

In terms of Navy procedures, Kiland was absolutely correct, for only by strict control over who could issue "doctrine" could conflicting information and orders be prevented. But as Hamilton notes, Admiral Turner, who had ordered the destroyers to picket duty and was responsible for promulgating useful intelligence and tactics, offered no insights to his subordinates and apparently saw no need. Hamilton credits Turner's habitual arrogance and, perhaps, his fondness for alcohol, as reasons for the failure to accept useful ideas from his subordinates.

In many instances, discreet, unofficial back channels distributed unofficially sanctioned information. Says Hamilton, "By the time of Okinawa, I knew all of the flag secretaries in the fleet and we had a sort of mutual-assistance society going." But in the matter of the kamikaze protocol, the case-hardened system stifled the dissemination of vital intelligence.

The problem surfaced in another area. Subsequently, Kiland's chief of staff persuaded his superior of the need for some evacuation plan for the area if meteorologists foresaw a coming typhoon, such as the storm that sank three destroyers a few months earlier. Notes Hamilton, "The admiral sent Captain Tomkins, his chief of staff, to see Admiral Turner and get permission to send this plan out. I guess the chief of staff felt lonesome and he knew something of what Admiral Turner could be like, so he asked to go with him. We went over, and I stood outside the cabin while he went in to see Admiral Turner. Turner was usually gassed by 10:00 A.M. and he was an irascible SOB anyway. He finally got through his head what Tomkins had to suggest. Turner said, 'If I want a typhoon procedure put out, I'll put it out. It's not your place to issue doctrine. Now I will give you thirty seconds to get off my flagship or I'll have you thrown off. Dismissed!' The chief of staff emerged from the cabin and we, left within the allotted thirty seconds." Some months later, the fleet under Kiland, with Hamilton and Sedgwick in tow, left Okinawa before a typhoon buffeted the anchorage. Fortunately, the damage was insignificant.

According to Hamilton, Turner was not the only top leader in the

The wounded Japanese battleship *Yamato* desperately maneuvers to avoid torpedoes and bombs. *(National Archives)*

Pacific fleet with a drinking problem. He suggests that Adm. Bull Halsey also imbibed so heavily that he would not or could not issue the orders that might have allowed vessels to change course and save themselves when they fell into the clutches of typhoons. Overall Pacific commander Adm. Chester Nimitz reprimanded Halsey for his poor leadership in these situations, but this was not an era in which alcoholism, particularly among successful commanders, was recognized as having potentially disastrous consequences.

With Japanese air and ground forces desperately engaged in the Okinawa campaign, the Imperial Navy threw its last remaining surface power into the TEN-GO game. Out of the naval base at Kure on the Inland Sea steamed the *Yamato*, at 68,000 tons displacement, the largest battleship afloat. It mounted 18.1-inch guns, more than a match for the mightiest ones on American or British dreadnoughts. Their biggest fired fourteen and sixteen-inch shells.

The *Yamato*, with a crew of more than 3,000, sallied forth on April 6, in the company of the light cruiser *Yahagi* and eight destroyers, designated Task Force II, a puny force, considering the massive number of ships available from the American fleet and a British one also in the vicinity. Worse, the *Yamato* sailed without any air cover. The notion that she could navigate the 600 miles to the Okinawa anchorages without discovery followed by an all-out onslaught from carrier-based planes could not even be sustained as a fantasy.

In the confused, conflicted and frustrated direction of Japanese military affairs, some hoped that at least the small task force, as part of Operation TEN-GO, could distract the American carriers sufficiently to allow the kamikazes of April 6 and 7 to reach their targets. If *Yamato* somehow managed to reach the Okinawa area, it could train its huge turrets on anything in range and, as a last resort, beach itself where it could provide a kind of artillery support for the Japanese ground forces. The operational plans went so far as to direct that when all ammunition had been expended in this last effort, the ship's crew should try to contact the ground forces and become infantrymen.

Some historians, like Morison, bluntly describe the *Yamato*'s voyage as designed for a one-way trip with only enough fuel to carry it to the Hagushi roadstead. But George Feifer in *Tennozan* points out that officers on the Combined Fleet staff scrounged enough oil to fill the battleship's bunkers three-quarters full, more than enough for a round-trip. While few held out any hope for survival, enough navy people were determined to give the *Yamato* at least a long shot at coming home.

Its crew was not sanguine. Sub-Lt. Sakae Kogono, a damage-control officer on the *Yamato*, says, "On the way home from the battle of Leyte in '44 [where the *Yamato* escaped from that disastrous encounter with minor injuries and was now considered a lucky ship], I heard secretly from some of the Nisei [U.S.-born Japanese, who knew English] that Japan was losing badly. Therefore, I did not have much hope from the time I left Japan for Okinawa.

"There was no tragic feeling in me about going on the suicide mission. I had to die one way or another. Therefore, I wanted to die with the ship. I wanted to return attacks to the enemy but my job was not of that nature. Some of my friends must have felt they would not see their families again. They sent money to their homes. But I was not married, did not have a fiancée. I was the last child of the family. For these reasons I had no special feelings about going away.

"Even I felt how reckless it was that the *Yamato* received a suicide mission, but I thought there was nothing to be done. It was too bad to waste such a ship, but the *Yamato* could not do anything unless it went. [There were naval strategists who wanted the *Yamato* kept at its Kure base for the final defense of the islands.] As a navy man, I thought I would rather die at sea. It was what you might call my fate."

Task Force II had barely cleared the Inland Sea at 5:45 P.M. on April 6, when the American submarine *Threadfin* detected the flotilla. The sub notified Adm. Marc Mitscher's Task Force 58, which was some 400 miles off and which included many carriers. Immediately, search planes began to prowl the skies, peering at the sea below for the quarry.

At dawn on April 7, a pilot from the *Essex* sighted the *Yamato* and her companions. Task Force II now endured continuous surveillance from aircraft based on as many as a dozen carriers, which stayed safely out of range of antiaircraft fire. The shadow team included flying boats based at Kerama Retto. Mitscher closed the distance to 250 miles and then launched a series of gigantic strikes—the first one sent up 280 dive and torpedo bombers.

The hunters swarmed over the targets while Task Force II responded with fusillades dominated by the *Yamato*'s six six-inch batteries, twenty-four five-inch guns and 150 machine guns. But only nine minutes after the *Yamato* spotted the first wave of attackers, a pair of bombs from Curtiss Helldivers struck near the mainmast, and a few moments later the first torpedo exploded against the thick armor plate of the port bow. Already, the *Yahagi*, victim of a bomb and a torpedo, lay dead in the water, while one of the destroyer screen had slid under the water bow-first, taking most of her crew down with her.

The *Yamato,* the over-size Japanese battleship, lies dead in the water after a series of U.S. carrier based torpedo and bomb strikes.
(Signal Corps, U.S. National Archives)

A brief respite ensued as the first attackers retired, but a second strike bore in less than an hour later. The hail of bullets and shell fragments toppled sailors on the supership. The *Yamato's* powerful engines and sleek design enabled it to dodge torpedoes for a time, and to the thick curtain of smaller guns it added its 18.1-inchers, training them low to the water, where they exploded great water spouts that might destroy aircraft skimming the sea as they prepared to launch their torpedoes.

Lt. (jg) Jack Speidel, a volunteer through the Navy's V–5 aviation cadet reserve program, had graduated from flight training at Corpus Christi, then did a tour at the aerial photography school in Opa-locka, Florida. From there he was assigned to pilot a torpedo bomber manufactured by General Motors from a Grumman design. With a crew of his TBM that included radioman Al Kerby and gunner William Groepper, Speidel flew from the "baby" flattop *Cabot.*

"We had our first crack at the *Yamato,*" says Speidel, "during the battle of Leyte Gulf. But we didn't do any damage. Then while we were attacking Chi Chi, a Japanese seaplane base, in February 1945, the ground fire punched a huge hole in my wing and wiped out the hydraulic system. I got back to land on the *Cabot* but couldn't control the plane well enough, so we had to go aboard the *Yorktown* [a much larger carrier].

"When we took off for the *Yamato* on April 7, we had one drop tank that gave us an extra hour of flying time. There was an overcast and one group never did find the *Yamato*. Everybody had to go through a single hole in that overcast, and there were so many planes, it was incredible.

"I remember colored bursts in front of us and splashes in the water from the enemy ships. I was concentrating on coming in the way I was taught. I didn't have any thoughts about the Japanese or the people on the ship. I only knew my you-know-what was on the line.

"We came in on the port side, not real low. Others had probably already hit the ship. After we dropped the torpedo [a 2,000-pound missile] and turned away, my radioman was watching and he screamed, 'We hit it! We hit it!' We returned to the *Cabot* and the entire mission took about five hours."

For more than an hour and fifteen minutes, the carrier aircraft, killer bees pouring out of many hives, stung the *Yamato*. Five more torpedoes

A wounded infantryman receives help. *(Signal Corps, U.S. National Archives)*

struck home after the initial blows, and the ship began to list. The commander ordered flooding of several compartments to correct the ship's attitude. The combination of that water, the sea pouring in through the holes created by the torpedoes, and steam escaping from ruptured boilers snuffed out the lives of several hundred Japanese sailors. The tactic failed to correct the list and, as only one screw continued to work, *Yamato* lost speed and any real maneuverability for defense.

Third and fourth strikes pounded away at the crippled behemoth, unable to respond to commands or to defend herself. Morison quotes Ens. Misuro Yoshida, "The decks were reduced to shambles, with nothing but cracked and twisted steel plates remaining. Big guns were inoperable because of the increasing list, and only a few machine guns were intact . . . One devastating blast in the emergency dispensary had killed all its occupants, including the medical officers and corpsmen."

At two in the afternoon the torment of the *Yamato* reached its peak. The assassins, with names like Dauntless, Hellcat, Avenger and Corsair, drilled her almost at will. It was hopeless. From amid the wreckage on the *Yamato* bridge, the admiral in command of Task Force II, Seiichi Ito, ordered the mission aborted. The ships still able to operate were to pick up men from the sea and from disabled vessels and try to make port. Then Admiral Ito shook hands with some officers on the bridge and locked himself in his quarters. He would go down with the *Yamato*.

The ship's captain, Kosaku Ariga, after making certain that the portraits of the emperor and empress would not suffer the indignity of capture—an officer in charge of the hallowed paintings secured himself with the artwork in his room—instructed a crewmen to bind him to a binnacle on the bridge. Ariga then calmly munched biscuits while awaiting his death.

With ten torpedo hits and five bomb blasts, as well as countless nearmiss explosions, the munitions aboard the *Yamato* administered the *coup de grâce*. Subterranean blasts sent up a 6,000-foot-high tongue of fire, and the smoke rose more than four miles as the mightiest battleship in the world expired after two hours of battering. One or two American aircraft, hovering over the battleship, may have been victims of the debris from detonation of the *Yamato*'s ordnance.

Sakae Kogono, the twenty-six-year-old sublieutenant responsible for repairs from air raids, sought to perform his duties as the first blows rocked the ship. Kogono realized the ship was already badly damaged. "Telephones were not working any longer and the ship started to heel. I left one of my men behind and took the rest to do the repairs. But while we were running there, a torpedo hit the right side of the ship. I closed the hatch and came up again. Our personal belongings were floating in the water, which came up to our knees.

"The flag could no longer be seen and I thought nothing more could be done. I tried to go back to my men but found it impossible because of the water. I called my men; there were eighteen of them and they came by. I ordered them to leave the ship, jump into the sea. They did not have enough courage to follow the order, so I jumped first. I say 'jump,' but it was really a matter of sliding down the side of the ship. My men followed.

"We kept swimming as a group for a while and saw the *Yamato* sink. We gathered some lumber and made a raft, putting the injured men on it. By now there were only five or six of my men with me. My glasses were already lost and, because I am very nearsighted, I could not see well after the *Yamato* sank. I had a bad feeling, for I knew there were sharks in the sea.

"American planes came strafing but after a while they were gone. Japanese destroyers began to appear, so we tried to swim to get near them. Because of the tidal current, we couldn't. Finally, we gave up and fell asleep on the raft. Then I heard voices and, when I opened my eyes, I found a destroyer, the *Uikkaze,* nearby. I swam near it and was expected to climb a rope ladder to the ship. I ordered a crewman on the destroyer to throw a rope down to me. I looped the rope around my waist and put one end in my mouth so my teeth could hold it while they pulled me up. My hands were too slippery to hold the rope, and besides, I was too exhausted.

"After I was rescued, I went to see one of my men. I offered him a cigarette but he could not take it. He was completely armless and legless. He died while on the destroyer. I will never forget him. At my mother's house there is a Buddhist altar. On it I placed a piece of paper with the names of my dead eight men.

"I also placed a poem I wrote next to the names. My mother said prayers for them every day. My poem reads, 'Though bodies might be left in the water, the sea of Okinawa, the battleship *Yamato* shall be kept. Although the bodies may be left in the sea of Okinawa, may there be left the spirit of the *Yamato.*'—which actually means Japan." [The Japanese sometimes called themselves "the Yamato people," after their ancient kingdom on Honshu's Yamato plain.]

The body counts for the destruction of Task Force II range from 3,700 to 4,250 lost; as many as 3,000 aboard the *Yamato* died. Along with the battleship, the Americans sank the light cruiser *Yahagi* and four destroyers. With the few survivors, like Kogono, plucked from the China Sea, the four surviving destroyers limped away. Mitscher reported his losses as ten planes and twelve airmen.

CHAPTER XV

KAKAZU RIDGE

Cutting Okinawa in half, the two Marine organizations swiftly trekked north, while the 96th and 7th Infantry Divisions headed south, with the former on the western side and the latter on the eastern. For the first few days after the Easter Sunday parade ashore, they encountered sporadic, light resistance. The gentle landscape enabled armor to support the foot soldiers. The climate, the landscape and the vegetation were far more attractive than the tropical, swampy jungle of Leyte.

For Mike Moroz, with the 382nd Regiment of the 96th, the idyllic quality ended abruptly. "It had been like a Sunday stroll until we came to a couple of huts. We burst in there with all of our weapons, BARs, rifles, grenades. There were a bunch of civilians in the corner of one hut, old people, women and children. They passed around a teapot while we stood there. Within minutes they were all dead, suicides by poison. Their minds had already been poisoned by the Japs."

Ellis Moore, the communications specialist with the 96th Division Deadeyes, passed an uneventful first few days on Okinawa and in a letter home wrote, "In the little orientation book on the island which we read on the ship, it said Okinawa is far from a tourists' paradise. I was pleasantly surprised at the terrain and landscape. While there are no Grand Canyons or Pike's Peaks, it is a pretty pleasing country to my eye. It is mostly rolling country covered with terraced fields of rice, cabbage and sweet potatoes. The villages [inland] are hardly damaged by bombs or artillery. They are usually grouped around the tree clusters and are very picturesque and quaint as you look down on them from a hill with their red tile roofs slanting through the leaves.

"The houses are just as the grammar school geography books always pictured them—wooden sliding panels dividing off the rooms; there are no tables or chairs, and the bedrooms consist of mats stretched out on the floor. Every house I've seen has a big fancy cupboard with Oriental designs all over it and the remains of red lacquer and china bowls strewn over it."

Bob Jackson, with B Company of the 382nd, recalls those first days as almost like a tour of an exotic land. "We were in reserve, behind the 381st and 383rd making the main attack. We crossed interesting, rather hilly country. The tombs that were to be a big part of the difficult fight ahead were deserted. On breaks we'd inspect them as best we could. We were still in fear of the highly advertised snakes [habu]. My only memory of action in these first days was watching as our company half-ton truck hit a mine and rolled over. There was small damage but I lost a Japanese bowl I'd found beside the road.

"When the forward regiments ran into resistance, our battalion, led by A Company, was committed and began receiving fire. A small hill had been invested by A Company, from which it was trying to move

Troops from the 2nd Battalion of the 382nd Infantry Regiment advance towards Kakazu Ridge. (*Signal Corps, U.S. National Archives*)

forward against strong resistance. We in B Company were behind them and could see the mountains where the Japanese had fine artillery emplacements. Company A was mauled pretty badly and had barrage after barrage of artillery thrown at them. This was our first experience with concentrated artillery fire and we were scared!" In previous campaigns, the Japanese had demonstrated a serious ignorance of the most effective use of artillery and limited themselves to a single shell at a time. On Okinawa, where they possessed ample pieces and ammunition, they showed Jackson they had learned how to use their heavier guns.

"About this time, the Japanese unleashed a previously unknown weapon, a 320 mm mortar. It blew a big hole in the ground and frightened us; it sounded like a freight train coming in. But it did little damage to the troops.

"On this hill I experienced my first abject and shameful fear. We had now relieved A Company and were preparing to move three platoons into position when we came under a severe artillery and mortar barrage. It was awesome. I understand one becomes inured, but that afternoon I tried to dig my way to the center of the earth. When the barrage lifted, I got up, shook the dirt off my fatigues and went back to work with my platoon. I have never forgotten, however, how I screamed in fear and how hard I shoved myself into the dirt of that Okinawa hillside.

"We had penetrated the outer reaches of the Japanese Main Line of Resistance (MLR) before the largest city, Naha. My company commander assigned my platoon to the left flank of the battalion. I was to occupy a small knoll facing away from the rest of the outfit. Because we had been together such a short time [Jackson had been reassigned from A Company just before leaving Leyte], I barely knew my men. I knew most of the squad leaders because they had been recruits back in the training days of Camp Adair. I have no memory of my platoon sergeant but must have known him by sight and reputation. I don't remember feeling close, which was a hell of a way to fight a war.

"Darkness was coming on as I took my messenger to the knoll while the platoon sergeant brought up the squads. The men were about fifty yards behind me as I gave instructions to a squad leader of where to place his BAR and have the men dig in.

"Suddenly, a Nambu machine gun ripped off a burst of fire. That has the sound of a cliché, but the Nambu was extremely rapid firing, and its sound was a frightening rip of noise. I was sloppy and had given no thought that the Japanese could have moved so close to our lines.

"At the same time this Japanese unit, probably five or six men, began lobbing knee-mortar shells at us. We used to joke that those shells would have to hit you on the head without a helmet to do any harm. The surprise of the concussive noise and the noise of the machine gun made us drop like tin soldiers. No one was hurt at that time. We were just scattered over an area of about fifty square yards. One of my squad leaders, looking for a site for his BAR, was about twenty-five yards off across a small swale.

"I had jumped into a shallow drainage ditch that ran toward the enemy line. The squad leader with the BAR and a couple of men occupied a similar ditch on the other side of the swale. We tried to fire at the enemy but the machine gun was well hidden as it searched for us with bursts of fire. I looked for the rest of the platoon and saw them running, helter-skelter across the fields, back toward their previous positions. I can see that still; they were in the last rays of the sun, a mob returning 'home' with all military discipline gone. I was angry, frustrated and very frightened.

"Waving and yelling, I tried to get the squad leader to work back to the former company position. He misunderstood and tried to come towards me. The Nambu opened up as he rose to run. He was hit and, I could see, badly. By then there were only the two of us and darkness was coming down fast.

"Crawling forward in my ditch, I came upon the sergeant, lying on his side, badly wounded and crying in pain. He was a mess in his middle where the machine gun burst had almost cut him in two. I had no idea what to do and doubted we'd get help. Every so often the Nambu or a knee mortar would fire. I got my poncho out of my pack, laid it in front of the sergeant, and, with great perseverance on his part, managed to get him onto the poncho. By dragging him a few feet at a time down the ditch, I got fairly close to the company line. By this time, something had happened to silence the Nambu and knee mortars—maybe they had just pulled back—and some squads from B Company came out with a stretcher. I went back to the company perimeter, sat down and shook. All night we remained under artillery and mortar fire."

Don Dencker, with Company L of the 383rd, reports a similar gradual involvement in the campaign. "Our first encounter with the Japs, except for a few sniper shots, was a heavy shelling from artillery early in the afternoon of April 5. We were still in reserve, but had moved up to about 600 yards of the front lines. Our CO, Captain Fitzpatrick, was seriously wounded trying to drag to safety a man fatally wounded by one of the first shells. This act of bravery cost us a damn good company commander. During the following days we were subjected to numerous artillery and mortar barrages. Our entrenching tools became our lifesavers."

Len Lazarick, with Company K of the 382nd, had settled in that first night with the modest luxury of being in reserve. "We didn't take it for granted that we had any guarantee of safety. We did our standard two hours on guard and four hours off vigil on the company perimeter. Although the temperature during the day was comfortably warm, I found the night chilly and stood guard with a blanket draped around my shoulders.

"We usually dug in three men to a hole and, when possible, in the shape of the letter Y. The foxhole was deep enough so that, from a sitting position, only our heads were exposed while on guard duty during the night. Farther south on Oki, we ran into hard ground and often were satisfied by piling loose rocks and coral just high enough to protect a sleeping comrade from ground-level shell or grenade fragments.

"I had carried ashore my trusty M–1 Garand rifle, bayonet, full cartridge belt, two bandoliers of ammo (close to 200 rounds total), two canteens filled with water, a snake-bite kit, standard first-aid kit, water purification tablets and a light field pack. That contained a poncho, a blanket, mess kit, foot powder, tooth brush, soap, razor, steel mirror, two pairs of dry socks wrapped in a waterproof sack, small inflatable pillow and extra K and D rations. Strapped to my cartridge belt harness, like suspenders, were two fragmentation grenades and two concussion grenades. All riflemen carried little specialty items in their packs or in packages—extra walkie-talkie batteries, front-line brightly colored marker panels for aircraft guidance purposes. The gas mask strapped to my leg was removed at our first stop and put in a pile near the beach, to be collected.

"I didn't own an OD jungle sweater until April 6, when I was able to remove one from the pack of a dead GI lying in a ditch beside the road we were marching along. The sweater was a pullover made of lightweight wool. It helped keep me warm during the chilly nights. Before I obtained it, I shivered a great deal with only a single blanket.

"When we moved out on April 2, and moved south, still in reserve, I was assigned to be the point. I don't know to this day what I did wrong to be so honored. It is not a comfortable feeling to be alone, 100 yards ahead of your column, searching for enemy snipers or stragglers.

"During one of our rest stops, Major Stell, the battalion exec, motioned to me to walk back to the rear. He had noticed that I had a fresh carrot stick in the elastic band on my helmet. We were told the natives used night soil to fertilize their crops, so eating fresh vegetables was a definite no-no. Major Stell ordered me to throw away my 'camouflage' and barked, 'We don't eat that stuff, Lazarick. Now get back on point.' That evening when I went back to battalion headquarters to get our rations and water, I noticed the troops there were boiling carrots in a big pot for their evening meal. That's the army!

"However, on Okinawa I was introduced to the army's 10-in-1 rations. They came in cardboard boxes and were such a great improvement over the K, C and D rations that I stopped complaining about the food for a week. The 10-in-1 contained bacon, sugar, oleo, cigarettes, cans of chicken, powdered fruit juices, powdered coffee and hard candies. We were issued small stoves so we could heat the bacon, warm up canned or powdered eggs and our coffee. The grease left over from the bacon was saved. When we had enough of it, we would heat it to boiling. The hard cracker rations were soaked in water until soft and then put into the hot bacon grease. When the crackers were browned, we took them out and rolled them in sugar to make what we called a poor man's donut. Hours after eating my 'donuts' I would have to belch and taste them all over.

"It was still uneventful as we dug in for our third night on Okinawa. Around nine o'clock, we heard rifle shots from a foxhole just thirty feet away. Not too many rounds were fired and then it was quiet. At daylight, we discovered that an elderly man and two women, one of whom had a baby, had been killed. We'd been told that pamphlets had been dropped on the island, instructing civilians not to move about at night. Either these people didn't know what to do or ignored the advice. It's a sad tragedy of war when the innocent are killed, especially babies.

"I was assigned to the detail digging a grave for the dead right on the spot. Pulling their bodies into the shallow graves, it was obvious that rigor mortis had set in and their skins felt cold and clammy. I wanted to wash my hands afterwards but I couldn't spare the water. We didn't talk much about what had happened."

Company K's rifleman addition on Leyte, Paul Westman, says, "The ground troops met very little opposition at first. We began to hope it would be a walkover. What opposition we did meet served as invaluable experience for untested replacements like myself. Later replacements wouldn't be so lucky.

"I remember the passwords and countersigns for the first days on Okinawa. They were glass/house; long/lane; forty/thieves; flimsy/skirt and fair/weather. We were told that the Japanese had difficulty with the letters L and R.

"When I first heard the cracks of rifle bullets going past, I thought,

'Man, you can get hurt! You don't have a target pit to hide in now.' Close rounds of artillery scared me worse. My mouth would get dry, my legs would go rubbery. I found out they would still function one morning when two shells came very close. The squad leader said, 'Let's get the hell outa here!'—and we did. Two others didn't. Three more shells hit and when we came back, one of the new replacements was lying outside the hole and his clothes were smoking. The other was still in the hole with a shattered leg and other wounds. Litter bearers took them away. I don't think either one of them got to fire his M-1 even once. That was the time I learned that if I paid close attention to S.Sgt. Jeff Brooks, I'd probably last longer."

According to Dick Thom, the S-3 with the 381st Regiment, the preinvasion instructions directed that civilians on Okinawa should be treated as if they were soldiers. "But one day after we landed, we received a brand new order that said for us to look to the welfare of the civilians we had been killing. At one point I saw fifteen people wearing tan uniforms in a rice paddy. I ordered a tank that was with us to fire on them with machine guns. They were all killed and I found out they had been in the homeguard, like Boy Scouts. They had all deserted but they didn't know enough to discard the uniforms.

"Nobody knew where the enemy was. Everybody seemed to be standing around and sucking their thumbs. It didn't help that we had a captain who was the CO of a rifle company and couldn't read a map. They brought in some civilians, prisoners, but the Nisei interpreter couldn't understand the language. But it seems that some Okinawans, as second-class citizens, had been sent to the nitrate mines in Chile, where they picked up a kind of bastard Spanish. There was a Mexican in our outfit, a tech sergeant medic who was an excellent soldier. He shouldn't have been a pill roller, but a combat soldier. He said, 'I can talk to them.'

"Instead, our intelligence officer sent them back to headquarters. About eight or nine days later, we were told it would be okay to interrogate civilians. The ones we picked up didn't seem to like the Jap army much. They freely told you where they were and their strength, if you found one who wasn't too scared. These were the only kinds of prisoners my regiment ever took. We never turned in an honest Jap soldier; quite a few of them showed up to surrender with a hand grenade."

On April 8, the fourth day of the contact with the enemy, Bob Jackson, with B Company of the 382nd, ate a noontime hot meal brought up from the company kitchens in the rear. The battalion commander called for a two-platoon attack on Tombstone Ridge, so named for the mauso-leum in the distance.

"The ground sloped away from our positions to a ditch running across our front," recalls Jackson. "Directly in the middle was a stone bridge. The company commander [Capt. George R. Gerrans], in textbook fash-ion, took me, as the leader of the two platoons, to the heights facing the front and pointed out the ditch as the jumping-off point for the attack. It was almost like an exercise at Fort Benning, with the captain even giving me a regulation five-point field order.

"I collected Lt. John Fox of the other attacking platoon and our platoon sergeants for a less formal battle order. I knew Fox only slightly; he was young, from another regiment originally, where he had received a battlefield commission on Leyte. Both of us had considerable battle-field experience but neither knew our men very well.

"We went down to the ditch, spread out, and in good order. When we were in position there, Lieutenant Fox, with his platoon on my left, informed me he was ready to go. I raised the antenna of my SCR-536 radio, ready to inform Company HQ to start the preparatory mortar barrage. It was to precede us as we moved toward Tombstone Ridge.

"I climbed up the side of the ditch, which was about seven feet deep, and called the company to start the barrage. When the shiny antenna rose above the ditch, a machine gun opened up from an enfiladed position to our left. It was impossible to see where it came from. But everytime I tried to use the radio, a burst of fire skimmed the top of the embankment. It would be suicide to try climbing the steep bank, get over the edge and into a running position. I scooted down and ordered the men to dig in until I could contact the company for further instruc-tions.

"Exposed as we were to enfilading fire, we'd lose most of our attack group if we tried to complete our move. We had no chance to take the objective. I tried to call in mortar fire by hand signals to the company commander in the position behind us. The captain was unable to read my signals in that deep ditch. I wasn't able to indicate anything but that the fire came from our left. The Japanese apparently moved the ma-chine gun about this time. It fired directly down the ditch into our positions.

"I was wounded twice in this first burst. I had been sitting against the wall of the ditch with my feet stretched out before me, trying to figure what in hell to do. I noticed the neat hole in the middle of my combat boot, turned over and started to crawl toward the left, from which direction the gun seemed to be firing. I was hit again in the upper thigh and that hurt! My runner, who was digging into the wall of the ditch right next to me, had a perfectly positioned, three-shot group through the top of his helmet.

"The men were panicking with fear; they didn't know where to fire or how to defend themselves. Neither did I, but I hauled myself under the stone bridge to Lieutenant Fox's platoon. He had taken a shot in the chest; it gurgled and he was very frightened. I have never felt so helpless!

"Some of my waving and motions must have gotten through to the CO, because mortar fire was laid on and the machine gun was silenced. The 81 mm mortars laid a heavy concentration of smoke around us.

"I figured," continues Bob Jackson, "that if we had to stay there until nightfall, I'd be able to crawl up the side of the ditch nearest the company and wiggle my way up to our positions. However, that wouldn't help those, like Fox, who were worse off than I. Just then several stretchers, followed by men from the company, came sliding into the ditch. I directed the evacuation and was loaded onto a litter to be carried out. Ever the pessimist, I remember looking over the side of the stretcher as I was hoisted up out of the ditch and searching for a drop place if that machine gun opened up again. I was looking out for Number One! I didn't know that, of the approximately sixty men under my command, eighteen had been wounded and two killed.

"Stupidly, after we were evacuated with the help of heavy smoke, the gung-ho assistant battalion commander ordered men back into that trap to bring in the dead. Several were killed and wounded in this foolish and futile operation. It never made sense to me to endanger fighting troops for the sake of bringing in the dead.

"My last memory of Okinawa is of lying on a stretcher near the battalion aid station with smoke swirling about and much feverish activity. The battalion surgeon, a good drinking buddy, came over and congratulated me on a 'million-dollar wound.' With a broken metatarsal, infantry duty was over for me!"

In the same area, half a dozen men, including Paul Westman from Company K, sought to scout a ridgeline. "The squad leader, Willard Johnson, had the SCR-300 radio. We were spread out, moving very slow when the first rounds cracked by. Sgt. Earl Neu hollered, 'Don't bunch up! Take cover!' About then, artillery rounds started dropping down the slope, walking our way. Rifle fire seemed to let up, and I recall hearing our radio operator calling the company, 'King, King, this is King One. We are receiving artillery fire. Is there friendly fire registered here?' He gave the coordinates and the answer was negative.

A dead Japanese soldier lies unburied with none to mourn his loss.
(*Signal Corps, U.S. National Archives*)

"By this time they were on us and Staff Sergeant Neu shouted, 'Back!
Go back! Scatter!' I got blast effects from one, enough to send me
downhill into some coral rock. I could see others heading back and
when I picked myself up, I couldn't put weight on my right foot. The
leg seemed badly scraped but not broken.

"Why I didn't draw fire, I can't imagine. I went back, using my M–1
as a crutch. It took quite a while to hobble back to the company and the
aidman there, and he told me to go to the hospital. On the way in an
ambulance, a medical officer asked me how I felt. I told him I didn't
feel so good after looking around at all those other guys, all shot and
burned to hell. All of them were in far worse shape than I. He put his
hand on my shoulder and said, 'Soldier, you wouldn't have been able to
do your company a bit of good.' "

The 1st Battalion of the 381st, with Thom as operations officer, had
continued to march south. By April 9, they faced the first element in the
basic defense for Okinawa, the Shuri Line's Kakazu Ridge, a steep, 300-
foot slope that stretched about 1,000 yards. On the western side it ran
down to the sea, and to the east a cut separated it from another escarp-

ment, the Nishibaru Ridge. A honeycomb of pillboxes, tunnels and caves, along with an infestation of mortars on the reverse slope, could shower every foot of approach with deadly fire. And before they could even attempt to climb the ridge, the GIs would be forced to traverse a deep gorge well targeted by the mortar positions.

The first of the Deadeyes to batter themselves against Kakazu were from the 383rd Regiment, Ellis Moore's outfit. As a radio operator with 1st Battalion headquarters, Moore and Fred Bauguss made up one of two teams with the thirty-six-pound SCR-300. One set went out to the observation post while the other remained at the command post for the unit and kept in touch with regimental headquarters.

"Our phony war of ten-minute breaks, feeling secure in three-inch foxholes and spending time enjoying the sweet-scented charm of Okinawa came to an end April 6. Suddenly we heard it—the long thin whistle ending with a thunderous WHAM! Even to our untrained ears, that meant artillery. The Nip observers had our positions. In a few minutes the first of those shells that we later nicknamed 'whistling death' landed in the CP. The first barrage lasted only ten or fifteen minutes but we had casualties, physical and mental. I saw my first psycho case then, a cringing, shaking, fear-ridden guy who, a few minutes before, was just as normal as I."

Moore admits, this and subsequent artillery barrages terrified him. "You just lie there in your hole while they land all around you and wonder where the next one is going to hit, and why it doesn't hit you. The whine of a shell as it passes over and the explosion as it hits are just as nerve-wracking as a shell exploding right next to you. After a while you find yourself ducking every time any shell goes over, even if it's one of ours, and we threw ten shells at them for every one they sent at us."

The following morning, when the outfit moved up to a hill held by the Americans, a wide-eyed Moore observed the results of a banzai charge. "About 150 of them had stormed up that hill towards our guys, and they said it was just like shooting ducks. You had to look or you'd step on them. They were scattered all over the place, so much abandoned equipment, these men with beards no heavier than mine, some with quarter-size holes in their heads; others with half their bodies blown away. A GI stooped down to one, jammed a cigarette into his mouth and muttered, 'Have a cigarette, you yellow son of a bitch. Sorry I don't have time to light it for you.'"

Moore also glimpsed his first dead GI. "The color that these men turn as soon as they die is the most horrible part of the scene. The closest approximation is to say it's the same color that appears on some men's fingers after they have smoked a great deal. The feet of the dead are grotesque. Usually, you only see them sticking out of a poncho, two boots with their toes pointed straight towards each other; or maybe just the opposite."

With the battalion exec, Maj. Kenny Erickson, who actually ran the unit in the field, Capt. Hugh Young, the S–3, and Bauguss, Moore, bearing the SCR-300 on his back, reconnoitered the ground in front of Kakazu. On the way back, the two officers crossed an open field without incident. "I followed and got halfway across, where I flopped behind a slight rise. After a few seconds pause, I raised up to cover those last thirty-five yards. No sooner had I started than rat-tat-tat-tat . . . Nobody had to tell me I was being shot at. The guys watching from the hill told me later the Japs had me bracketed perfectly—two or three bursts hit a foot in front of me, then a couple to my rear. It was just like that guy on the stage who throws knives at women to see how close he can come without hitting them.

"About five yards from safety behind the rise, I went sprawling, probably a combination of the thirty-six-pound radio on my back and my feet moving faster than they were intended. Erickson and Young thought I was shot and started to pull me in. I was up on my own and in with them in a second. Captain Young said, 'Goddamn, Moe, that was close. It's a good thing you can run.'"

But when the line companies of the 383rd started their advance on Kakazu, they could neither run nor hide. Moore, however, as a radio operator with battalion headquarters, could obtain at least temporary refuge from the terror of artillery in a tomb. "You crawled through on your knees after you removed a stone slab secured in the entrance by a putty substance. The tomb was high enough for us to stand up, with a plot of about six feet by six feet. There were stone shelves covered with iron and clay urns. They evidently died in this family at all ages. The big skulls and bones were in the larger vases, and the little ones held remains of what must have been very small children.

"We hauled out the urns to let their occupants get a feel of good fresh air again. With a little further policing up, we had a fairly decent and safe habitat with sleeping room for at least seven. Every tomb along the ridge was broken into sooner or later. It was an unwritten rule that, if the tombs offered needed protection, it was okay to open them up. But we weren't allowed to mention the raiding of the dead's resting place in our letters." Japanese authorities' mistaken belief that American reverence for the dead would preclude use of the mausoleums held only for military public relations.

On April 8, just before dawn, the 383rd made its initial assault on Kakazu. A fearsome downpour of artillery and mortar shells fell upon the defenders, and the advance started, led by Able (A) and Charlie (C) Company, with Baker (B) in reserve.

"There was to be no firing," says Moore, who left the safety of the tomb to occupy a spot at the OP. "They were to get up the hill unnoticed. We just sat there while time dragged by. At about five-thirty Able radioed that they were almost to the top. It looked like it was going to work.

"Then all hell broke loose. The Japs must have been watching all the time. They struck at just the right moment. Machine guns from both flanks cut Able and Charlie to ribbons. Japs on the top of the ridge looked down at our guys, ten yards below, and threw everything in the book at them—rifle fire, machine gun fire, hand grenades, satchel charges, even sticks of dynamite. Both Able and Charlie radioed for help. Since Able was farthest up the hill and catching the most hell, Erickson decided to send Baker up behind them.

"We got a call from Able's CO, Capt. Jack Royster. He asked if he couldn't order a retreat. Said more than half of his company was lost. Erickson replied, 'You've got to hold the ground you've got, Jack, or else all that's happened will be useless. I'm sending Baker up to help you and the two of you ought to be able to reach the top.'

"A few minutes later Royster called again. I've never heard such a pitiful voice. 'Listen, Major,' he pleaded, 'I've been hit and can't see a thing. There are only five men in my company left. There's no sign of Baker Company up here. Will you please give me permission to withdraw what's left of my company?' Erickson replied they were to hold their ground.

"But where the hell was Baker Company? I got them on the radio and they said they'd no sooner gotten out of their holes than they were pinned down by mortar fire and machine guns. They were trying to advance in short rushes, but the Japs had them in their sights and they were suffering heavy casualties."

All three of the units assigned to charge Kakazu experienced the same disastrous results. Remnants of the trio managed to link up, but they were reduced to a disorganized band, desperately seeking self-preservation rather than to overcome the enemy. "Behind these men," says Moore, "was the bulk of their companies, men still pinned down in shallow shell holes, men wounded and crying for help that was to be a long time in coming and men for whom there would never be any help."

At last convinced that the battalion had all but been destroyed, Erickson finally countenanced a withdrawal. It was about three hours after the abortive assault had begun and the enemy continued to inflict casualties. Litter parties, made up mostly from headquarters personnel, were shot down while on their errands of succor.

Moore, with the battalion staff, had remained at the observation post. "The Japs had kept their mortar fire out in front of us," says the former communications specialist. "But now, all of a sudden they started dropping in our sector. They were falling like raindrops in a cloudburst. You

Debris explodes as U.S. soldiers seal one of the thousands of caves manned by defenders of Okinawa. *(Signal Corps, U.S. National Archives)*

don't have any warning with these mortars, but we all dove in a trench as the first one hit. [Floyd] Gore, the battalion commander's orderly, was at one end with me and four others beyond us. We hugged the ground and I closed my eyes. It must have lasted only five minutes but I'd swear that 100 rounds hit within a radius of fifteen yards of our hole. The second it stopped, the three officers took off in the direction of the CP. One of them [Byron] yelled back to me to stay at the OP.

"Then I heard a groan and became conscious of Gore next to me. He must have received a direct hit from a mortar. His whole side was ripped away and his insides were gushing out with every breath he took. The flesh on his right thigh was peeled down over his knee. While I was trying to comprehend the sight, Gore raised up on his elbows, twisted his head so he could see his body and then fell flat. He groaned a minute or so longer and then died.

"I was shaking like a leaf as I called the CP, explained I was the only one at the OP and requested permission to return to the CP. An officer said for me to stay there, that I was safer up there. Another ten minutes and I asked again, and this time Captain Young told me to come down. [When I got there] I told him about Gore and that finished one of the regimental officers. He was a beat man. He hung his head in his hands and muttered over and over, 'Gore gone, Gore gone.' That night he went back to regiment and that was the last we saw of him."

Those trapped on the slope kept calling for smoke shells to cover their retreat and eventually the artillery expended all it had. The defenders continued to spray the landscape with murderous fire. A supportive strike by Navy planes missed the mark and bombs fell on the hapless GIs. Not until dark of that dreadful day could they escape, slinging makeshift litters from ponchos and shelter halves on rifles to remove the wounded.

According to Moore, the count of able-bodied soldiers showed that, of the roughly 450 involved in the attack, 128 remained. On the following day, the 383rd sent its 2nd Battalion into the maw, and they too were chewed up with horrendous losses and little real estate to show for the investment of men and equipment.

The divisional command now threw the 1st Battalion of the 381st into the battle. Its S–3, Dick Thom, says, "The 2nd Battalion was on a little knob to our right, west of us. The 3rd Battalion was to the extreme west. General Easley was there with the regimental commander and the regimental S–3. Easley said the 383rd Regiment was up on the ridge. " 'I want you, Cassidy [Lt. Col. John], to take your battalion in a column of twos on the double, with an attached heavy machine gun platoon up there. Commit the 3rd Battalion when you're ready.'

"The company commanders got the order and we crossed the gulch between us and Kakazu. We went up to the top of a little hill. When we got there, there was an army up there, all right, but it wasn't the 383rd Regiment. All hell broke loose. Our men came tumbling down, their rifles falling. I got behind a big rock and saw a light machine gun off to my left chipping away at my rock. I was not happy. We lost half our rifle companies from the battalion. We had two company commanders either killed or wounded, along with a number of lieutenants. By the second or third day in these positions, we had only one active officer per company.

"On Okinawa, each battalion had a destroyer or cruiser assigned to it. The ships would fire five-inch shells for illumination—fifty-second flares that burst over the area. We endured a series of counterattacks, and after what must have been the twelfth one on a dark night around 3:00 A.M., we pleaded for illumination. The cruiser assigned to us said, 'There's a red alert, possible air attack.' They couldn't give fire and give us illumination but they said, 'We'll give you the baseball scores.'

"Then I got a call from one company commander who was kind of a nasty bastard. He said there are hundreds of Japs in our positions. I sent about fifty of them your way. Their artillery was also coming over. Things didn't look too bright. I thought we were done for. I couldn't think of what to do. I called for the 81 mm mortars to fire almost on our positions—we were all in holes, which we got into at 7:00 P.M. and never came out of until morning.

"T. Sgt. Beauford Anderson, who was the section leader for a 60 mm mortar team in A Company, had been busy with the mortar, and he was down to six rounds, and the mortar was no good anymore. They were swamped with Jap soldiers. I saw Anderson pull the pin on a mortar shell, bounce it on a rock to knock out the detent which keeps the shell from going off while you're handling it. Then he heaved it by hand, so it would land on its nose and explode. Four out of the six went off and then, although his arm was busted, Anderson took a carbine and went up and down the gorge shooting Japs. He had seemed like just an ordinary soldier, smallish, cheerful, a guy who did his job. He just went ape that night. Later, his company commander put him in for the Congressional Medal of Honor and I was a witness. [Thom received a Bronze Star for his own efforts.]

"They finally pulled us out, but there wasn't too much to pull. We left 700 dead Japs up there but we had fifty-three fully able enlisted men left from the three rifle companies of our battalion which had attacked Kakazu." Thom blames much of the carnage upon General Easley. "He was too damn brave, too gung-ho. We were all going to get killed following him." Certainly, if Thom's recollections are accurate, Easley should have known that the riflemen from the brother regiment had pulled back from their tenuous hold on the forward slope of Kakazu.

Unlike Jackson, Dencker, Lazarick, Thom, et al., Herman Buffington underwent his baptism of fire that first week on Okinawa. "I was assigned to K company, 3rd Battalion, 383rd Regiment of the 96th, which was in about the middle of the island. Right off, I was appointed first scout for my platoon. My job was to go first, about fifty yards ahead of the others, as we went through the villages, checking houses. The countryside had pine trees and reminded me of home [Rome, Georgia].

"A machine gun opened up at one village. There was popping all around and we were in a field approaching a village. I tried to get up and go forward, but bullets were all about. One of our tanks came forward to help. But the enemy machine gun couldn't be located. Mortars were falling. It turned out that a native woman in a village house had that gun.

"We reached what was called the 'Little Siegfried Line,' and they said it was better fortified than the one in Germany. It was the Japs' first line of resistance. We were caught in a crossfire but I got about halfway up a hill. The Jap tactic was to wait until you go up and then hem you in." As the Americans soon discovered, the enemy had perfected techniques for defenses established on the reverse slopes of Okinawa's ridges.

"We couldn't get back," says Buffington. "Some of the men were wounded. It was late day and under dark we finally did make it back to our lines. Mortars and artillery shells fell on us all night. But there was no counterattack. Next morning, we shove off, up the hill. I was plenty scared. Some of the guys were cracking up—there was a rumor that some thought it would be an easy way to get off the line. I was busy trying to figure out how to stay alive and wasn't worrying about why some went back. I had wanted to see action. But by this time, I'd seen all I wanted to. But there was no backing out.

"We got plastered up against a bank and they opened up on us. We were young and green, and when someone behind ordered us to 'mush on,' no one moved. The lieutenant came up. As scout, I was in the lead. I wanted to be sure that before I struck out, the others would come on up. 'What's wrong?' he asked. I said, 'Nothing.' He retorted, 'Then let's go!' He said if I'd move, they would.

"I was down in a ditch—he was some yards behind me, and so off I finally started, first edging up while looking to see if the others were coming. They were and I ran across an open place. I stopped between two big rocks. The Japs opened up on us and cut us to pieces. The rocks saved me. Later, we knew we had to pull back. I ran toward our lines. Seeing a wounded soldier, I grabbed him and tried to drag him back with me. As the shelling continued, we both fell into a hole. I tried there to tighten my belt around his bleeding leg, then I jerked him out and finally got back off the hill. We tried again that day to take this hill and several times the next day. After nine days on the line, and still not having taken that hill, we were pulled out. We were pulled off the line because we had lost three-fourths of our forty-two man platoon."

Mike Moroz also endured the Kakazu battle. "I was lucky. A shell fragment actually hit me in the temple and punctured a vein. I thought half my head had been blown away. But I just about cured myself, just holding a hand on the wound. I went to a hospital in the rear for a week.

"I went to the Philippines as a private and made Pfc. after that campaign. On Okinawa, because of casualties, I became first a squad leader and then a platoon sergeant. It wasn't due to superior abilities, just that I stayed on my feet."

"Our three line companies," says Ellis Moore, "started the battle of Kakazu Ridge with an average complement of 150 men each and emerged Able Company twenty men, Baker sixty-five, and Charlie forty-three. In spite of the beating we took, there is evidence that we gave the Japs a bloodier time than they gave us.

"We hung around that position for two or three more days, sending out feeler patrols and trying to reorganize the battalion. Major Erickson took over the battalion, and his main idea was to get us in the frame of mind again for the attack, whereas everyone was wondering, 'When will we be relieved?' Erickson's efforts to get us in a fighting mood weren't helped by the artillery we kept receiving. It would start every night at dusk; you could set your watch by it. A few minutes after the Japs commenced, our counter battery would tear into them at a rate of about ten shells to one. The Japs would soon cease firing until the next hour.

"About two days before we were relieved, rumors started flying around that President Roosevelt had died. Nobody believed it and we attributed the talk to the efficiency of the Army rumor system, where a man can start one and have it spread through the battalion in a half-hour. Not until we were back in the rest area and heard the shocking news over the radio, did we learn the truth. We reacted much the same as people throughout the world must have reacted. Disbelief, grief and even fear mingled with anxiety about what would happen to our country now. Most guys didn't even know Truman's first name. Most were skeptical about his abilities in following the Great Man's footsteps." To his Aunt Jane, Moore wrote, "I think most GIs regarded him as one of the soldiers' best friends and had faith in his plans."

Like the troops of the 96th, those from the 7th Division welcomed the absence of serious resistance at the shoreline. Pushing east, they were impeded only by minefields, cleared by engineers, and some lightly defended pillboxes.

Maurice Reeves, the 1st sergeant with the 13th Combat Engineers, recalls, "We moved across the island and then south on the east side. We then traveled south looking for a site to set up headquarters behind the line. We found a nice house, and inside I came on a red, hardback book, the diary of a young lady of Japanese ancestry from Hawaii. She had been visiting relatives when the war caught her in Okinawa. According to the diary, she was dating a Japanese officer who wanted to marry her. She loved this officer but wanted to return to Hawaii after the war, and therefore refused to marry him." Reeves and his colleagues settled in for a number of days as the 7th Division forces jabbed at the defense stretching east of Kakazu Ridge, where the 96th traded knockout punches with the enemy.

Gage Rodman, the platoon leader with Company G of the 17th Regiment, also enjoyed a largely uneventful first two weeks on Okinawa. He wrote home, "There is not much doing as yet. The infantry position in this one is so far like standing between two people bent on killing each other and to hell with the middle man [exchanges of artillery fire].

"I've got a three-room apartment, below street level. In fact, I am almost below sea level. Anyone who wants to know about subterranean strata in the Ryukyu Islands can come to me. If I were to jump into my foxhole without a parachute, I'd probably break a leg.

"My sunglasses took the count finally. A shell fragment went through the case. I hope those other ones get here. I've been riding (bareback) horses again and I'm all stove up. I had a Jap cavalry or artillery horse and he was a razorbacked critter for sure. I still think this is a pretty island and the nights are still cold. I am getting used to it."

Capt. Gene Prather, the executive officer for the 1st Battalion of the 7th Infantry's 32nd Regiment, says, "We expected an opposed landing but met no resistance and moved all the way across the island, then turned towards Mount Yonabaru. Then the Japanese defense scheme became apparent. Our battalion was in the rice paddies along the coast with little opposition, contrary to what units on the ridge encountered.

Consequently, we advanced more rapidly and then came under prereg-istered artillery and mortar fire."

The brother regiment of Prather's 32nd, the 182nd, advanced on the right flank of the 96th Division and, like the Deadeyes, ran into a wall of fire, dominated by a height known as the Pinnacle. According to some researchers, the expedition led by Commo. Matthew Perry, nearly 100 years before, hoisted the American flag on this site. On April 5, 1945, a 110-man contingent of Japanese soldiers repulsed two American as-saults backed by artillery, tanks and mortars. On the third try the GIs prevailed. It was a small triumph, for the main line of resistance lay dead ahead. Subsequent movement farther south encountered increas-ingly aggressive enemy forces. Not even the added power of fifteen light and heavy tanks from the 711th Tank Battalion could enable the 184th to overcome the foe, who swarmed about the armor with satchel charges and flaming rags. The units from the 711th retreated after losing a number of tanks.

Gene Prather's outfit, the 32nd Regiment, after making good early progress, had deferred to the 184th, protecting its left flank. But when it tried to renew the drive, the enemy responded with artillery barrages from the heights. Notes Prather, "After three days in this situation, we were ordered to withdraw out of range and, essentially, to the flank of the units on the ridge above us. As I recall, I lost one killed and three wounded from my communications section while we manned the origi-nal command post covering the withdrawal. I presume the strategy was all right, but most of us felt we should have withdrawn earlier."

The pullback gave Prather his worst experience of the campaign. "I had established the new CP to our rear and was alone, on my way back forward to the old one. About halfway there, I met a junior officer separated from his unit, walking alone, heading to the rear, totally disregarding the incoming shells dropping around us. When I spoke to him, he did not respond or stop, but stuck his carbine in my belly and ordered me out of his way. There was no recognition of me on his part, though we had been together in the battalion and were friends for more than two years.

"He was obviously hysterical and unaware of what he was doing. I was afraid to move and began talking to him to calm him. After what seemed an eternity, he suddenly dropped the carbine and collapsed, crying, on the path between the rice paddies. After getting him far enough to the rear and headed for the aid station, I returned to my old CP and found the casualties. It was a crushing blow to lose my men who had been with me over three years, on top of seeing a fine young officer and friend become a shell-shock victim.

"The officer was sent to a division-operated rest and rehab area. He returned to duty about a month later, though not to any front-line job."

Like everyone else in the 7th Division, machine gunner Solomon Berger, with division artillery, expresses surprise at the lack of enemy along the shoreline. The briefings had led him to believe this would be a bloody assault.

"Our headquarters battery was well behind the lines and, luckily, was never infiltrated by individual Japanese, even though we had to maintain round-the-clock vigil on our perimeter with barbed wire and machine guns. On a number of occasions we fired the machine guns, usually nights, at what was thought to be the enemy.

"Our greatest danger came from enemy counter-battery fire which killed several of our men. The Japanese had a very great concentration of field artillery, more than in any other campaign."

Both sides slugged it out at long distance for several days after the 96th and 7th Division advances halted. The Japanese stubbornly hid in their underground redoubts while their artillery, with a strength never before seen by the Americans, continued to pound away. The U.S. forces, anxious to reorganize themselves, found themselves kept off balance by counterattacks and the incessant forays of infiltrators.

CHAPTER XVI

THE MARINES GO NORTH

The 4th Marine Regiment, part of the 6th Marine Division assigned to conquer the northern half of Okinawa, encountered its first stiff resistance the second day ashore. A fierce firefight engaged Company L from the 3rd Battalion. The skirmish cost it all but ten men from one platoon, but the fight eliminated 150 of the enemy. The 1st Battalion then reported it slew 250 more as the division set its sights on the town of Ishikawa on the eastern coast. Having tightened the belt across the Okinawa midriff, the 6th Marine Division worked its way back west, focusing on the Motobu Peninsula that poked its head out towards the nearby island of Ie Shima.

Ahead moved the Recon Company commanded by Tony Walker. "Early in the operation," says Walker, "we made a patrol out in front of the division. When night came, we formed a perimeter defense and hunkered down to get some rest. Trouble was, we had left our packs behind at our base camp. No one froze, but no one slept. After that night we always carried our knapsacks with rations and blanket roll wherever we went, even in the assault.

"During the night, a noncom or officer was checking the lines to make sure everyone was awake. A newly joined replacement opened fire on him from the far end of the line. We removed this fellow's rifle and next day transferred him to the 29th Marines, where we heard he became a tiger in combat."

The Recon Company traveled in strength during these first days. Sgt.

Harry Manion comments, "Someone did good planning. Along with us were five 75 mm gun tanks and one dozer tank. If the enemy wanted to commit himself, he would find one small and ready 140 Recon men and six solid Sherman tanks. Moving ahead of the infantry, we presented a lucrative target."

Walker says, "We led the division up the road towards the town of Nago, supported by tanks and moving with some care to avoid an ambush. Col. Victor Bleasedale, commanding the 29th Marines, kept pushing us, urging us to go faster."

Manion recalls that incautious, hasty pace of the 29th. "Sometimes, after an all-night patrol, our men would be lying in the road's drainage ditch, resting. Along would come the guys from the 29th Marines. Surprised to see us, they would ask, 'Who are you? Recon! What a racket. Try the infantry if you want some action.' We would laugh. Some day these rifle-slung Marines would find out to be more alert."

Chick D'Angelo, the runner for Lt. Justis Smith, in command of an 81 mm mortar platoon, says, "It was a twenty-mile forced march. I was the rear guard for us, and they were moving so fast I lost them. I finally caught up just as they were getting ready to bivouac. One or two of the companies got involved in a firefight. The colonel became an observer for us with the 81 mms and later they counted twenty-seven confirmed kills."

Tony Walker regards the engagement as a blunder. "At Nago," says Walker, "we had pulled off to the right and let the 29th go by. They continued on to the Motobu Peninsula and ran into a major ambush. Bleasedale was relieved of his command."

"It was at Nago," also remembers Walker, "that an Army brigadier general, assigned by Gen. George C. Marshall, Army chief of staff, to observe Marine tactics, attached himself to us. When we were ordered to make two patrols at the same time, he offered to lead one of them, which he did. He took one of our platoons and a tank through Nago to the coast road around the Motobu Peninsula, where they ran into mine fields, and then returned. The remainder of the company crossed the base of the peninsula without serious opposition. The general was right to take my patrol because he wanted to see for himself, the mark of a good officer.

"We were told to take prisoners, if we could, mainly for intelligence purposes. We had a Japanese-language man with recon. Civilians were to be sent to the rear for Military Government to handle. We took very few prisoners; I can remember only one. Our men were not angels and they killed civilians on occasion. Jap soldiers were killed on sight."

Scout-sniper Jim Smith recalls "an unoffical patrol" in which he and three companions came upon a pair of men wearing robes. A search uncovered army uniforms beneath the robes. "A suggestion that we bring them in for interrogation was vetoed by BAR-man Ray Miller. He shot both of them. Miller was the most cold-blooded killer in the company. Earlier, while on patrol, we had captured two Jap soldiers. As we were discussing what to do with them, we were fired on by a lone gunman who was beating a hasty retreat into the hills. As we got to our feet, the two prisoners on the ground were the recipients of a burst from Miller's BAR. That ended the problem of what to do with the prisoners."

Chick D'Angelo recalls one of his encounters with a forlorn enemy soldier whom he was given custody of. "I made the mistake of bringing him up to the front lines," says D'Angelo. "Lieutenant Smith said to me, 'Kill him.' I said I couldn't do that, execute a man. Two other guys volunteered to do the job. You couldn't take a prisoner up to the guys on the line who maybe just saw a buddy killed."

A few miles from Noda in northern Okinawa, a Marine totes a bazooka. (*Signal Corps, U.S. National Archives*)

As Dick Thom, with the 96th Division, indicated, there was an official policy to at least spare civilians, if not soldiers. The Marines were issued a sheet with phonetic commands in the Japanese language. The phrases included "Surrender" (KOH-FOO-KOO); "If you do" (SHEE-TAH-RAH); "We will not kill" (KOH-Roh-Shee-Nah-EE). Other locutions instructed soldiers or civilians to leave pillboxes, put their hands up, drop their weapons, and offered food, tobacco and medical help.

"We were thoroughly briefed en route to Okinawa about the official way that both citizens and prisoners were to be treated," says Stormy Sexton. "We were even cautioned not to use or desecrate the Okinawa tombs. Prisoners were always sought for the information that they might provide."

Intelligence from the few individuals taken prisoner, and from aerial reconnaissance, determined that the enemy planned to make his stand amid the stubby, mountainous series of slopes that comprised Motobu Peninsula, whose land area was as great as Saipan and considerably more rugged. Considering how much it cost Marine and Army units to overwhelm the division-size garrison at Saipan, the 6th Division commanders were wary. They had learned that the principal stronghold lay on Mount Yaetake, a 1,200-foot-high pile with heavy scrub-pine forest at the base, which thinned out into rock and ever sparser shrubs at the higher elevations.

Col. Takehko Udo commanded the defenders, a mix of army troops, Okinawa conscripts and navy personnel drafted from a now useless base. The sailors contributed a pair of 6.1-inch naval guns capable of blasting any target within a range of eight to ten miles. Colonel Udo could call on batteries of 75 mm and 150 mm artillery along with an arsenal of small arms. The Motobu brigades, like their comrades elsewhere, had dug deep into the crust of Okinawa to hollow out a complex of caves and tunnels, all wired for quick communications. The Japanese also mounted an effective, swift transportation system in the near roadless wilderness by means of horses. To maintain this weapon, there were paddocks, corrals and even veterinary supplies. Udo was certainly under no illusion that he could defeat the invaders, but the Americans believed that he intended to mount a guerrilla campaign after his positions were overrun. The best means to prevent that troublesome form of warfare lay in a quick, decisive victory.

On April 9, as the GIs of the 96th Division to the south prepared for their ill-fated drive on Kakazu Ridge, the three 29th Regiment battalions engaged in a pincer movement with the leathernecks from the 4th Marine Regiment. Platoon leader Merrill McLane participated in the assault on Mount Yaetake, where enemy gunners taught him to be more circumspect.

"I was leading my platoon around the base of the mountain," says McLane, "and I took out my map and unfolded it in an open space where I could look up at the mountain. I had no sooner begun to look at it when 'Wham! Wham!' big gun shells fell around me. They came from a Japanese gun on the ridge of the mountain. The gun crew had probably been watching me with binoculars. They wasted no time in firing at me as soon as they saw me open the map—which told them I was a worthwhile target, either an officer or a senior noncommissioned officer. I scurried away before they could fire again."

Harry Manion, with his recon colleagues, adept at scrounging and improvising, quickly sought to exploit the available means of transportations. "We came across some horses and caught some. Several recon men took fast rides across the landscape and we used horses as pack animals. As usual, the high command put a stop to that."

Manion also reports on a practice that was to become a common tactic twenty-five years later in Vietnam. "While we had been moving up the island, we also were putting the torch to all huts. High command put a stop to that too."

Subjugation of Colonel Udo and his determined, skillful troops atop Mount Yaetake required a week of painstaking and bloody effort climaxed by a futile banzai charge. When the last of the hand-to-hand combat from this counterattack ceased, 347 Japanese lay dead. The Marines counted numerous other corpses in the dugouts and emplacements, victims of shelling by air, from the sea and from artillery.

Although the bastion had fallen, groups of enemy soldiers continued to strike at the invaders. "Recon Company," says Walker, "had taken a position across a road coming down from the hills, not far from division headquarters. We set up a machine gun covering the road, manned by Corp. Bill Ellis. Iolo Evans, my operations sergeant, and I were sleeping in a shelter tent right behind the gun.

"We had worked hard that day and with nightfall everyone was asleep, including Ellis. At midnight, an enemy force of about fifty, with fixed bayonets, came down the road in a column. A religious fellow, Ellis said God woke him up just as the leading enemy soldiers reached his position. Not having time to use the machine gun, Ellis picked up his .45 lying by the gun and fired five times, knocking down five Japanese soldiers. These were wounded, not killed, and all reached for hand grenades.

"Quick as a wink, Evans, with his rifle, was out of the tent and firing, killing all five enemy soldiers before they could activate and throw a single grenade. Ellis opened up with the machine gun on the remaining Japanese, and the whole firing line, now awake, joined in. At daylight, we mopped up."

Jim Powers, a communications specialist with the 8th Antiaircraft Battalion, was in support of the 6th Marine Division during its push to the north. "When our battalion was defending Nago, I was assigned to reconnaissance patrols and to holding a foxhole on the defensive perimeter. We not only had to provide AA protection for shore installations and ships in the harbor (Nago Wan) but also to cope with guerrilla attacks launched by units which escaped the trap on Motobu or had come down from northern Okinawa.

"One night while we were in Nago, the Japanese launched a night guerrilla attack on our battalion HQ area and several of our gun batteries. I was sleeping behind an L-shaped hedge in the mud. Cpl. Tony Viscona was also trying to catch some shut-eye. We had both had a very busy day and were totally exhausted.

"A Japanese machine gunner began raking the area. His bullets passed over our heads, trimming the top of the hedge as though they were a garden clipper of some sort. People were getting hit and yelling. Tony poked me in the ribs and said, 'Jim, wake up! The goddamn Japs are shooting at us!'

"I was so tired that my responses were off. It didn't sound reasonable that someone would shoot at us at 0200 in the morning. 'Don't worry,' I replied confidently. 'They're not shooting at us.' More leaves fluttered down from the hedge. But Tony was so tired that my answer sounded logical.

"Then the gunner lowered his fire so that we could have gone home just by sticking a hand up. Leaves from the hedge were flying all over. Tony came alive. 'What the hell do you mean, they're not firing at us! What the hell do you think they're doing?'

"I had to admit he had a point. We remained pinned down for a time until our people counterattacked and chased the Japs off. Eventually we ambushed and annihilated this Jap force."

Nolen Marbrey, with Company K of the 5th Regiment in the 1st Division, spent the early hours of the first night gazing at the heavens, "a cloudless sky, stars twinkling like distant candle flames. The buzz of a plane caused us to sit upright. Soon, I could separate sounds of two airplanes, and when they were overhead, the shapes identified one as a Corsair and the other a Zero. They circled and dipped, swerved and turned, playing a game of tag. A Morse code of flame would issue from one, then the other until the tail of the Zero burst into a blaze of fire and smoke. It then glided silently toward the beach. The Corsair lifted its nose and zoomed upward, then out of sight. Silence fell, like a curtain on the last act. The crash of the Zero was the final burst of applause.

"We settled down, and Hill took the first watch. It seemed as if I had only been asleep a few minutes when Hill shook my shoulder. I was awake instantly and could hear the voices babbling close in front. Down the line an M–1 came alive and screams of pain rent the air. Shadowy figures ran closer to our line of holes and I let loose with a clip of ammo. I loaded another clip into the tommy gun and raised it to shoot. Hill had been firing steadily as dark figures ran straight towards our foxhole. One fell, his hand dangling in front of my face.

"I heard a small cry and wondered why a child would be with a banzai attack. The firing ceased suddenly as one man shouted, " 'Oh my God! What have we done!' "

Marbrey explains that the Japanese had run the majority of the civilians in a village at the Marines, while screaming in the background, knowing the leathernecks expected an attack at any moment. Their strategy accomplished two things: expenditure of ammunition and a drop in morale for the Americans.

"We sat in our foxholes the rest of the night, shamed and stricken with remorse as we listened to the cries and wails of the wounded and dying. At first light, corpsmen were out tending the ones that could be helped, gently pulling an injured child from its dead mother's arms, bandaging torn bodies.

"The rising sun brought to light the enormity of the shooting. I stood, tears streaking my cheeks, looking out on the night's work. The hand that had dangled in front of me belonged to an old man, his thin arm disappearing into a Japanese soldier's jacket. Three or four feet away lay an old woman beside a little girl of five, their hands clenched together.

"In the next foxhole, Hare was vomiting convulsively and Bens stared vacantly into space. Hill, next to me, just looked at his hands and cried."

Marbrey says he tried to comfort his companions. His platoon leader and company commander passed among the shaken soldiers and offered reassurance. Within a few days, says Marbrey, the men of Company K had regained their composure and their sense of purpose.

As they trekked west they were bothered briefly by an enemy plane whose strafing run wounded a single man. "We walked for the better part of the day with only one incident," says Marbrey. "Bens shot a sniper out of a tree, and afterwards was like a man refreshed from a long drought. He joked, laughed and told us over and over how he had shot the sniper.

"'You want to know where I shot him, Bama? Shot him right in the nose. I looked at him and his nose was just a hole all the way through.' Hare remarked on the change in Bens's attitude and Bens answered, 'Just wait until you kill one, then you'll know how good it feels. I hope I get one everyday.'"

A day or so later, Marbrey, on a patrol, sniffed a vaguely familiar smell and farther on caught the gray-green glint of the ocean dappled by the sun. They had marched clear across their sector of the island without encountering serious opposition.

For Bob Craig, with the 2nd Battalion of the 1st Marine Regiment, and the others in the 1st Marine Division, the experience of northern Okinawa was quite similar. "Our division was assigned the middle sector of Okinawa and intelligence predicted that, with two major airfields, Yontan and Kadena, in that area, there would also be a substantial number of ground forces there to defend them. It soon became apparent after the landing that whatever forces were there had been withdrawn before we made direct contact with them. We spent that whole month trying to locate the line of resistance but the only contact we ever had was an occasional sniper."

On his second day, Craig noted in his diary, "Dug in for the night on a hillside above the road. Some time during my two hours off some of my boys got jittery and shot at something that moved. Next morning we found some barefoot prints so assumed it was some scared gook (native).

"Had our first Company casualty (death) this night. One of Cat's (Lt. Catterton, 1st platoon) boys got out of his hole during the night, presumably to relieve himself and when he came back his buddy thought he was a Nip and killed him."

By the third day, some Marines of the 1st Division had far outstripped their supply sources. The diary notes, "Nothing to eat except parts of K-rations we brought from the ship. Water is the real problem. We tried sucking on sugar cane stalks, but that was a big mistake because it only made us thirstier. Will have to get some [water] today or resort to local stuff which is supposedly infected with fluke that cannot be killed by halazone tablets [water purification chemical issued to GIs]."

Craig's outfit, having traversed the island from the China Sea landing to the west, now set up a base camp on a ridge overlooking the village of Gushikawa by the Pacific Ocean in the east. "We split up into combat patrols with the mission of trying to make contact with the Japs and force a fight. The work contrasted with reconnaissance patrols that normally work less exposed in order to obtain information about troop strength, weapons, etc., without making direct contact with the enemy.

"For the next three-plus weeks we made daily forays into the hills around our base but the contact was pretty much limited to individual snipers and civilians who may or may not have been enemy soldiers in disguise. Our first big discovery was a hidden eight-inch coastal gun, camouflaged back into the hillside, hardly 500 yards from our base.

"I was given the order to spike it. We had no training on how to do that to such a huge weapon so I told my demolition men to place explosive charges—Composition C–2—all around it and also in a stack of shells ready for loading into the gun.

"The fuzes were lit and we headed back to our base on the double. When it blew up, the whole top of the ridge went with it because our charges set off the rest of the ammunition stored back in the hill. If the gun crews or other soldiers were hiding back in there, they were either killed by the explosion or buried alive.

"On another occasion, we found a small extensively tunneled hill and with fresh footprints that gave the appearance of being occupied. I called for two of our company flamethrowers to position themselves at the only two entrances I could find, and at the given signal, they emptied raw napalm in and ignited it. The idea was to suck all of the oxygen out of the cave and suffocate anyone in there. But we got a real big surprise a few minutes after the napalm was lit. A terrific explosion lifted the top of the hill about six feet in the air and then it fell back into the collapsed tunnels. Smoke, flame and dirt blew out of the two openings. Platoon Sergeant Bridges got part of the blast in his face and had to be taken to a field hospital in the rear area. That hill was an ammo dump and we, with luck on our side, blew it up.

"We did this type of work for almost a month. Our recreation was to watch the nightly air raids, to see whether it would be AA or Black Widow night-fighter planes that would knock the Jap planes out of the sky. We preferred to see the Widows up there because the AAs showered us with their spent shrapnel which was just as dangerous to us as bullets and artillery fire. When the AAs were firing, if possible we would stand up and put on our helmets in order to offer the smallest possible target for that shrapnel. Some pieces would weigh several pounds."

Don Farquahar, as a replacement officer in A Company of the 7th Marine Regiment, and yet unblooded, had been anxiously anticipating an opportunity to use the special bayonet training he had assiduously practiced. "The first firefight we were in, occurred on the second day. Lieutenant Conklin got shot in the stomach and was evacuated. But there was no extensive action. We spent about a month in the middle of the island, not doing much of anything."

Another replacement, Gunnery Sergeant Elmer Johnson, the erstwhile bandsman and armorer, with others in his draft, worked on the beach breaking down the cargo ferried ashore by the likes of Coast Guardsman Joe Roddy and other boat teams from the transports that continued to jam the area. "For the first ten days," recalls Johnson, "we were strafed almost every night. On the tenth of April, the Japs seemed to send everything that could fly and lost just about all. In one forty minute period I saw ten planes, bombers, go down and from that one spot, I could only see so far. During the entire period I was on Okinawa, I never saw any Jap bomber escape. There was no way to know what happened to fighters that strafed us, but if they flew out over the ships they were shot down."

Earl Rice, now a rifleman with the same A Company as Don Farquahar, unlike the replacement lieutenant, was pleasantly surprised by the quietude of the first few days. "We didn't run into anybody until the third day, when we encountered a Jap patrol. Pop Wilson killed one and got his rifle. He carried it around with him a good part of the time. After that, we moved here and there and after a few more days, we even stopped moving about. We stayed in one place.

"The very first night that we dug in those damn hills, I dug in with a guy named William Arndt. He come over as a corporal, I think because he had some sort of pull, in Washington. He was the group leader. We were chatting; there wasn't anything else to do. Meanwhile, the Navy is getting pounded. You could hear the suicide planes coming over, one after another. They had that distinctive sound; their motor was so different from our planes. You could hear all those bangs. The ships were getting just blasted.

"Arndt and me were talking. He told me that he went with Truman's daughter. I didn't even know who Truman was. He said he wasn't much involved and met this other girl; she was the daughter of some bigshot on the St. Louis (Post-)Dispatch. Arndt was a nice guy, highly intelligent.

"We were still sharing a hole a few days later when we got the news that Franklin Delano Roosevelt had died [April 12, 1945]. That's how I knew who Truman was for sure, since he'd be the new president.

"We had a few tiny encounters. Speedy Martin, one of my closest friends, whom I owed thirty bucks, was hit by some damn Jap sniper, shot him through the stomach. I talked to Speedy, chatted with him. I thought he was going to be all right, but Speedy passed away.

"When we got to areas where we stayed for a few days," Rice continues, "I would go out on my little tours, most of the time taking somebody with me. I usually went to the tombs because that's where most everything was. I didn't realize there were so many damn snakes though. I'd go into there, get my souvenirs. I sent my cousin a whole bunch of beautiful silks, one of the flag with a painting on it. The folks at home loved everything until they found out that it came from the tombs. Then they threw it all in the garbage. That really teed me off. They coulda wrapped it up and saved it for me.

"It was probably wrong to take the stuff but that was then. One time I went with Parkinsinger, whose father had been a thirty-year marine. When we come back, the damn company had moved out. He started to bawl about his father and that we'd get a court-martial and get kicked out. I thought he would have a hemmorhage. I told him not to worry; I'd take the blame.

"It took us an hour but we found the company. One lieutenant wanted to run us up for a court-martial. But all we had to do was dig a latrine, a big hole. Last time I ever went out, I was alone and I got the biggest scare. I got to the tomb and there was a horse there. I thought I could hear water, like from a faucet. But it was blood dripping off the horse. That was my last time I ever went into a tomb looking for souvenirs."

Accounts from 1st Division Marines almost make their first month on Okinawa seem like a gambol in the country. But there was a grim side and danger for the unwary. "There were no heavy engagements with the enemy when we moved north," says Jim Moll. "It was more like trying to find the enemy and getting caught in ambushes.

"One day, a platoon from one of the other companies went out and never returned. The next morning, I had to take a patrol to try and find them. We had been on so many patrols the week before and it was our turn to rest. I asked for volunteers, and ten of us took off about four o'clock in the morning so that we could reach the area they were supposed to patrol before daybreak.

"Just before the sun came up, we found the whole platoon dead, on top of a ridge. It looked like they had been ambushed. Ahead was a much higher ridge. We climbed it and fortunately found one of their guards [Japanese] asleep at his post. We silenced him with a K-bar knife.

"A little further ahead, we could see a trace of smoke. We snuck up and surrounded the area. We found about ten Japs sitting around a fire, preparing to have breakfast. For security reasons we had to eliminate all of these men. We continued our search but could not find any more Japs.

"I've often thought about the Marines killed in that ambush. It looked as if they never had a chance to fire their weapons and I would have thought some would have jumped for cover to return fire. I suppose whoever led the patrol should not have taken them onto the crest of the ridge, but maybe he had a reason. It baffled me then and still does.

"A short time before all this happened, some men in our platoon went out on a patrol and were ambushed. One of the guys by the name of Grier had asked me if he could borrow my Marine binoculars. I said okay, but don't come back if you lose them. Grier was wounded and didn't come back to the company again. But on this patrol where we found the Japs at breakfast, I found my binoculars among the possessions of one of the officers."

Ernie Pyle chose to accompany elements of the 1st Marine Division. He wrote: "You may have wondered why I was carrying three life belts on dry land. Well, I knew what I was doing all right. I just blew up my three life preservers, spread them in the foxhole, and I had the nicest improvised Simmons [mattress] you ever saw. We finally got onto that trick after a few invasions in Europe and all one summer in France . . . [Marines stare] and then say, 'Well I'll be damned. Why in the hell couldn't I have thought of that.' "

On that first night, Pyle ate K rations like the troops, staved off the chill of the Okinawa evenings, heard the occasional shots and shellfire "—the exciting, sad, weary little sounds of war"—and indulged in stargazing.

"Just at dusk three planes flew slowly overhead in the direction of the beach. We paid no attention, for we thought they were ours. But they weren't. In a moment all hell cut loose from the beach. Our entire fleet and the guns ashore started throwing stuff into the sky. I'd never seen a thicker batch of ack-ack. As one of the marines said, there were more bullets than there was sky."

Pyle's stint with the Marines exposed him to no combat and focused on the American passion for souvenirs. "One marine had a Jap photo album in his hand. One had a wicker basket. Another had a lacquered serving tray. They even had a Columbia phonograph with Jap records strapped onto a horse. Many of them wore Japanese insignia or pieces of uniform." The Marines with Pyle occupied a small village, where they seized the opportunity to launder their single set of filthy clothes, wearing liberated kimonos as they scrubbed away. "Later an order came out that any Marine caught wearing Jap clothing would be put on burial detail. Maybe that was to keep Marines from shooting each other by mistake."

A pair of youthful Japanese soldiers surrendered, enabling one Marine to add an enemy weapon to his bag. "That rifle was the envy of everybody; the other boys tried to buy or trade him out of it. Pop Taylor offered $100 for it and the answer was no. Then Taylor offered four quarts of whisky. The answer was still no. Then he offered eight quarts. Ossege [owner of the rifle] weakened a little. 'Where would you get eight quarts of whisky?' Pop said he had no idea. So Ossege kept the rifle."

Pyle continued his stock in trade, brief paragraphs describing a soldier, with his hometown carefully appended. His willingness to share the hardships and danger of the lower ranks, plus this technique that

GIs from the 77th Division train their rifles on enemy positions on Ie Shima. (*Signal Corps, U.S. National Archives*)

gave a man a brief moment of notice in the local newspapers, endeared him to his companions.

After two weeks on the island, he remarked, "The boys of my regiment were continuously apologizing to me because the Okinawa campaign started out so mildly. They felt I might think less of them because they didn't show me a blood bath. Nothing could have been further from the truth. I was probably the happiest American there about the way it turned out for us. I told them that kind of campaign suited me . . ." But in fact, the lack of fighting in his area gnawed at Pyle. When he heard that troops from the 77th Infantry Division would be landing at Ie Shima, the small island off the northeast coast, he arranged for a transfer to that operation.

The two Marine Divisions would spend roughly one month securing the northern half of the Great Loochoo. The 6th Division reported a body count of more than 2,500 dead, with forty-six prisoners. The outfit mourned 236 dead, 1,061 wounded and seven missing. Figures for the 1st Marine Division were considerably lower. While, in terms of Okinawa real estate, the Marines could boast of capturing a substantial portion of the territory, the figures reveal that, at most, they had defeated three or four percent of the enemy. Close to 100,000 of the defenders, in accordance with Colonel Yahara's strategy, had manned the redoubts south of the beach landing sites.

CHAPTER XVII

IE SHIMA

Well pleased by the success of the Marine campaign on the upper half of the island, even as the Army divisions to the south reeled from the savage response of the enemy, the brass advanced the schedule for possession of Ie Shima, an island a mere three and a half miles off the northwest coast. Its ten square miles, dominated by a large plateau, promised to provide an excellent airfield for the final assault upon Japan, and the invasion was set for April 16. The 77th Division, aboard troop transports since the capture of Kerama Retto a few days before Love Day, received the assignment.

Intelligence estimated a force of 2,000 defenders, a mix of battle-experienced soldiers who had fought in Manchuria and labor units. The Japanese command on Okinawa, realizing that Ie Shima's forces could be expected to hold out for only a few days, directed the airfields on the island be destroyed with ditches and holes pockmarking the runways, pimples of rocks and dirt to hamper any reclamation project. To further deter use of the facilities, an elaborate net of mines awaited the unwary.

The resident troops constructed defensive positions around Mount Iegesugu, a 600-foot-high rocky tower known as "the Pinnacle" or "the Needle" to soldiers, and which overlooked the remainder of the largely flat terrain. From the Pinnacle, excellent fields of fire covered the gentle, southeastern beaches, nominally the prime site for invaders.

Because of the strength of these emplacements, the Japanese, burrowed in well-concealed and protected caves, tried to seduce their foes into the belief that the southeastern beaches were more vulnerable than the steeper shores to the west. To deceive the Americans, the defenders held their fire when recon parties had approached the bait; one U.S. serviceman actually strolled a few yards along the shore, surveying the area without drawing a single round. The well-disciplined Japanese soldiers hid themselves from the prying eyes of observation planes that flew as low as 100 feet over the site. On the other hand, anyone attempting to gather information about the more vulnerable beaches quickly came under fire, as if these places were where invaders could expect intense opposition.

In spite of all of the guile and camouflage, the 77th Division brass spotted the trap. They drafted plans which specified landings on the south and southwest coasts by the 305th and 306th Regiments supported by field artillery, including one unit set up on a sandy islet four miles off Ie Shima. The third regiment of the 77th, the 307th, minus a battalion maintaining control over Kerama Retto, was not immediately available. The Tenth Army had nominated it for another feint at one of the Okinawa beaches as part of an April 19 push.

The beach choices dismayed those charged with supply because high, jagged coral reefs limited the use of landing craft. General Bruce's staff, however, believed that a quick breakthrough would enable them to open up easier access. And the Americans committed one serious blunder; with aerial inspection unable to find Japanese soldiers, they undercounted the number of hostile forces awaiting their arrival. Bruce advised the Tenth Army commander, General Buckner, on April 6: ". . . original estimate of enemy is considerably reduced. It is planned to take entire division to target area; secure island quickly with minimum forces, less heavy equipment."

While the top echelons plotted their future, the troops remained on the transports. "Following the *Henrico* incident," remembers Frank Barron, "our ships moved to the south to get farther away from the kamikazes. We got our weapons and ourselves cleaned up, did calisthenics on the main deck, had Sunday church services, conducted by yours truly, and studied the half-dozen operational plans any one of which we could be ordered to execute. We were informed of the new regimental staff, and we heard, too, about the death of President Roosevelt [April 12].

"About April 14, we received word to prepare for an assault landing on Ie Shima. Division landed three battalions of artillery on Minna Shima, a small island just south of Ie, so that, in addition to Navy and Air support, we had our own artillery shelling the beaches just ahead of

Mt. Iegesugu towers over the rest of the island of Ie Shima off the northwest coast of Okinawa. *(Signal Corps, U.S. National Archives)*

our landings. It also gave us the availability of artillery any time we needed it."

During the three-day period prior to the debarkation of the GIs on "W-Day," naval guns and aircraft furiously bombarded Ie Shima. A cloud of smoke and dusk soon enveloped Mount Iegusugu until it faded from sight. Said Bruce, aboard the U.S.S. *Panamint,* "On the morning of April 16, the skies were clear; the sun warmed the chilled air; the seas were calm, the most magnificent weather conditions I've ever seen for an amphibious operation."

And when the Liberty Division soldiers headed for the beach, it seemed almost a repeat of Love Day. Bruce noted, "Our good fortune continued because we landed, apparently, where the Japs did not expect us. Only scattered light resistance was met during the first hour or so."

"Light resistance," while gratifying to upper echelons, still means casualties, and those upon whom injury is inflicted can find little solace in the term. Buckner Creel describes the landing for his outfit as "rather uneventful, although the amtracs on either side of mine in the first wave hit aerial bombs planted in the ground. One was blown upside down; the other lost a track." These incidents aside, Creel and companions made swift initial progress. "We swept over the airfield with virtually no opposition."

The experience for Barron and Company A of the 305th replicated Creel's. "The landing went off like clockwork and we had little opposition. As soon as we moved inland, we encountered land mines. They ranged from hand grenades triggered by trip wires to 500-pound bombs buried in the roads. We lost two lieutenants almost immediately from land mines. One of them, battlefield-promoted Lt. Donald Flower, formerly my C Company 1st Sgt., was placed on a jeep ambulance with several other wounded. En route to the beach, they hit a mine that blew them all up."

Promoted to executive officer of Company C, in the 706th Tank Battalion, William Siegel commanded a tank that first day of the invasion. "My tank had no sooner come ashore when I was immediately ordered to rescue an infantry platoon pinned down by Jap small-arms fire on a plain about 300–400 yards from the beach. We were able to bring this unit out under extreme small-arms fire with no casualties by backing the tank up and the infantrymen using us for cover.

"When we had landed, we had water cans and cases of 10-and-1 rations tied on the outside of the tank, but due to the apparent urgency of our mission, we did not have time to remove these items. When we completed the mission, all the water cans were bullet-riddled and the canned goods had exploded, leaving food and tomato sauce running down the sides of the tank."

Larry Gerevas, a newcomer to Company K, 307th Regiment, while it recovered from Leyte, considered himself lucky, first having escaped injury when a kamikaze smashed into his troopship off Okinawa, and then when the regiment remained in reserve for Kerama Retto and Okinawa. However, he now found himself on a landing boat headed for Ie Shima. "There was no enemy fire as we pulled into this small cover. The beach was surrounded on three sides by a steep, crescent-shaped slope rising about thirty feet to the island's plateau. We dug in as well as we could in the coral sand. That night, we repelled a banzai attack. An old man was killed while trying to spear one of our men. Heavy explosions shook the ground during the night, caving in foxholes dug in the coral sand slope. We thought it was Jap artillery, but it was the Navy underwater demolition team, blasting the coral reef to open way for supply ships."

Earl Miller, who had given up a draft deferment as a farmer, joined a weapons platoon machine-gun squad on Leyte, with Buckner Creel's outfit. "In the Philippines, I got in on the 'mopping up' and had been accepted immediately by the combat veterans, and being placed with them probably saved my life. I learned very quickly from them." On Kerama Retto, Miller helped plant an American flag. But the level of combat intensity stepped up on Ie Shima.

Concrete pillboxes halted Miller and his associates. "Navy airplanes were called in to soften up those positions. After the five planes made one pass and started a second one, a Corsair was hit by one of our own artillery shells and exploded into a thousand pieces in front of us. The poor guy never knew what hit him."

Joe Budge, the Scottish-born, Hawaiian sugar-plantation technician, now a sergeant replacement in a mortar section with Company D of the 305th, boarded an amphtrac in the belly of an LST for the final ride in. "Meanwhile, various kinds of hell were turned loose on the island from at least one battleship and two heavy cruisers. I remember one of the cruiser guns blowing a perfect smoke ring which sailed off into the clouds. Most impressive of all was the rocket ship, an LST with banks of rockets fired in waves from its deck, a fearsome sight and even more fearsome to hear . . . roaring and screaming of rockets and a thunderous echo from the shore, which disappeared under a gray blanket of smoke sparkling with red flashes.

"Someone wondered out loud if anyone could live through that, and a sergeant said not to worry, there would be plenty left. 'Right now,' he said, 'they will be running around a-jibber-jabbering to themselves and a-sharpening their swords.' He asked me if I was scared and I said not yet. He said, 'Well, you better be sceered [sic] and stay sceered. That way you will react quicker. Adrenalin or something.'

"Someone had asked him what the island looked like as an objective for infantry. He peered at it for a while, noting that it was a flat plain, dominated by a pyramidal-like hill, militarily uninviting [one might ask if any place is militarily inviting for invaders confronting hostile forces]. He grunted and, obviously with unfond memories of the South Pacific, found something good to say. "Waal, anyway, there ain't no goddamn palm trees on it."

"At the moment," says Budge, "I was more worried about our mode of transport than the Japanese, so I unbuckled my ammunition belt, which meant that if it came to swimming in a hurry, I could shrug off all my equipment and retain my rifle, with which we had been trained to swim. One soldier was crossing himself and muttering prayers.

"Presently, the man beside the driver of our conveyance winked at me through a small hatchway and then slammed it shut. We roared down the ramp and bobbed reluctantly up to the surface, then roared across a submerged sandbar to the accompaniment of a few pillars of water that suddenly appeared near us, without apparent cause.

"As soon as the tractor heaved itself up on the beach, it dropped its rear ramp and we debarked to run as fast as we could through scrub bushes into the open that lay beyond. The riflemen among us pushed on while we set down the mortars and waited for further orders. A few yards away lay another amphtrac, fitted with a turret like a tank, but which now lay upside down with a huge hole in its bottom. Someone asked about the crew but the rest of us just looked at the smoking, shattered hulk and said nothing.

"A certain amount of small-arms fire passed overhead and we could hear our own infantry also at work. One could sometimes tell what was happening [from the sound] . . . the chatter of a Nip machine gun getting more and more erratic as the boys closed in on it under cover, from the slow thump-thump-thump of a BAR, and a spattering of our own rifle fire. Then might come the thud and whine of a U.S. hand grenade; the whine being the flying fragments, and the Nip gun would cease forever. Sometimes there was no whine, which meant the grenade had been thrown into a pillbox.

"A jeep came down, this one fitted with brackets to hold litters. There were four litters, all occupied. It stopped by us and one of us recognized a friend and walked over to see him. There was a tremendous explosion under the jeep and the spare tire went humming over our heads. A few pieces of metal remained of the jeep and nothing of the men except for the GI who had been walking toward it.

"Now, he was on the ground, crawling frantically away from the site of the explosion, dragging a leg, until somebody got to him and made him lie still. 'If that was a mine, it was the damndest mine I ever saw,' said someone. We found plenty of them, large sea mines or airplane bombs, sticking up through the ground, with a rubber tubelike fuze visible above the surface.

"Someone said that ——— was on that jeep. Someone else said, 'Christ, he had a wife and three kids.' From the moment of that explosion, the GIs had assumed their combat faces—gray, grim, tired and unchanging, whatever befell.

"Odd scraps of news reached us . . . the regiment had covered the whole western plain of the island with little opposition and was sweeping towards the pyramid. We were still to wait until our heavy mortars were needed. So we stayed there the rest of the day and then dug in for the night around a series of rock piles."

According to Bruce, during the first day, the advance on the right flank fell short of its goal, but the regimental team on the left succeeded in occupying its objective by midafternoon. The infantrymen, like Budge and Creel, bedded down until the next morning.

The achievements on W-Day left in their wake hidden dangers. J. G. Haynes, a sergeant with the 132nd Combat Engineers, had arrived with the initial assault waves and encountered no enemy fire. "After all the available supplies had been landed and stored," says Haynes, "a bivouac was established. Late in the afternoon, a nearby cave was discovered. Two fellow sergeants and I decided it should be investigated. [Everett] Rankin and I felt that members of a line company, which was better trained for such a task than men from a Headquarters and Supply Company, should be approached to do the job. [Bernard] Perrault, who had just received a 'Dear John' letter from his fiancée, really was in a kind of 'I don't care what happens' mood, said we were being overcautious.

"Since he was the noncom in charge of plans and training and was a tech sergeant, while we were staff sergeants, we allowed him to prevail. He had only taken a step into the mouth of the cave when there were rifle shots. Since he did not reappear, we assumed they were not his and that he'd been hit. The noise had brought an officer and some members of a rifle company to the site. The cave could not be sealed or grenades thrown into it until it was determined if Perrault were still alive at the bottom of the shaft.

"But before the body could be retrieved, Sgt. Robert Devers, a platoon leader from C Company, was killed. At that point, grenades were thrown into the cave. Five Japanese soldiers ran out of another entrance. Before they were killed, one of them wounded WO Elroy Titus of our company, who was resting near the camouflaged alternate entrance to that cave.

"Progress that afternoon was much slower. While a couple of miles had been gained in the morning, the most any of the battalions moved in the afternoon was about 300 yards. A few mines had been placed near the coastline, but greater numbers were detected as the troops moved toward Iegesugu and the town of Ie. Fortunately, most of them were aerial bombs, buried nose-down, and were crudely laid and poorly camouflaged. Still, time had to be taken to mark their locations until they could be removed.

"A ceramic object that was discovered was at first regarded as a possible new type of land mine. Later, a bomb expert identified it as a sealed burial urn. Although the mines were, for the most part, easily spotted, the mere fact they were there made the use of tanks, self-propelled guns and other mobile equipment almost impossible for the first and most of the second day. That, in turn, made it much more difficult to clean out hundreds of caves which were nests for snipers and small mortars."

Gunner Dick Forse, with a Cannon Company M–8, self-propelled 75 mm gun, climbed up to remove waterproof tape around the turret after arrival on the beach. "I heard a machine gun and couldn't tell whether it was a U.S. or Japanese one. But I dropped down on my hands and knees. I tried a second time to strip off the tape, and when the machine gun went off, I knew it was a Japanese one because of its rapid rate. I tried a third time to get to the tape, but that machine gun opened up again and I gave up for the moment.

"We had another M–8 coming in from the sea, and I tried to signal them there was a machine gun firing at this beach. I saw spouts of water around the M–8, but they weren't paying any attention. They were lucky, because that gunner must have run off. Lt. Jesse Gershberg, our platoon leader, and two others went back for orders. A machine gun opened up, hit a nearby pine tree, and a piece struck Gershberg in the forehead. But he stayed with us.

"We started up again and found we were all by ourselves. There were no targets and I didn't know what we were doing. Then we came across a bunch of guys from our company, and they warned us to go between the tape [put down to indicate a safe path through mined areas]. It was nervewracking; there were so many of them, aerial bombs buried in the ground, and the pressure of a finger could set them off.

"But you could see where the mines were, even though they tried to camouflage the spot. They would plant grass around them but it died, turning yellow, while in the safe spots, the grass was really green.

"Gershberg learned that the road up ahead wasn't secured. We entered a field where there were a bunch of Americans moving towards a woods. I watched guys creep along, like they were reluctant to move out. Then one would get up, run and then drop. Boom! I thought, boy, these Japs are accurate with their mortars. I saw what I thought was a knapsack but it was half a body; he must have triggered one of the mines.

"We settled in for the night and it was peaceful for a while, and then there was an explosion. They were attacking with satchel charges and grenades. I heard a clang against the side of the tank. It must have been a grenade. In the morning I found a bone, a human knee bone. It must have come from a Jap who ran at the tank and blew himself up with one of the satchel charges."

General Bruce reported that similar events occured every night, and "progress was slow, the fighting became more intense." Indeed, at the conclusion of the first day, with his forces stopped by intense mortar, artillery and machine gun fire, Bruce conceded, "It was necessary to reorganize and get set before an attack. Meanwhile, there were several accurate air strikes on Mount Iegesugu, and naval gunfire ringed three sides of the mountain."

On April 19, the day the big push for Ie Shima town and the Pinnacle started, Sgt. Henry Lopez of C Company, 307th, was on a landing craft off the Pacific coast of Okinawa. "We were making a feint landing toward the Minatoga beaches. Most of the landing craft were empty except for navy personnel that manned the boats." The operation had nothing to do with Ie Shima; it was intended to keep reinforcements from moving north to aid the hard-pressed defenders along the Shuri Line.

A few days later, as Bruce realized the degree of difficulty confronting his forces, he would recall elements of the 307th Regiment, which, having performed a mock invasion to fool the enemy, would come ashore to add their weight to the attack.

At sea on the *Goodhue,* Ed Fitzgerald, of the 307th's Service Company, fell into conversation with Sgt. Joe Price, a former New York City doorman and amateur showman who amused his companions with a soft-shoe routine and a ditty titled, "Down at the Corner of Thoity-Thoid." Says Fitzgerald, "I told Joe he had missed out on the landing at Ormoc in the Philippines and he ought to come with us, even though he could have stayed on the ship. 'You'll always remember being in on this,' I said to him. 'And you'll get a D-Day arrowhead [decoration for an invasion].' Joe never forgave me for talking him into it.

"They had told us it would be a walkover at a briefing. The company commander and I lived together. He told me the bombing from the air and the shelling from the sea would leave nothing. That night we dug a slit trench and there were low bushes around us. By morning, every one of those bushes had been chopped into tiny pieces. Instead of a walkover, it was going to be three or four days of unremitting combat."

"That first evening," says Barron, of A Company, 305th Regiment, "I had a man shot through the calf of his leg. It was too late to send him back to the beach. The aid men, who were totally dedicated, efficient and courageous, dug a slit trench for the wounded man after dressing his wound and giving him a shot of morphine.

"During the night, I was awakened by voices. It sounded like an argument but a brief one—then a rifle shot—then quiet. At daybreak I learned that the wounded soldier, lying flat on his back, awoke, and standing over him was a man with the point of his bayonet inches away from his belly. The soldier slapped the bayonet to one side, screamed and struggled with the man. A friend nearby dived into the fray. Someone said, 'It's a Jap!' Someone else insisted, 'It's not a Jap!' Then, 'It is a Jap; hold him!' It was a Jap and the single shot killed him.

"When we had a man wounded, the Japs often would allow a litter team to come forward, administer aid, place the wounded soldier on stretcher, and when they raised it for carrying out, the Japanese then would open fire on the group."

On April 17, the 77th welcomed the presence of Ernie Pyle, who had chafed at the relative absence of action with the Marines on Okinawa. Pyle once explained the lure of the battlefield. "The front does get into your blood and you miss it and want to be back. Life up there is very simple, very uncomplicated, devoid of all the jealousy and meanness that float around a headquarters, and time passes so fast it's unbeliev-able. [I tried] not to take any foolish chances but there's no way to play it completely safe and still do your job."

After the kamikaze hit on the *Henrico* wiped out the two top officers of the 305th Regiment, command fell to Lt. Col. Joseph Coolidge. Pyle began his tour on Ie Shima with Coolidge's organization. In a memoir twenty years later, Coolidge wrote: "Every man in the outfit anticipated this visit with pleasure and pride and with the hopes of meeting this great little fellow who had portrayed the lot of the doughboy in Europe with such moving simplicity. Now we would have our chance to show him that fighting in the Pacific was just as rough and dirty, and a lot more unglamorous than that in civilized Europe."

The correspondent joined a group at an observation post overlooking a plain that led to a village at the foot of the Needle. According to Coolidge, two or three other reporters, "acting like general aides," accompanied Pyle. The regimental commander noted that when the other reporters stood up to get a better view, the defenders apparently noticed the activity and began dropping mortar shells. Those who had come with Pyle "had seen enough and left us. Ernie remained in his corner until the final action of the day."

Coolidge says that when the newspaperman left his jeep to talk to a group of soldiers, it seemed as if he wanted to speak to them as much as they wanted to chat with him. "In the twenty-four hours that he was with our regiment, he talked little but listened lots. He was a most retiring, shy individual. Around officers he seemed to try to keep out of the way, but around soldiers [Coolidge made this odd distinction between enlisted men and the commissioned ranks] he was at home, and much of the shyness dropped away . . . he was considerate and understanding, interested in everyone around him. He must have promised many that when he returned to the States, he would send a card to the family of each man . . ."

On the following day, Pyle visited with General Bruce at the 305th command post. Among other topics, Bruce spoke of the necessity for intensive operations to eradicate enemy soldiers "who had been hiding as much as 48 hours or more in cleverly concealed positions and who would suddenly pop up behind and execute a raid or deliver sniper fire." After scrawling autographs for several GIs, Pyle accepted a ride with Coolidge—bound for an observation post, according to Bruce, although Coolidge claimed their destination was division headquarters. Five men packed into the jeep, a driver, two members of the regimental staff, plus the lieutenant colonel and Pyle.

"Our route," wrote Coolidge, "lay well within the area we had already 'secured'; it paralleled a coral cliff about 300 yards to our left. We fell in behind three trucks and another jeep [with military police]. Just ahead lay a road or cart trail junction. On either side, two infantry battalions had bivouacked the night before and were packing up after breakfast, getting ready to move up to the fighting. Just as we reached the road junction, a burst of machine gun fire exploded around us; our jeep, with two flat tires, stopped quickly, and we, in turn, exploded from the jeep to the ditch on either side of the road.

"Ernie and I, on the right side of the jeep, landed in the ditch away from the line of fire; the others, we hoped, had found shelter on the left side of the road. I had seen Barnes, our driver, jumping to the left. Ernie and I were quite safe; the ditch dropped off three feet from the side of the road. The jeep, fortunately, had taken the brunt of the burst, two flat tires, a jagged hole in the bumper and a hole in the radiator. Ernie reported he was safe.

"I told him to keep down while I checked the rest of the party; I raised my head and called each man in turn. They all reported that they were safe in the sheltering ditch. Then, another burst from that machine gun. One shot kicked dust in my face, but ricocheted over my head. I ducked and turned to Ernie. He was lying on his back; his hands, resting on his chest, were holding a knitted arctic cap, which he was known to carry at all times. His face was composed. It must have taken an appreciable time for me to realize that he had been hit; no blood flowed, and only after I looked at him more closely, did I see the hole through each temple. His bullet had not ricocheted."

In a scene that presages war in Vietnam twenty-five years later, flames, ignited by GIs, burn huts during the battle for Ie Shima. Shortly after the photograph was taken, the soldier at right was killed. (*Jack Lewis*)

"A platoon was dispatched to search out the machine gunner, but hidden in the coral crevices which honeycombed the entire island, that Jap might well have escaped for another day. A tank was sent in to pick up Ernie's body.

"The ironic element to the story is that the two battalions on either side of the road knew only that machine gun fire had hit quite close to them. The men felt no danger nor did they know the tragic loss of this fine Little Man [*sic*]. The machine gunner must have located himself well back in the crevice so that his line of fire was limited to the road junction, and he patiently awaited a vehicle carrying personnel, a far more valuable target than the lumbering two and a half ton truck which preceded our jeep."

Coolidge's statement implies that the area and road seemed relatively inactive, and Bruce remarked, "Many vehicles had been over [the road] and we all thought [it] was safe." But to the infantrymen near the site, danger lurked constantly. Joe Budge, with his mortar section, recalls, "That night I kept really far down in my foxhole for two reasons. One was that a U.S. machine gun was firing protectively very close over my head. Another was that a Japanese heavy machine gun was chipping dirt off the lip of it all night." When morning came, Budge observed a jeep with an antenna—a sign of a radio and of personnel of some importance —run along a road the troops knew was covered by enemy fire and clearly visible to spotters on the Pinnacle. Budge saw the occupants of the jeep fling themselves into the roadside ditch and then watched as one lifted his head for a peek at the action. "The gun fired a short burst and the man was dead." Only later did the sergeant learn the victim was Pyle.

Frank Barron was also in the vicinity. "Things were fairly quiet. Every once in a while a Jap would fire a few rounds at us; once or twice a few Jap mortar rounds landed near us. I was discussing our situation with my platoon leaders when a jeep with four or five people drove into my company area. They drew Jap fire, so the driver stopped quickly and all aboard piled out behind a low bank that paralleled the road.

"A minute later, my company radio operator came over and said somebody was trying to get our regimental commander, Colonel Coolidge, and he thought he was in the ditch by the jeep. I had heard the shot when the jeep stopped and someone said, 'I believe they got the driver.' So I told the operator, "Callard, take the radio over and let the colonel take the call. But take it on the double; I think the jeep driver just got hit." A few minutes later, Callard was back—he only had to go twenty or thirty yards. He said, 'Captain, that wasn't the driver. That was Ernie Pyle and he's dead.' "

Remarks Budge, "Everybody makes mistakes in war but the colonel who ran that jeep up that road needed his head examined. Running an obvious command jeep along a road which, like everything else on the island, was under direct observation was an incredibly foolish thing to do."

Coolidge glossed over the necessity for him and the other survivors from the ill-fated jeep to crawl along the ditch to gain their safety. Because of the continuing bursts from that machine gun, which defied even tank fire, the body of the correspondent could not be recovered until hours later, after the dark of night masked movement.

When Bruce learned in a series of somewhat garbled messages of Pyle's death, he immediately sent a message to Tenth Army headquarters, "Regretfully report Ernie Pyle who so materially aided in building morale for troops killed by surprise Jap mg fire while standing beside regimental commander of foot troops, 77th Division, Lt. Col. Coolidge on outskirts Ie Shima town about 10:15 today."

To the press Bruce said, "It's hard to tell how much Ernie Pyle meant to the men of our services . . . The Jap machine gun sniper who hid within our lines caused the death of a buddy of the 77th Division." And

Coast Guard photographer Jack Lewis (left) and *Time-Life* correspondent Bill Walton flank the marker erected by the 77th Division in honor of reporter Ernie Pyle on Ie Shima.

when the GIs hastily erected a crude memorial, Bruce decreed an inscription: AT THIS SPOT, THE 77TH INFANTRY DIVISION LOST A BUDDY ERNIE PYLE, 18 APRIL 1945. The body was at first interred in a cemetery for Liberty Division dead on Ie Shima and later transferred to the Punchbowl military graveyard on Oahu.

His death was mourned by many American fighting men, including those whom he had never encountered. Ellis Moore, with the 96th Division, wrote to his Aunt Janie: "Ernie Pyle's death came as quite a blow to all of us. We all sort of feel that we knew him personally. He is the only correspondent I have read who has been able to convey the full horror and suffering of war without resorting to exaggeration and misleading facts . . . Ernie Pyle was the only one who seemed to be able to write accurately about this plain day in and day out weariness which is actual combat."

CHAPTER XVIII

BLOODY IEGESUGU

Joe Budge recalls that on the day the machine gun cut down Pyle, he moved along the shore as the troops encircled the town. "A brigadier general, our assistant division commander [Edwin H. Randle], was strutting around the beach with a walking stick, a habit he had picked up from the British in Libya. He encountered a little yellow sparrow of a soldier using a mine detector on the beach, but with a very bad case of the shakes.

"Son, where is your officer?" inquired Randle.

"Dead, sir" stammered the GI.

"Then where is your NCO?"

"Dead, sir."

"Where is the rest of the bomb disposal squad?"

"Sir, I *am* the bomb disposal squad."

Budge reports the general gulped and said very gently, "Son, get on that landing barge and come back to the ship with me." According to the mortar section sergeant, booby-trapped aircraft bombs planted as mines had wiped out almost all of the disposal experts.

Larry Gerevas and Company K of the 307th left the comparatively quiet beach area and marched along a dirt road above the beach. "Within minutes machine gun bullets were cracking all around us and we ran for cover. No one was hit and it seemed the firing came from a great distance. There were a lot of trees and brush at the sides of the road, so we took advantage of this cover as we continued on our way.

We all knew for sure that our movements were being observed by the Japs on the Pinnacle.

"Later, as we tried to climb over a saddle on a small ridge, mortars began falling on the only path. The mortars landed every thirty seconds. As soon as one hit, the platoon leader would point to one of us and tell us, 'Go!' The path was very slippery from the rains and when it was my turn, I started to run. About halfway there, I fell and started sliding down the slope. My rifle flew out of my hands and I knew it was only a matter of seconds before the next mortar shell exploded. There wasn't time to retrieve my rifle. I dug my fingers into the muddy path and pulled myself over the hill just before the next mortar blast.

"On the other side of the hill I expected to find the rest of my platoon, but there was nobody in sight. Here I was, without my rifle and alone. I knew that I had to find my group quickly. Nearby I found a group of tombs. I decided to hide in one for a while until I could make a plan. I decided to retrace my steps to see which direction the others went after they came over the hill. As I was doing this, I saw some medics placing a wounded man in an ambulance. I ran over and asked for the rifle of the wounded man. They handed me the weapon and I found my platoon."

Enemy infiltrators and nighttime attacks bedeviled the U.S. troops. Shortly before dawn on April 19, some thirty Japanese soldiers suddenly materialized in the bivouac of the 304th Field Artillery near one of the beaches. Armed with everything from spears and clubs to machine guns, they surprised the Americans in foxholes. Exploding satchel charges and grenades, slashing knives, spear thrusts and club blows punctuated a few frenzied minutes of struggle.

In his reports, Bruce recounted some details from Lt. Col. Elbert Tuttle, commander of the 304th Artillery Battalion, who had been sound asleep in his pup tent. Tuttle told Bruce, "It was pitch dark. I was awakened by the sound of several rounds of small-arms fire and then heard a grenade go off very near me. Then I heard something in my tent and an explosion by my head. I was cut in the neck by what I knew was a Jap grenade. I sat up to get a bandage from my aid kit when I heard gutteral sounds and shuffling around, then a long pole thrust into the front of my tent.

"It caught me directly amidships and although it hurt, it was not disabling. I grasped the pole and struggled with it. In the meantime, the right of the tent had been slashed by a knife or a saber and I got tangled up in the canvas. I pulled myself out along the pole. While I struggled with the Jap, a second one started beating me over the head and shoulders with another club. As we fought up hill, I must have pushed the first Jap into another officer's foxhole because I later learned that a Lt. [John] Holt had shot and killed a Jap crawling out of his hole. The other Jap also fell backwards, for some reason which I did not understand. He was later found dead, having fired his last grenade into his stomach."

Tuttle scuttled in the direction of the aidmen for help with his wound. "I saw a figure, which I hoped was Corporal Becker, busily stabbing a Jap whose head was just over the edge of the hole. I hoped it was not the reverse. It wasn't. I was in the hole back of them and found a second aidman there. They handed me some gauze and got out a carbine and a .45 just in time to see a figure crawling within three or four feet of our hole. We challenged him for fear it was another one of our people, but he made no sound and kept sliding down the hill, so the two men killed him firing the carbine and pistol."

The first exchanges of rifles, pistols and grenades awakened many in their foxholes or tents. A Japanese rifle butt knocked a shelter half down on Sgt. Eugene Hendricks, entangling the American in a web of canvas. However, the enemy soldier failed to follow up his advantage and vanished. The sergeant freed himself and grabbed his pistol. He saw three infiltrators setting up a light machine gun. Hendricks killed one, wounded another, and thereby prevented a probable massacre in the battalion.

Two vague forms loomed out of the darkness, advancing on Tec/4 John Sinclair. Another sergeant, John Haley, saw the threat as a ray of light gleamed from a saber swinging down upon Sinclair. Haley fired but the sword glanced off Sinclair's carbine and then bit into his left forearm until only a small strip of flesh connected it to the upper arm. Sinclair managed to empty his carbine into the attacker, using only his right arm.

With that pair of intruders routed, Sinclair staggered in search of help. Sergeant Hendricks, now armed with his M–1, was about to shoot the wounded man coming out of the darkness when he recognized Sinclair's voice. Hendricks applied a tourniquet and medics later preserved the near-severed limb.

When the melée ended, they found seven American wounded, but their nocturnal excursion left twenty-five infiltrators dead, including several who blew themselves up with grenades.

Gerevas and his companions were also dug in for that night. "One man in our platoon was nearly frozen with fear. He was really dangerous to everyone around him. We wouldn't let him have grenades during the night because he would throw them anywhere without thinking. Usually two shared a foxhole, but nobody wanted to be with him.

"That night the Japs attacked our position and we managed to kill them or drive them off. During the attack there was a lot of gunfire and grenades. When things quieted, we could hear a baby crying. We continued to throw grenades toward the sound until it stopped. The next morning we found dead Jap soldiers and women who carried spears. One of them had a baby strapped to her back. I don't think I will ever forget the sound of that crying baby.

"The really frightened guy survived the night. The following day we had to run across an open area under sniper fire to reach wooded cover. After we arrived there, grenades started falling around us. Many were duds. The scared GI was sitting with his legs spread and one of the grenades landed between his legs. He didn't move—just sat there and stared at the grenade. He was paralyzed. Thank God, it was a dud. All of us were afraid but we all felt sorry for this man who was filled with terror every moment."

In contrast to Bruce's originally somewhat optimistic outlook, Buckner Creel, with G Company of the 306th, says, "We were not led to believe that there would be light resistance. On the contrary, we were expecting moderate to heavy resistance, and that was the reason for a two-regiment assault landing." However, Alanson Sturgis, with the 292nd JASCO, recalls a briefing that described the defenders as largely unarmed Korean laborers.

Alanson found himself one night with enemy soldiers to his front and one flank. "They didn't know where we were but they started to look for us with mortars. They were close enough so that we could hear the Japanese officer giving his fire commands. That was too close. Luckily, they never found us or hit anyone. If they had wounded somebody and he yelled, then they would have realized where we were and we'd have been in real trouble.

"The next morning, the naval officer, a scout and I were drinking coffee on a stone wall when our battalion medical officer came along and gave us each a jolt of medicinal alcohol in the coffee. It looked as if it would be a better day than we thought. Then a Jap machine gun opened up while we were sitting there. We went off the wall in a hurry. The medical officer had his helmet snatched off; he found a couple of bullet creases in it. None of us were hurt but it was close."

Meanwhile, other elements from all three regiments united in an effort to capture the town and participated in the final bloody effort to eliminate the tenacious defenders hunkered down in the deep bunker-

age of Mount Iegesugu. Backed by artillery, the 305th initially gained
some ground in Ie town starting April 19, but a buzzsaw of machine gun
and mortar fire drove the attackers back from a hill that overlooked the
town. The same deadly reception met infantrymen seeking to enter the
town, where defenders hid themselves in the concrete rubble created
by incessant bombardment. Tanks and self-propelled guns halted for
fear of the abundant mines. Engineers could not clear these obstacles
because any open space lay exposed to withering scythes of bullets.

Among those advancing on the objectives were Gerevas and his buddies. "As we reached the foot of Iegesugu Mountain, an American tank
and some infantry came into an opening about 150 yards below us and
immediately started firing at us, thinking we were Japs. Our squad
leader frantically removed a bright orange banner from his pack and
held it up. The machine gun firing from the tank and the infantry rifle
fire stopped. This was the closest I came to being killed by friendly
fire."

On April 20, two battalions of the 307th pressed forward in spite of
intense fusillades from above them to finally occupy a major objective,
the town's Government House atop a hill. Their triumph proved short-
lived. A battalion of the 305th, which had seized a flanking hill, withdrew without notifying the GIs around Government House. The enemy
swarmed back onto the position vacated by the men of the 305th and
rained fire down upon the 307th's troops. Running low on ammunition
and now highly vulnerable, the infantrymen pulled back.

The 706th Tank Battalion added its armored might to the battle.
William Siegel, now executive officer for Company C, says, "Our tank
was disabled and set on fire by a satchel charge. My crew and I were
forced to abandon it and wound up in a close-quarter fight with three of
the enemy. Cpl. Kenneth Rogers was killed in this action, but we were
rescued by another unit from my platoon."

Joe Budge, as a mortar sergeant with the 305th, endured prolonged
terror. "Heavy artillery or mortar fire can be seen in any war movie, but
it is usually toned down because nobody would believe the size of the
explosion one is expected to live through. Sometimes you can hear them
coming. Usually there is too much other uproar going on, as in this case.
These shells kept making great thunderous explosions in our midst, and
flat on the ground—as flat as the human form can get when frightened
—we felt the ground viciously kick us in the belly. Things flew around,
helmets, bits of rock, bushes, branches, sometimes bits of soldiers.
There was nothing to be done except to lie there and try to be ready to

receive the horde of nasty men with bayonets and swords who were likely to show up the moment the barrage stopped.

"Then the rifle company we were supporting told us to pull back and we went with it. I grabbed the base plate of one of the mortars and proceeded to walk out of that hellfire spot toward a ruined building in a field. A standard Japanese reaction, the moment they saw anyone retreating, was to pour on the fire. This time was no exception. Unfortunately, when we pulled back, so did another rifle company, leaving a gap at the edge of the town into which the Nips poured some infantry. Every Jap weapon in or out of range opened up, mostly mortars, machine guns and rifles, but including one small field gun.

"The forty-pound mortar base plate jumped energetically and a bullet screamed off it. With considerable relief, and after resisting a strong temptation to run, I reached the ruins and lay down in a sunken road. I felt comparatively safe until a jerrycan lying by my feet jumped up with a clang and exhibited a neat bullet hole. One forgets that bullets have a dropping trajectory. We set up the mortars to be ready for any Nip attack, which, the book would have it, should come any moment. But they were too smart to charge us across a wide-open field in daylight.

"Our battalion commander had been promoted to fill one of many vacancies from the slaughter of the regimental staff on the *Henrico*. We had inherited a major who, for good reasons, carried no respect from the troops. He showed up with his radio operator. The latter squatted on the ground with his set. The major walked round and round him, actually wringing his hands and wailing out loud, 'What should I do? What should I do?'

"The radio operator's head, like an owl's, swiveled about watching him in amazement. If the troops had respected the major, this might have become a bad situation, the nervous collapse of a battalion commander at a bad moment. But the men had no expectations of anything better because of incidents with him on Guam.

"An old sergeant—or maybe he just looked old and tired—said, 'Oh, shit!' Then he calmly started giving orders. Other noncoms followed suit—there were no other officers around. Within minutes a call came over the radio for the major to report to the beach. Maj. Eugene Cook, a fine officer, took his place. We went back to where we'd been in the morning and reorganized."

Budge and his mates remained for the moment removed from the worst of the fray. "A few Nips came our way but they seemed to be stragglers. When we shot at them or threw grenades, quite often there'd be a pause for a few seconds and then an explosion of a Nip grenade and a body would fly into the air. They were blowing themselves up, being afraid of capture and incapable of figuring out a more profitable method of committing suicide, such as taking one or more of us with them.

"Throughout the night continual heavy action continued in the town around the Pinnacle. There was one particular U.S. machine gun that seemed to be firing all night. It must have used up several barrels and thousands of rounds of ammunition. One could see the constant stream of cherry red tracer bullets encountering some target at quite close range, and disappearing or ricocheting off into the night. From the opposite direction came an equally constant stream of yellower Japanese tracers.

"We discovered later, this fight ended in the CP of the 3rd Battalion with clerks, cooks and the battalion commander in hand-to-hand combat. The stubborn machine gunner, Pfc. Martin May, earned a posthumous Congressional Medal of Honor."

Nevertheless, the noose around Iegesugu tightened as the American forces enveloped the base. For Buckner Creel, with G Company of the 306th, the assignment was the northern slope of the Pinnacle. To con-

The bodies of Americans killed while fighting for Okinawa were interred in a new cemetery. (*Signal Corps, U.S. National Archives*)

solidate the attack, his outfit temporarily acted under 1st Battalion control. At 1430 on the afternoon of April 20, the troops jumped off, preceded by a concentration of shells from the 304th FA in addition to what tanks and self-propelled howitzers could toss onto the Pinnacle. C Company of the 306th led off, sprinting, falling, rising and then running again across 200 yards of open, fire-swept ground. Rushing forward in the tracks of C Company and on its flanks came the others in the assault, including Creel with G Company.

Earl Miller, the replacement machine gunner with G Company, recalls the final push up Mount Iegusugu. "It was a volcanic hill with caves three stories deep. Also a field gun on tracks behind sliding doors —all of this looking right down our throats!

"On the morning of our assault, we charged through a mine field and barbed wire on the run, stepping in the tracks of the man in front. We all made it to the base of the hill. It was the first time I had heard bullets snap and crack around my ears.

"Right after we charged through the minefield, and fell behind a big rock to catch our breath, I saw my first case of battle fatigue. ——— was not hit, but he could not move. The medics gave him a shot and sent him to the rear."

While, as Miller saw, an occasional soldier flinched, the assault brigades reached the steep slopes where the entrenched foe could only be routed with bayonets, flamethrowers, satchel charges and grenades. An observer from the War Department in Washington marveled, "It was the most remarkable thing I have ever seen. The attack looked like a Fort Benning demonstration. Why, I saw troops go through enemy mortar concentrations and machine gun fire that should have pinned them down. But instead they poured across that field and took the mountain against really tough opposition without even slowing down."

Over a period of three days, units from all three regiments fought, bled and died on the slopes, taking ground, retreating in the face of devastating onslaughts and counterattacks, and then regrouping to climb ever higher.

Even after the GIs gained the northern slopes of the 600-foot tower, groups of well-concealed, determined resisters fought on. "We were 'mopping up,' " recalls Creel, "and destroying pillboxes. We made attempts with a Japanese-language interpreter to get them to come out. Rarely would they do it. On one particular occasion, we had tried to get an unknown number of Japanese soldiers to come out but to no avail. So I gave the order to blow it. An engineer demo man 'capped and fuzed' a satchel charge, lit it and threw it into the emplacement. We waited and nothing happened. We figured it was a dud, so we threw another one in. Nothing happened; a third satchel charge followed—nothing.

"I got a hold of the engineer platoon leader, 1st Lt. Charles E. Sears, who was part of my landing team. Together we figured out that the Japanese must be pulling out the flaming fuzes on the charges as they came in. Sears got a satchel charge and he and his demo man rigged it up with about ten to fifteen fuzes, all different lengths. The last five to be lit were capped and live. When all the fuzes were lit and spurting fire, he heaved the satchel into the open door of the emplacement.

"We got down behind the berm and could picture the Japanese in there furiously pulling out the fuses, wondering which one was live. A tremendous explosion shook up all of us. All the ammo in there, as well as the three earlier satchel charges, went up at once in a sympathetic detonation."

Creel also recalls a grim moment of levity while tenuously perched on the side of Iegesugu. "We had a platoon sergeant who was quite a womanizer and considered himself very much the ladies' man. He had been bragging to the guys in the company that he was going to be the first one in G Company to get some of that Japanese 'poontang.' On the night of the 19th or 20th, we had several attacks, which we repulsed. During some of them, individual Japanese would come out of holes and caves on the mountain above us. They would have satchel charges strapped on their backs. They would come running down the mountain and when they reached our positions, they would blow themselves up and hope to take some of our guys with them.

"One of these attacks was made on our Lothario sergeant. At first light our standard practice was to sweep the area, checking for infiltrators. When the troops reached our lover, he was unhurt although very shook up. Straddling his foxhole was the lower half of a Japanese torso —obviously a female. The men informed him that he had finally gotten his wish but they thought he should not have been so brutal about it. Needless to say, we heard nothing more from him about his potential conquests."

Company K of the 307th approached a clearing on the third day of the operation. Gerevas recalls an Okinawan woman accompanied by two small boys. "When they saw us, they ran as fast as they could to escape. We caught the woman but the little boys were too quick and got away. However, as soon as they were far enough off to feel safe, they stopped and watched to see what we were going to do with their mother.

"I was holding her by her arm as we walked along a dirt road. Suddenly, she tried to pull away and kick at a wire that ran across the road. Another soldier grabbed her other arm and we lifted her over the wire. We examined the wire and saw that it stretched from a stake on one side of the road to a 500-pound bomb on the other. When we continued down the road, we spotted three more of these booby traps and lifted the woman over each. The small boys kept us in sight. When they saw we were not harming their mother, they came up. Later we turned all three over to a group collecting civilians. They were loaded on a truck and driven away."

A few days later, Gerevas's unit was ordered to secure a small hamlet. "The day before, a squad from another company had tried to enter the village and nearly all were killed or wounded. My squad was now picked for this attempt and I was made the scout. Up to that moment, I thought I had been very lucky but now I felt my luck had run out. The scout leads and is at least twenty yards in front of the others. He is the bait for a sniper and usually the first to be hit. If the scout is wounded, the rest of the squad might retreat and abandon him to the enemy. I know that's not what it is like in the movies, but it is what I saw happen in real combat.

"I knew someone had to do the job and it was my turn. We moved through the streets, expecting to be machine-gunned at any moment. When we had walked through the entire place, we turned and came back. Not a single shot was fired. The Japs had left during the night.

"During the last week of April, we dug in as we had every night since we arrived on Ie Shima. Two of us would dig one foxhole. We would sit, facing each other. One person would sleep for an hour while the other kept watch, alternating throughout the night. About midnight we were attacked by a small group of Jap soldiers while I was sleeping. The firing of the rifles awakened me with a start. I sat up quickly. My head came up alongside the muzzle of my foxhole companion's rapidly firing automatic rifle. My head felt as if it had exploded. I thought that I had been shot. The muzzle blast caused concussion deafness in both of my ears. Still, I was able to grab my rifle and fire at the gray shadows around us. Soon they were either dead or driven off.

"When morning arrived, my hearing had not returned. No one knew of any aid station nearby, so I had no choice but to stay with my unit until we returned to the ship. It was especially frightening to continue in combat without being able to hear. But I had no other option."

On the third day, a small patrol of GIs with mountain-climbing experience scaled the last fifty-foot cliff guarding the peak. Although snipers peppered the area, one soldier waved an American flag from the summit while others below tried to bring up a flagpole for a replica of the Mount Suribachi scene on Iwo Jima. Intense fire forced the GIs to abandon the project.

Still, a day later, two U.S. banners waved atop the Ie Shima peak. Bruce wrote his wife, "That morning it dawned on me that it was the 21st of April 1945. I sent instructions . . . that I would like to see a Texas flag go up in honor of Texans. I sent [a] message to the governor of Texas, 'The 77th Infantry Division after a bitter pillbox to pillbox, house to house, cave to cave fight, planted our American flag on the highest point of the strongly defended mountain temple at Ie Shima. Men from Texas planted the Texas flag on the bloody ridge at the base of the Pinnacle fortress in honor of those gallant Texans who gathered together at Corregidor to remember San Jacinto Day, the 21st of April 1942.' "

To the troops, Bruce also issued General Order 56: "Ie Shima is captured. Thank you, tough guys."

Not until April 27, when the last substantial U.S. forces boarded ships, leaving behind a small garrison, could the battle for Ie Shima be regarded as actually finished. Sandwiched between the relatively easy landing and the final few days eliminating small pockets of defenders had been six days of fierce combat that Bruce compared with other bitter battles, like Iwo Jima.

The Americans estimated about 4,800 dead enemy, including as many as 1,500 civilians who put on Japanese uniforms and bore arms. As Creel's anecdote indicated, even women served the emperor on Ie Shima. The division's 239 KIA, 897 WIA and 19 MIA nearly equaled its 1,143 casualties for Guam, a campaign that lasted three times as long. In comparison, Iwo Jima required twenty-four days to subdue with 24,000 Marine casualties, including 1,600 classified as "combat fatigue," while the Japanese dead totaled well over 20,000. Navy losses at Iwo Jima ran around 2,700 killed, wounded and missing.

To go along with his Silver Star for Leyte, Buckner Creel received a Bronze Star for his role in the ascendance up Iegesugu. To Miller, the six days of Ie Shima ranked equally desperate with his subsequent grueling weeks of combat on Okinawa itself.

"Ie Shima was a tough fight," says Barron. "They attacked and counterattacked and at night they attacked or infiltrated. We killed them inside our lines every night. We killed women dressed as soldiers and soldiers dressed as women."

For J. G. Haynes, with the 132nd Combat Engineers, Ie Shima

would become home for the duration of the war. He and his others from the outfit remained on the island constructing projects designed to transform the bloody battleground into a base that would supplement Okinawa.

Temporarily ensconced on the beach, the GIs of the 77th could see the wrack of war on Okinawa. Budge remembers, "There was constant artillery fire and flares. One could see the shells, redhot from the guns, soaring off towards the front, losing their color as they went. It did not look very inviting and, from what we heard, it was turning into a WW I type of operation. We also heard that one army division had been badly hurt and was completely stalled and worthless."

CHAPTER XIX

INTO THE BREACH

With parts of the 96th Division shattering against the Kakazu wall, the Tenth Army summoned the 27th Division from its reserve status. [During World War I, General O'Ryan commanded the 27th, and the organization became so closely identified with his name that the subsequent shoulder patch punned his name with the constellation of Orion.] The former New York National Guard organization arrived on the line April 12, toting along with it all the usual baggage of war plus controversy and a dubious reputation.

The questions about the 27th initially arose during the invasion of Makin Island. In the capture of that island, the division operated under Rear Admiral Turner, historian Morison's "man of steel", whose command included the V Amphibious Corps led by Marine Lt. Gen. Holland M. ("Howling Mad") Smith. The 27th's CO was Maj. Gen. Ralph Smith.

Fewer than 1,000 defenders backed by scant artillery faced off against roughly 6,500 in the assault force, which also had the benefit of a prelanding naval and aerial bombardment. However, irregular tides misled the intelligence experts and the opening day arrivals fell far behind schedule. The atoll was declared secure on November 23, four days having elapsed from the start of the invasion.

Naval historian Morison presents a devastating critique of the Army performance—"miserable, dilatory . . . trigger-happy soldiers"—and observes, "Gen. Ralph Smith in the regimental command post had such poor communications that he knew little of what was going on. . . . the troops should have overrun this weakly defended island by nightfall." He concludes with a brief description of a furious Howling Mad Smith endangered by confused Army snipers firing bullets through the command post tent where Marine Smith was visiting Army Smith.

A second joint operation of Marines and the 27th at Eniwetok again generated negative comments from naval sources like Morison. He chastised the soldiers. "Too long they were held up by groups of defenders not one tenth their strength. The men were all right but their training and leadership alike was poor." Under the circumstances, the assignment of the 27th to join the Marines under Howling Mad Smith in the assault upon Saipan seems a dubious choice. Tony Walker, the Recon Company commander who became a career Marine, insists the Marine 2nd Division was the obvious choice to serve in reserve but Army brass, jealous of Marine successes, preferred one of their own units.

Charles Hallden, reared in Jersey City, had graduated from college, where he majored in banking and finance, in the early 1930s and spent ten years in the New York National Guard, whose elements would compose much of the 27th Division. By 1940, Hallden had gone on active duty with the now-federalized 27th Division.

At Saipan, Hallden held the post of CO for Company L, 106th Regiment. "The first mistake was aboard ship as we sailed toward the Marianas," says Hallden, "for the invasion of *Guam* [italics Hallden]. We had maps, photos, landing area, objectives and general information about roads, buildings, harbor installations, natives, on Guam. All of these were intensely studied. After about a week at sea, plans suddenly changed. We would now participate in the Saipan operation as reserve for the 2nd and 4th Marine Divisions there. When we sailed on June 1, there were nineteen alternate plans for possible employment of the 27th. On June 9, they added three more."

D-Day for Operation Forager against Saipan began June 15, 1944, and a quick conquest of the island would set up the next target, Guam. But the 30,000 or so Japanese defenders survived the customary prelanding hammering from ships and planes. Their leader had adopted as his credo, "Destroy the enemy on the beach." And when the Marines began the amphibious phase, they encountered intensive fire, often with devastating results.

In spite of all of the Japanese artillery, mortar and small arms, the leathernecks procured a narrow beachhead, although well short of their objectives. Small craft dodged shells while ferrying many wounded and dead back to the transports. The 27th no longer could be kept in floating reserve and, one day after the Marines set foot on Saipan, the Army troops arrived. "All previous twenty-two plans," says Hallden, "were now discarded."

The defenders retreated slowly and after a week of bitter fighting, a line of Americans stretched across the island. The two Marine organizations took the flanks while the Army occupied the area between them, an area which would become known to the 27th as "Death Valley," with adjoining terrain dubbed "Hell's Pocket" and "Purple Heart Ridge." That set the stage for the great Saipan dispute. "To me," says Charles Hallden, "it was a mistake to have a divisional boundary or dividing line along the top, on the eastern edge of Mount Tapotchau. In my opinion, the 27th should have had control of the top of the mountain so it could flush out an enemy in the caves overlooking Death Valley. The Marines made no attempt to clean out these caves, and the Army was afraid to fire into the mountain or caves, which technically were in the 2nd Marine Division zone.

U.S. soldiers fire at the enemy across a ravine.
(*Signal Corps, U.S. National Archives*)

"A third mistake was that the Army could never make contact with the 2nd Marine Division on its left, even after the regiment sent out an entire company to contact them."

As the CO of Company L, Hallden, with only 133 soldiers, relieved two Marine units that included 185 leathernecks. Hallden was disconcerted to find the positions occupied by his predecessors did not square with the locations on maps. He later concluded, "Marine officers never report any problems or losses of ground when pulling back, and several I met didn't understand the lines on their maps or were poor map readers. Seldom did they report critical information to higher authority."

In the period of three days, June 22–24, Hallden and the rest of the 3rd Battalion of the 106th Regiment suffered about 100 casualties as the enemy hit them with small arms, mortars, artillery and tanks. "During the entire day of action, June 24," says Hallden, "Maj. Gen. Ralph C. Smith [Division CO] was at the front line keeping in touch with every phase of the critical situation. With his front line riflemen and small unit commanders, he studied and tried to solve the terrain puzzle in the area. It became evident that to push forward in a frontal attack, without cleaning the Japs off the cliff side which infiladed the valley, would mean a heavy cost in lives."

Efforts to break through wrought fearsome costs. Hallden notes, "The L Company attempt to seize Hill King had not stopped. It had simply melted away. The commanding officer [himself] soon found himself all alone with none of his assault platoon left." When he finally dodged from cover to cover and safety, he discovered the 1st and 3rd Platoons each numbered only twelve able-bodied men, nominally the number for a rifle squad.

Perhaps the worst of the Saipan experience was the fate of a five-man patrol from Hallden's outfit. "I was requested to send them out, through the front lines with the mission to capture a prisoner for interrogation. They failed to return. Several days after the fierce attack in the vicinity of Death Valley, our men came across the five-man patrol, legs bound with wire, hands behind their backs tied to bend them over, with a bullet hole in the backs of their heads. This was a shock and the troops soon turned angry. They said, 'We'll never take another live prisoner.' I myself was very angry and disturbed by what happened. Prior to this incident, we had turned over to Battalion Intelligence prisoners who surrendered. Word of our 'take no prisoners' stance filtered through Battalion and the upper echelons of command. An officer from Division visited us, stating we were to adhere to the voluntary surrender code. But to put it bluntly, the experience demonized the enemy."

Like Hallden, Gordon Larkins served with the 106th Regiment of the 27th. A miner's son from Kentucky, Larkins describes himself as a "meek kid and an average student. We always had a radio, as my Dad listened to the news—Lowell Thomas—the whole family took an interest in world affairs and we also read a daily newspaper. As World War II started, we felt the Japanese were inhumane and really not worthy of mercy. My brother Henry fought them on Guadalcanal before I was drafted in November 1942, so I already had a hatred for them."

Larkins received his basic training in Hawaii and then made the beachead on Eniwetok with the 27th Division as part of a machine gun section. "That first day, my partner Alonzo Schumann and I had been

Soldiers from Company M, 105th Regiment, 27th Division advance during the early May attack. (*Signal Corps, U.S. National Archives*)

lying on the ground behind a big rock. I looked over and saw soldiers we had considered goldbricks and they were digging foxholes. I said to Lonnie, 'Look over at Robbie and Duke. They know something we don't, so let's dig.' We lost a lot of men and after three days of hard fighting, we knew the enemy pretty well. They were skilled soldiers. Eniwetok was mosquito and fly infested. Everyone had dengue fever.

"On Saipan, we dug in at an enemy naval base. It started to rain at night and we couldn't keep the guns dry and free of sand. Sometime during the night, I heard the enemy whispering. I knew they were close and Lonnie wouldn't wake up, until three enemy officers jumped in our foxhole. We all came to life. Lonnie and the number one ammo carrier killed their men, hand to hand. I finally shot my jammed-up carbine to get the third officer.

"As daylight came, so did the enemy soldiers. Schumann and I fired thousands of rounds from the machine gun as the enemy made their sake run. Saipan had some very rough terrain through the middle of the island, and that's the segment our division had. Of course, we were not as gung-ho as the Marines and would not take chances, especially up those high rocky crags. We all knew of the feud between the Smith generals, but we fought to save every precious life we could. The Marines thought they were the only ones fighting that war, and I'm sure each of our men thought as I did, let them have their glory. We want to go home. But I do feel the 27th had a communications problem."

Nobuo D. Kishiue, a Nisei from Hanford, California, endured the typical military experience meted out to men of his ethnic background. An excellent student, number two in his high school graduation class, Kishiue followed the family occupation of farm worker when he completed his course at Hanford High.

He paid little attention to the world beyond California until drafted a month before the Imperial forces sank much of the U.S. fleet at anchor in Pearl Harbor. "There was no prejudice towards us among the troops, but the Nisei were then taken off KP and guard duty. [Presumably, the brass feared they might poison the food or permit sabotage while serving as sentries.] Others envied us because these were the most despised duties.

"We were allowed to complete basic training [at Camp Roberts] and then all Nisei on the West Coast were shipped inland. I was sent to Camp Robinson, Arkansas, and assigned to the rifle range."

At Camp Roberts those who spoke Japanese had been interviewed by officers for possible assignment as interpreters and intelligence specialists. "I did not hear anything further," says Kishiue, "until I had been at

Camp Robinson for nine months. "The interviewers came there and I recognized the officer who had questioned me in California. He remembered me and asked if I would go to language school. I answered that I was in the U.S. Army and would serve wherever they wanted me to. Two days later I received my orders to attend the school at Camp Savage, Minnesota.

"We spent twenty-six weeks there, learning about the military tactics of the Japanese army and military terms, things we never learned in the civilian schools which I had attended. We did not receive any definite instruction on our duties, just general information.

"I joined the 27th Division at Schofield Barracks in Hawaii in June 1943, and worked with ten other linguists as a team. There was no discrimination against us and we were accepted by the troops. We trained along with the troops, learning all we were expected to do as soldiers in the field.

"I had my first combat experience on Makin in the Gilberts. We came under fire as I participated in the beachhead landing. Through captured documents we passed along information on the units and order of battle for the Japanese on the island. We received a commendation from the G–2 [intelligence] colonel for this work after the campaign.

"On Saipan, I went out to the front lines when they captured a command post or some important materials. There were very few prisoners captured but when we talked to them, they were relieved as we assured them that we would treat them in a humane way. They would then open up with whatever information they had. We had a rough time getting civilians to come out of caves or hiding because of the propaganda they got about the American soldiers. At times we literally had to go in and pull one or two out in order to convince them we meant to do no harm. The prisoners of war were treated fairly in the camps and the civilians went into internment camps for their protection."

Bob Cypher, fortunate enough to receive a transfer from the category of rifleman to division finance before Pearl Harbor, spent his time with the 27th Division, well behind the front lines. But he toured the site of a final, futile 3,000-man banzai charge that temporarily overran some 27th Division positions. "The front of the attacking force managed to penetrate and were followed by others without weapons, but bearing sharpened bamboo stakes with which they stabbed the wounded. I saw the bulldozed grave mounds with signs showing the number of Japanese killed, fifty here, 100 there."

Holland Smith, described by author J. Robert Moskin in his book,

The U.S. Marine Corps Story, as "hard driving, bad tempered," and who was overall commander of the ground forces on Saipan, became choleric over the inability of the 27th Division's pace through Death Valley to keep up with the Marine progress on either side. The sag in the line exposed the flanks of both Marine organizations.

Although Holland Smith later professed he considered Gen. Ralph Smith "a likable and professionally knowledgeable man," he advised his superiors, Admirals Raymond Spruance and Richmond Kelly Turner, "Ralph Smith has shown that he lacks aggressive spirit, and his division is slowing down our advance. He should be relieved." The Navy brass concurred and the 27th received a new commander. Dismissal of an Army general by a Marine could be expected to breed rancor among the ordinary GIs as well as the highest circles of the Army. Bob Cypher says he detected no drop in morale around division headquarters after Smith was relieved, but others disagreed and some were irate.

Nobuo Kishiue explains the dismissal of Ralph Smith, "The Marine General Smith, known as 'Mad Dog Smith,' wanted glory. He wanted to finish the campaign in a few days in order to turn the fleet loose. It was said—I did not hear it directly but from other sources—that he ordered the Marines to advance into enemy fire, as they were 'expendable.' Army General Smith wanted more naval and artillery bombardment to soften up the front lines. Saipan was cut off from reinforcements and twenty-four hours did not make a difference in the outcome. The Army general thought about his troops and because of this, everyone of them would have, as they say, 'gone to hell and back with him.' Which is why the Marines had more casualties in all conflicts. I don't care who he is, if a person tells me to cross a field when it is zeroed in, I would tell him to lead the way and I'd follow." While the "Marines are expendable" quote attributed to Holland Smith may not be factual, Kishiue's sentiments mirror those of many.

Much of the unfavorable comment on the 27th Division stemmed from basic differences in the approaches taken by the Marines and the Army. In the words of Morison, "The Marines consider that an objective should be overrun as quickly as possible; they follow up their assault troops with mop-up squads which take care of any individuals or strong points that have been by-passed or overlooked. Marines dig in at night and attempt never to fire unnecessarily, because night shooting seldom hits anyone but a friend and serves mainly to give one's position away. They allow the enemy to infiltrate—keeping good watch to prevent his accomplishing anything—and when daylight comes, liquidate the infiltrators. Such tactics require good fire discipline of seasoned

Riflemen cover a soldier with a flame thrower.
(*Signal Corps, U.S. National Archives*)

troops who have plenty of élan but keep their nerves under control. The Army, in World War II, preferred to take an objective slowly and methodically, using mechanized equipment and artillery barrages to the fullest extent, and advancing only after everything visible in front had been pounded down. Army tactics required enemy infiltrators to be shot on sight."

This is, of course, a critique from an expert whose main sources and affinities lay with the Marines and who had the luxury of a military life well removed from foxholes on the front lines. The debate over whether one should operate on a "damn the torpedoes, full speed ahead" basis —the doctrine accepted by Marine officers like Stormy Sexton, who warned against being "too careful"—or move more cautiously using all available supporting fire, continued well after World War II. There were Army leaders, particularly in the armored forces, like Gen. George Patton, who enthusiastically endorsed speedy advance as a means of minimizing over-all casualties, while accepting initially higher ones. Other strategists insisted haste wasted men and pointed to the low losses absorbed by men under Douglas MacArthur's more deliberate campaigns. The body count issue becomes further confused by the

A flame throwing tank hurls napalm at Hill 115.
(Signal Corps, U.S. National Archives)

A flame thrower tank works with infantrymen from the 96th Division.
(National Archives)

nature of the missions assigned to Marines and Army troops—small coral atolls like Iwo Jima and Tarawa present different problems from the Philippines or Okinawa.

On Saipan, the 45,000 Marines involved listed more than 2,300 dead and missing, an additional 10,500 wounded. The 27th's 16,400 force recorded killed and missing of more than 1,000, with another 2,500 wounded. From a percentage standpoint, the Marines took more of a beating than the Army.

Morison's remarks about infiltrators seem less supportable. With one incendiary bullet, a single infiltrator on Saipan blew up an ammunition dump, resulting in numerous Marine dead and wounded. The notion that any combat troops could allow enemy infiltrators to freely roam among them until daylight is less credible, and that became particularly true on Okinawa.

A case can be made for the strategies and tactics of either branch of the services. But when plans and operations called for cooperation and a unified effort by Marines and Army, the differences could lead to devastating consequences. Those in command throughout the Pacific theater had never come to grips with this dilemma, and Okinawa would be no exception.

The 27th Division moved into positions formerly occupied by the 96th Division along its western area of responsibility. Dick Thom, as the plans and operations officer for the 1st Battalion of the 381st, watched the relief operation as his own organization drifted toward the rear. "I never saw such an ugly bunch," says Thom. "They were nasty; morale was awful. They had to cross one hot spot and men refused to do it. I saw a lieutenant colonel grab men and drag them across. They were the fuckups of the Pacific, never had a successful campaign. In retrospect, I feel sorry for them. They had a hard background, called up before the war and they kept failing tests to see if they were qualified."

Regardless of how they may have seemed to Thom, the newest plan of attack called for the 27th's 106th Regiment to cross the Machinato Inlet, which bit toward the flank of the infamous Kakazu Ridge. Once beyond the inlet, the 106th would meet the brother 105th Regiment in a sweep behind the ridge that had brought so much grief to the 96th Division.

A captured Japanese document insisted that Americans, while firing at artillery at night, ordinarily do not take offensive action after dark. And indeed, the prevailing philosophy of the U.S. forces was to hold their positions after sundown. Maj. Gen. George Griner, now in command of the 27th, decided to confound the enemy by launching his attack at an unexpected hour. Because the area lay under Japanese observation, the engineers responsible for preparing bridges to ford the inlet and grade roads to the objective cleverly disguised their efforts and worked at night.

At midnight of April 18–19, the first GIs from the Orion Division marched across a footbridge. Before the enemy became aware of the advance, troops of the 106th gained command of a strategic escarpment and the 27th achieved the success forecast for the plan. Now, all along the line, the Americans pressed the defenders from the air, sea and land. The heaviest concentration of artillery ever employed in the Pacific theater poured 19,000 shells on the enemy lines.

It seemed doubtful that anyone could have withstood this intensive blasting. But the Japanese had prepared themselves for this kind of warfare. Several days earlier, a directive went to all of those with command responsibility. "Spiritual training within the cave must be intensified. . . . Useless work should be avoided; whenever there is free time, get as much sleep as possible . . . Have the men go outside caves at night at least once or twice and perform deep breathing and physical exercises . . . Latrines should be built inside and outside the caves and, above all, kept clean . . . Take precautions against diarrhea and epidemic diseases resulting from drinking water which has been left untreated because of the inconvenience of having fire."

Not only did the Japanese prescribe basic measures to promote the emotional and physical health of their well-disciplined forces, but also they constantly improved the quality of their underground bunkers. The subterranean warriors were instructed to add reserve positions into which troops could move swiftly when cave positions became vulnerable. As a consequence, in spite of the massive tonnage of explosives, the overwhelming number of defenders under fire remained alert and available to repel an attack.

CHAPTER XX

FIRST RING OF
THE SHURI

On the drawing board, the 27th Division could have been listed as a fresh infusion of combat-ready troops. In fact, it was significantly below the others in strength, and many of the men were combat weary.

Following his experiences on Eniwetok and Saipan, Charles Hallden was appointed executive officer of the division's 3rd Battalion, 106th Regiment. "We were understrength in the 3rd Battalion for Okinawa, plus most of the enlisted men and junior officers were replacements with no combat experience. Because of this condition, the new replacements required intensive individual training simulating combat conditions and methods in fighting Japanese soldiers. The battalion also had extra instruction in the use of grenades and satchel charges to clear out spider holes and caves."

Like all of the divisions involved at Okinawa, the 27th brought along a Joint Assault Signal Company. On paper, the mission of these special units was to establish beachhead and beach-party communications, but in fact the JAS companies often served other purposes. On Okinawa, the 594th JAS Company filled slots as communications replacements for the understrength 27th Infantry Division.

Bob Riddel, a sergeant in the company, came from a family that had spent three years on home relief during the Great Depression before his induction through the peacetime draft in September 1941. "I didn't have much interest in what was happening in the world except I became very bitter about Hitler and the Japs. But I felt the Nisei were treated rotten and really screwed by our government. I had two Japs in my barracks, George Hikaido and Yoshio Nakazawa, on December 7, 1941. December 8, they were both gone and I never saw them again. Both were great guys."

Riddel says he "conned" his way into radio school but could back up his boasts because, prior to military service, he achieved excellent grades studying in that field. For three years he served with a California-based aircraft warning battalion before joining the 594th.

"The 27th had been horribly shot up and, even though in JASCO we carried only a .45 pistol as a weapon, we were actually considered replacements because they were so understrength. We were attached to the 3rd Battalion of the 105th Regiment on Okinawa for air support. I was the air liaison staff sergeant. We would call in carrier-based Navy planes but our infantry battalion commander, a major, was not impressed with that ability. Instead, he would use us to replace the communications men lost in action."

The all-out attack on the front of the Shuri Line defenses added not only the 27th Division, but also 1,200 replacements filled some of the empty slots in the rosters of the 7th and 96th Divisions.

One of the newcomers was Roland Lea, born in March 1926, a son of an electrical engineer and his artist wife. "I was raised in a middle-income environment and we lived comfortably in St. Louis. I was a good kid, never in trouble. When schooling allowed, I worked as a stock boy for an electrical contractor, as a farmhand and on a ranch in California."

He gave little thought to international events other than to realize the likelihood of being involved. "I looked forward to serving my country in the military." Lea received his summons from the draft while still in high school. Allowed to complete the semester, he entered the infantry replacement training center at the same Camp Robinson where Kishiue tended the rifle range. "Weapon knowledge homed in on basic infantry arms. Jungle training included enemy weapons knowledge, survival in the jungle environment, and amphibious landings in the various type crafts. During basic training, the squad of twelve men was lined up by height, from tall down to short. The tallest in my squad were illiterates but made leaders. They were lost in map and compass exercises but this didn't change during basic.

"I became a replacement with the 7th Division, B Company of the 17th Regiment after the Easter Sunday landing while my company was in reserve. On a mop-up patrol of a bypassed pocket of the enemy, I came under fire for the first time. I controlled my emotions and fears like the others. You did your job and did not panic. It took a while to be accepted. You were sized up by the experienced soldiers, and how you reacted under fire determined their confidence and trust in you. It went both ways, the new to the old and the old to the new infantrymen."

Lea quickly learned whom he could count upon. "My platoon sergeant actually ran the platoon and led it in combat. Our lieutenant was not officer material and always lagged behind. He did make cookies for us while in rest reserve, heating graham crackers topped with tropical chocolate, and provided us with his whiskey rations. He was our nanny and we protected him from harm.

"I had a problem with another replacement assigned to assist me by carrying extra magazines for my BAR. Twice during the night in our two-man foxhole, he fell asleep when it was his responsibility to stay alert while I rested. The second time he felt the steel tip of my knife in his butt, and I told him to leave the foxhole. I never saw him again. The irony is that he probably was awarded a Purple Heart for the wound in his buttocks at some aid station in the rear.

"Fighter pilots, both Navy and Marine, were the best friends to the ground fighters. They provided tremendous and constant support in reducing enemy positions and strong points by strafing and napalm runs. We also liked their whiskey when they came to our rest areas to trade for souvenirs.

"There wasn't any discussion about the treatment of prisoners. We didn't take any. We were wary of civilians who often fought us as the Japs. We were never next to the Marines and able to see them in action, but we did fight alongside both the 77th and 96th Division, and I always felt all of the units did well."

The American Army also added several more weapons to its arsenal. The U.S. artillery began using the VT or proximity fuze. Placed in the nose of a shell, the fuze relied on a miniature transmitter and receiver which detonated the shell at a predetermined distance from its target, rather than upon impact or at a set time after being fired. The system sent out a radio beam that, upon striking a solid object, reflected back to the receiver, which then tripped the fuze switch. Proximity fuzes were lethal for anyone above ground and stripped away the protection ordinarily afforded by trenches or foxholes.

Antiaircraft guns around London used proximity fuzes first, and then ground artillery added them during the battle of the Ardennes—the Bulge during the winter of 1944–45. The two ammunition ships sunk by kamikazes on April 2 took most of the proximity fuzes consigned to Okinawa, but new ones quickly reached the gunners.

Even more useful against an enemy holed up in caves, tunnels or concrete bunkers was the flamethrower tank. It was not a new invention. Fire as a weapon dated back to British experiments in 1915. During the Italian campaign in World War II, both the British and Canadian forces employed portable, mechanical flamethrowers. U.S. experts in ordnance and armor disaparaged the idea of mounting a fire cannon on a vehicle. After viewing a demonstration of the British Crocodile tank, which carried the flamethrower in the place of the bow machine gun on a Mark VII Churchill tank, General Patton had sneered at the result as a "piddle." In Europe, the leading proponents of armor thought in terms of tank versus tank warfare rather than assaults upon deeply imbedded bunkers.

While Crocodiles accompanied British troops to Normandy on D-Day, June 6, 1944, ten months before Love Day, U.S. soldiers in the invasion of France relied on the individually manned system, a cannister of napalm on the back of a soldier who carried a hose that sprayed and ignited the fluid. And it was not a favorite among the GIs, both for its cumbersome weight and its ability to attract enemy fire.

As early as Guadalcanal, however, Marines enthusiastically adopted the flamethrower, even though the first versions often failed to produce the requisite conflagration. Marine tank commander Bob Neiman, who participated at Tinian, Saipan, Tarawa and Iwo before coming to Okinawa, was well acquainted with the development of flamethrower technology. "The Marines had been experimenting with them in the tank corps and when we landed at Saipan, the 4th Marine Tank Battalion, fully equipped with regular Shermans, brought along a company of old light tanks and installed flamethrowers on them. They were used with some effectiveness, burning out cane fields, pillboxes and caves. But these flamethrowers still left a lot of room for improvement. They burned bunker fuel, diesel oil, that spread out in a rather wide flame. There was no pinpoint accuracy and the range was about fifteen yards. The only advantage was, a light tank could carry more fuel than an infantryman. The tanks also deflected small-arms fire."

Army engineers improved the fuel mix, introducing napalm as the combustant. "Napalm was a vast improvement," says Neiman. "You could shoot it a distance of 100 yards with pinpoint accuracy. The gunner would discharge his raw napalm at the target, and when he saw it hit a pillbox or aperture of a cave, he could press a solenoid switch that lit up the napalm he was now shooting. That thin stream of flame then ignited what was already on the target. We practiced diligently on Maui [Hawaii]. Anytime a tank could get within 100 yards of enemy fortifications, it was the ultimate weapon, able to squirt flame right into the position better than any other thing we had."

When first designed, says Neiman, "the tube ran alongside the regular 75 mm barrel. But that made the flamethrower tank too obvious and an obvious target. We decided we had enough 75s in each platoon and we'd rather hide the identity of the flamethrower tanks, making them look like all the others."

At Tarawa, the Marines borrowed sixty of the newest flame throwers from the Army. They were critical in the effort to breach the sea wall defense pillboxes. An after-action report suggested all units involved in a landing should be equipped with one flamethrower in each rifle platoon.

The Marines deployed nine armored flamethrowers in each tank battalion, distributing them evenly among the companies. The leathernecks credit the fire-shooting vehicles with a major role in overcoming the near-impregnable positions held by the enemy on Iwo Jima.

Some negative comment arose from those who labeled the weapon as excessively cruel, while advocates unsuccessfully promoted the flamethrower as humane since, they argued, it killed instantly. The horrendous loss of Americans at Tarawa and Iwo squelched complaints.

While the Marines already had flamethrower tanks on Okinawa, the Army did not begin to use them until almost three weeks after Love Day. The 713th Armored Flame Thrower Battalion unloaded on the Okinawa beaches April 7, but their first use in the field occurred on April 19. The "Zippos," as infantrymen quickly nicknamed them for the common cigarette lighter, quickly created fans among the GIs. The efficiency increased with techniques that enabled the 713th to run a hose from the tank up 200 feet of cliff in order to spray enemy nests.

As part of the general attack all along the U.S. lines, the 7th Infantry Division struck in the eastern sector at Skyline Ridge and Hill 178. Medium tanks and armored flamethrowers preceded the foot soldiers, hurling explosives and fire at those entrenched on the heights. The blend of shells, shot and flame blasted and burned the defenders on the forward slopes and crest, enabling the infantrymen to seize their ground.

On the western flank, Stephen Behil acted as a forward observer for the 27th's 249th Field Artillery Battalion in support of the infantrymen from the 105th Regiment. "We had been moving forward, up ridges and through valleys with the 3rd Battalion, when we were stopped by a burst of enemy machine gun fire.

"Everyone took cover and started looking for the source. The only possible place was a clump of trees right on the next ridge. It was thoroughly shelled by our machine guns and rifles. Hearing no return fire, one of the men decided to advance and was promptly wounded.

"As if on cue, five jeeps brought up supplies. The officer in charge placed a driver and machine gunner in each jeep and told them to charge the clump of trees with machine-gun firing. The first one got about fifty yards before he either tipped over or was shot. The officer immediately sent out the second jeep, who traveled only a little farther. The third jeep finally reached the top of the ridge and fired his machine gun into the group of trees. Then he waved us all on. It was a kind of casual wave, like he did this all the time for a living."

The Japanese, as they would demonstrate so often on Okinawa, artfully counterpunched from the reverse slopes, where they were more or less immune to artillery. They blanketed the Americans with preregistered mortar and machine gun fire until forward movement became impossible. Indeed, the troops of the 32nd Infantry retreated to slightly less vulnerable positions.

The maneuver by the 27th Division opened up a route around the stronghold of the defenders of Kakazu Ridge, allowing units from the 96th Division to get beyond the heights where they had shed so much blood and life. But some enemy soldiers still remained on the ridge, and from behind the U.S. lines they trained their weapons on the GIs.

Herman Buffington, who had become a member of K Company, 383rd Regiment in the 96th on Love Day, had participated in that first confrontation at Kakazu Ridge. "After nine days on the line and still not having taken that hill," says Buffington, "we were pulled out. We were pulled off the line because we had lost three-fourths of our forty-two-man platoon. Now we were about a mile back of the line and I felt like a house had been lifted off my head. I pinched myself to see if I were really alive.

"We rested and listened, more intently than before perhaps, to the chaplain. We were regrouped, incorporating about forty new men into our unit. I remained as the first scout. After a few days of rest, we went back. The hill held so stubbornly by the enemy had been taken in the meantime.

"We were now getting to their second line of defense. Shortly after taking the new positions, I, as first scout, was ordered to cross a sugar cane field. As I ran, I saw three dead Americans and I learned, by experience, that a sniper was nearby in a tree.

"I carried a lot of stuff, including a bright-colored flag—the front line banner, water, food and a small stove. To give me more speed I threw away the stove and fuel. The sniper's shots were getting close when I tripped and fell over some of the cane. I lay still, as though I had been killed by the shots. Above five minutes later, I jumped up and ran. The sniper shot at me four or five times before I saw a ditch and plastered myself in it.

"The second scout," continues Buffington, "came right behind me. Other members of the platoon, along with the lieutenant, hit the ditch too, unfortunately ignoring my warning about not getting to a certain spot I knew the sniper had been hitting. The officer was struck near the nose and the shot came out at his throat. I felt so helpless as the man writhed in agony, his blood mingling with the water in that far-from-home ditch. We patched him up and sent him back. The last time I saw him, he was going back across the cane field and I never knew whether he lived or died.

"We finally learned the Jap sniper was actually tied in a tree. We hit him at last and he fell, but hung from his perch. We left him hanging there.

"The enemy finally pulled back. We had some new recruits and several of us went into a little village to check out each of the old houses there. Many native civilians were about and they bowed and bowed to us, offering popcorn all the while. They apparently were afraid we'd kill them. Some were killed with hand grenades when they wouldn't come out of their houses.

"At one time we saw some Japanese soldiers walking toward us, hands behind their heads as though surrendering. We set up a horsehoe stance and let them walk into the mouth of it. One of our men went over to the side and saw something strapped to their backs. We found they had satchel charges of machine guns on their backs. We shot all of them before they got too close. It was unpleasant but just something we had to do.

"Orders came down later that we could not take prisoners if they were surrendering for no apparent reason. 'Just shoot them' was the word we got. I don't think it meant take no prisoners but it was interpreted that way.

"We dug in that night outside the village in a place that overlooked a meadow. There was a problem of 'civilians' coming back through the lines, and some were enemy soldiers dressed as civilians. So we were ordered to shoot some of these people. Some Americans, I'm sorry to say, shot kids."

George Brooks, the former Air Corps and ASTP soldier who'd been wounded on Leyte, was impressed with the newly named leader of the

1st Battalion of the 382nd Regiment, a change made on April 17. "Lt. Col. Franklin Hartline was trained at West Point. Once we were stopped, thrown back several times and seemed to be stalled. He came up to the front, examined the terrain in front of us very carefully with field glasses, asked questions of other officers. When he was ready, he organized an attack and went right along with the men until the objective was gained. That was in contrast to one of the replacement officers, a platoon leader. This lieutenant said he couldn't see without his glasses and one day during an attack he broke them. He was sent back and got a replacement pair. Very soon after, he broke these also. After that happened several times, the company commander sent him back for good.

"I don't recall any indoctrination on how to treat civilians or Japanese soldiers who tried to surrender. The soldiers almost never surrendered, but we did capture one or two. We weren't sure if they were Japanese or Okinawans in uniform.

"We treated the civilians the best we could under the terrible circumstances. Our planes dropped leaflets telling them how to surrender. The trouble was that many would try to get through our lines at night, and of course most of them were killed. Those that surrendered during daylight were treated with first aid if necessary and then sent to the rear. Toward the end there were so many, they needed trucks up front to carry them back.

"I vividly recall one little boy, about one or two years old. He had a bullet hole through his left thigh and his left eye was gouged out, probably by shrapnel. Maggots were eating the dead flesh in his eye. I cleaned out the maggots as good as I could, poured the eye socket full of sulfa powder. I then bandaged him up, gave him something to eat and drink. His mother had been killed, and we tried to get one of the women on the truck to take care of him but they all refused. Finally, one of our men shoved his fist in a woman's face and threatened her if she didn't hold the boy. She couldn't understand the language, but I think she got the idea of what his fist meant. The truck took off and the last we saw of it was the little boy still on her lap."

Company L, with Sgt. Don Dencker of the 3rd Battalion, started up against the nemesis of Bob Jackson, Tombstone Ridge, in a combined operation with the 1st Battalion. But Dencker and his associates could not advance in the face of the withering blasts from the defenders. The intensive exchanges lasted throughout the afternoon of April 20, with the Japanese even counterattacking in a bayonet charge amid their own knee-mortar fire. "Our morning report for the day," says Dencker, "listed thirty-five casualties for the company."

Company K's Len Lazarick says, "We were instructed that there would be a major attack launched. Very early in the morning, the artillery opened up on the Japs holed up in the area of a place called Tombstone Ridge. As we assembled to our line of fire, my squad leader fell to the ground and began to cry, uncontrolled sobbing and pounding his fist into the ground. This combat veteran had been in charge of my squad since our stateside days. He fought all through the Leyte campaign and did okay on Okinawa until now. People had different names for it—combat fatigue, maladjustment, rock happy, etc. But whatever the name, it was not a pleasant sight.

"We could not even tend to this soldier because we would be attacking in a matter of minutes. We left him there where he fell and I never saw or heard from or about him again. I hope he made out okay because he was married and had children. I often wonder what made him crack. There were many times before and after this episode when I thought I might crack up and become a basket case.

"The artillery was rolling its barrage forward and our 60 mms and M Company's 81 mm mortars were firing. Then the light and heavy machine guns opened up. When they stopped, we were on our way, charging across a small, sloping field heading for the northern tip of Tombstone Ridge, which ran mostly north and south.

"Surprisingly, the resistance in our area was light and we managed to get to the top by the afternoon. From that vantage point I could see about eight tanks deployed in a field about 300 yards to our west. They were shelling another ridge to the south and a town called Nishibaru. The tanks came under artillery fire and several were hit. They began to smoke. I could see infantry running ahead of the tanks, through a deep gulley between one end of Tombstone and Nishibaru Ridge.

"A machine gun was firing from one of the ancestral tombs. I was ordered to blow it up. The hill above the tomb was steep, so I removed all of my gear and set it aside with my rifle. The others covered me as I carefully slid down the slope on my belly, dragging a satchel charge. When I was over the top of the tomb itself, slightly to the right, while still on my belly, I armed the charge. I tucked the fuze under the flap of the satchel, then used the strap on it to swing the charge like a pendulum. When I figured I had enough amplitude, I tossed it into the entrance, about eight feet away. Luckily, it landed right in the entrance. Seconds later it exploded and no more was heard from within the tomb.

"As I crawled back up the hill, I suddenly saw a young, unarmed Jap soldier in a clean, well-pressed uniform walk no more than ten feet in front of where I lay on my belly. He looked straight ahead. He was between me and my rifle, which he could easily have picked up and shot me. Maybe he was in a daze from the earlier shelling, or maybe he was on drugs or sake. What happened to my buddies who were covering for me? Turns out, they were ordered to continue moving south and told that I could catch up later. I cannot understand how that mystery Jap soldier paraded through our lines without being shot but I never saw his body after our encounter.

"At this point, our platoon was reduced to fifteen men and no officer. We were down to a single BAR, where normally we had six. All the shellings, skirmishes and patrols had taken their toll." The next day we continued south along Tombstone Ridge, with L Company in the lead while we mopped up behind them."

Len Lazarick had spied tanks bearing down on Nishibaru. They were part of a mechanized advance that included as many as thirty tanks, self-propelled guns and flame-spouting armor. Mines, antitank guns, individuals who suicidally bore twenty-two-pound satchel charges to hurl at the thinnest sites of steel plate, knocked out all but eight of the tanks. The enemy explosives frequently disabled tanks without killing the occupants. But the Japanese troops who forced open turret lids and jammed in grenades slaughtered many hapless crewmen. The defense that turned back the armor was a skillful piece of tactics; the Japanese commanders dispatched special squads and set up their machine guns to winnow out the infantrymen who accompanied the tanks. Once they drove off the foot soldiers, their task of sneaking up on the vehicles became much easier.

The confrontation between the Imperial Army and the 96th and 27th U.S. Divisions on April 20 had produced more casualties among the Americans than the Japanese. The 27th, in fact, suffered 506 dead, missing and wounded for the single day, the most for an Army division in the campaign. It is believed this was the only time during Operation Iceberg that the invaders suffered greater losses than they inflicted.

Pfc. Gordon Larkins, the 106th Infantry Regiment machine gunner, had escaped serious injury at Eniwetok and Saipan. On Okinawa, he found himself pinned down for three days. "We had no food or water and at night they would bombard us with artillery. My good friend Cleatus Cessna killed a Jap officer at night when the officer jumped into his foxhole and stabbed Cleatus in the chest with a bayonet. Cessna shot the officer with his sidearm, a .45.

"We moved out on our way to Naha. As soon as I set up my machine gun, our whole squad was wiped out. Every man was wounded. As a result of my injury, I lost my left kidney."

On the morning of the third day, on the left flank of the 27th Division, Lazarick and his companions breakfasted on a K ration of cold scrambled eggs from its can, crackers and coffee. They heated the beverage by burning a one-inch cube of the explosive Composition C–2, which had the consistency of putty and burned white hot with a smokeless flame. As they prepared to move out, Lazarick saw his first spigot mortar shell. "It was huge and traveled so slowly, clanking along in an arc, that a soldier could run from its path. But it left a crater ten feet deep and forty inches in diameter. It was an awesome but not a militarily effective weapon."

The troops from two other K Company platoons entered the village of Nishibaru while Lazarick and his 3rd Platoon deployed behind a small rise just short of the town. "We could hear bullets whizzing and crackling over our heads, when along came a Captain Brown from regimental headquarters. He had been shot in the arm and was supporting the wounded limb with his other arm. He was bleeding pretty bad. He screamed at us, 'The second platoon is trapped in the village!'

"We jumped up onto the higher ground and stared straight into the face of a company-strength counterattack. The lead Japs were no more than twenty feet away. We were shooting and reloading as fast as possible. Pfc. Costanzo, firing his light machine gun, was killed almost immediately. Pfc. Jim Peters took over the machine gun and handed me his BAR. While we were pumping lead at the Japs as fast as we could. About twenty feet to my left I saw Sgt. David Dovel, of M Company, had dragged his water-cooled .30 caliber machine gun up the rise and was firing it from the hip. There was no time to set up the sixty-two pound piece on a tripod. Our own 60 mm mortars were firing almost straight up and sending shells into the midst of the Japs. I don't know how long it lasted but we were able to hold them off. Some Japs who turned to run were shot down. Several hid in the waist-high grass, and one crawled within feet of Sgt. Dovel and was preparing to toss a grenade when he was cut down.

"After the counterattack was repelled, I noticed blisters on my hands. I had burned them on the hot barrel of the BAR. A bullet had grazed both of my legs and my face was peppered with small grenade fragments. I went to the Battalion Aid Station to get patched up. The medic treating me remarked, 'You know we don't give out Purple Hearts for scratches.' I told him I already had a Purple Heart from Leyte and to just patch me up so I could get back to the company."

That night, the seven remaining men from the platoon prepared their positions. "It was mostly a matter of piling rocks and debris," recalls Lazarick, "but Pfc. Peters and Pfc. Fitzgerald were able to dig down a foot or so before hitting rock. They excused me from taking a turn digging because my hands were bandaged. I stood watch and a lamb with its hindquarters burned come towards our hole, bleating. Peters didn't like the lamb hanging around, making noise and pinpointing our hole. I threw some rocks and he did scurry away, for a while. But in five minutes he was back making a nuisance of himself. I ran him off again and promised I would kill the lamb if it returned.

"The lamb, of course, returned and Peters and Fitz looked hard at me. I turned my back on them and confessed, 'I can't kill it.' They both laughed and called me chicken. No matter, when darkness fell the lamb disappeared. Our ammo, which was almost out, was resupplied. We also received rations and fresh water. Best of all, we got news that tomorrow we would be relieved and go back to a rest area." And in the morning, GIs from the 383rd arrived to occupy the positions held by Lazarick and his buddies.

The initial success of the 27th Division drive stalled before a formidable pair of obstacles, the East and West Pinnacles, rocky promontories honeycombed with natural and man-made vaults that concealed and protected defenders with their weapons. Casualties mounted and the enemy continued to soak with shot and shell the ranks of the latest entry into the Okinawan campaign. The GIs yielded much of the ground which they had occupied, some soldiers fleeing to lines behind them.

Overnight, the troops were reorganized and doggedly resumed the push towards the escarpment and the two pinnacles. Armor, both conventional and flamethrowing tanks, burrowed into the ridge, painstakingly eliminating one cave stronghold after another. Meanwhile assault companies of infantrymen closed the distance between themselves and the foe, leading to hand-to-hand, bayonet, club and grenade exchanges. S.Sgt. Nathan Johnson, of C Company in the 105th Regiment, was credited with killing thirty enemy soldiers. In one brief deadly encounter, he cut down eight with his rifle, then clubbed four more to death. Johnson received a Distinguished Service Cross.

At the same time, isolated bands of Japanese soldiers ambushed even the wary. A sixteen-man patrol from Company A of the 105th passed through the village of Kakazu without incident and pronounced it secure. But fire from all directions scattered the patrol as it sought to recheck the streets. One man escaped; three others were rescued three days later.

Along the eastern stretch of the line, the progress was equally costly, yards won and then lost, many men dead, wounded or missing. Skyline Ridge, dominated by its tallest feature, Hill 178, blocked passage along the coastline. From Skyline Ridge to the west lay a series of concrete emplacements and fortified positions along ground designated "Rocky Crags." For four days, regiments from the 7th Division struggled against enemy mortars, artillery, machine guns and counterattacks from the entrenched defenders. Again, flamethrower tanks played an important role. When the GIs finally swept the last Japanese soldier from the scarred earth and the burned and blasted battlements, they counted 500 enemy dead on Skyline Ridge alone.

During the night of April 23–24, Japanese artillery laid down its heaviest barrage, with every front-line U.S. regiment the recipient of at least 1,000 rounds during the dark hours. When the first rays of daylight tried to pierce the gloom of a morning fog, the Americans discovered that their opponents had abandoned the positions immediately before them. The first ring of the Shuri defense line no longer posed a threat.

CHAPTER XXI

REINFORCEMENTS AND REPLACEMENTS

The 17th Infantry Regiment of the 7th Division, like its brother organizations, after cracking the first circle of the Shuri Line, prepared to resume the drive. The objective now was another of those natural defensive fortresses, Kochi Ridge. Units constantly relieved one another along the front as the Japanese intermittently rained high explosives upon those most forward.

As 3rd Platoon leader for G Company of the 17th Regiment, Gage Rodman, on April 26, was told to have his group take the place of a matching outfit from A Company. "The company commander," says Rodman, "ordered me to send a patrol to the front. Rather than send a runner, I decided to go myself and tell my second squad leader to take his men about 500 yards to the front to establish contact with the enemy.

"About that time, we began receiving mortar fire in the area where my platoon was deployed. Trying to move only in the intervals between bursts, I was running forward toward an irrigation ditch. As I hurled myself forward to land lengthwise, a mortar shell exploded against the side of the ditch close to me. My eye caught a flash of black falling, which I suspect was the mortar shell. The next thing I knew, I was seated on the ground instead of running forward. I knew I was shot but the only blood I could see was on my leg. Then I caught sight of what seemed like several yards of pink tubing on the front of my trousers.

"I propped myself up and looked around. Then I noticed a man in the bottom of the ditch where I would have landed, had I jumped. He was hit in the leg. A man stood up and came towards the A Company soldiers—we were in the process of changing areas, so we were overlapping.

"He administered a morphine Syrette to the A Company GI and, seeing he was a medic, I asked him for a Syrette for myself. I knew my wound would start hurting soon. Working as fast as he could, he bandaged the man in the ditch, then turned to me and gave me a Syrette.

"One of my assistant squad leaders, Sgt. Carl Wilson, stood up and walked over to me, breaking out his first-aid dressing which he carried on his belt. He made a temporary covering for my exposed intestines. Two litters had been called for and they came up in a matter of a very few minutes.

"The A Company man, a GI named Outlaw, was loaded on one and I

American riflemen hunt an enemy sniper.
(*Signal Corps, U.S. National Archives*)

on the other. We were carried to Battalion Aid, then put on a jeep ambulance for a very rough trip to the division clearing station. The 102nd Portable Surgical Hospital had been set up there. I was operated on for the removal of the majority of shell fragments and the manufacture of a colostomy to replace my severed bowel function.

"During the operation I must have started to come to, because I heard, as from a great distance, a voice that said, 'Captain, we have used 260 grains of pentathol and we're running low. Better finish up under ether.' Then another voice close to my head said, 'We're going to give you some ether. Don't fight!' With all the strength I could muster, I answered, 'With what!' "

The enemy clung to Kochi as stubbornly as it had elsewhere along the line. Interlocking fire provided by deeply entrenched Japanese troops devastated a series of assaults. Once again, the resistance frustrated U.S. commanders as the hemorrhage of casualties flowed almost unabated.

The losses and stalemates wrought a number of strategic decisions by the topmost brass. Even before his 77th Division headed for Ie Shima, Gen. Andrew Bruce had suggested to the Tenth Army commander, Gen. Simon Bolivar Buckner, that his troops assault the southern Minatoga beaches, forcing the Japanese to pull away troops from their Shuri Line strongholds. Bruce argued the maneuver would enjoy the same success achieved when his forces surprised the enemy with an end run to Ormoc Beach on Leyte. The defenders also recalled that strategy; they expected a strike on Minatoga.

Initially, according to Bruce, the Navy chiefs favored the idea. But subsequently, Buckner rejected the second front. Reconnaissance and intelligence experts pointed out dangerous differences from the Ormoc expedition. There was no gentle, sandy strand at Minatoga. Instead, jagged reefs limited access and a jumble of rocks lined the shore, behind which rose a fifty-foot high cliff, undoubtedly teeming with well-shielded armaments. Furthermore, the ability of the Navy to find enough vessels to haul and maintain the ground forces was dubious. Buckner and his aides remembered the military disaster at Anzio in Italy, where the U.S. troops became isolated on a narrow beach pocket. The question of an end run at Minatoga, however, would continue to generate second guesses about the conduct of the Okinawa campaign.

While Buckner had discarded that second-front proposal utilizing the 77th, he realized the urgent need for added forces against the recalcitrant Shuri Line. The 77th Division, once its labors on Ie Shima were completed, had always been ticketed to join its three brother divisions.

But with the northern two-thirds of Okinawa secure, the Tenth Army also decided to commit the 1st and 6th Marine Divisions. At one point, the availability of the Marines briefly raised anew the Minatoga option, but a lack of ships ended further consideration.

Of the three Army organizations manning the line, the 27th seemed in the worst shape. It had started with far fewer men than the 7th and 96th and, whether through failures of leadership or the bad luck to run up against the worst that the Japanese could dish out, it was in wretched condition. However, the courage of individuals and the valor of small units notwithstanding, the 27th no longer had the trust of the Tenth Army command.

On April 30, the Old Breed—the 1st Marine Division—replaced the 27th Division on the western end of the U.S. lines. Bob Craig, with G Company of the 1st Marine Regiment, notes that on April 29 he heard official word that their search and destroy mission was over. "We were being sent south to relieve the 27th Infantry Division. They apparently had been taking a terrible beating from the Japs, so needed to be pulled out of the line for a rest and replacement of their many casualties.

"We unloaded from the trucks at Miyagusuku, a small village east of the Machinato airfield, a fighter plane strip. We proceeded south on foot. We were appalled at what appeared to be a disorderly withdrawal by the men of the 27th Division. There seemed to be no organized line of march, many had no weapons at all, and there were rifles and BARs all over the nearby ground.

"At first I ordered my men to pick up all the weapons they found, remove the firing pins—standard procedure for destruction of weapons we couldn't collect for reuse. It quickly became apparent this was too much of a task because it slowed down our march.

"I did see one soldier lying up against a bank, fast asleep. He had a Thompson submachine gun. Here was a weapon I really wanted in combat. I told Lecklightner, my runner, to go and get it, along with the ammo belt and extra magazines. I had Leck take my carbine and leave it with the soldier so he would at least have a weapon when he awoke. We laughed about what he must have thought when he found his tommy gun gone."

As the Marines took over the front, the 27th traveled north, assigned to keep the area captured by the two Marine organizations secure.

Meanwhile, Craig and his platoon arrived at the base of what maps designated as "Hill Nan." Eventually, the 6th Marine Division would insert itself to the east of the Old Breed, but at the time Craig reached

Hill Nan, their immediate neighbors were remnants of the 96th Division, which was in the process of being relieved by the 77th Division.

Atop Hill Nan, a portion of the fairly level ground lay exposed to enemy fire. Recalls Craig, "As we prepared to dig in, I noticed two stretchers containing the bodies of two Marines. Curiosity caused me to check the dog tags of one, probably because he looked vaguely familiar, even though the atabrine we took to prevent malaria turned his skin very yellow, like a Jap's. The body was that of Bob Brundage, one of my classmates in the Special Officer Candidate School at Camp Lejeune.

"We did note a dead Jap about five yards down on the other side of the crest. After it got dark and the air cooled, we became very much aware of his presence, caused by the smell of rotting flesh. We never tried to move him because that would have exposed us to the Japs in the caves all around us.

"Things were fairly quiet for the first few hours, nothing more than a few artillery or mortar shells thrown our way, which was the Jap way of letting us know that they were out there. Occasionally, one of them would yell in English, 'Marine, you die!' or something similar. We never bit, even though the temptation to yell back was great. Also, our Navy would send up star shells (flares) intermittently to light up our front, but all movement and sounds stopped while they were up. In that respect, they served a useful purpose.

"Sometime after 2:00 A.M., when no flares were up, we knew we were in the middle of the battleground as we heard blood-curdling screams for several minutes. Then it became very quiet. We had no idea what was happening, whether the Japs were going to make an attack or were just infiltrating our lines. It was so dark, you could not see your hand in front of your face. The standing order was to stay in your foxhole and do not attempt to get out, even if it was to try and help a buddy.

"At the earliest moment of daylight, Leck and I went to the area where we heard the screams come from. We found two of my men, Corporal Pike and Private First Class Harrell, had been stabbed to death, with literally hundreds of stab wounds all over their bodies. I can only speculate that both were asleep at the same time, instead of one sleeping while the other took a two-hour watch. One or more Japs must have come out of the caves at the base of our hill, crawled up and then massacred them. It was ironic that both men had been involved in the battle for Peleliu. They were not inexperienced in warfare.

"Much of the reason for their deaths was because our earlier mission on Okinawa was limited pretty much to patrolling, cave-blowing, rounding up civilians, and generally mopping up rather than having any real, direct confrontations with the Japanese Army. This resulted in a natural complacency or carelessness, instead of the instinctive fear for one's life when about to face an enemy whose only objective is to kill him.

"We had been somewhat prepared mentally for what was to come after seeing the havoc wreaked on the area and the looks on the faces of the soldiers walking back to the rear. But it was a real awakening when we lost our first two comrades. The starkness of this tragedy was horrifying. The fear that grabbed me then, quite honestly, was momentary because of the realization that I was responsible for the lives and well-being of these men. Quick removal of their bodies and a stern reminder to be on the alert all twenty-four hours of the day with the buddy system was the method of allaying fear in the platoon.

"I was just as scared as any of the guys, especially each night when you depended on your buddy—in my case, Lecklightner—to stay awake during his watch. But one of the secrets of leadership at this level is to build confidence in yourself first, and then by example you are able to have your men believe in you. The fear is always there, but the self-confidence dominates and suppresses the fear. We had known all along that Okinawa was not going to be a piece of cake, because in three years of war, the enemy had proven themselves to be capable, though fanatical fighters. That day was horrendous but it proved a valuable lesson.

"Dixie Koiner, the company commander, came up later that morning to determine what could be done to protect our hold on Hill Nan. He discovered several caves around the base of the hill, but because of the extreme possibility of exposure to immediate enemy fire, he decided not to use our demolition men to blow them shut. He called for flamethrowing Sherman tanks to burn them out, or at least suck out all of the oxygen, thereby suffocating anyone inside.

"Two tanks came in to do the job. Unfortunately, while maneuvering into position, one struck a land mine that flipped it over on its side. Only the tank commander survived, because he had his hatch open and was blown out. The other tank then finished the burning procedure.

"Later the same day I was sitting in my foxhole, trying to repair one of the BARs we had picked up earlier on the road, when suddenly the foxhole started to collapse around me. I felt I was being buried alive. A Jap artillery shell had come in right over my head and, without exploding, landed at the far end of the hole. Fortunately for Leck, he was at the Company CP, or he would have been killed.

"It was not unusual to have duds in Jap artillery shells. We estimate as many as sixty percent duds. We thought the reasons were, they used picric acid as the base of the explosive charge, and it was so unstable that in the course of time it deteriorated."

For a bare few days, the men of the 77th rested from their endeavors on Ie Shima and received replacements in equipment and manpower. Then they sailed to Okinawa and moved and plugged into the line as April ended. The 77th Division commander, General Bruce, had come from Ie Shima to Okinawa on April 27 to assume responsibility for the central zone of the line on the last day of the month. His troops were probably in better shape than the men they would replace, but not much. Like the other organizations, units of the Liberty Division were understrengthed, physically and emotionally tired.

Buckner Creel, as CO of G Company in the outfit's 306th Regiment, had reboarded their LST 649—the same vessel that carried the men to Kerama Retto, to Ie Shima and now would take them to Okinawa itself. "The Navy crew was rather shocked by our casualties [on Ie Shima] after the stiff time we had there. Altogether we had spent about a month on that ship and made a series of landings from it. Many friends had been made between the Army and Navy men. And there were many empty bunks when we returned enroute to Okinawa. But at least we had a chance to bathe, shave, clean clothes, hot meals and clean sheets. As a result of this respite, we were fairly fresh and rested when we went into the lines. However, there was not the usual bantering between units that there had been earlier. Perhaps because we were all combat veterans or perhaps because this was a very serious time.

"I recall passing columns of troops on the road [GIs from the 96th] as we were moving up. They were coming back and they all looked like Willie and Joe [the combat cartoon characters of Bill Mauldin], typical of GIs who had been in combat, tired, dirty, downcast. Actually, they looked the same as we would after a month on the line."

"Just before dark on our first night on Okinawa," remembers Joe Budge, the mortar crewman, "we were joined by a number of replacements, thirteen of whom came to our company. Within a week we had lost eleven to death or wounds. They were lads who had been in service a little over three months, a poor substitute indeed for the three years most of us had under our belts.

"I had been issued a carbine and now was offered what I wanted, an M-1 Garand, which was much more reliable and hard-hitting. I got the M-1 from a kid who was issued my carbine because that's what his duties specified. I immediately stripped the M-1 and found it was so gummed up with congealed grease that there was no way it would have fired one round, let alone any more on semiautomatic."

"The division," says Buckner Creel, "had a replacement training policy and would both train and indoctrinate the newcomers before sending them on to their units. That worked well and when the replacements reported to the line companies, we would try to orient them further and, when possible, put them with an old-timer for their first few days in combat. While in division reserve, I usually ran around in a khaki tee-shirt, khaki trousers and no insignia. My 1st sergeant would meet the new replacements and then send them to my tent to be interviewed by the 'old man.' Most were a little disconcerted upon meeting the youngster 'old man'. I was a 21-year-old 1st lieutenant about to be promoted to captain. However, when we went back into the line, there was no question about who was in charge."

There were officer replacements as well as enlisted ones. Creel recalls, "Several were 'retreads' who had been commissioned in some other branch and then became surplus to the need of the original service. They took crash courses at Fort Benning, then transferred to the infantry. We had men from armor, coast artillery and the air corps ground crews. The anxiety quotient was high but I don't believe any showed themselves incompetent or unable to accomplish their jobs as platoon leaders.

"For the most part, replacements of any stripe were accepted eagerly, as we all realized that the tasks would be easier if we were at or close to full strength."

Creel confesses that quite by accident he continued to develop his persona as a leader of men. "While in the rear area, they showed movies at night on a bed sheet we had 'liberated' off one of the Navy ships. For three nights in a row, we tried to show *Mutiny on the Bounty*. Just about the time Charles Laughton was bellowing 'Mr. Christian' at Clark Gable, the Japanese would bomb the airstrips at Yontan and Kadena and interrupt the show. We were quite frustrated by the third night, when a Jap Betty flew over our area after having bombed the airfield. It was picked up by searchlights. I pulled my .45 pistol from my shoulder holster and let fly a magazine at it. About a minute after I finished firing, smoke came out of one engine. On fire, the Betty crashed into the sea near our position.

"The troops cheered and I became the hero of the hour. My driver painted a downed airplane and a Japanese flag on my jeep. Deep down, I believe the plane was hit by ack-ack during its bombing run. But I never expressed any doubts in public."

Richard Spencer, as a staff officer with the Liberty Division's 307th Regiment, was among the party that worked out details for relief of the

96th Division. "While we were talking to them, a few artillery shells fell just out of range. One of our company commanders fell to the ground, moaning. He was a psychiatric casualty, otherwise unhurt. When I accompanied C Company officers to examine their position, I noted how deeply the 96th was dug in.

"The battalion commander, Colonel Cooney, began things with a probe between the pinnacles around the end of the escarpment. The lieutenant in charge of the platoon soon came walking back with a bullet hole in his chest and minus two men.

"On April 30th after a fairly quiet night, three of us were eating breakfast in our shallow hole at the top of the saddle. A 155 mm Long Tom artillery piece, miles behind us, was firing a mission over our heads when one round fell short. It burst right beside me, moving the earth in around my waist and sending small shell fragments into the hole. The S–2 was hit in the hand and I was covered with black powder and powdered coral.

"When I recovered from the concussion, I looked back at a horrible shambles. There were dead and dying all around. None of these people were in protected areas or holes, since the enemy could only reach us with mortars and we hadn't experienced their attacks as yet. We were 'blind-sided' by our own artillery."

After being checked out by the medics for a concussion and some scratches, Spencer became his battalion commander's "eyes" at the observation post. In this capacity he witnessed the A Company drive for a foothold atop the ridge. "These brave men climbed up, one by one, and were shot down from hidden pillboxes on top. Some of them, wounded, made it back to the ladders and slid down, headfirst." Spencer maintained communications on the escarpment for close to a week, escaping serious injury when a dud mortar dropped beside him.

When the 77th Division had reached the front and replaced units of the 96th Division, Alanson Sturgis, with the 292nd JASCO, was dismayed by what he saw. "The 96th had had an awful time of it on the escarpment. To show how bad it was, they left some of their dead behind. That didn't sit well with us. We thought you ought to evacuate your own dead, no matter what."

The GIs from the 96th Division boarded trucks and hiked back to a rear area near the Yontan air base. Len Lazarick, with K Company in the 382nd Regiment, settled in at what had once been a farm. "Our first order of business was to establish a perimeter, dig foxholes and slit trenches." Even behind the front, the potential for infiltrators, aerial attacks, artillery or even a sudden breakthrough demanded precautions.

"Next," says Lazarick "it was clean clothes, a good shower, a hot meal and then letter writing. Our living conditions were primitive. But we tried to add some comforts of home, like a roof over our foxholes made of ponchos. The only tents in the area belonged to the medics and headquarters.

"To supplement our rations we would stroll down to the airstrip and trade souvenirs for canned peaches, coffee, flour, and sometimes a deal could be struck for the tiny whiskey bottles fliers were issued when they returned from combat missions. We had a collection of bayonets, rifles, Jap flags and assorted artifacts like fountain pens, billfolds, photos and currency. The aircrews were delighted to do business with us but we were careful not to saturate the market with our wares and reduce their value.

"Our uniforms were fatigues, helmet liner, helmet and combat boots. We were required to carry a rifle and cartridge belt whenever we left our rest area. The reason given was that we were in a combat zone and could run into the enemy at any time. Rear echelon troops, however, were not so encumbered, although they were all issued weapons. I resented the different treatment but my bitching fell on deaf ears.

"During our rest period, both Peters and Fitzgerald were promoted to staff sergeant. The original platoon was down to seven men and they needed noncoms. I was made sergeant, assigned to Peters as his assistant squad leader. I had made Pfc. by an act of Congress by having served honorably in combat. Now I made sergeant by surviving.

"I don't know of any combat troops in the Pacific theater who wore insignia. Even our medics did not wear arm bands. It didn't make sense to advertise that you were a person with responsibility or special skills because the Japs knew the difference and acted accordingly. Officers were not addressed by rank in combat.

"While we were in our rest area, replacements arrived. I was only twenty-one, but some of the new riflemen seemed awfully young to me —eighteen and nineteen years old. A smaller group, more mature, were in their twenties. None were in their thirties. All of these replacements had gone through infantry basic training. They knew how to fire a rifle, dig a foxhole, handle a bayonet, march in step and do KP. We wanted to train them in how to survive against a tough and wily enemy.

"Towards this end, squad leaders held informal bull sessions passing along their experience to these new men. During one of these sessions, headquarters requested one man from each squad for a detail digging a slit trench lavatory. As assistant squad leader, I asked Jim Peters if he would mind if I performed the work instead of one of the new men, who could sit and listen to his pearls of wisdom. Some of the new guys were puzzled at seeing a noncom doing a private's job. They didn't realize the importance of what they were hearing about, but Peters and I did."

A wandering cow spotted in the area offered a taste of steak. One of the newcomers with previous experience in a slaughterhouse offered to serve as butcher. The animal was carefully concealed from other units and superiors until the appointed time. Within two hours, the bovine entered the food chain, its entrails and other inedible parts buried. Company K dined on beef with gusto for several days.

"We did our best to get to know our new buddies," remarks Lazarick, "but not too well. Old friendships could be snuffed out in an instant and the closer the friendship, the harder to face the loss when death came.

"We saw some movies, got some mail, played cards and caught up on world events. Fitzgerald acted as our 'information officer' and held forth every other day to let us know what was going on in the outside world. The clock seemed to tick a little faster when we were in our rest area, and the time was approaching when we would have to 'saddle up' and go back to the front."

Paul Westman, who had become a member of the same Company K while the division recuperated from its combat on Leyte, had left the line earlier after an artillery blast rolled him down hill, injuring his right leg. After a stay at the 74th Field Hospital, Westman returned twelve days later. "My buddy, Shelby Allen, had made it through but he was a bundle of nerves. He told me of seeing our squad leader Kermit Ellis get hit, then the assistant squad leader John Willis go down. He was beside Albert Grossman when he heard Albert groan and pitch on his face, dead.

"His reserve broke and the strain was too much as he relived moments when his life hung by a thread in his first face-to-face encounter with a Japanese soldier. 'We were in some brush and all of a sudden, there he was, and we just stood there, a second. It just stu-u-un-ned me and then I shot him; I fired the whole clip into him and I was just st-u-un-ned. I was standing over the Jap shaking when the squad came.' Shelby was so broken up that he had begun to stammer.

"It was a moment of pure terror, my own would come when we went back into the line. But the 383rd for now had been pulled out. Days of death and destruction had made Shelby subject to violent starts while sleeping but he seemed fairly normal during the day. We did some roaming around in secured areas and it was SOP to carry arms outside of the company area. We visited the Marine flyboys at the Yontan airstrip and inspected their F4U Corsairs, which we loved to see when they were making their strafing runs on Japanese targets.

"One day, I suggested we visit the division cemetery. We were appalled at the number of white crosses in just thirty days. About the time we were leaving, an Okinawan civilian suddenly appeared at the gate. I heard Shelby growl, 'You dirty-eared son of a bitch.' I turned in time to see him swing his rifle toward the civilian. I reached out and deflected the rifle, hollering, 'Don't do it, Shelby. You could get court-martialed.' He was shaking and it took a while to calm him down. I think he was near the breaking point."

Lazarick's regiment had been relieved by the 383rd but that outfit, having been battered also, pulled back on April 30 to a rest area. Ken Staley, a replacement during the effort to oust the enemy from Kakazu Ridge, says, "The seven-man squad I had joined was now down to five men—one injured, one killed. During the ten-day rest period, new replacements came in and our squad was built up to a full twelve-man squad. One of the perks at the rest camp, besides hot food, was a pond to bathe in."

Ellis Moore mentions that on a second visit to Kakazu Ridge his 383rd Regiment brought along truckloads of replacements for those lost during the first failed attempt to capture the site. "This second time up we had a rash of self-inflicted weapon wounds, all in the foot. At least twenty men in the battalion shot themselves, all of them either new men or old-timers who still were in a daze after Kakazu. There was a big fuss over these shootings, with orders that all who did it be court-martialed. It was difficult to pin it on a man unless he was actually seen shooting himself. I think most of them got away with it and ended up back in the States."

To his Aunt Jane, Ellis Moore wrote of his off-the-line sojourn, avoiding descriptions of the fighting he had witnessed. "Back in a rest area you can really enjoy the scenery of the island. The weather is just about perfect. It reminds me of spring at home, in fact the two things I think of when I close my eyes and take a deep breath of this air are springtime in Washington, especially around the lagoon where the cherry trees are, and track season in high school, when we used to run on balmy days like these."

After a few paragraphs describing the countryside and what he had seen of civilians, Moore closed, "Peggy and I will have been married a year in a few weeks. It's hard to realize since we only had twenty-two days together, but I'm certainly glad we decided to marry before I came over. Knowing that she is back there waiting for me, and at the same time is with me here through all the times makes all the difference in the world. Every day I realized what a lucky guy I am."

The replacements mentioned by Lazarick included junior officers as well as enlisted men. But unlike the raw riflemen fresh from basic training, some of the new lieutenants brought considerable combat experience. Among them was Robert Muehrcke, orphaned at an early age in Chicago, where from boyhood he had worked seven days a week, delivering both morning and afternoon newspapers, with extra hours on Saturday cleaning windows.

"I joined the Illinois National Guard not only because it provided income for the family needs but it was the patriotic thing to do. I was nineteen when the Guard was federalized in March 1941. We felt the United States would eventually enter World War II. Fellow guardsmen discussed it many times with me, probably mainly as a fight against the Germans. When Pearl Harbor was bombed, I was with the 132nd Infantry Regiment in Camp Forrest, Tennessee."

The regiment, embarking at New York City on January 22, 1942, was the earliest Army line outfit shipped out to the Pacific. Muehrcke learned about war in the jungle training in the mountains of New Caledonia and the Fiji Islands. Among Muehrcke's closest friends was T.Sgt. Jack Fitzgerald, another Chicagoan from the Illinois National Guard.

Fitzgerald from a "modest home and modest family" had signed up in high school with three buddies, Kenneth Pearson, Richard Mc-Laughlin and Thomas Edwards. While in New Caledonia, Fitzgerald and this trio spent an evening swilling beer with friendly Australians who had fought at Crete. That night, Fitzgerald dreamt that the quartet would suffer three casualties in their first battle.

In December 1942, the 132nd arrived on Guadalcanal to fight along-side two other Army regiments, the 164th and the 182nd. The trio comprised the infantry component for the Americal Division, the only nonnumerical organization of that class. The Americal Division relieved the 1st Marine Division, which had engaged in a desperate struggle with the Japanese occupiers of the Solomon Island outpost since the summer.

On January 2, 1943, at Hill 31 near the vital airstrip, Henderson Field, Fitzgerald's group attacked a Japanese pillbox. A burst from a Nambu machine gun instantly killed S.Sgt. "Swede" Pearson and shattered Staff Sergeant Fitzgerald's shoulder. Sgt. "Plug" McLaughlin, a few yards from Pearson when the bullets mortally wounded him, was untouched. But he broke down and developed a chronic mental illness, spending most of his adult life in veterans hospitals. Only Edwards escaped unscathed, as the premonitory dream of Fitzgerald, who returned to duty after a month, had come to pass.

Muehrcke notes, "There was a great deal of battle fatigue early in the war. We referred to them as 'in the burn-out syndrome.' There was more battle fatigue on Guadalcanal than on Okinawa. Once soldiers would adapt to battle, they gained confidence in their leaders and themselves. They would feel their prime duty was to support their fellow soldiers and keep each other alive."

Following the successful outcome on Guadalcanal, Muehrcke and the 132nd moved to Fiji for recovery and training and then to Bougainville, at the upper end of the Solomon chain, in January 1944. The densely overgrown mountains, the rain forests and the determination of the 45,000 to 60,000 enemy soldiers made Bougainville a difficult site for combat, but a classroom for men like Muehrcke and Fitzgerald.

"One important leadership quality for all infantry officers, as well as noncoms," says Muehrcke, "is the confidence built within the combat soldier and officer. Moreover, they must also instill this confidence in the men they lead."

On Bougainville, the opportunity for him to develop the qualities of a leader, presented itself. "My first main role in personal combat experience," says Muehrcke, "occurred there as the 2nd Battalion S–2 sergeant. Our battalion commander requested me to accompany almost every combat and reconnaissance patrol sent out. He especially assigned me to go with new officers and lead platoon-size patrols into the Bougainville jungles."

His tours on Guadalcanal and Bougainville taught him to respect the prowess of the enemy. "Japanese infiltrators and sniper infantrymen were always a problem. They camouflaged themselves and were excellent soldiers. Rather than hating the Japanese soldier, we more likely admired them. In general, they were cunning, tough and brave. They did a superb job. We never underestimated them, although we could not understand their wasteful banzai attacks."

Fitzgerald also developed a high regard for the effectiveness of the enemy. "The Japanese soldiers were good but not as resourceful as the American GI. After all, we had beaten them on every island from Guadalcanal to Okinawa. We all recognized their respect for death and their fierce battle attitude."

After Bougainville, Muehrcke, Fitzgerald and other noncoms who had demonstrated ability and intelligence returned to the United States to attend the Infantry School at Fort Benning. When they graduated, the newly-minted second lieutenants promptly returned to the Pacific theater. "The previous officer classes," notes Fitzgerald, "had all been sent to Europe to replace the depleted ranks following the Battle of the Bulge."

Muehrcke took over a platoon with Company F in the 383rd Regiment, while Fitzgerald joined Company G with the 17th Infantry of the 7th Division. Says the latter, "I was well briefed on the situation. We were beginning a new offensive. Thirty-two months in the Pacific theater, sixteen weeks at Fort Benning at intensive training, and four years greater age—I was twenty-three—all helped me survive and provide experienced leadership to a platoon of nine men, down from the usual complement of twenty-eight. Most had been casualties but some were lost for illness. Most of the remaining were rather new replacements.

"I was well received by the officers and men. While the unit I joined had been depleted by combat, the men, for the most part, had the ability to fight all day and to take heavy artillery fire at night. The officers, many of whom had been in Attu, Kwajalein and the Philippines, were well experienced. The 17th Infantry was a proud outfit dating back to 1812."

Muehrcke formed a similarly favorable opinion of his new associates. "The caliber of our platoon sergeants and squad leaders greatly impressed me. They had adapted to the stress of battle. They became very dependable, and would give excellent suggestions and opinions when asked. They were battlewise. Together there was a sharing, an unusual sharing and cooperation in combat experience. This reduced our men killed.

"No one informed us on how to treat Japanese prisoners, should we take them. At times our division general officers offered a case of either beer or hard liquor or both for us in an exchange for a Japanese prisoner. In addition, they gave us the time to drink it. This was for intelligence purposes, valuable information. In general, we would take captives, especially as the war was drawing to a close. We treated them with respect. We did not push them around, beat or abuse them. However, we made absolutely certain they had no hidden weapons such as hand grenades in their loincloths. [Because surrendering soldiers sometimes concealed weapons in their outer garments, GIs often forced would-be prisoners to strip to their underwear.]

Fitzgerald, like Muehrcke, thought the Americans more or less handled the problem of prisoners humanely. "I did not like the term 'gook.' I realize the less educated GI used it to support his insecurity in a strange land with strange, to us, people. Nevertheless, I believe our treatment of captured enemy soldiers was evenhanded and fair, as was our treatment of the indigenous people."

Their opinions differ markedly from those of others like Dick Thom, from the 381st Regiment in the same division as Muehrcke, as well as numerous noncommissioned GIs. Many Marines also disdained mercy or even the value in taking a prisoner.

Muehrcke arrived while his division was still in reserve, recovering, refitting and replacing. Fitzgerald, however, would have little time to acclimate himself, for the 7th Division was the one organization not pulled back. It would remain in place until the 6th Marine Division, now on the march south, made its way into the line next to the 1st Marine Division while the 77th occupied the adjacent eastern sector and the refurbished, refreshed 96th could relieve the 7th.

With the insertion of additional units, as well as the return of some in reserve and resting up, the Tenth Army was poised to hammer at the second ring of the Shuri Line.

CHAPTER XXII

CHRYSANTHEMUMS

While the soldiers inland traded lives for hillsides, only a few short miles away the war took on a surreal quality. Coast Guard lieutenant Joe Roddy continued to supervise the laborious job of transferring cargo from the *Cepheus* to the shore during the daylight hours, running LCVPs and LCMs back and forth.

"We all had the impression that everything was going fine on the island. On the ship we had an ice cream machine. It was in great demand; one of the things we sent to an aircraft carrier that had been hit by a kamikaze was ice cream, and we kept trading the stuff for souvenirs to soldiers who came back down to the beach.

"One day, some of the boat crew wanted to look around to find their own souvenirs. It wasn't supposed to be done but I let them explore a nearby cave. They didn't bring back anything except fleas. On the ship there was a demand for who was responsible, and I had some cross words from the medical officer and the captain.

"But at night it was a different story. We all left and went back out to the open sea. The radar picket line would pick the kamikazes up, and we knew they were on the way even before they became visible. Then you would see them coming. How they could get through the screen and then keep coming in spite of all the firing was impossible to understand." The *Cepheus* officially was authorized to claim it shot down three Japanese planes; the silhouettes of two Bettys and a Val were painted on the bridge. According to Roddy, with every vessel throwing up shells and machine gun rounds, no one could really be certain who deserved credit.

The *Cepheus* remained in the Okinawan waters until April 16, when it sailed off to Saipan to perform a new mission. It had escaped any damage, although one attacker crashed close by. Other ships in the fleet, particularly among the destroyers, were far less fortunate. In the first week of Operation Iceberg, a total of thirty-five ships were sunk or damaged by bombs, kamikaze hits or mines.

The Imperial Empire's aerial offensive struck almost every day. Sometimes only a single attacker or clusters of two, three, even twenty, appeared. In addition, the Japanese mounted massive raids called *kikusui*—floating chrysanthemums. The 355 aircraft *kikusui* launched on April 6 had sunk the destroyers *Bush, Colhoun* and *Emmons;* the cargo ships *Hobbs Victory* and *Logan Victory;* had rendered five other destroyers and support vessels unfit for further wartime duty and damaged four others.

Six days later floating chrysanthemums, numbering 185, bore down on the Americans again. Among the victims was the *Mannert L. Abele,* a destroyer first crashed by a Zeke that put her dead in the water and then sunk by a *baka.* The *Abele* earned the dubious distinction of being the first victim of this rocket-boosted glider carried to the scene under the belly of a twin-engine bomber and then released. A suicide pilot guided the *baka,* with its 2,600-pound warhead, to the target. Because the initial dive of a *baka,* boosted by its rockets, propelled the small-size missile to a speed of 500 knots, the weapon neutralized defensive gunnery.

On April 15–16, a contingent of 165 *kikusui* set out to ravage the U.S. ships. At Picket Station #1, one of the furthest outposts, more or less directly north of the Hagushi beaches, the U.S.S. *Laffey* faced off against a flock of about fifty bogeys, some of whom sought other targets. But the *Laffey* crew counted twenty-two separate attacks on them in a period of eighty minutes. During this encounter, no less than six separate suicide aircraft, four bombs and strafing fire all slammed into the *Laffey.* But sixteen planes were splashed by the battered *Laffey,* two Landing Craft Support (LCS) ships and the combat air patrol.

On the bridge, during the height of the action, Cmdr. Frederick Julian Becton insisted, "I'll never abandon ship as long as a gun will fire." The *Laffey,* with only four 20 mm guns still shooting, thirty-one killed or missing, another seventy-one wounded, somehow remained afloat.

Ten days now passed before the Japanese could muster another batch of floating chrysanthemums with somewhat less success than achieved earlier. However, in the bright illumination of the moon, one pilot spotted the Hospital Ship *Comfort*, fully lighted, in accord with the Geneva Convention, and steaming away from Okinawa towards Saipan. The kamikaze, unimpeded by any defensive gunfire, dove into the superstructure and exploded. An entire surgery staffed by medics tending patients was demolished with extensive loss of life.

During the first week of May, the fifth suicidal wave struck at Picket Station #10, the westernmost outpost, about seventy-five miles from Okinawa. On duty, monitoring the approach, were a pair of destroyers, the *Aaron Ward* and the *Little,* plus the rocket-firing Landing Ship Medium 195 and Landing Craft Support (LCS) 25. It was about six-thirty in the evening and visibility was excellent.

Ed "Andy" Anderson, with advance training as a torpedo and gunnery officer, was on the bridge of the *Little* on May 3. "My father was in

Andy Anderson served as gunnery officer on the destroyer *Little,* sunk by a kamikaze.
(*Andy Anderson*)

real estate and insurance, my mother served as postmaster at Royers-
ford, Pennsylvania, while I was growing up," says Anderson. "I was
moderately athletic and studious and won a regional scholarship to
Lafayette College. I disliked the Japanese and Italian leadership because of their bombing raids on China and Ethiopia, respectively.
Hitler's Germany seemed reprehensible because of the invasions of
Czechoslovakia, Poland and France. I disliked the Japanese government even more because of the sneakiness associated with the Pearl
Harbor attack."

In his senior year, when that event occurred, Anderson, after graduation, attended Midshipman's School at Northwestern University to become a "ninety-day wonder" with an ensign's commission.

Anderson had not been excessively concerned over his safety, and
while the *Little* participated in the Iwo Jima invasion, he and his shipmates had never come under kamikaze attack. "I don't think there is
any question that the kamikazes were much more unsettling than the
more conventional air raids. The possibility of kamikaze attacks caused
more apprehension on the part of some of the crew. Most probably
shared my fear and awe at the willingness of the Japanese to commit
suicide for their country. May 3 was our first and last encounter with
them.

"Prior to the May 3 attack, our action report shows enemy planes
began to appear on the radar screen at 1415, but it wasn't until four
hours later that they came after us. Two fighter aircraft—Corsairs—had
circled over the ships on Radar Picket Station #10. They had then just
returned to their ground base on Okinawa, when more than twenty
nondescript planes flying in a ragged formation became visible off the
starboard bow. Their bearing dropped aft to about 135 degrees relative
bearing. From there one of the lead planes started a glide toward the
Aaron Ward.

"That ship, which was steaming astern of the *Little,* commenced
firing but was struck near the waterline with an accompanying burst of
flames." In fact, gunners on the *Aaron Ward* had set the Val afire, but
the pilot managed to control his plane until he crashed into the sea 100
yards or so short of his quarry. However, sheer momentum hurled the
wreckage of the engine, prop and part of a wing into the destroyer,
causing minor damage but no casualties. Even as the *Aaron Ward*
sailors deflected that threat, a Zeke (Mitsubishi Zero, a Navy fighter) set
afire by antiaircraft, persevered long enough to drop a bomb whose
explosion ignited fuel. A temporary respite enabled the vessel's dam-

age-control parties to dampen fires, seal flooded areas and even administer medical aid.

But the attacks resumed and all four ships reeled from the blows. Five more kamikazes rammed the *Aaron Ward*, leaving her almost dead in the water, fires blazing, ammunition exploding.

While her sister ship fell victim first, the *Little*, with Andy Anderson, absorbed fatal strikes. "The kamikazes split up and attacked at various directions and glide angles, with most diving from angles approaching the vertical. The captain [Cmdr. Madison Hall] ordered 'All engines ahead flank,' 'left full rudder' and 'right full rudder' in an effort to run an evasive course, hoping to cause the planes to miss the *Little*.

"One or more may have been shot down by the 20 mm machine gun fire, but overall the *Little*'s firepower was overwhelmed by the coordinated kamikaze attack from various angles and numerous directions. Two of them plowed into the *Little* on the port side amidships. I didn't see one actually hit the ship, but they did, with a deafening explosion—both my eardrums were ruptured—caused perhaps by the explosive they carried combined with the detonation of two of the ship's boilers and/or the high pressure air flasks in our torpedoes. The keel broke and the sea poured in.

"I was on the bridge when the order to abandon ship was given. I think everyone knew the ship was doomed. The captain gave me the code books, which were weighted, and I dropped them over the side. I simply stepped into the water on the starboard side, and I believe I was one of the last to leave the ship. The depth charges had been put on 'safe.' They detonated, apparently so deep that no one was hurt by them.

"Don McClelland, a ship's cook, second class, had the presence of mind to go below and pick up empty powder cases. These were thrown over the side and did much to keep a number of shipmates, including Lt. Stew Norris, afloat. A number of men performed heroically while we were in the water. Ernie Flanagan, a seaman first class, credited Machinist Mate Second Class John Cairns with saving his life. 'That boy would get me when I was going down.' Ed Seiford, quartermaster third class, stayed with Ted Schalk, a torpedoman, keeping his head above water until a rescue ship arrived."

The *Little* sank in 850 fathoms of water, breaking apart in less than fifteen minutes after the first of what were actually four successful kamikazes. While the *Little* survivors struggled in the water, the *Aaron Ward* crew nursed their stricken vessel and also looked for help. Neither of the smaller support ships could provide much assistance after taking hits themselves, with the LSM 195 joining the *Little* on the ocean bottom.

The deck log for LCS (L) 83, signed by Lt. James M. Faddis, tersely recounts its efforts at succour and what its crew saw [some numerical and alphabetic designations eliminated]: "1800–2000 Underway . . . changing courses every half hour . . . speed six knots. 1827 Sounded General Quarters; 1828 *Aaron Ward* has enemy plane under fire. 1830 Plane crashed into *Aaron Ward*. 1832 Planes crashed into both *Aaron Ward* and *Little*. Proceeding independently to the stricken ships. 1845 Both ships burning and out of control. LSM 195 fell behind because of engine trouble. . . . 1855 *Little* appears to be broken amidships. 1902 *Little* sunk . . . 1906 Opened fire on plane attacking LSM 195. Plane hit LSM 195. 1910 Plane took mast off LCS 25 in suicide dive. 1912 Plane missed *Aaron Ward* after another hit it amidships. 1915 Picking up survivors. Plane attacked us from port side. All guns to port firing. Plane out of control crashed in water about fifty feet over our bow. LSM 195 burning furiously. Plane coming in on our stern shot down, fired at us as it hit the water. 1920 Lowered life rafts, men on them to pick up survivors. LSM 195 exploding. 1926 Another plane crashed into the *Aaron Ward*. 1942 LSM 195 sank. . . . 1959 still picking up survivors."

The doughty LCS pulled alongside the *Aaron Ward*, taking aboard several injured and handing over pumps to crewmen seeking to save the ship. It then continued to search the area where the *Little* and the LSM 195 had foundered. Around midnight, the landing ship counted at least seventy-six sailors taken from the sea (including Andy Anderson) or from the hulk of the *Aaron Ward*. One man had died of his injuries. All of the survivors were transferred to a patrol escort craft.

From the two destroyers and the sunken landing craft, eighty-three men were listed as dead and another 144 injured. Nor could the *Aaron Ward* return to the wars. After six weeks of repairs, and limping on a single engine, the destroyer managed to make it to a navy yard in New York, where experts deemed her not worth further effort.

Simultaneously with the siege upon the *Aaron Ward* and *Little,* a batch of suicide planes hurled themselves at the destroyers *Macomb* and *Bache* prowling Picket Station #9, southeast of Picket Station #10. The *Macomb* suffered a hit but the *Bache* escaped injury.

A day later, enemy planes smashed nine Navy ships, sinking four, including a pair of destroyers. Art Replogle, a supply officer who had graduated from Washington and Jefferson, where he earned a letter in baseball, was on duty aboard the *Luce*. Replogle received academic instruction in his Navy specialty at the Harvard Business School, which was supplemented by practical work at an amphibious base in Little Creek, Virginia.

The *Luce*, officially commissioned in June 1943, had performed patrol duty and some island bombardments before Replogle caught up with it at Manus in the Admiralty Islands, Christmas Day, 1944. "I had crossed the equator the day before as a passenger on a destroyer-escort. They had roughed me up quite a bit—my hair was cut, my head painted with yellow chromate paint initiating me as a 'Shell Back.' I reported aboard the *Luce*, my confidence shaken by my physical appearance, a bit scared, homesick. Everyone was getting mail except me.

"The next day we took off for the invasion of Lingayen Gulf, and I found out the supply officer on the *Luce* traditionally stood duty watches, the same as line officers. I had not gone to midshipmen's school and knew little about navigation, gunnery, etc. Eventually, beside doing my supply and disbursing duties, I stood watch in the CIC [Combat Information Center] and even JOD [Junior Officer of the Deck]. My battle station was assistant gunnery officer in the Director, which automatically controlled the firing of our five five-inch guns.

"Life aboard a destroyer is cramped, monotonous, hard work, but on the *Luce* it was like a family, with a minimum of formality. We had an experienced crew that had been battle tested. The skipper [Comdr. J. W. Waterhouse] was older, and a Naval Academy graduate. He was not a gung-ho type of leader but quiet and laid back. The exec was also an Academy man.

"We had heard vague references to kamikaze pilots prior to Okinawa. We knew this was a desperate attempt by Japan to prolong the war, but I never knew the extent or the official strategy of the concept. We thought these nutty Jap pilots were an aberration and just a part of being at war with the Japanese.

"On May 4, we had been on the picket line for thirty-four days. We became bored, tired, testy with all the General Quarters. We became careless. It was hot in the Director, so most of us did not wear our bulky kapok life jackets. We heard about other sinkings but never thought it would happen to us."

Replogle's destroyer on this day patrolled Station #12, some sixty miles off the west coast of Okinawa and on a slight northwest heading. Around 7:50 on a hot, sticky morning, a handful of aircraft started runs at the *Luce*. Antiaircraft splashed several. One, apparently badly damaged, crashed in the sea, brushing the side of the destroyer. Its bomb went off, temporarily knocking out all radars as well as automatic settings for the guns. When a second pilot bent on suicide bore in on the port quarter, the gunners could only track him manually. There was little time to fire before the plane blasted into the vessel.

"After the first plane sideswiped us," recalls Replogle, "our electricity was blacked out. We knew we were hit when the second plane exploded the Number Four gun mount. I heard the explosion and felt the ship shudder."

The Zeke, its bomb and whatever ammunition it carried combined to gouge a forty-foot-long hole in the starboard side of the hull. It was 8:11 in the morning. Three minutes later, the *Luce* began listing heavily. Commander Waterhouse recognized there was no hope for his ship.

"My phone to the bridge," says Replogle, "was knocked out, so we got no word to abandon ship. I realized we were sinking, so I went through the hatch to the sonar room below and then clawed my way to the port side of the flying bridge. By this time, the deck became a bulkhead, since we were listing so fast. The water was already up to my knees. I grabbed an inflatable life belt but it came off as I slid into the sea. I remembered you weren't supposed to inflate it until in the water. I also remembered not to take off my shoes and socks because your white flesh could attract sharks.

"I am not a strong swimmer but I paddled around in the warm water and grabbed onto some shell casings. One of our stewards was panicking, so I calmed him down by both of us saying the Twenty-third Psalm together. At no point did I think I wouldn't make it. I knew I would survive.

"The calm sea carried many dead bodies floating in life jackets. Some were badly burned, some still alive and moaning. Since there was no formal abandon ship, everyone was scattered and surviving the best he could without float nets or whale boats. I was in the water about half an hour and saw the *Luce* sink vertically, stern first, with its 522 glistening in the sun. A shipmate refused to let go of the jackstaff and went under with the ship. It was hard to believe we were sunk so quickly by only one kamikazae."

Almost immediately after the *Luce* disappeared under the China Sea, a violent explosion wracked its corpse. That brought additional death and injury to some in the water, but Replogle escaped any hurt. "We were all covered with Navy Special Black Oil. We looked like minstrel-show players and it was difficult to recognize your shipmates. For weeks afterwards it was hard to get the oil out of my hair, and my pillow cases carried dark stains.

"I was picked up by an LCS. After I scrambled aboard I saw sharks around the ship. I was thankful none had been near me in the water. To my knowledge, however, nobody was attacked by them. Jap planes came in and strafed us on the LCS. I thought how ironic it would be to survive a sinking and then be shot on a rescue ship.

"Most of our men were lost below decks. They didn't have time to get out and I often think, what a horrible way to die, trapped below deck, no communication and unable to see what was happening." The toll for the *Luce* was 149 dead, 94 wounded, including the skipper, from a crew of 335. At Station #1, the same morning, the destroyer *Morrison* counted even heavier losses—159 killed, 102 injured—as it perished from kamikazes, including blows from a pair of ancient wood-and-canvas, twin-float biplanes.

Task Force 58, which had snuffed out the last vestiges of Imperial Navy surface power through the aerial strikes upon the *Yamato* and its escorts, went through the May 3–4 *kikusui* sorties without serious incident. However, on the morning of May 11, a pair of suicide planes somehow escaped radar detection and broke through the clouds right by Adm. Marc Mitscher's flagship, the carrier *Bunker Hill*. The first, a Zeke, smashed onto the flight deck, careening through parked aircraft, igniting numerous fires before skidding into the sea. But before it tumbled over the side, the plane's 500-pound bomb ripped through the wooden deck and went off inside the ship. As the crew sought to cope with this disaster, the second assailant, a Judy (Japanese Navy bomber), dove in from the stern, releasing its bomb prior to touchdown, and then pierced the flight deck at the base of the island. Flames spurted through openings in the superstructure. The decapitated Judy engine wheeled into the flag office, killing three officers and eleven enlisted men on the admiral's staff.

Some five hours later, with assistance from other ships, the *Bunker Hill* could report fires under control. But the thick smoke and intense heat were largely responsible for the deaths of 353 and 264 wounded or injured. Another forty-three were carried as missing. *Bunker Hill* now became part of those invalided out of the war. Mitscher shifted his flag and staff survivors to the *Enterprise*.

Two days after the *Bunker Hill* disaster, the *Bache* again sought to fend off kamikazes, but less successfully. The *Bache*, commissioned in 1942, accompanied the naval force covering the invasions at Attu and Kiska, where the 7th Division eventually routed the Japanese. As part of the Seventh Fleet, the *Bache* supported landings in the Cape Gloucester area of New Britain and New Guinea, sites of operations of Marine

Raiders and the 1st Cavalry Division. The destroyer had also supplied firepower for the army troops hitting the beaches of Leyte.

Her greatest triumph came in the great sea battle of Surigao Strait, where the U.S. fleet drove off a serious threat to progress along the Leyte beachheads. As a member of a destroyer squadron, the *Bache* was credited with sinking an enemy battleship, cruiser and destroyer. After its tour shelling defenders at Iwo Jima, the ship had become part of the destroyer screen around Okinawa, in a sense putting it together with land units it had served elsewhere

One of the Bache's officers, Henry Bergtholdt, was raised in Auburn, California. With a family fruit ranch and nursery business as the background, Bergtholdt was able to attend college, expecting to major in agriculture. But the death of his father while Bergtholdt was halfway through his higher education forced the sale of the ranch and nursery. The student switched to business administration, earning a master's degree in that subject as well as a secondary teaching credential. Bergtholdt chose pedagogy and began a career as a teacher in the nearby Porterfield's high school and junior college.

"Because of my profession, my upbringing, and as an avid reader of history, I was up to date on current world events. Having gone to a high school where one-third of the class was Japanese and having worked with them on the ranch and nursery, I had nothing but good feelings for the American Japanese. But I thought the country of Japan was crazy to attack the U.S. Hitler and his actions in the European countries had been a concern but, having several relatives who lived in Germany and corresponded with the family, I felt no animosity towards the German people."

After Pearl Harbor, Bergtholdt tried for a commission in the Navy, but he was originally only offered an opportunity to enlist as a boot. He did fill out papers for the Supply Corps, USN Reserve and continued to teach while awaiting orders. When a draft notice arrived, Bergtholdt hurriedly arranged to be sworn in as an apprentice seaman on inactive duty. Not until the spring of 1943 did his commission and orders finally arrive. After several months of instruction, Bergtholdt attended the same course as Art Replogle at Harvard's Graduate School of Business. From Boston, Bergtholdt traveled to Hawaii for assignment, only to be shipped back to San Diego for transport to Alaska and a post on the *Bache,* ostensibly still engaged in the Aleutians. But, having completed its mission in the Bering Sea, the destroyer had now headed towards the South Pacific. New orders directed Bergtholdt elsewhere. He continued his wanderings in search of his ship. Three months and 25,000

Kit Hall (left), Mike Shiminity, Art Bowman and Harry Lord were part of the *Bache* crew. *(Kit Hall)*

A kamikaze hit badly damaged the *Bache* amidship. *(Kit Hall)*

miles after he received orders to the *Bache,* Bertholdt caught up with the destroyer.

As a supply officer, Bergtholdt's battle station was the coding room. On the bulkhead of the station hung a clipboard which, during fire from one of the five-inch guns, would shake off its hook and bang Bergtholdt on his head. But the clipboard also bore a personal message: MR. BERGTHOLDT, THIS MACHINE [for coded messages] IS MORE VALUABLE THAN YOUR LIFE. DESTROY IT BEFORE ABANDONING SHIP IF ORDERED TO DO SO.

Berghtholdt remembers the early days around Okinawa as uneventful as the ship protected transports involved in the landings. "On the fifth day after, we escorted the transports to Guam. The day after we left, one of our squadron's ships was sunk and one damaged by kamikazes. That day in the wardroom we had turkey for lunch. When the captain [Lt. Comdr. A. R. McFarland] asked why, I answered, 'Thanksgiving, for having left yesterday before the kamikazes.' It made him mad that we had missed the action, and he ended up by betting those in the wardroom that when we got back to Okinawa, all the kamikazes would be gone and we would be left out of the turkey shoot.

"It took us seven days to reach Guam, about five more to receive orders to escort tugs and tows back to Okinawa. That voyage required another eleven days. All the time Comdr. McFarland was champing at the bit to get back into the operations zone and shoot down some of those Japanese planes.

"When we had returned, Admiral Turner's flagship directed us to refuel and report to a picket station north of Okinawa. We spent five days there without much action. Radar would pick up planes either going to or coming from Okinawa who would be heading for our ship. But when we fired on them, they veered off.

"In the beginning of May we were assigned a station between Okinawa and Formosa. On May 3rd, while on patrol with the *McComb,* we came under attack from kamikazes. Since there was nothing to do in the coding room, I had stepped out on the deck and saw two planes overhead. I thought they looked like fighter cover, but then one peeled off and headed straight for the bridge. Fortunately, he was not strafing us, for if he had, I probably would have been hit. I froze and watched him dive down through the flack we threw up. Just when it seemed like he would hit the bridge, he veered slightly, crossed the bow, carrying away the forward lifelines and leaving part of a wing wrapped around the anchor windlass before crashing on the port side.

"The other plane dove on the *McComb* and crashed into the handling room under the Number Four mount. The *McComb* suffered some casualties but was not in danger after putting out the fire. It required no help to return to Kerama Retto.

"About this time we received a voice message that an adjacent station was under attack and the LSR 195 was sunk. We went to the rescue and picked up survivors [sixty-seven according to official reports], several of whom were in serious condition due to wounds and burns from the rockets which had been aboard and exploded during the fires.

"Ten days later, we were on picket duty near the area we had patrolled May 3. Just as before, Japanese planes from Formosa came in toward us, but this time there were more of them. Our group shot down several but one got through the air cover and was coming in low toward us. The Marine pilot of a Corsair asked that we hold fire until he got within 5,000 yards. When he couldn't shoot him down, he told us to open up. The Jap and the Marine came through the flack until the kamikaze hit us.

"The plane hooked our after stack on the port side and crashed on deck on the starboard side, right outside the supply office. Once again, because of no activity in the coding room, I was outside on the deck and watched the planes come in. When it hit, I was going forward, yet when it was all over, I had a small piece of shrapnel on the right side of my face, a small hole on the edge of my ear, a hole burned in the right front of my shirt, with bruised skin beneath that hole, and two more holes in my right leg. When I had surgery on my ankle in 1992, the doctor showed me the final X-ray. There was a piece of metal about the size of a pea next to my shin bone. The doctor said that was not a piece he had inserted.

"The fire was burning under the warheads on the torpedoes in the forward tubes. A machinist grabbed a fire extinguisher and was putting them out. Because the plane had hit the after stack, the after fireroom was useless. When the bombs exploded on the main deck outside my office, they broke not only the steam line from the forward fireroom to the after engine room but also put shrapnel in the reduction gear in the forward engine room, so we were dead in the water and without power.

"Everyone in the forward engine room was burned by 800-degree steam. Some had seen that they couldn't make it up the ladder out of the engine room, so they had gone down in the bilges to escape from the steam. They waited there, rising with the water that was being poured into the ship by an LSM alongside on the port side for help in the emergency. When the space above these men cleared of steam, they came up out of the bilges just as engineers tried to get steam from the forward fireroom, unaware that the line was broken. I don't remember that anyone got out of the forward engine room without being burned, some of them clear down into their lungs from breathing the steam.

"As we were towed into Kerama Retto, several of us assisted the doctor in treating the injured or trying to ease the pain of those for whom there was no help. The doctor had lost his pharmacist mates from sick bay because the bomb blasts had blown the supply office, sick bay and emergency radio off the port side.

"I lost fine men out of my division, including 1st Class Storekeeper Walt Alestack, who, with four others from the starboard midships 40 mm gun, were never found, probably having been blown overboard by the blast."

Harry B. Gunther, son of a Memphis cotton broker, grew up savoring the lore of the Navy, thanks to an admiral uncle. Persuaded that a career at sea would be "fun and rewarding," he obtained an appointment to the U.S. Naval Academy at Annapolis. "Furthermore," says Gunther, "with war brewing in Europe, I thought life in the Navy better than what the Army could offer."

He was still a midshipman at the time of Pearl Harbor. "I was appalled at what happened to the fleet and the attack made me dislike the 'slant eyes.' The training at Annapolis was more adequate than that of most ensigns and made me a more valuable officer than most ninety-day wonder types. But some of the finest officers I knew were reserves with little formal navy training. On the other hand, much of what I was taught was already out of date. For example, the Ordnance Department at the Academy did not have a modern fire-control system of the type then being installed in destroyers under construction and in the fleet."

Upon graduation, Gunther's entire class attended a ten-week course at the Naval Air Advanced Training Command in Florida. A key feature of the program was instruction on recognition of friendly and enemy aircraft and ships. Gunther remembers hours spent while silhouettes of these would flash on a screen for a fiftieth or hundredth of a second.

Assigned to the *Bache* as a gunnery officer, Gunther participated in bombardments of enemy shores, barge hunts and escort duty. He was at his place in the five-inch gun director as the destroyer squadron steamed down the Surigao Strait. "We fired five of our ten torpedoes at a range of 13,000 yards or more. This was far too great a range, and although we may have hit something, I seriously doubt it".

The *Bache* altered its course and, with its sister ships, closed on and took under fire, the Japanese cruiser *Mogami*. "We raked her over with

255 five-inch shells at as close as 5,300 yards. I don't think she ever fired at us. During this entire action, the torpedo battery matched up with the fire-control director and should have blown the *Mogami* out of the water. The torpedo officer and the combat information center chief requested permission to fire our five torpedoes, but we were refused permission by the captain, who was the third officer to command the ship. He said he had no instructions from the squadron commander to fire torpedoes. This captain simply sat in his chair on the bridge and did nothing. I think he was scared. Later he got a Navy Cross for this and I think he should have been court-martialled. He happened to think well of me, but I thought he was a poor destroyer skipper, and so did most of the crew."

Captain number four [McFarland] took command after the *Bache* entered a shipyard in Oakland for repairs. Off Iwo Jima, Gunther, when assigned the role of officer of the deck, became responsible for keeping the ship from colliding with numerous small craft in the area while maintaining a proper bearing on target for nighttime star shell illumination. It was the busiest four-hour tour in his memory, notes Gunther, who adds, "Captain Number Four [McFarland] had a good night's sleep. We all liked him."

Gunther says he relished the voyage back to Guam after the first few days around Okinawa. "At thirty knots, no zigzags, no planes, no enemy. Coming back, with the tug pulling a floating dry dock, it was one and a half knots, slower than a man walks. During our return we received numerous reports of picket line destroyers being hit by kamikazes and of destroyers shooting down (or claiming to have) many Jap planes. The captain was fit to be tied because we were missing all of the action and there wouldn't be anything left for us. Personally, I was enjoying the trip and in no hurry to get back to Okinawa."

Gunther recalls that first brush with a kamikaze. "Two planes attacked. One hit the after gun mount on the *McComb* but the other, a Zero, attacked from our starboard side. We were firing everything we had at it when the captain said to me over the battle circuit, 'Cease fire. It's an F6F [U.S. Navy Hellcat].'

"The plane crossed our bow, just forward of the Number One gun mount, knocking down the life lines before going into the water on the port side. The 'Meat Ball' [Japanese red circle insignia on the wings] was very evident to all of us. Captain Number Four called and apologized. He was a great guy and my recognition training had paid off."

Gunther regards kamikazes as doubly difficult to defend against. "A pilot who is willing, or more likely, wants to kill himself is certainly a tough target to stop because he is not distracted or deterred by fire at him. He can approach his target using evasive maneuvers, whereas a pilot trying to bomb or strafe must, at some point, fly a steady course. I don't believe we tried to understand the mentality of the kamikaze pilots. I think they were brainwashed and, possibly, somewhat drugged."

On May 13, according to the *Bache* gunnery officer, radar detected incoming aircraft and General Quarters sounded. "There were several Vals; it was an old dive bomber with fixed landing gear. Two were shot down but a third Val attacked from the port side and we ceased fire momentarily for fear of hitting an F4U pursuing the Val. We resumed fire and I remember hitting the Val, knocking off his landing gear.

"But he continued to come at us and crashed into the base of our after stack. The Val crossed over to starboard when his bomb detonated above the main deck. Fragments entered the forward engine room, rupturing main steam lines. There must have been a big blast when the Val struck the ship and then the bomb went off but I don't remember hearing anything. I had on a sound-powered headset which would have diminished outside noise.

"The usual sightseers—radio men, sonar men—had rushed to starboard, thinking we would be hit on the port side. They were badly punished by fragments from the bomb blast. There was heavy damage amidships. Sick bay, the galley, laundry, supply office were all wiped out. All power was lost. There was no radio communication. There was no sound-powered phone communication with the after part of the ship. There were fires there and we were dead in the water.

"Some time after the kamikaze hit us, an enemy plane approached but was driven off by our forward, starboard 40 mm machine gun, under local, manual operation. The entire crew performed extremely well during this engagement and the members of the engineering department were outstanding. If there is any criticism, it should directed at me, as gunnery officer, for we failed to shoot down all of the kamikazes."

Clement R. McCormack, on duty May 13 as Fighter Director Officer in the Combat Information Center of the *Bache*, actually located the trio headed for their area. A college graduate from Massachusetts and former U.S. Immigration Service employee, McCormack had enrolled in an officer training program in May 1942.

Buried in the Combat Information Center (CIC) during operations,

McCormack had witnessed little of the *Bache*'s on-deck operations. "In the battle of Leyte Gulf, I was so busy with ship handling and CIC that I really was not aware of the shooting until we retired from the torpedo attack and then saw gunfire overhead from our heavy ships. When the Japs launched kamikaze attacks in Leyte Gulf, they were directed at larger warships. I saw one hit the *Honolulu* [light cruiser] and didn't really understand that it was a kamikaze. However, I saw the damage inflicted on other DDs and I was very fearful.

"Soon after I came on watch, radar reported an air contact seventy miles due west. It then disappeared. Shortly thereafter, our Combat Air Patrol (CAP) said it would have to leave, as it was nearing sunset.

"On a hunch I vectored the CAP thirty miles due west, and very soon I heard, 'Tallyho—three bandits.' CAP engaged the kamikazes and, I believe, shot down two. [Gunnery officer Gunther claims credit for the pair.] The third one hit us. A hot breeze came into CIC, even though we were quite forward of the hit. My assistant CIC officer was also damage control officer, and he immediately left for the damage site.

"After determining that all radar equipment and communications equipment was inoperable, I headed for the forward medical station—the wardroom—and did what I could to assist the medical officer.

"Two radarmen had come to me as the shooting began and asked if they could go on deck to watch. Usually they were glued to the radar screen and unable to see the shooting, so I acceded to their request. Eventually, as they saw the kamikaze approaching under heavy fire from us and CAP, they ran to get inside but were killed by the bomb blast at the hatchway on the starboard side. I found them there without a mark on them. They had been shipmates a long, long time and I will never forget these two fatalities."

Bache shipmate Seaman Kitt Hall grew up in the small city of Keene, New Hampshire. "My Dad worked in a manicure implement factory and later as a contract painter. As a teenager, I never gave much thought to any world events, just did my homework and held small jobs. I graduated from high school in 1941, and on December 7th of that year I was working in a gas station when the owner ran in and said, turn the radio on. It was unbelievable to hear of the Japanese attack on Pearl Harbor."

To avoid being drafted, Kitt Hall hitchhiked forty miles to Fitchburg, Massachusetts, in search of a Navy recruiting office. With his parents' signatures on the forms, he headed for the Newport Naval Training Station a few weeks later. "The training consisted of three weeks of marching, a lot of sentry duty, firing ten rounds of a .22 caliber rifle and handling boats under oars." That perfunctory exercise completed, Hall spent almost a year at the Quonset Point Naval Air Station and then received assignment to the *Bache,* reporting to the ship while it was at New Guinea.

His duties included the anchor windlass room, where ship's materials were dispensed—chipping hammers, paint, lines. His battle station during General Quarters was a five-inch gun, Number Three on the ship, just aft of a torpedo tube site.

"On May 13," recalls Hall, "it was Mother's Day and at seven minutes to seven, General Quarters was sounded. Several enemy dive bombers were hitting all the picket stations and one, a Val, made a successful attack on the *Bache.* It came from the port side, crossed and came in amidships on our starboard side. All steam and electrical power was lost. There was some confusion, but everyone pitched in and did their best to save our ship.

"One officer, Ens. Arthur Peterson, did fire the aft torpedo tubes, which had been damaged and probably would have blown up. In about thirty minutes all the fires were brought under control. One seaman, Charles Poteat from Alabama, during the previous week while on gun watch, read the Bible. We believe he knew his time had come. Another, Gunners Mate J.H. Pittman, just before going to his battle station, handed his wallet to his buddy and asked that he see that his wife would receive it if anything happened to him."

With its fires extinguished, the ship was towed by a fleet tug alongside a repair vessel at Kerama Retto. "It was much like a funeral march," recalls McCormack, "especially as the number of casualties [forty-one dead, thirty-two wounded] became known. There was an air of disbelief that it could happen to us, because our gunnery had been so good."

"The midships was a mess," says Gunther, "with bodies and wreckage everywhere. I think we found the jawbones of the Val pilot. He had gold fillings in his teeth. At some point on the afternoon of May 14, the doctor disbursed medicinal whiskey. It was the first time we ever had whiskey aboard ship."

At Kerama Retto the bodies of the dead were taken ashore and interred at an Army cemetery. The survivors stayed aboard the *Bache.* Supply officer Henry Bergtholdt says, "They took a steam line from another destroyer which had been hit worse than we. They welded steel plates to the deck and I-beams to strengthen sections. They replaced the Number Four and Number Five gun mounts with two which had been damaged on other destroyers. One mount had an ashcan blow up under it and was stuck at a ninety-degree angle, while the other had blown the barrel and the shield bowed out."

With one engine room and one fire room functioning, the battered *Bache* crept away from Okinawa for a long voyage to New York—the West Coast repair yards were fully occupied with damaged destroyers.

CHAPTER XXIII

CAP, YONTAN AND THE GIRETSU

Apart from their own antiaircraft, the fleet depended upon the Combat Air Patrol to deal with *kikusui* and the smaller raids of kamikazes. The CAP, working with Fighter Director teams in the Combat Information Centers installed on the radar picket ships, operated both from aircraft carriers and the captured airfields of Kadena and Yontan on Okinawa.

The land bases housed both Army and Marine squadrons, but the former's responsibilities lay mainly in support for B–29s on their runs to Japan and Formosa. (A minor payoff for the kamikazes was the shifting of targets for the huge bombers from the enemy cities to the home fields of the suicide planes.) The leatherneck fliers, as members of the 2nd Marine Aircraft Wing, directed their efforts at interception of kamikazes or conventional air attacks and tactical support for ground troops.

The strategic decision of Colonel Yahara to cede the ground north of the Shuri Line enabled the defenders to concentrate their resistance. But it was a questionable tradeoff. In giving away Yontan and Kadena, the Japanese provided a pair of airfields that added to the resources for defeating kamikazes and allowed easy access for tactical support of U.S. ground forces. Stung by the air power operating from Okinawa, the Japanese sought to neutralize the bases with regular bombing runs, usually during the hours of darkness.

For the residents of Yontan and Kadena, the climate added operational difficulties at ground level. The heavy downpours rendered much of Kadena to muck, and fliers from that field developed a habit of using Yontan, to the dismay of that field's ground crews. But even there, the inhabitants contended with muck. Al Rose, a radio technician with VMF(N)–533, a nightfighter squadron at Yontan, notes, "When it rained, it was a sea of mud. When it didn't rain for some period, Okinawa was a cloud of dust. We lived in tents, dugouts during the bombing raids. These were holes in the ground, perhaps five feet deep, covered with logs which were topped off with sand bags. Hot food was a long time coming, as were facilities for medical treatment. In the early days we used K rations and C rations.

"But the pilots were superb airmen, particularly those who flew night interception missions."

Among these fliers was George C. Axtell, who, as a kid in Pennsylvania during the 1920s and 1930s, developed an ambition to become an aeronautical engineer and pilot. "My goal was to do something more interesting than work in the industrial environment of western Pennsylvania." An honor-roll student in high school, Axtell, as an adolescent, worked forty hours a week in a dairy store, while avidly devouring accounts of current events and fiction.

He took the first step towards his chosen career at the University of Alabama, where he studied aeronautical engineering. "I participated in the glider club that had primary and intermediate gliders in need of rebuilding. The club made me flight instructor, and though none of us had soloed, we taught ourselves to launch the gliders through a high speed tow, then circle the field and land." While in college, Axtell also earned a private pilot's license.

As a student at Alabama, Axtell read magazine articles on current events, discussed world affairs with classmates and reserve and active duty officers connected with the university. "I do not recall any personal animosity toward the Germans, Italians or Japanese as a group of individuals. The philosophy manifested by the leaders of these governments, their political structure, national goals, aggressive nature of their military and foreign affairs was, in my view, something that could not be tolerated by the democracies of the world. Appeasement as a national policy was intolerable. It was either their rule or standard of government or ours. The challenge was clear and unambiguous. The democracies had to resist. The United States must participate to assure the freedom of the countries that were being invaded. War was inevevitable."

At the end of his second year at the university, spurred by these convictions, Axtell, in May 1940, decided to join the military and become a fighter pilot. The Army Aviation Corps rejected him as underage at nineteen. The Navy refused his application for the same reason. Learning of the Marine Corps aviation arm, Axtell hitchhiked to Washington, D.C.'s Anacostia Naval Air Station, where a Marine captain listened to his request. "He remarked that the British were successfully utilizing 'boys' of my age as fighter pilots and observed that the Corps should waive age requirements. He said I would hear about my application in a month. I didn't expect anything would happen, but I thanked him for his time, returned home and accepted employment as a draftsman at a steel fabricating plant in Ambridge, Pennsylvania."

To Axtell's astonishment, the Corps accepted him, and in July 1940, he embarked on the long, arduous path towards his dream. He completed flight training in May 1941, but because he was still only twenty and ineligible for a commission, he served as an aviation cadet instructor. But within a few weeks, a waiver allowed him to become a second lieutenant.

After a tour at Pensacola with an instrument training squadron, Axtell

The members of Marine fighter Squadron 323 include, (back row, left to right) aces George Axtell, Jefferson Dorrah, Jerry O'Keefe, William Hood; (front row, left to right) Charles Allen, Herman Theriault and Edward Abner. *(George Axtell)*

attended a fifteen-month course at the Naval Academy. During his time at Annapolis, the Japanese struck at the United States. "Pearl Harbor and the conduct of the Japanese military in China and Southeast Asia revealed that the military defied the Geneva Convention and that they were very cruel. Barbarians! But war is hell!"

Subsequently, Axtell became commanding officer of Squadron VHF 323, with the job of building it into a combat-ready unit in six to eight months. He started from scratch with personnel who had only just learned the basic rudiments of fighter pilot duty. But instead of VHF 323 then going off to combat, most of its pilots were detatched and shipped overseas as replacements. Axtell rebuilt his squadron of thirty-two F4U Corsairs and the outfit received assignment to Okinawa.

"We were one of the first aviation units to be land-based at Kadena," says Axtell. "We launched from the carrier that transported the squadron within 100 miles of Okinawa, the ninth of April. We flew our first combat mission at dawn the next morning. Twenty-four aircraft took off in atrocious weather—300–400 foot ceiling in heavy rain topping in excess of 25,000 feet. We were assigned to combat fighter stations under control of the picket radar destroyers. The high command wanted an early demonstration of land-based fighters to combat the large flights of Japanese aircraft causing heavy damage to the fleet. The mission aborted due to weather conditions that prohibited visual sighting.

"My first encounter with the enemy could have been my last. With my wingman, 1st Lt. Ed Abner, I was assigned to a combat control point under radar control of a picket ship. We were at 25,000 feet in clear weather, and during the first hour we were repeatedly intercepted by Navy carrier-based F6Fs. We turned into them, made identification and each flight broke off. Because the land-based and carrier combat flight controllers operated separately, overall coordination of operations was loose. Our patrols overlapped and each flight had to identify any apparent bogey—aircraft whose identification was in doubt.

"After several hours of these false encounters, radar control directed us on a heading to intercept a large flight of unidentified aircraft at a lower altitude some distance to the northwest. As I added full power, we turned to the assigned heading. I made my usual visual check in all quadrants and glimpsed what appeared to be F6Fs, high above us, coming out of the sun, making an apparent pass in our direction. Since we were under a radar controller's direction, and this type of activity had been going on all morning, I told my wingman, 'Oh ***, a couple of F6Fs are making another pass. Let's press on.'

"Shortly thereafter, I noticed red flashes going all around and into my aircraft. Simultaneously, I saw in my mirrors the large insignia of the setting sun on two Frank [Japanese Army fighter] aircraft. I executed a violent snap roll. I ended up behind the two Franks, while my wingman took evasive action by diving for the deck.

"I was mad, embarrassed and determined to close on the Franks that were heading north. At full power, I was barely keeping them in range while I fired in bursts most of my ammunition at higher and higher angles of deflection in an attempt to score hits. When I finally took stock of my situation, I realized my aircraft was damaged. My engine was losing oil that streamed over the canopy. I aborted the flight and, under very low power, made it back to Kadena. Ed Abner had landed about an hour earlier, reported the incident and, due to no word about me, had started to assume I had been shot down."

A much more successful encounter occurred around dusk April 22 during an eighty-plane raid upon the picket ships. In the furious scramble of carrier- and land-based U.S. fighters, Axtell became an ace, credited with five planes knocked down.

"My encounters with Japanese aircraft after that first one, usually kamikazes, were under poor visibility and bad weather conditions. You'd be flying in and out of heavy rain and clouds. Enemy and friendly aircraft would wind up in a big melée. You just kept turning into any enemy aircraft that appeared. What appeared to be a big flight would be badly dispersed by the first attack of our flight. It was fast and furious and the engagement would be over within thirty minutes.

"Others had somewhat different experiences with flights of two to four against two to ten of the enemy, and active dogfights took place. I flew hundreds of hours, through instrument conditions night and day, low ceilings of circling over radar picket ships and then ones of holding at 25,000 feet over a designated control point under radar control, awaiting an assignment to intercept.

"I had the opportunity to engage enemy aircraft three times, if memory serves me correctly. It was a crap roll, plus the willingness to fly weather, to cruise most economically, to fly at night and operate from airfields with minimum ceilings and heavy rain, utilizing primitive navigation aids." He added one more victim to his total in his last meeting with the enemy.

Dueling with kamikazes and other enemy aircraft was only part of VMF 323's task, and the figures indicate that aspect as not the most dangerous. "My recall," says Axtell, "is that roughly half of our missions were in air-to-ground support of both Army and Marine units. These were very important and were also very gratifying, as we received reports of the accuracy of the delivery of ordnance on target and statements attesting to the effectiveness of these missions.

"The pilots made extremely low-level passes to increase the accuracy of the deliverance of bombs with ten-second delay fuses, napalm and rockets. The attack runs carried them through friendly artillery and small-arms fire as well as enemy small arms, mortars and artillery trajectories directed at them, as well as antiaircraft ordnance. Small-arms fire and heavy antiaircraft fire were intense at times. We suffered considerable material damage to our aircraft and, unfortunately, lost pilots and planes from ground fire."

In fact, while Axtell's squadron listed half a dozen pilots lost in its Okinawa tour, none were shot down in aerial combat. The casualties all came from the close air support missions or operational accidents.

Axtell handled the depressing assignment to write letters to the families of the dead. "I emphasized the positive, what an outstanding squadron mate he was, and cited specific contributions he made for the benefit of the unit, and I expressed our love and affection for him."

For all of the handicaps and the apparent difficulties in closing with the foe in the air, Axtell's VMF 323 counted a record 124-plus kills off Okinawa. Twelve members earned the rating of ace. He attributes the record-setting statistic to the skill, determination, tenacity of the aviators and the outstanding work of the ground crew technicians. "We started as green kids and gained skills and maturity over a year and a half before entering combat."

Living conditions at Kadena and Yontan, while infinitely superior to those of units seeking to crack the Shuri, began on the primitive side. The men were housed in tents and relied on slit trenches for latrines. Personnel rigged up showers and facilities to wash clothes for one amenity.

"The food was outstanding due to our mess officer, Sol B. Mayer, an enterprising individual and a frustrated grunt," says Axtell. "I honored his request for a week or so 'temporary duty' with the infantry on the front lines. My jeep was made available, plus several cases of bourbon for his use in potential bargaining.

"Mayer had several goals. First, he wanted to prove his manhood by participating in actual combat. He was quite successful in this endeavor and performed quite professionally. Second, he was determined to obtain Japanese souvenirs with the idea that he could trade them for food with members of the fleet lying offshore. His salesmanship was outstanding. The squadron mess after the first two weeks was furnished with white table cloths, silverware and the fare included eggs and steak. The mess was open twenty-four hours a day and fed anyone who stopped by. Needless to say it gained notoriety, island wide."

Vigilance against kamikazes and other aerial predators required round-the-clock efforts, making patrols after sundown a must. Earlier in the war, night fighter planes had roamed the dark skies of Europe, with German pilots attacking the RAF and U.S. flights of bombers while American and British airmen who accompanied the bigger aircraft tried to intercept the specially equipped Messerschmidt 110s and Junker 88s with their own modified machines.

The U.S. night fighters first deployed P–38s and A–20s using added radar. The Army then chose the P–61 Black Widow as its weapon of choice for night work. The Navy and Marines opted for a version of the Grumman Hellcat, although some Marine night fighter squadrons flew Vought Corsairs.

VMF(N)–542, a Marine squadron charged with this duty, used the Hellcats while based at Yontan. A similar outfit, VMF(N)–533, made its home at Kadena. VMF(N)–542, under Maj. William Kellum, touched down at the airfield on April 6 to start the nocturnal patrols. In pairs, pilots roared off at dusk to begin their four-hour searches for bogeys. Usually, the dusk-to-dawn duty meant sixteen of the Hellcats prowled the appointed sector before the sun rose.

Ten days later, VMF(N)–542 recorded its first kills as radar controllers vectored 2nd Lts. Arthur Arceneaux and William E. Campbell onto a pair of would-be maurauders. The Hellcats shot down a Zeke and a Frank. The sweet sense of triumph was muted by the collision of two Hellcats racing down the runway to take off. One pilot died instantly; the other succumbed after several days.

As a boy, Lloyd Parsons, growing up on a nonelectrified farm in northern Missouri, gazed at solitary airliners overhead and started to dream of becoming a pilot. He recalls the rumors and talk of war he overheard in the mid-1930s. "It was said the only way President Roosevelt could end the Depression and stop the killing of little pigs [part of the government effort to maintain the price of pork] to prevent overproduction was to have a war. A ten-year-old in full naiveté wonders how a president can cause a war. At age seventeen, December 7, 1941, while listening to a battery-powered radio, the wondering stopped. It became a reality but one did not question who or what had caused the war. The United States had been attacked by the Japanese."

With college ordinarily out of the question, Parsons applied for the

V–5 Naval Aviation cadet program and, with his Marine 2nd lieutenant's commission in hand, reported for instruction on night fighters.

"I had hoped to become a fighter pilot but this was a newly created field. How could fighter aircraft engage the enemy at night? The answers weren't too long in coming. Once we survived the learning to fly at night, everyone went off to the new night fighter squadrons, where training really began in earnest.

"At the Marine Corps Air Station at Cherry Point, North Carolina, we learned to fly the plane and to watch the radar scope at the same time. I am still astounded that the equipment worked, with its maze of wiring, miniature tubes and bulkiness. How the antennae stayed on was a mystery, since it turned at 18,000 rpms out there on the right wing tip."

Parsons received additional and intensive instruction on Guam while attached to a squadron there before coming to Yontan with the 542nd. He named his night fighter *Melancholy Baby*. He recapitulates his unforgettable experience. "On the night of May 13, Mother's Day [the same night that the kamikazes struck the *Bache*], I found myself on patrol in that dark, seemingly endless starlit sky, routinely flying vectors and occasionally talking to 'Delegate'—code name for ground-control radar.

"Suddenly the controller said, 'There's a bogey in your area. Find him!' That's not the way it is supposed to work. The controller is supposed to vector you into a trailing position, giving you altitude, speed and direction information. However, the ground-control radar was not working properly. So with the adrenalin flowing, all senses alerted, hands flying around the cockpit in almost total darkness to adjust knobs, turn switches off or on and still trying to fly upright, the search began.

"The almost total darkness in the cockpit was necessary to eliminate the possibility of being seen by other aircraft and for the prevention of night blindness. Our eyes had to remain adjusted to see in almost total darkness to enable visual sighting on an intercepted aircraft. We were forbidden to fire our machine guns until then to prevent the unforgivable mistake of shooting at friendly planes.

"When our radar, known as AIA for airborne, intercept and attack, was working properly, it scanned in front a sixty-degree cone extending out to nearly 100 miles. My set worked this night and my grateful thanks went to the squadron ground people.

"So I searched. I went one way for awhile, then turned, then dived, turned, climbed, turned and searched—with not a word from ground control regarding the bogey. I was desperate. Still nothing. When I was about to give up and return to patrol, the radar suddenly came to life. There he was, six miles straight ahead and at the same altitude. Don't lose him! More speed! The *Melancholy Baby* roared to life as the throttle was jammed forward.

"Look again, I'm closing—too fast, slow down, damn, he's coming straight at me, less than a mile. Throttle closed, slow down, too late. How close did we come to each other? He had to have just passed under me. Turn around fast and relocate him. What's my direction and what heading do I turn to?

"All these thoughts run rapid-fire through my mind as the Hellcat is tortured in a hard-over turn. Then the search begins all over again. 'He's gone. He must have seen my backfire and flames from the exhaust and was taking evasive action. Please, Lord, help me find him again.' No luck, time was running out and still no help from ground radar. 'He's gone, admit it. Go back on patrol. Climb back up to 6,000 feet and relax. But keep watching that radar.'

"Whap! Propeller turbulence and that beautiful radarscope paints him again. This time I know I'm behind him and at the same altitude. 'Now close in. This time it is for real. Faster, don't let him get away. Get that closure rate going. Now, good. One mile and closing, one-half mile, one-quarter mile, closing too fast—slow down. Power, cowl flaps open, gear down, flaps down—please slow down—200 yards and closing, 100 yards. My God, I'm going to overshoot!

" 'Stay below, don't hit. There he is, silhouetted against the stars—twin engines, not a friendly. Please don't have a belly gunner. Blue flames from my exhausts with the engine at idle are a dead giveaway.'

"Fifty feet back and twenty below and finally the *Melancholy Baby* matches speed and ever so slowly starts backing off. The gunsight—turn it on. Damn, can't find the switch in the dark and can't take my eyes off the enemy. Forget it, pull the nose up and fire.

"Six fifty-caliber machine guns roar momentarily. I'm covered with oil. Both engines on the enemy bomber burst into flames. The big red meatball shows up vividly in the dark night sky. 'Get out of here—he's going to blow up.' Full back stick, hard left rudder and aileron and full power. The Hellcat responds instantly and with no room to spare. The Japanese bomber blew into a million pieces and went drifting, burning towards the South China Sea.

"It's over. Now assess the situation. That sweet-sounding Pratt and Whitney engine was pure music to my ears but I can't see out. The *Melancholy Baby* is completely soaked with oil from the Jap bomber. 'Delegate Control from Topaz 29. I can't see out of my windshield. Give me a vector home.' 'Okay, Topaz 29, turn left twenty-five degrees and that'll take you home. Congratulations.'

"The return home was uneventful but I did have to make the approach and landing with the canopy open in order to see the flare pots that lined the runway. It was a night to remember and what a Mother's Day gift. Only God knows whether the bombs in that Jap Francis were diverted from killing some of our mothers' sons."

Throughout April and into May, the enemy continued to harass the two air bases. Unable to seriously interfere with operations, the Japanese plotted a spectacular surprise assault with five twin-engine Mitsubishi Sallys, each carrying about a dozen heavily armed soldiers from a specially trained, airborne attack unit. At 10:25, according to the official reports, one Sally sped in towards Yontan at a very low angle. Perimeter AA guns knocked it down. The remaining four also swooped down as if to land, and three more fell victims to the ground fire, where the Americans continued to believe they were fending off a regular bombing raid. The fifth member of the group succeeded in making a belly landing within 100 yards of the control tower. The battered plane had hardly skidded to a halt before the soldiers burst from it and quickly started to destroy whatever they could along the flight line, tossing grenades or fastening them by suction to parked aircraft.

Jack Kelly a member of the 542nd Night Fighter ground crew, says, "Until May 24th, night life on Yontan was hazardous, lively and routine. In the early evening we would listen to Tokyo Rose spin a few records after beginning with 'Strike Up the Band.' Then she would give her spiel on the U.S., all negative. We thought it very humorous. This was usually followed by air raid alerts and then Jap bombers overhead. At the confluence of our two fighter strips, a large foxhole housed all the ground personnel working on the flight line. When the Nips started laying in their bombs, the ground crew Marines would hole up in this large shelter.

"The evening of May 24th began quite sanely but would progress into the wildest experience of my life. As we prepared our first flight of F6F night fighters, the air raid sirens sounded. As the evening wore on, searchlights picked up several Jap bombers. They kept flying around, out of range of our 20 and 40 mm guns, dropping bombs and acting as a diversion for what was to follow.

"After a few hours, a Jap bomber crashed into one of our fuel dumps and caused instant daylight. Shortly thereafter, another bomber, loaded with Giretsus—Japanese commandos—came directly onto the landing strip with his gear up. The aircraft careened along the fighter strip, generating a myriad of sparks as metal mashed against coral. They ground to a halt about 100 yards from our bomb shelter. I couldn't believe what I was seeing! Out came the Nips, loaded with incendiary devices, grenades and rifles.

"In our bomb shelter were about seventeen Marines, unarmed. Our carbines, M–1s and other small arms were all back in the tent area. The Nips were scurrying about, burning aircraft, firing their rifles and were positioned directly between us and the tent area. All we had were screwdrivers and other assorted tools. I have often thought, if only one of the ground crew had taken a rifle to the flight line, many casualties could have been avoided, equipment and supplies saved. We could have picked off quite a few of the Giretsus as they exited their plane and staggered down the strip with their heavy loads.

"We were defenseless in the bomb shelter and at their mercy if they had seen us. One Jap grenade thrown into the shelter would have KO'd the whole group. Three Marines, at the other end of the strip, came to our rescue—Ordnance officer, Bucket Campbell, Sgt. Chan Beasley and another Marine with small arms were a welcome sight. We pointed out several Nips nearby. They were identified as Nips and shot.

"Campbell established a perimeter defense around the shelter using a few of us out on point. I manned one, armed with a screwdriver. After being out there a short time, I heard a voice shout, 'Whoever goes there better answer up,' and a shot rang out. I was hit in the foot. I had no time to answer with the password, issued fresh each day to every Marine on Okinawa.

"I hollered back, 'Hold your fire, you dumb son of a bitch!' and the firing ceased. A few buddies came running over, saw my problem and cut my boondocker off with a K-bar. They applied sulfa, dressed the wound quickly, and helped me to the rear."

Bruce Porter, a major, who, only forty-eight hours earlier, assumed command of the 542nd, had flown a fruitless mission earlier in the evening and had landed less than half an hour before the arrival of the Giretsu. Porter had retired to his tent. "I no sooner sat down on my rack to pull off my combat boots than I heard explosions from the field below our hill. [At Yontan, the men lived in tents erected on slightly higher ground off to one side of the field.] "Before anything else sank in," says Porter in his memoirs, *Ace*, "a field telephone beside my cot began ringing. I grabbed the handset and shouted, 'Major Porter!' A frantic voice I could not place bellowed news that all hell was breaking loose on the airfield and the Japanese were *landing* planes on our runways."

Porter says he strapped on his shoulder holster with his automatic pistol and stepped outside. "I had already heard several new explosions and could hear small arms popping from below our hillside bivouac. I hit the door just as a huge light flared into the darkened sky. I was certain that someone had blown up a gasoline dump.

"Below my vantage point, I saw that many lines of tracers were flying across the runways and onto flight lines and tent camps on all sides of the airfield. It was totally chaotic down there. It was very evident that I could contribute nothing to events below except the seeds of more confusion. I decided to sit tight, and I ordered everyone within hearing distance to do the same."

Indeed, chaos, rather than disciplined resistance, marked the first reactions to the sudden appearance of the enemy amidst the Americans. Those able to find weapons opened fire with submachine guns, carbines, M–1s and pistols. As Jack Kelly indicated, friendly fire was at least as much to fear as hostile weaponry.

Flight surgeon John Ellis, on "meat wagon" duty near the tower that evening, crouched in a foxhole with his corpsman. Ellis had only a .45, while the medic carried a carbine. From the tower, Ellis heard a controller yell, 'I got one of the SOBs.' Moments later he cried out, 'Oh my God, they got me.' The corpsman with Ellis, disregarding his own safety, climbed the tower ladder, hauled the wounded man to the ground, commandeered a vehicle and drove through the melée to a Navy hospital. Recalls Ellis, "That sailor should have been awarded the Navy Cross. As he drove away, he said, 'Doc, you must stay here until something serious happens.' Then a B–24 parked a couple of hundred feet down the strip, all gassed up and loaded with bombs, blew up. I thought, this has got to be the end, but all the debris missed me."

At Kadena, only a short distance away, George Axtell says he was alerted to something unusual by the intense antiaircraft fire thrown up that night. "We observed some spectacular fireworks and assumed an attack was in progress."

The shooting went on throughout the remainder of the night but slowly the Marines organized themselves into effective search-and-kill teams. Tanks trundled back from the front lines to assist. As dawn began to illuminate Yontan, the last of the Giretsu fell.

T. Sgt. Jerry Reubel was appalled by what he saw at daybreak. "Bodies everywhere, Japs and ours. Planes on fire and blowing up. People moving all about. At some point in time, I saw one of the Jap attackers behind or in one of our blown-up aircraft. My only thought was to get him. I crawled to a closer range with my carbine and just screamed at the Jap. What I screamed, I don't remember. The Jap came out and we faced off. He threw a grenade at me and I fired at him at the same moment. The grenade landed nearby but never went off! My carbine fire killed him." Credited with killing the last living Giretsu, Reubel earned a Bronze Star.

James Powers, as a member of the Marine 8th Defense and Anti-Aircraft Artillery Battalion, was off duty the night of the Yontan raid. From his vantage point near the coast he could see both kamikaze attacks on the fleet and the activity around the air bases. "One of our .50 caliber crews scored direct hits on a Japanese troop-carrying, twin-engine aircraft coming in low over Maeta Point. The plane caught fire, turning into a blazing comet. It was part of the Giretsu operation. As I dived for what little cover there was, the aircraft roared over my head just a few feet above the small trees among which I had been standing, crossed the highway beyond our Battalion HQ compound, hit one hill, bounded over an intervening hill and crashed in flames on a third one just beyond. Aircraft parts and enemy dead were scattered all over the place in a gruesome pattern in the ensuing morning.

"When our gunners hit the approaching aircraft, it seemed aimed directly at me, and all my sins passed in review as my day of reckoning seemed at hand. As the plane passed overhead, I could feel the heat from its flames. When my hour of deliverance came, I knew that Jesus Christ, the Sergeant Major or somebody, was looking out for me!"

Although Powers says orders were to take prisoners wherever possible, some men failed to follow the script. "Two of our men were court-martialled for killing a Japanese major they captured after the Giretsu attack. They found him asleep in the boonies, with his briefcase of maps and shot him in the head. The Navy was furious because he would have been worth his weight in gold after surviving the crash of his plane."

Two Marines died and another eighteen were wounded during the uproar. The nocturnal desperadoes destroyed three Corsairs, a pair of PBY flying patrolboat planes and four transports. Another twenty-nine aircraft were damaged and two fuel dumps blew up. However gratifying the opportunity for the doomed to demonstrate their fealty to the emperor, the raid did nothing to reduce the combat air patrols or the pressure applied to ground forces.

CHAPTER XXIV

X-DAY, MAEDA ESCARPMENT AND CONICAL HILL

Capt. Tsuneo Shimura, the twenty-three-year-old commander of the Imperial Army's 2nd Battalion, 32nd Infantry Regiment, ordinarily commanded 700 men. With the addition of 100 Okinawans and an infusion of many men from construction and other service units, Shimura started April with nearly 1,500 soldiers. On April 25, the outfit replaced a depleted 62nd Army Division. According to Shimura, who accompanied the foot soldiers on a horse until they neared the front, they entered the fray with morale high.

Headquarters directed Shimura's organization to mount an offensive against the Americans advancing on the Maeda Escarpment, a rocky ridge named for a village at the base. The 96th Division referred to it as Hacksaw Ridge and the series of hills and plateaus climbed about 500 feet above sea level.

Shimura regarded his orders to attack over unknown terrain, without information on enemy positions, at night as "contrary to common sense, a classic miltiary blunder." He dispatched scouts ahead in the afternoon and then counted upon stealth to surprise the invaders. But the moonlit night brought mortars that erased his hopes and his concern deepened with "fire from tanks and more mortars."

His men hid in caves and tombs. "But in the morning, the American tanks came out, firing into each hole and tomb." Shimura hid with four others in a mausoleum and shuddered as the tombs on either side crumbled. Cut off from the main body for the entire day, Shimura

A grenade explodes in front of a trio from the 77th Division.
(*Signal Corps, U.S. National Archives*)

slipped back to his outfit under the cover of dark, only to find new orders to attack.

Now he at least knew something of the topography and, instead of having his forces advance in a line, Shimura directed them to travel in a column. They followed a small stream bed and, while several were killed en route, the main body gained purchase over turf previously held by the enemy. In the course of the attack, the Japanese rescued sixty to seventy fellow soldiers from another unit.

Pushed to carry the fight to the Americans, Shimura, who described himself as a "hands-on" leader, issued the instructions, although he says he and his men knew it meant sure death. "The power and strength of the Japanese military was shown in this willingness to obey." And indeed, two platoons were quickly wiped out. Control of "this evil upland" was in dire jeopardy. Reinforcements hauled themselves up with rope ladders. The attackers at last drove the Americans backward.

Shimura and his battalion originally fought against the elements of the 96th's 381st Regiment. On April 29, during a brief respite, the 77th Division settled into the area previously assigned to the 96th Division.

Frank Barron, with the 305th Regiment of the 77th, considers his second day on the main island probably the worst. "Our battalion commander was a very good officer, but at this point in time, very inexperienced. He had been given a jumping-off time that was totally impractical. My A Company led the attack. With virtually no reconnaissance and under the illusion that our left flank was protected by friendly troops, our leading elements moved forward like a Fort Benning demonstration.

"Suddenly, from our left rear, Jap machine guns opened up. I believe every one of about a dozen men leading the advance was killed or wounded. The Jap fire came from a cave in a rocky ridge that was impossible to approach on foot. I sent back for a tank and a couple came up. By now Jap mortars were falling all around. Suddenly the tanks disappeared but the Jap machine guns were still there. I called again for tanks; they came forward but the same thing happened.

"I sent back, too, for a squad—about six men at this point—and as they approached, I realized I had never seen the leading man before. He was one of six replacements that had joined my company the previous evening. As he came within half a dozen feet, a Jap knee-mortar shell exploded between us. I felt a blast of sand sweep over me, harmlessly. But my recruit doubled over with a fragment in his side.

"I turned him around and said, 'Keep walking and keep asking for the aid station.' He was the only one of the six newcomers that I ever laid eyes on. All of them were casualties that day. About twenty-five feet away, a lieutenant was on his knees, obviously in pain. I moved toward him and he flopped over, unconscious from the mortar shell concussion.

"The third time I got a tank to come help us, I told a platoon leader lieutenant to climb on the back of the tank before he came under fire, have the tank commander unbutton or open the cupola and tell him, the tank commander, he would not come out alive until he eliminated the Jap machine gun we could not get to. I told the lieutenant to stay on the tank until they did it. Frankly, I didn't expect him to come out of it intact, but he did and they got the job done. The lieutenant was wounded later in the day.

"I would estimate that our battalion consisted of about 400 officers and men that morning, and over 140 were casualties by afternoon. I saw some awful things. Perhaps the worst was a machine gunner of D Company. He sat behind that gun for hours. It was originally positioned to support our attack. During the hours that he waited, there was nothing he could do to help—no enemy he could see or shoot at. He only watched enemy mortar fire, and the dead and wounded of friendly troops. I happened to turn towards him, and as I saw his face, he started to shiver and the look in his eyes was indescribably pathetic and haunting. Some buddies had to carry him away.

"What a hell of a day! And we didn't gain a yard."

The 292nd JASCO coordinated artillery and naval support. Alanson Sturgis says, "Our basic weapon was a destroyer with five-inch guns. Occasionally we called on a cruiser with six- or eight-inchers. Naval gunfire was extremely accurate and the great thing was that if a ship couldn't hit the target from where it was because of hills, it could move.

"One day we were beating our brains out against a concrete bunker. A platoon of tanks had fired on it and didn't make any impression. Neither did my destroyer do any good. I asked for a cruiser and they said none were available but they did have a battleship with sixteen-inch guns that fire 2,000-pound projectiles. I fired thirty-nine rounds from the battleship at the bunker. They never scored a direct hit but they filled up all of the firing slits with dirt, trees and other debris, so the Japs abandoned the place."

The 1st Marine Division had replaced the Army's 27th Infantry Division on the eastern end. The same fierce resistance that had broken the Army units now fought off the leathernecks. Casualties piled up, a deadly stalemate pervaded the entire front, and the 6th Marine Division started its long trek from the northernmost tip of the island to reinforce its brother regiments.

Although Colonel Yahara's strategy that concentrated the bulk of the Japanese resources in the caves and fortifications along the Shuri Line continued to bleed the invaders, the Imperial Army headquarters, General Cho, deputy chief of the 32nd Army, as well as the heads of the 63rd Brigade and the 24th Division, chafed at the purely defensive mode imposed on the troops. They disdained a war of attrition.

In the deep recesses of the 32nd Army command post, with sake flowing freely, the overall leader, General Ushijima, his staff and the top officers of the army furiously debated their options. Tokyo advised of the massive *kikusui* being organized to strike the American fleet on May 3–4. The time seemed propitious for a massive counteroffensive.

An ambitious plan evolved. The 24th Division, on paper largely intact with 15,000 men, would spearhead a drive punching into the center and eastern sectors. The 32nd Army Command acted as if unaware of the savage punishment absorbed by Shimura's regiment. The script envisioned other units would follow the 24th Division, exploiting the openings and forcing the Americans to retreat or face annihilation. Several hundred engineers carried by barges would float ashore behind the U.S. soldiers, where they could destroy tanks and artillery.

Unlike some earlier attacks, this was not construed as a banzai mission solely aimed at killing as many of the foes as possible in a suicidal venture. The operation directed units towards specific objectives with an eye to gaining strategic advantages. Artillery, the handful of tanks available, communications technicians, medics, indeed all support troops, were to carefully coordinate their efforts with the infantrymen as part of the overall goals. May 4 became "X-Day."

The kamikazes had opened their phase of the battle at dusk on May 3 and through May 4 registered considerable success, although the warships sunk or damaged meant little to the developing fight on land. Similarly, planes from Kyushu tried to destroy U.S. ground support Corsairs at Kadena and Yontan, but these added up to empty gestures rather than serious interference with operations from the two airfields.

The barges bearing the 26th Shipping Engineer Regiment, plotted to land behind the Marines along the western coast, committed a fatal error in navigation. At 2:00 A.M. on May 4, they turned for a beach guarded by well-entrenched members of the 1st Marine Division. Riflemen behind a sea wall spotted the ten barges and poured volleys of shot into the engineers. Naval vessels, alerted to the attack, lofted star shells that lit up the scene. Mortar sections lobbed explosives into the boats and several flamed up.

Many of the Japanese scrambled through the shallows to shore, some even able to work their way south back to their infantry comrades. But most were cornered in the village of Kuwan, where the Marines systematically killed them all. To the east, the same maneuver, designed to place some 500 from the 23rd Shipping Engineer Regiment behind the 7th Division on Skyline Ridge, met the same fate. Maurice Reeves, the first sergeant of Company C in the division's 13th Engineer Battalion, recalls, "We had set up two-man foxholes not far from the beach. The Japs' end run landed some troops from small boats just about right on top of us. They brought us under fire but we killed or captured all of them in our area." Ships and soldiers from the 7th Division, assisted by the U.S. 776th Amphibious Tank Battalion, wiped out several hundred of the foe.

American intelligence detected movement of enemy artillery but concluded the deployment of the heavy guns might signify a Japanese withdrawal from the forward positions on the Shuri Line. In fact, large pieces were being shifted to spots where they could better support the attack. (The absence of prisoners—the 77th Division, for example, reported 3,500 Japanese killed by May 6 without a single prisoner counted—handicapped evaluation of information.)

About four-thirty in the morning, the Japanese artillery opened up with massive barrages, delivering 8,000 rounds into the 7th Division and another 4,000 upon the 77th Division. It was the biggest effort mustered by the defenders during the Okinawa campaign.

The 32nd Infantry Regiment was designated lead force for the ground attack. Capt. Koichi Itoh, commander of the 1st Battalion of the 32nd Infantry Regiment, a graduate of the 1940 class at the Japanese Military Academy, came from a military background. "My father was an officer who had graduated from the Naval Engine School but voluntarily resigned his commission at age thirty because of tuberculosis."

Although Itoh might be presumed to endorse the belligerence generally attributed to pre–World War II Japanese from that sort of environment, he says, "Before the war, I never once thought that the United States was a threat. But I did feel dissatisfied about the Washington Treaty, which placed unfair numerical restrictions on Japanese naval power. Before the war, I never had any intercourse or contact with an

Working with the 96th Division GIs, infantrymen from the 77th Division support an assault along route 9. (*Signal Corps, U.S. National Archives*)

American or westerner. I think there was a lot of anti-American sentiment fifty or sixty yers ago. I believe a lot of it was caused by misunderstandings rooted in cultural differences."

Referring to the Japanese assault on Pearl Harbor, Itoh says, "I do not believe that an undeclared war is proper. I understand the declaration of war was delayed due to a breakdown in communications." (If this is a common perception among Japanese of any age today, it would appear their reading of history differs from that of most people.)

"I was not at all confident that we could win the war. Based on my understanding of world strategy, I do not think that Japan was in a position to wage a war." In this regard, Itoh recalls a discussion with Kiyohiko Miyoshi, a contemporary who later commanded an artillery company on Okinawa, while the two of them were still in Manchuria.

"In July 1944, Miyoshi and I were the only two remaining in the officers' mess. 'Hey, Miyoshi. Now Saipan, too, has fallen.'

"Miyoshi answered, 'It was really vulnerable, wasn't it?'

"This means that Japan has lost. Everything must be built again from scratch. We must resign ourselves to twenty years of reconstruction." Miyoshi agreed, and Itoh remarks, "This kind of talk was never to be

While in Manchuria, Koichi Itoh, a battalion commander for the Japanese on Okinawa, wore cold weather gear. *(Koichi Itoh)*

indulged in by soldiers on active duty, such as we were, but there was nobody else around, and so I spoke right from the heart to young Miyoshi."

Itoh's 32nd Regiment had pulled out of Manchuria and arrived on Okinawa August 6, 1944. Every day thereafter they worked to build fortifications or at drilling. However, he never accepted the strategy dictated by Colonel Yahara. "The Japanese were mistaken in their judgment of the point of landing by the Americans from the beginning. The disposition of the Japanese forces was lacking in any determination to annihilate the enemy forces. If there were indeed such annihilating measures, then we should have marshalled all our powers to that end."

On the eve of the Japanese counteroffensive, men from the 307th Regiment of the 77th Division were still locked in the contest for control of the Maeda Escarpment. Sgt. Henry Lopez of C Company was jolted by the sight of thirty-foot scaling ladders and Navy cargo nets slung from the rocky edges of the ridge at its eastern end.

"An abrupt ascent up the scaling ladders brought the company out on

An army nurse administers whole blood to a wounded man.
(*Signal Corps, U.S. National Archives*)

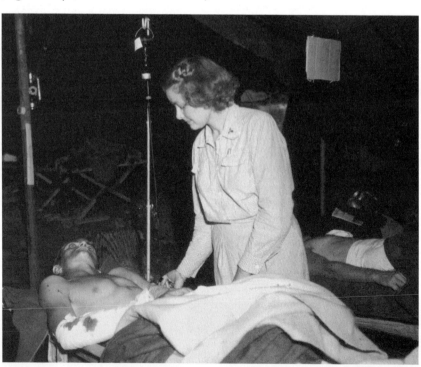

the brow of a rugged and sheer fifty-foot precipice, with a narrow plateau to the front, which gradually widened out until it was 150 feet across. The men fanned out in single file. Enemy grenades, knee mortars and 81 mm mortar shells were exploding. A three-foot high rock wall offered protection from snipers as long as one crouched. Lt. Martin Tamasy, who was the lead man for the 1st Platoon, glancing over the low rock wall, saw four Japs lying side by side, rifles in hands but helmets removed. Lieutenant Tamasy and Sgt. Alfred Junkin quickly killed all four."

The enemy stepped up the pace of its fire and attempted a counterattack. Mortars broke up that effort. As night darkened the slope, the GIs, unable to dig in the rocky terrain, piled stones around them and hunkered down in the face of Japanese artillery. A burning fuel dump shed light upon the escarpment, making infiltrating foes easy targets as they emerged from their spider holes and caves.

With morning, the Americans, using their ladders and nets, hauled up boxes of grenades, five-gallon cans of gasoline and the ubiquitous satchel charges for use against the maze of caves and dugouts. Lopez reports, "Three satchel charges were detonated in a deep shaft. Legs,

A halftrack stalls in the mud after heavy rains late in April and early May. (*Signal Corps, U.S. National Archives*)

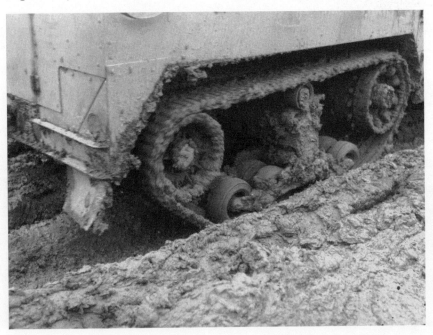

arms, and other assorted fragments of Japs, guns and equipment blew out of connecting tunnels, forty feet or so in the air."

The enemy not only refused to yield but raked the GIs with their weapons; a grenade killed Lieutenant Tamasy; rifle and mortar fire felled others. Shell fragments from big guns decapitated two and wounded a number of men. After seventy-two hours of fierce fighting, its last officer evacuated for an injury, C Company started to withdraw, down the rope cargo nets. Of the 162 soldiers on the roster April 29, when they came up on the line, only eighty-two remained. The entire 1st Battalion that had ascended the Maeda Escarpment with about 800 had retreated, with 324 survivors.

Henry Lopez pays special tribute to Company C first sergeant Carl Stanick. "He proved his capable leadership as well as his courage during the see-saw battle to take the escarpment. We were ordered to withdraw during an intense artillery barrage and, as all of the officers were

Infantrymen advance during the battle for Okinawa. (*Jack Lewis*)

either killed or wounded, he took command of the company and withdrew the men down the cargo nets. He quickly reorganized what was
left of the battered unit and then led the men back up into the escarpment. After subsequent attacks and blasting caves with explosive, seal-
ing them from the reverse slope of the ridge, he returned to the valley
below. Through this action, Company C helped to clear its sector on top
of the ridge. For this he was awarded the Bronze Star.

A medic gives water to 77th Division Pfc. James Smith after a sniper bullet tore
into his shoulder. *(Signal Corps, U.S. National Archives)*

"In the valley, Stanick and the men joined up with some tanks. He was seen walking on the open slope, exposing himself to heavy rifle fire while personally directing the fire of three tanks on heavily protected enemy positions. That action added a Silver Star to his decorations."

Lopez himself was among the wounded. "I was evacuated from the battalion medical station after receiving blessings from the regimental chaplain, Father Daniel Hunt. They transferred me to a hospital ship in the bay, but unfortunately that vessel had been strafed and bombed by Jap planes, which killed a number of wounded soldiers, sailors, doctors and nurses. I was moved to a troopship with limited medical facilities and staff. It headed for Saipan, and many of the wounded were injured sailors from picket duty on destroyers. My first view when I boarded the ship was a row of dead men on the deck, with tags on their big toes. I felt rather ashamed of myself with only a gunshot wound on my upper left arm."

The body count for the Maeda Escarpment battle would have gone

Infantrymen from the 96th Division aim their M-1 rifles at defenders on Big Apple Hill towards the end of the campaign.
(*Signal Corps, U.S. National Archives*)

even higher in the Liberty Division were it not for a single medic, Pfc. Desmond T. Doss, the Seventh-Day Adventist who, during training camp, had shunned a rifle as against his religion. During the struggle atop the escarpment, Doss climbed the ladders to the ridge on at least four separate occasions. He was always the last of Company B to leave.

On May 4, his superiors, noting his blood-crusted uniform, scrounged fresh clothing for him. On Saturday, which Doss by religious belief honored as the Sabbath, and therefore spent the day in prayer, Company B received orders for another visit to the escarpment. The company commander voiced his dismay at not having a medic to succor the troops. Doss supposedly overheard him and said, "Sir, I will go with you but you will have to wait while I read my Bible." Fifteen minutes later, Doss accompanied the soldiers of Company B.

It was another bloody and fruitless endeavor, an exchange of as many as 1,000 grenades during a three-hour battle. It ended with the GIs forced to escape down the ropes. Doss, however, was not with them. Those down below the ridge were amazed to see him wave from the cliff thirty-five feet above. For the next three hours, he stayed on top, lowering wounded, one by one, by means of improvised rope litters. In this fashion, he rescued about fifty soldiers, earning himself a Congressional Medal of Honor.

Two weeks later, during a night attack, a grenade seriously wounded Doss in his legs. Rather than risk the lives of others who might be mistaken for infiltrators should they come to his aid, Doss kept silent and treated himself. After five hours, litter bearers reached him but the group came under fire. Doss directed his companions to attend another injured man. While he waited for aid, another explosion fractured his arm. Doss then strapped a rifle to his shattered limb and crawled 300 yards to safety.

The Liberty Division thrust at the Maeda Escarpment had been frustrated. But the 307th Infantry's GIs had killed and wounded hundreds from the forces chosen to lead the X-Day counteroffensive. Itoh's original complement of roughly 1,200 now stood at only half that. The fighting had shattered the 2nd Battalion, commanded by Capt. Tsuneo Shimura. The 1,500 Japanese who started so cheerfully for the Maeda Escarpment now numbered about little more than 300, most of whom were trapped in one of the cave networks.

On X-Day, Itoh's battalion began its advance in the wake of the artillery's attempt to open gaps in the American lines. Within half an hour, Itoh, his soldiers and those of other units encountered stiff opposition by well-entrenched GIs from the 77th Division's 306th Regiment.

The tanks expected to aid in a breakthrough never contributed. U.S. cannons caught some on the roadway, and Pfc. James Poore, using a bazooka, knocked out the only pair of medium tanks that neared the American positions.

Itoh's battalion incurred horrific losses; the original 600 were reduced to 470. But by nightfall he decided to press the attack. The objective was Tanabaru, a small town at the base of the Tanabaru Escarpment, 1,500 yards behind the American lines, and which GIs had seized ten days earlier. He was under no illusion, however, that whatever he achieved, the tide of World War II would turn. "I did not think it was possible to defeat the enemy or anything like that."

One of Itoh's subordinates, Capt. Shoishi Oyama, led the 2nd Company of the battalion, which had distinguished itself repelling earlier enemy advances. He approached Itoh after receiving his orders. According to Itoh, "Oyama smiled audaciously and said, 'For us to go to the Tanabaru Highlands, that should be a good thing.'" Itoh says he responded that he would accompany the troops and, "the hearts of the battalion commander and the company commander were surging with mutual confidence and trust."

In a column of twos, the 1st Battalion stealthily hiked towards the enemy line. Some GIs claim they heard the sounds of marching feet but assumed they were friendlies. By dawn of May 5, Itoh and his men occupied a portion of the Tanabaru Ridge. "I think the main reasons for the success were in discerning the weaknesses of the deployment of the American forces and the selection of the method [the use of a narrow column instead of a broad skirmish line]."

But to his dismay, Itoh found himself isolated. "I expected that, once my battalion had succeeded, other Japanese forces would join together and advance. We could achieve a temporary tactical victory in a small region." Not only was he cut off from his countrymen, but communications broke down. Aware of his presence, U.S. artillery rained down on the Tanabaru Escarpment and small-arms fire tattooed the ridge. Itoh could not obtain permission to retreat until the night of May 7. A sniper's bullet snuffed out the life of his friend Oyama.

While GIs continued to shoot at Itoh's abandoned positions atop Tanabaru, he led the remnants of the the 1st Battalion back to the temporary safety of the Shuri Line. The meager, temporary gains achieved left his outfit with only 250 soldiers. The entire offensive had become a military disaster. With their positions reversed, the GIs, now in protected defensive venues and bolstered by superior air, sea and ground weaponry, slaughtered the Japanese, now out in the open and shorn of their cave cover. The figures for the two days of battle list 5,000 dead among the attackers, while more than 700 Americans were carried as KIA or WIA. General Ushijima, who bore ultimate responsibility for the offensive, tearfully advised Colonel Yahara that henceforth he would abide by his strategy. The militant General Cho remarked that defeat was now inevitable.

Buckner Creel's G Company in the 306th Regiment helped stave off the second day of the offensive after being in reserve the first night. Creel was bemused by an incident involving one of his soldiers. "I had a Pvt. David Kellner, a very devout Jewish man. On Leyte, while we were on a ridge line in tall Kunai grass, we received our first counterattack. I was moving up and down our lines encouraging the troops. I came across David Kellner, sitting down with his back to the attack, calmly firing his rifle into the air.

"I hollered at him and jerked him to his feet—he was much smaller than I—demanding to know what he was doing. He explained that he didn't want to kill anyone. I informed him that this was a kill or be killed situation and he had better hop to it.

"As part of our field equipment, we carried a canteen on each hip and a large 'Jungle Aid Kit' on the back of the cartridge belt. As Kellner stood up, with enemy rifle fire whipping around us, he yelled, 'I'm hit.' I asked him where and he said his leg. He turned and I discovered that he had been shot through the canteen on his right hip and the 'blood' he felt running down his leg was water. As he showed me this, he was shot through the canteen on his left hip. As he showed this to me, he got shot through the Jungle Aid pouch.

"At this moment, David said to me, 'Lieutenant, you're right. They are trying to kill me.' As he turned to face the advancing Japanese and raised his rifle to his shoulder, a bullet went through his rifle stock. I've never seen so many close ones on only one person.

"Now on Okinawa, we were engaged in mopping up infiltrators after the attack, David Kellner and a couple of the boys were wandering around—I always figured they were souvenir hunting, which we discouraged—but they denied this. They came upon a cave and David entered it. According to the guys with him, there was one helluva roar that came out of the cave—gunfire, grenades, etc. When things quieted down, David strolled out with a few nicks, scratches and a little hard of hearing, but all right. When his mates checked the cave, they found from twelve to fifteen dead Japanese. We recommended that Kellner get the Silver Star, but I believe he received the Bronze Star."

Slightly wounded on Leyte, Leonard Schweitzer, a Pfc. with Company K of the 306th Regiment, dodged another bullet a few days after he arrived on Okinawa, when one pierced his helmet but only nicked the back of his head. With his squad leader down, Schweitzer replaced him, and on May 11 around 7:30 A.M. he climbed out of his foxhole as part of an attempted advance. "We got to the top of a knoll and started down the other side. All hell broke loose. I hit the ground and was looking for cover. I saw no comrades, not even wounded, only ones who had been killed.

"I got up to go further and I got six or eight hollow-point bullets in and above the left hip and one in by my spine. As I was falling to the ground, I got another in the left knee. I saw Japs quite near me and didn't want to give my location away. I did a lot of praying.

"About an hour or so later, three or four stretcher bearers came up to carry off the wounded. They were all killed. Three tanks tried to come up but they were knocked out and the crews killed. About three or four in the afternoon, they shot over a lot of smoke. I knew that this was my only chance. I could not walk or run or stand. I prayed, I cried; I heard others at a distance doing the same thing.

"I finally got in the track left by a tank, set my wounded leg on my good one, pulled myself with my elbows up the hill and started down the other side. I supposed I crawled eighty yards in that tank track. I looked up and there was a tank at the bottom coming towards me. They drove over me, stopped, pulled me up through the bottom. All the time there was rifle and machine gun fire hitting the tank. While one man held me, the tank turned around and headed for the rear. If ever a tank went forty miles an hour, that one did."

Evacuated in that fashion to a point where he could ride a stretcher mounted on a jeep, Schweitzer reached a field hospital. Around midnight, a surgeon started to work on him. "He said, 'You're bound for the States.' I said, 'No, sir.' He insisted I was. I couldn't believe it.

"Morning came, the doc called out our names and we answered. He said to me, 'I didn't think you'd be here.' That makes you think." Another jeep with a stretcher hauled Schweitzer to an airfield. "They put my stretcher on a fork truck, then hung me on the wall of a C–54 and flew me to Guam."

The 96th Division's brief respite had ended May 9, as it relieved the 7th Division holding the eastern end of the line across Okinawa. "We were still beat and tired," says Ellis Moore. "You could hardly see any difference between us and those we relieved, except we had clean uniforms. In our new location, we could see the town of Yonabaru, and the Pacific Ocean. Conical Peak, which looked like a giant ice cream cone, was off to our left. It was raining hard, the mud gave us trouble getting food and supplies up. Things would get so bad on the roads that they started dropping things to us by parachute."

The peak of Conical Hill stuck some 500 feet into the air and the Japanese exploited the elevation as an observation post. It allowed them to direct accurate artillery fire on any U.S. forces approaching the site. Breaking the Shuri Line at the eastern side of Okinawa demanded capture of the natural tower. Jack Fitzgerald, one of the OCS graduates, after a record of service on Guadalcanal and Bougainville, had been with the 7th Division troops driven off Gaja Ridge, a finger of high ground that led northeast from Conical Hill, during the Japanese offensive.

At Conical Hill, Bob Muehrcke, Fitzgerald's classmate at Fort Benning and, like him, a veteran of Solomon Islands battles with the Americal Division, now a replacement platoon officer with Company F of the 96th's 383rd Regiment, faced his first combat on Okinawa. On May 11, Muehrcke led his 1st Platoon along the slopes of Gaja Ridge.

Muehrcke moved cautiously, slowly, deliberating carefully before committing his troops. He was intent on preserving their lives while gaining the objectives. A combination of artillery, white phosphorus, satchel charges and smoke grenades enabled the platoon to eliminate eleven pillboxes without suffering a single casualty.

But that good fortune, the residue of luck and Muehrcke's tactics, could not last indefinitely. Says Muehrcke, "T. Sgt. Elmer Wood, the heavy weapons platoon leader, jumped into my foxhole on the front lines at Gaja Ridge. He wanted to know where the Japanese were. After two push-ups from the parapet, he was able to locate them. But on his third look, he took a bullet in his forehead and was killed immediately. I tried to pull Sergeant Wood out of the foxhole. I did manage to roll his body over the parapet and down the hill. While doing this, I was wounded in my arm and shoulder by a single, small, rifle bullet.

"It was a superficial wound. Capt. Robert Becker cleaned and dressed it and I rejoined the platoon. In the heat of the Okinawa battle, I did not want to leave my platoon, the men who fought with me. They were short on sergeants and line officers. The pain was bearable and after two days, the shoulder and arm, while still sore, were healing."

A day later, Muehrcke met with his noncoms for a battle plan that would rid Gaja Village of its resident Japanese soldiers. The infantrymen would be accompanied by two Sherman medium tanks and a trio of flamethrowing ones.

The platoon moved out, crossing rice paddies, with a squad of men right behind each flamethrowing tank in a mutual protection arrangement. About fifty yards from the objective on the ridge, the machine guns and 75 mm guns on the two Shermans began firing. At thirty-five yards from the enemy positions, each flamethrowing vehicle spewed a long stream of concentrated fire that saturated the targets. The flames burned for at least fifteen minutes and, to Muehrcke, seemed an eternity. He remarks, "The smell of roasted human flesh resulting from these tanks was never to be forgotten."

As the defenders tried to flee, the 60 mm mortars and light machine guns from F Company's heavy weapons platoon chopped them down. Muehrcke ordered S. Sgt. Edward "Lefty" Mankunas to sweep the area. "Mankunas," says Muehrcke, "was a man with a sense of humor about himself, even in unusual battle situations. However, when he left the tanks to clean up the Japanese positions, he discovered he was all alone. He used a few choice words to move his squad forward."

The 383rd's 2nd Battalion consolidated its front line at the approaches to Conical Hill itself. And on May 13, word came from Gen. Simon Bolivar Buckner, "Take the summit." In midmorning Muehrcke's platoon, with the other elements from the 383rd, pressed forward. "During the ascent of Conical Hill," says the 1st Platoon leader, "we encountered a machine gun position just below the summit. It briefly held us up but we disposed of it in a few minutes with satchel charges.

"Within the machine gun cave we found a Japanese knee mortar and about seventy or eighty rounds of ammunition. While at the Infantry School at Benning, we received instructions in the use of this weapon. Several of my men carried the knee mortar to the top of Conical Hill and then brought up its shells. At the crest, I taught Sergeant Mankunas how to use it."

Atop the peak, Muehrcke and his people looked out over the Pacific for a front row seat as kamikazes called on the fleet. Muehrcke remembered his anxiety as an infantryman aboard a troopship, the insecurity of being trapped below deck while planes attacked ships above.

He had little time for sightseeing, however, because, although they encountered only light resistance while making their way up the strategic hill, the GIs expected the enemy would seek their ouster. A Piper Cub spotter plane saw the Japanese massing for this purpose. The pilot radioed the information to the 921st Field Artillery Battalion. A time-on-target barrage in which all pieces fired together, combinations of air bursts and point-of-contact explosions brought down a storm of shrapnel upon the assembled soldiers.

Exhausted GIs from the 96th Division sack out at Big Apple Ridge.
(*National Archives*)

Lefty Mankunas added to the devastation with deft use of the captured knee mortar. In addition, the blow at the counterattackers included ordnance from the 88th Chemical Mortar's 4.2-inch weapons
and the 60 mms of the heavy weapons platoon. From its vessel offshore,
the Navy protected the GIs with illumination flares during the night,
sharply reducing the effectiveness of infiltration tactics. The Americans
on Conical Hill beat off three separate attempts to evict them. However, the struggle to retain control came at a high cost. Mines, mortars,
snipers and other enemy fire killed and maimed many in Muehrcke's
group.

To the west of Conical, the 96th's 382nd Regiment coped with another sector formerly occupied by the 7th Division. Len Lazarick recalls, "It was raining the day we packed our belongings, boarded an
Army truck and headed south along some very sloppy roads. MPs stationed along the way directed the trucks to the proper route. These
were 96th Division MPs and, to a man, they waved at us and shouted
good luck.

"Our trucks took us to within a mile of our ultimate destination. We
slogged through the mud and up some slopes overlooking Item and

Zebra Hills. As we replaced the 7th Division troops and took possession of their foxholes, they wished us luck. I saw the relief in their eyes. They knew the score and their good wishes were sincere. We all belonged to that same, exclusive fraternity, combat infantry.

"During the first night on the front lines, some of our replacements did some loud talking and laughing. Some were careless about lighting and smoking cigarettes. Clearly, they had not heeded the advice and instruction given back in the rest area. Attempts to quiet these raw recruits down with stage whispers, 'Shut the f—— up!' were either not heard or obeyed. No one was going to leave his foxhole and crawl around trying to rectify the situation, because he would probably be dead by morning. We got through the night without incident, but there was plenty of hell raised the following morning, with heavy emphasis upon what happens when you do not follow nighttime perimeter discipline.

"On May 10 we were ordered to launch a frontal attack on Item Hill, immediately to our front. It was midmorning when we charged over the top of our own hill and were met by very heavy machine gun fire. Several riflemen were hit instantly and our squad leader, S. Sgt. Jim Peters, fell to the ground like he had been hit with a sledgehammer. Within minutes we withdrew from this withering small-arms fire and tended to our dead and wounded.

"I ran to Jim Peters's side to see what I could do to help him. He was in great pain. I cut open his fatigues to expose a gunshot wound that had gone clean through his leg. I could see the ground below; the hole was the size of a half dollar. 'How bad is it, Laz?' he asked. I told him he had a winner—a ticket to the States—but he should be okay. He replied, 'Fine, give me a shot of morphine and get me outta here.'

"As we talked, I poured sulfa powder into his wound, wrapped it with a bandage from his kit and tried to fashion a splint for his leg with his rifle. Our company aid man had his hands full with other casualties, but eventually a medic got there and gave him a shot of morphine. A litter moved him off the hill. When he was out of earshot, I quietly began to cry. My best friend was gone—the war was over for him—and I was now in charge of his squad, which was already down to seven men. My tears were both of joy and sorrow for old Jim Peters. Now he could get home to see his wife and baby daughter, and I silently prayed he would not lose his leg."

In midafternoon, Lazarick, with the others from Company K, again rushed Item. To their amazement, the fierce resistance of the morning never erupted. They owed the ease with which the objective fell to a one-man assault force, Lt. Seymour Terry, company commander for B Company of the 382nd, who by himself eliminated an intricate, heavily fortified system of caves, tunnels and gun emplacements, using phosphorus grenades, his carbine and satchel charges. For this exploit, along with two similar ones that followed, Terry would earn a Congressional Medal of Honor.

The advancing infantrymen discovered they had bypassed a number of caves that still harbored enemy soldiers. "One of our medics," remarks Lazarick, "armed only with a carbine, silenced two caves, so he could get past with wounded GIs on litters. It's an ugly war when medics are armed and expected to use their weapons." When K Company dug in for the night, Lazarick, grimly notes, "The foxholes were quiet and no cigarettes in sight. The surviving replacements were learning quickly."

On the following day, the outfit scrambled over the crest of Zebra Hill. When they started to descend along a gentle slope of open ground, the well-zeroed-in Japanese mortars and machine guns killed or severely wounded many GIs. Lazarick escaped injury and when the shelling died down, he and others began to minister to the stricken. A smoke screen enabled the withdrawal of the able-bodied and walking wounded. Lazarick carried out one soldier, then volunteered to return to the fire-swept area and help evacuate another pair of downed Americans.

On May 12, Lazarick watched members of the antitank company drag their 37 mm cannon up Zebra Hill to add some support for the next attempt to evict the enemy. He was bemused by the sight of a ring of GIs throwing rocks at two habu snakes, the vipers everyone feared infested Okinawa. "It would have been crazy to try and shoot the snakes because a stray bullet would hit or ricochet into our people."

When the signal to move out came, Lazarick led his squad for fifty uneventful yards. "All hell then broke loose with mortar and small-arms fire. I realized that a very good marksman had me in his sights. Bullets were whining around me and crackling over my head—a sign they were very close. I was all alone, out in the open. I decided to run back to the squad and find cover. I was at a full run when the shooter finally hit me in the left shoulder. The shot knocked me down and my rifle flew out of my grasp. My entire left side was numb and my arm limp. To this day, I'm not sure if some GI in L Company [off to the flank of Lazarick's unit] mistook me for a Jap 100 yards away. The bullets that missed me earlier seemed to be at a rate of rapid fire very hard to achieve with a bolt-action Japanese rifle. But it could have been a Jap with a captured M–1, or two different soldiers.

"After I was hit, I managed to make my way up the slope. I stuck my left hand between the buttons on my fatigue blouse for a crude sling that would keep the arm from dangling. My shoulder didn't hurt as much then. Once over the top of the hill, I was greeted by some medics who tagged me, gave me a shot of morphine and got me a seat in a nearby ambulance. I was surprised how quickly the morphine went to work, because it wasn't long before I was feeling no pain. A very pleasant euphoria set in as the ambulance, with two litter cases and four walking wounded, took us on a bumpy ride directly to a field hospital set up on the beach, near our initial landing spot.

"The field hospital was a depressing experience. We were all put in a waiting room upon arrival. It was wall-to-wall litter cases. The walking wounded had to stand because there wasn't room for a lot of benches. Some of the wounded were moaning, some were crying and one GI was

Marines jump off for an assault. The lead leatherneck bears communications wire. (*Signal Corps, U.S. National Archives*)

calling for his mother. Those who couldn't fit in the waiting room were set up in ward tents and told not to wander off.

"I went for X-rays and then back to a ward tent, which I preferred to the waiting room. I had clean dressings on the wound and my left arm was in a sling. The effects of the morphine had worn off and I was in some pain. They gave me pills and told me to lie down.

"Eventually, I saw a doctor, who examined the injury. He took a very thin wire and probed the hole all the way through, front to back. I asked him what he was doing and he told me he was checking for any piece of uniform that might be in the wound and could cause infection. He explained I was very lucky because the bullet went clean through. It missed the socket of my shoulder and arm, missed all the bones except the shoulder blade, and that only had a hole in it. And most fortunately, the bullet missed the apex of my lung. I was luckier than he knew. I had left the front in one piece and would sleep on a cot that night.

"Father Le Clerc, the chaplain, came around. I spoke to him for about fifteen minutes and asked him to write a letter to my parents and explain that my wound was not life threatening. He agreed. I mentioned that I heard a couple of medics bitching about how much work

Pinned down U.S. forces receive supplies through air drops.
(*National Archives*)

they had to do, and could Father arrange to have complainers sent to the front? He smiled and said complainers didn't realize how well off they were. Don't misunderstand me. I give the U.S. Army medics very high marks for the care they gave me, and the company aid men and litter bearers are the unsung heroes of the war.

"During the night they sounded an alarm for an air raid. The noise alone scared me. I had only one good arm, no rifle, no grenades, no helmet and stood in a ward tent in hospital pajamas. I felt naked and helpless. No one instructed us to go to an air raid shelter. We just had to sit tight. After a short stay at the field hospital, I was evacuated to Guam by air."

Some months later, division headquarters recognized Lazarick for his actions in rescuing wounded soldiers by awarding him a Bronze Star.

Paul Westman, also with Company K, already aware that his close pal Shelby Allen was near the breaking point, was told by Allen he had bad news. "The CO just made me a squad leader." When Westman tried to offer congratulations, Allen responded, "All it means is that I won't be going home." Subsequently, Allen accosted Westman and handed him a slip of paper with an address for Mrs. Shelby Allen in Cincinnati. "He said, 'When you get back, I want you to write to Eliza and tell her I love her and to take care of our babies [two daughters].' I gave him my address and he was surprised there was no street number or even a box. I explained we lived so far out in the sticks that they had to pipe in sunlight. Didn't even bring a smile.

"On the second day in our new positions, I was cleaning my BAR in my foxhole when my new squad leader, Jeff Brooks, stopped by and with no preliminary, said, 'I have to tell you that your buddy Allen was killed a few minutes ago.' My heart did a few flip flops and then Jeff said Shelby had tried to get at a sniper. Without a word to anyone, he had crawled out in front of the company lines and hadn't gone but a few yards when his helmet flew off and Shelby was gone. I asked Jeff to let me be alone for a few minutes. I was okay when the platoon leader, shortly afterwards, said move out.

"We had some savage firefights as we closed in on Shuri. Arza Smalley won a battlefield promotion on Leyte and was well liked. On this one day, he was out in front, after having led us on a wild charge across an open area with no real cover. When I ran up and we were face to face, it was evident he was in big trouble. He and another man had been at the mouth of a cave and about to pitch in a grenade when Smalley was hit twice in the chest. The fellow with him got whomever it was in the cave but Lieutenant Smalley was in a bad way.

"He stood there, with his legs braced and gritting his teeth. I think he was already in shock. I could see the two bullet holes; he was losing considerable blood but he refused to go down. He just stood there, swaying and sort of shivering. I had to leave, but the thought went through me, 'My God, what a man!' He probably never heard someone say, 'Good luck, I think you'll make it.' To my surprise, he did; I saw him more than forty-eight years later at a reunion.

"During this period, along towards midnight the sounds of a life and death struggle brought the entire company to a high state of readiness. About four holes away from mine, a desperate battle was underway and flares started to light up the area. You could plainly hear the GI, 'Die, you blankety, blankety blank! Damn you, aren't you ever going to die!' There were squeals mixed in with the curses, the sound of something heavy hitting flesh and bone again and again. Finally, the noise stopped and I heard a few more heartfelt curses, then I thought someone sobbing. I felt sick to my stomach and it was a while before I could quit shaking. It was all so totally unreal and eerie; no wonder it made people crack up.

"At daybreak, a big redhead from M Company stood up outside his hole and announced to the whole world, 'Hey guys, look what I got last night.' He had a big grin on his face. He got a big hand from everyone near. But I'll bet he hated to face each night from then on."

The 382nd's objective at the moment was a portion of Dick Hill, in reality, a ridge with three main peaks and two smaller ones, which on detailed maps became Dick Able, Dick Baker, Dick Right, Dick Center and Dick Left. The Imperial Army's artillery lashed the Dick Hill area constantly with both artillery and lesser forms of lethality.

Crawling up Dick Center, Westman briefly glimpsed the Chinen Peninsula, the East China Sea and Conical Hill on his left flank before he scraped a hole in the jumble of rock, earth and debris near the top. "There was a machine gun dug in about fifty feet away and the GI there stood up, facing sideways to me. A single shell hit the top of the ridge some ways from his emplacement. Fragments or flying rock spun him around to face me. He had no face left. There was no blood for a moment or two and then it turned into a gory mask. He may have stood there for three or four seconds, then fell forward. I don't suppose he had any sensation after the impact. He must have been dead almost instantly. When Jeff Brooks and Roland Irish came back from a squad leaders' conference, I think they only half believed me when I told them what had happened. It was that peaceful.

"From where I was, I could see Lt. Howard Tway and a companion in a sharp angle of the ridge. The Japanese were obviously aware of activity near them; they were only a few feet away. One of them heaved their version of a satchel charge. Tway or his comrade instantly grabbed it and threw it back over the ridge. It should have exploded but did not. Maybe it was a dud.

"Lieutenant Tway had now armed his own satchel charge and threw it. At the same time, another Japanese one came sailing over. It went off and so did Lieutenant Tway's. It was like a dream to see the lieutenant's body momentarily suspended in the air. The jar, when he came down, must have been terrific. I couldn't believe it when I saw a person rise out of the smoke and dust, arm another charge and let fly again. Apparently, he had already done the job, for no more explosives came over the ridge.

"My estimation of that two-man team rose about 2,000 percent. I wish that violent action, maybe a minute in duration, had been witnessed by a high-ranking officer, as well as a private like myself.

"On that evening of May 14, my last on the line, while Roland Irish and I were digging in, there were two sharp cracks. I felt a burning on my left shoulder and found a slit in my fatigue jacket where a bullet had grazed me. Irish had been peppered with coral fragments. We both dropped instantly, and I guess the Jap thought he got us both. But he stayed put for a while.

"I could see part of a rock ledge about 100 yards away but it couldn't have held a body. I raised up, a little at a time, until I could see another ledge below. There looked to be a knob showing. I reached out on the edge of my hole for my rifle and got in position. I put the sights on that knob and waited. It moved just a bit and I fired. A body rolled off the ledge, bouncing off some rocks. I stood up and drilled him with a couple of more shots. I heard somebody shout, 'By God, he got the SOB. Nice shooting, Deadeye!' It was the first time I'd ever rated a word of approval and it made me feel good.

"That night it started to rain and it kept on all night. Foxholes filled up with water and all you could do was to sit and take it. Daylight came and it was still raining but not quite so heavily. Company I got the orders to take the hill. They were on our right and moved up in a spread-out formation. Just as they crossed over the ridge, the reverse side of the slope came alive. You could hear the machine guns open up, the spaced shots, then the cough of mortars and then bodies were falling. Some would get up and move forward, then go down again.

"The sky was thick with mortars and not all were falling in the area of I Company. There was an instant when the world turned white and a terrific crash. I ceased to function. I couldn't even reason as I tried to climb out of the hole. I wasn't aware of any movements or sounds from Irish or Brooks. I fell several times and then came to, briefly, on a litter at the battalion aid station.

"The 1st squad had been down to three on Jeff Brooks, Roland Irish and myself. With the mortar round that dropped in our foxhole, the 1st squad temporarily ceased to exist." Lieutenant Tway saw to it that Brooks, Irish and Westman got to the battalion aid station. "I recognized Tway's voice and I asked about Jeff Brooks. Somebody on a litter beside me spoke, 'That you, Westman?' Then silence. Our litters were side by side and his head was a bloody mat of dressings. The next thing I can remember is being loaded on a big silver plane.

"As well as a concussion from the mortar that ruptured both of my eardrums, my left thumb was amputated, metal fragments were imbedded in the knuckles of my right hand, a three-quarter by four-inch chunk of flesh from my upper right arm was torn out, and pieces of shrapnel were lodged in my right shoulder and left bicep.

"Roland Irish survived also, the only one of the new replacements to last more than five days. He received a Bronze Star."

CHAPTER XXV

DAKESHI, WANNA AND SUGAR LOAF

As a platoon leader with G Company of the 1st Marine Regiment, Bob Craig and his men were on a reserve status when the Japanese counter-offensive of May 4–5 began with the predawn seaborne expedition that sought to place Japanese soldiers behind the Marine lines. Leathernecks on G's right flank dealt with the threat. "We knew something was going on," says Craig, "because Navy star shells and land-based flares lit up that area all night long.

"The next morning, Jim Paulus, the company exec, came up from the CP to see how things were. He looked over our left flank and saw a little smoke coming up from down below. He said to me, 'I think some gook is cooking chow down there.' I replied I didn't think so; it was probably some timbers in the cave still smoldering from yesterday's burn-out by the tanks, but that I'd check it out."

Craig approached the area from his ridge position. "As I looked over the edge, I saw a Jap at the entrance to the cave. At the same time, he looked right up at me. I quickly pulled a hand grenade from my pocket, yanked out the safety pin, released the activator handle, counted a fast one-two and dropped it. It had hardly left my hand before it went off. After the handle flew off, only three seconds elapsed before the grenade exploded. Of course, the Jap had ducked back into the cave when he saw me, but my concern was the apparently fast fuze.

"Jim Paulus and I immediately went back to the Command CP to check the supply of grenades. We found that they had sent up a new model with three-second fuzes, instead of the original five-second models we had been using. No one had advised us concerning the new model, and I would have been killed if I had held onto it for the time we had been trained to do with the five-second version. The reason for holding on was to avoid giving the Jap time enough to pick up the grenade and throw it back, as they had done earlier in the war. I warned all my men to check the fuze model numbers on what they had and any new ones they got."

Around noon, Craig huddled with a forward observer for the 11th Marine Artillery Regiment as that organization selected targets for its 105 mm howitzer barrage in preparation for an attack the following morning. "Before the forward observer left," says Craig, "he asked me where I wanted protective fire laid in, in case the Japs attacked that night. I told him to put it right down in the draw in front of us. He was somewhat reluctant because, he said, the area of dispersion for 105s might result in some shells falling short into our position. I told him I couldn't afford to leave the draw wide open without protective fire.

"About ten o'clock that night, I saw a smoke screen thrown up on Hill 60 [in front of Craig's position on Hill Nan]. I used the phone to call for an emergency barrage because it looked like the Japs were either going to make a night attack or were making troop movements behind the smoke screen. Within less than one minute the first of thirty rounds came over and appeared to burst right overhead, not in the draw where they were supposed to fall. I thought the FO had made a miscalculation in laying in the target because the rest of the rounds burst in similar fashion.

"No attack came and the next morning I got with the FO to find out what had happened. He explained that the shells had proximity fuzes which caused them to explode so many feet above the ground, throwing shrapnel into anything or anyone below. We had suffered no injuries or death from this event, solely because howitzers fire at high-angle trajectories. The shells we thought were landing among us actually burst as they came down on the forward slope of Hill Nan. It was another near miss for my platoon."

Craig's 3rd Platoon jumped off around 10:00 A.M., seeking to make its way past Hill 60. "We didn't get very far before a counterattack by Jap mortars stopped us in our tracks. The 1st Platoon then tried to relieve the pressure on us, but it too was hit by Jap mortars. Only fourteen escaped without injury. [Forty-nine officers and enlisted men ordinarily make up a Marine infantry platoon, but the number available by this time was somewhat less.] Lt. "Cat" Catterton, their platoon leader, could only hold the ground he had taken, waiting for relief or support."

Those in command committed the 2nd Platoon of G Company, but everyone was forced to fall back, and needed tank and heavy machine guns even to accomplish a successful retreat. The second day of the battle produced similar results, large numbers of casualties and a retreat back to the foxholes from which the attack was originally launched. Craig, Company Commander Dixie Koiner and Paulus were now the only officers from G Company still on their feet. The officer ranks for other units in the battalion were also badly depleted.

At midnight, the Japanese tried to overrun the position. "When this battle started," says Craig, "I was off watch trying to get some badly needed sleep. My runner, Leck, and another rifleman were on watch— we were using three men in a foxhole to avoid what had happened earlier on Hill Nan. Leck later told me he couldn't arouse me, presumably because I was so exhausted, but I didn't believe him and reamed him out. I have no recollection of that night, and, thank God, those two, with the rest of the platoon, stopped the counterattack.

"About 4:00 A.M., when it was over, I came to, probably because the sudden silence prodded my inner senses. I saw dead Japs, all over our area, maybe eighteen or twenty. As a matter of security, Leck and I ventured out of our foxhole to check them out and make sure none were faking dead. Sure enough, one was lying on his side, still holding onto his rifle. When I kicked the bottom of his foot, he flinched, then tried to rise up and shoot me. The slugs from my tommy gun knocked him back down."

The Marines renewed their drive and the battalion, with G Company, advanced southeast towards Dakeshi and Wanna Ridges, natural ramparts that guarded the town of Shuri and the anchor of the defenses bearing its name. Craig became pinned down by a Nambu machine gun in a large shellhole, half full of water. With him were Lecklightner and a wounded Marine. "I concluded we were going to be there for a while since there was no cover and we would not leave the wounded man there by himself.

"One of our tanks appeared and I attracted his attention. The tank commander told me he would drive the tank right over our hole, open up the escape hatch at the bottom, take the wounded man up inside. He did this and then Leck and I crawled out on the side of the tank, where we were not exposed to Jap fire. We walked back to a little knoll with the tank and waited for a corpsman and stretcher bearers. I could see bullets bouncing off the side of the tank. I hoped there was no antitank gun nearby, since the tank just sat there protecting us."

While the Marine 5th and 7th Regiments engaged the enemy on Dakeshi Ridge, the cohort with Craig dug in near Wanna Ridge. The Marine Air Wing flew in rations, water and ammunition, dropping the supplies by parachute, and for several days, the 2nd Battalion remained in a precarious state, flanks exposed, subject to murderous mortar and artillery fire from Wanna Ridge. Both Koiner and Catterton were wounded, making Paulus the company commander.

After four days, the strategists determined the position of the 2nd Battalion untenable and under cover of darkness the Marines retreated. "The happy surprise for us," says Craig, "was that we continued to march back to a rest area. For the next four days we got some cooked meals, daily showers, and brand-new clothing. We had been wearing the same uniforms for forty-four days and mine just about stood up by itself. We also received replacements for the three platoons, and, in

Marines, advancing on Naha, cautiously approach a cave.
(*Signal Corps, U.S. National Archives*)

addition, two new platoon leaders. But Jim Paulus's original slot as executive officer was not filled, which indicated a shortage of experienced officers."

Gunnery Sgt. Elmer Johnson, the onetime military bandsman shipped to Okinawa in a replacement draft, had labored on the beach pumping items into the supply pipeline. On May 5, with the Japanese attack stifled, at some cost to the Marines, Johnson was called up to C Company of the 1st Regiment.

"The company was still made up of well-trained men," says Johnson. "They had been in combat the better part of a month and we were all green, poorly trained replacements. I was assigned to accompany a sergeant who had been wounded twice in previous operations. This was how I was to be trained.

"The next morning we were ready to go at 0900, but the tanks couldn't move because of the rain the night before. We had to sit until noon. Then we moved out and the shit hit the fan. We were to take three small ridges that lay 200 to 500 yards to our front, and then swing right to the side of a small mountain. As we started out, all I could think about was that this is what it is all about; for over five years I had drawn pay as a Marine and wondered how I would do if it ever came to this. And I knew this was where men die! In any combat zone you learn to live with fear, but this was different. This was it!

"In a matter of minutes the Marine beside me was shot in the shoulder. He dropped his rifle, swore, picked it up and headed for the aid station. After that, as I ran from one hole to another, I turned to signal the man behind me to hit the dirt. As he dove into the hole I had just left, he and a mortar shell hit the hole at the same time. I went to go back to him but the sergeant signaled me, 'No!'

"Shortly after, the sergeant and I came upon another Marine and tried to get some information from him. But he had been shot right through the mouth. This sort of thing continued for four hours. We took those ridges, but our platoon of forty-six men numbered five. My first day in combat, the sergeant was gone and our lieutenant was gone. The company commander ordered me to turn in a casualty list. Hell, I hadn't known the name of anyone in the platoon but the sergeant. Our division history makes note of how this sort of thing played havoc with the compilation of casualty lists.

"The next night I was ordered to take a squad and set up a defense around the battalion CP. I was told to set trip flares and didn't know how. (I bluffed my way through, and by the following night knew what to do.) During the night, a Jap worked his way to within a few feet of the colonel's foxhole, which was covered by a pup tent. I doubt if the Jap knew it was the colonel's, but anyway the sentry with me spotted him at daybreak. We didn't know what to do because he was so close to the colonel.

"I took the sentry's M–1 and shot at him. What a mess that stirred up! The Jap ran and the colonel came out swearing, along with a lot of Marines. The next shot finished it off but I can still hear the colonel holler, 'You son of a bitch, that better be a Jap!' "

Johnson's company subsequently occupied a modest ridge on the edge of Wanna Draw, a lowland that was overlooked by the bastion of Shuri Castle. "They were firing at us with antiaircraft guns set to burst right over our heads and the Japs were on the high ground above us, giving it to us with mortars and small arms. I tried to set out flares for our artillery to help us. A bullet struck my tommy gun right between my hands; otherwise it would have hit me in the guts. Blood flew everywhere from my hands and I was knocked down, scared silly. However, I wasn't hurt very bad.

"A while later, I was in a large crater with several others. I felt uneasy because one shell could kill all of us. I crawled out and was lying on the ground when a mortar exploded right at my feet. I knew I was hit and again was scared very badly. I refused to look at my legs because I was sure I didn't have any. When the corpsman cut away my pants, he said I wasn't hurt very badly but I had better head for the battalion aid station. I didn't know where it was but I was told I'd have to walk out because no stretcher bearers could get to us."

In company of another Marine shot through the hand, Johnson worked his way back through windbreaks of scrubby bushes that separated otherwise open fields. They evaded the occasional bullets directed their way until they reached the company command post. "There was a lieutenant there from another company. His platoon was completely gone. He had been shot through the arm but wouldn't leave. He took the smoke grenades I carried to mark our flanks and said he would handle it. We took off for the aid station, which lay under artillery fire."

Evacuated farther back to an Army field hospital, Johnson, who had eaten nothing except the sulfa pills he gobbled after being wounded, stuffed himself at the mess tent. He then passed out, awakening to find himself on a cot with his still-dirty mess kit and his tommy gun on the dirt beneath him. "I gave the orderly hell for not cleaning my mess gear and demanded a pair of pants, as mine were bloody and cut away.

"He refused to give me any, even when I threatened to shoot him. He went off to report me, and while he was gone, I busted into his

Aided by tanks, Marines move into the city of Naha.
(*Signal Corps, U.S. National Archives*)

footlocker and took a pair of pajama bottoms. He returned with an
officer and I told them the only way I'd give up these bottoms was for
him to take them off me. The officer turned on the orderly and gave
him hell." Johnson was flown to a fleet hospital on Guam for treatment
of his injuries.

As an acting platoon sergeant in A Company of the 7th Marine
Regiment, Jim Moll and his unit had been pinned down by artillery a
day or so after they relieved the 27th Division soldiers. "I told Sgt. Vern
Smith, acting as platoon guide, we were all going to be dead ducks
unless we did something soon. With deadly fire coming in from behind
us, the only way out would be with a few tanks to cover our rear. I told
Smitty that whoever tries to get back to headquarters had a very slim
chance because he had to run along the ridge we were on, run down
through the draw and climb the only footpath up to the higher ridge. I
told Smitty I would go, but he insisted it would be better if I stayed with
the platoon. He took off his pack to lighten the load and shook hands
with me. A few minutes later, word came back to me that Smitty was
killed.

"I dropped my pack and took off. When I got to the spot where
Smitty was hit, they opened up on me with heavy machine guns and

Jim Moll found this photograph of a Japanese officer who died on Okinawa. (*Jim Moll*)

mortar fire. I dove into a small, shallow hole which left my feet and legs exposed. I felt two bullets hit my left shoe, but no pain. A few seconds later, a mortar exploded next to the hole. The blast knocked the stock off my weapon and me cold. When I came to, I jumped up and kept running until they tackled me. The bullets had passed right through the heel of my shoe but barely nicked me. Later, just before dusk, the Marines dropped smoke shells and got everyone off the ridge.

"That evening, we could see the Japs building up a heavy concentration of troops on a ridge about 200 to 300 yards in front of us. I had never seen such a massing of Jap troops, and I was concerned because we had no protection on our right flank. I had to send a man back to bring me a telephone so I could get some artillery support. Our machine gunners wanted to open up on the Japs but I knew then all hell would break loose. I had them hold back until I got the phone. The Japs started to blast hell out of us with their artillery and I finally contacted the 11th Marine Artillery. Unfortunately, I had no map to pinpoint our position. The Marine at the other end said they would fire three rounds and I should let him know where they landed. But with all of the Jap shells, I couldn't hear anything at first. Then during a short pause in the action, I thought I heard the three more rounds they fired way off in the distance. After about a dozen more tries, shells began landing between us and the enemy. I told them to start at that point and work their way outward on a path about 400 yards wide. I never witnessed such a masterly display of artillery. They literally blew the Japs off the hill."

Also with A Company of the 7th Marine Regiment, Lt. Don Farquahar had moved south as the leader of the machine gun platoon. "We started fighting on the 10th of May at Dakeshi Ridge. Lt. Doug Demler, who had the first platoon, had just made it over the ridge and down into the valley when he was hit, KIA. [This is the period described by Jim Moll, when the acting platoon guide Sergeant Smith also was killed.] I was sent down as his replacement, and it was then that I was glad I had joined the division early. [He had volunteered for quick assignment while in a replacement draft]. As I passed guys in the stream bed and in the valley, they told me where to be careful, where to hurry and where to duck.

"I finally found my platoon; it got late and we weren't going to make it to the top of the next ridge. We called for smoke and, under its cover, picked up all our wounded and climbed back to the ridge.

"The next day we started back down in what we began to call 'Death Valley.' We made it to the top this time but couldn't move sideways. There was a gun emplacement holding us up. I took a squad from the 1st Platoon and ran across and lost three guys. It was about seventy-five yards to the Jap gun. When we got there, some of us fired our weapons into the firing ports so they couldn't shoot at us. The rest ran to the top of the hill and raked the Jap position with BAR and tommy gun fire. We couldn't get any further that day, so we picked up our wounded on the way back to the company and returned to the ridge.

"The next day we made it all the way and along the ridge to Dakeshi town. Then we went into what was called 'Wanna Draw.' Lt. [Robert] Romo, the company commander, called all the officers to him. We were standing in a wrecked house, leaning over Romo, who was reading a map when a Jap in the rubble shot Romo through the head, killing him. Our exec officer, shortly thereafter disappeared, along with his runner. Temporarily, I took over the company and tied us in for the night. The following morning, Lieutenant McCall joined us as company commander."

Earl Rice, with A-1-7, headed toward southern Okinawa, coping with a swelling anxiety. "On May 9 we were moving up and I seen all these bodies, the maggots already on them. There were so many dead on the way up. You'd think they would have got them outta our way—because when you see they're dead and you know that's where you're going, you realize you can be killed. On Peleliu I didn't have that kind of fear, but on Okinawa I did.

"On May 10 we started to cross a big field, with hills in front of us, and on each side, I believe there were machine guns on at least two, or maybe on all three. Machine guns frightened me the most. The shit hit the fan; they opened up on us something awful, coming through a gulley. I said to Bill Arndt, who was our group leader, 'You better get your head down.' Him, being a corporal, thought he knew it all. I don't think five minutes went by when, bink! I could see the hole right through the helmet. I hollered for a corpsman and pulled his helmet off. Damn bullet went right through the helmet and the helmet liner but never touched his head. Amazing.

"A lot of guys got killed that day, like Vernon L. Smith—also, our platoon leader, Lieutenant Demler, one mean, rough son of a bitch, a sadist, I thought. He had guts though. He was using the field phone and had that phone, got shot over and over. The machine guns went after the stretcher bearers. One of them taking Demler back was killed. May 10 was awful. We got very little sleep, 100 percent watch during the night. The Japs were all over us. Next day, Lieutenant Cook walked from one place to another, but a skinny kid running full blast through the same area got shot through the heart."

Nolen "Bama" Marbrey, with K Company of the 5th Marine Regiment, and his fire team, Hill, Benson (Bens) and Hare, received orders to serve as a patrol led by Sergeant Lesperance into Shuri itself for intelligence purposes. Concealed by darkness, the team sneaked into the city. The Marines hugged the walls of buildings, gingerly picking their way lest their boots on the brick walkways alert the enemy.

"We ducked into the doorway of a large building to figure the best route. I could hear noises inside, murmurs that were too low to even make out the language they were speaking, but I didn't for a minute believe it was English. Once in a while a chair would scrape, and a voice would raise momentarily, as if in mock anger. Two indistinct shadows slid across the roof on the other side of the street, but I knew we couldn't have been seen yet or an alarm would have been given.

"Lesperance stepped out of the doorway and we followed. Turning the last corner, I saw the tank sitting in the middle of the street, flying a white flag with a red spot in the center. A couple of Japs stood near it talking. Without a pause in his end of the conversation, one of them pulled out his dick and pissed. We had come up behind the tank, which faced the direction of our front lines, and luckily, the Japs weren't worried about anything to the rear."

The patrol retreated through another door. In the gloom they discerned a number of enemy soldiers sound asleep, secure in the knowledge that the tank outside guarded them. The only possible escape route away from both the inhabitants and the tank lay in a stairway to a second floor. But as Marbrey climbed up to explore that route, a scuffle erupted. One of the soldiers had awakened and engaged in a silent, deadly struggle with the intruders.

"I hurried down," says Marbrey, "pulling my knife as I went. Another Jap raised his head just as Bens ran a bayonet through him. We got most of them while they were still asleep, all but the one that grabbed Hare and split his throat under the chin. Hare's blood spurted into the Jap's face, as three bayonets drove into his back."

Having killed all of the enemy soldiers swiftly and quietly enough to avoid outside awareness of their presence, the patrol headed up the stairs and out a window to a back alley. Marbrey carried Hare's dog tags, weapon and canteen. They sifted through the lines back to their outfit. Barely had they completed their report when the company started forward for another attack on the positions around Shuri.

Marbrey recalls a nightmare kaleidoscope of snapshots. "I drew up short, hearing a piercing scream. I looked again, a Marine, standing in the middle of the street, holding his crotch with his left hand and his rifle in the other, blood formed in a puddle at his feet, the seat and legs of his trousers changing color rapidly from mottled green to red.

"We covered the last two hundred yards on our bellies. I made it to a precariously leaning chimney. I called to Hill and Bens to join me; it was important to keep my team together. Two Japanese tanks rolled towards us, bricks and stones crunching underneath the massive treads, the snout of its weapon swinging back and forth seeking a target.

"As the lead tank drew near, Bens pulled the pin on one grenade and threw it, jumping back under cover before it hit. A damned dud! The second grenade bounced off the rear end before exploding ineffectually on the ground. His third one burst just under the left tread, slowing it down.

"Hill lost his balance but pitched the grenade at the tank as he fell. It hit the damaged tread, breaking the belt. A flamethrower shot a tongue of flame at the second tank, stopping it dead. Hill grabbed his rifle and, yelling as he ran, started for the second tank. Maybe he saw something we didn't.

"Another round of heavy artillery caused us to jump for cover. I looked for Hill. He was lying next to the tank, face down. I carefully picked my way to him. I rolled him to his side. A piece of metal protruded about six inches from his chest. He tried to speak, but red-ringed bubbles formed at the corner of his mouth. He lifted his hand toward my face; it then fell lifelessly. Bens, kneeling beside me, wiped Hill's face, saying 'Hold on, buddy, we'll get a corpsman,' knowing there'd be no answer."

Dazed, Marbrey broke into tears. But within hours, the Marines resumed the attack. "Something rolled by, leaving a faint trail of reddish-brown splotches. It came to a stop a few feet behind us, a head with its eyes open and staring. Our wounded and dead lay scattered over the area. If we could, Bens and I moved the living behind piles of bricks or oversized rocks till they could be seen to.

"I felt more alone and scared than ever before. God! I thought. If Uncle Sam doesn't have anybody better than me to fight this war, we're lost. I raised up on one elbow and a force hit me like a tornado. I felt myself rolling or flying until something solid got in my way. When I opened my eyes again, I couldn't tell which part of me wasn't hurting. My back was ablaze with pain but my head hurt, too. My teeth moved when my tongue touched them, but they were still connected to my gums. My hand was covered with blood, and I tried to see if I had all my fingers by counting each one as it wiggled. But I would forget which one wiggled last. My next memory was of being lifted onto a stretcher and placed on an amtrac for a long, bumpy ride to the beach."

Portions of the 1st Marine Division, with Craig, Moll, Farquahar, Rice, et al., still on their feet, had slid to their left, shortening the outfit's lines as the 6th Marine Division completed its journey south and assumed the most western positions.

"Major Walker ordered me south, ahead of the division," says Harry Manion, of the 6th Reconnaissance Company. "It really didn't give us any advantage. The company and the division were moving as fast. We first set in along a railroad track with good observation out to sea. The Navy was shelling inland. Some of our guys needed the help."

Everything was slowed by the torrential rain. "The mud conditions were so bad," says Stormy Sexton, "that even tracked vehicles bogged down. For approximately ten days, all supplies were brought up to the front lines by individual Marines. The mud was so thick, it grabbed a person's feet up and over the ankles."

The 6th Marines halted short of the first natural obstacle to progress, the Aswa Kawa—Aswa means 'morning' and Kawa is the word for 'river.' A bunch from the recon company helped the engineers unload and then erect a Bailey bridge to cross the river.

On May 11, Gen. Lemuel Shepherd, CO of the 6th Marine Division, signaled for the tanks to lead the way as the 22nd Marine Regiment led off the assault. Exposed to enemy artillery for a distance of 3,000 yards of level ground, the Marines slogged on through the mud until they reached the Asato River estuary, that lay in front of the city of Naha. The assault teams paid heavily; the spearhead Company C of the 22nd lost thirty-five killed and another sixty-eight wounded from the original 256-man contingent.

Instead of focusing upon the town, the strategists concentrated on Sugar Loaf Hill, a citadel of well-armed, well-dug-in Japanese troops who could count on additional firepower from comrades dug in on two lesser neighboring slopes. Overcoming the defenders of Sugar Loaf and its supports required the Marines to cross the upper reaches of the Asato and then take on the entrenched foe.

For five days, men from the 6th Division battled to reach the heights of Sugar Loaf. Stormy Sexton's K Company, from the 4th Marine Regiment, was among them. Says Sexton, "When we encountered the Japanese MLR [Main Line of Resistance], it was vicious, hand-to-hand combat. And to aggravate the situation, the heaviest fighting coincided with the rainy season."

Francis Hepburn of G Company, dug in behind K Company, which was the focal point of an enemy assault, noted what he saw in a diary, using somewhat overblown prose. "From the very first shot fired by the Japs, our own artillery and Naval gunfire, every available unit, immediately swung their huge muzzles towards the oncoming Japs. For better than an hour all batteries delivered rapid fire for K Company and sporadic but intense fire afterward.

"In my hole, I listened with amazement at the shells whistling overhead, howling and screaming, never the same pitch as each raced to the ground to explode. Streams of missiles of large caliber left spark trails behind from the smouldering charge that sent them skyward and arced overhead lighting up the sky along with the star shells the Navy was sending in from the ocean. In addition to our shelling, the Japs laid down their own barrages from behind the hills and in caves north of Naha. All I could see was the tracers from our shells. The Japanese were receiving a horrible pasting.

"The meager reports I heard the next day didn't tell of any terrifically large numbers of Japanese but since they all struck at one narrow point in our lines it was a real job keeping them off. There were 400 to 500 in the attack coming through a narrow 500-yard vale east of Half-Moon Ridge and Sugar Loaf.

"The usual tactic by the Japs was to hit in number, sweep over the foxholed Marines and go as far as possible. This meant a mixture of Japs and Marines all over the vale, with mostly Jap artillery falling on the combatants. Troops caught in the zone were either dead or wounded, or would be. Anguished and fearful shouts filled the air. Men shouting to their comrades, Japs and Marines trying to identify movements, rebuild lines in the dark. 'Who's that?' 'Sound off or I'll shoot!' 'You okay?' 'There's a Nip; shoot the bastard!' Shouts, curses, open prayers and flashes of grenades made the K Company area a black hell until dawn. Many Japs were still milling around the foxholes, killing, sneaking and killing again as dawn faintly appeared.

"When vision was possible, machine guns were quickly placed on the flanks of the battle area, and in the early morning light they killed off the last of the infestation. In the gray light of day human bodies were strewn about, sprawled, wasted and broken. A blue pallor of gun smoke hung overhead, mingling in men's nostrils with the other smells of freshly plowed earth, mud, sweat, blood and pure rain. The drizzle kept up a light pattering as if nothing had happened the night before. Our losses lay uncounted, heaped in profusion among the numerous Japanese dead. Some far behind the line were killed by the engineers back there.

"After daylight some twenty Marines were killed in hand-to-hand skirmishes. Pieces of bodies were seen everywhere, thrown down in the oozy mud or splashed against boulders flanking the valley. As I passed through the area, I could pick up a hunk of shrapnel wherever I stood. I was careful where I stepped, lest I step onto a body.

"The awful specter of decaying bodies and the smell did not detract from the small squarish ridges of earth that were Marine foxholes, now lumps of mud with pieces of weapons, bandoliers of bullets, live grenades lying about among the flesh. Where flesh could not be identified positively, I assumed it was Japanese. Many times I could see the black letters USMC printed on blouse pockets or Marine dungaree jackets. Leather Marine boondocker shoes were easy to identify. No one walking through or along the area dared to disturb anything. By moving a shoe we might learn there was a body under it. A cartridge belt meant there was a torso under it. We dared not lift a helmet."

"It was during the Sugar Loaf phase," notes Stormy Sexton, "that battle fatigue cases began appearing. This was the first time I had encountered such a problem, but, happily, someone a lot smarter than me had thought of a very sensible remedy. It was to take a man in question and send him back to a rear service area. There he would work on loading cases of ammo, supplies, and rations that were destined for the front lines. After several days, the individual would accompany the supplies to the front. And then later he would be returned to his unit.

At the time this duty was called 'the bun run,' because often hot buns were a part of the supply package. I actually had men who went through this process and returned to duty. They all performed well on their return."

A retired Marine top sergeant involved in the abbatoir-like grind of these days speaks of the difficulty of keeping track of the casualties. "We had replacements arrive without dog tags. I cut up K-ration boxes, got them to put their names on the cardboard and had them put these in their pockets."

Harry Manion had a front row seat to observe the carnage and the difficulty. "Moving forward was slow; the infantry were catching all kind of hell from the deeply dug-in enemy. The caves were a big problem. We used everything we had against them, white phosphorus, bull dozers, flamethrowers and any other available ordnance. Throw in a smoke grenade and watch for where the smoke comes out the air openings. Pump in gasoline and bang. Some caves had many levels and complex entrances. There were no simple solutions but we continued to underestimate the Oriental fighter. He can dig."

Anthony Walker credits General Shepherd for his steadfast performance. "He handled the division well, relieved a couple of regimental commanders, and gave the best orders he could under the circumstances of Sugar Loaf Hill and other blood-stained terrain. He got to the front and he knew what was going on. He didn't have charisma but he was a consummate professional, liked and admired."

CHAPTER XXVI

CHOCOLATE DROP, WART, FLATTOP AND ISHIMMI

The push by the two major Marine organizations were part of a general advance. From the second week of May to the end of the month, the U.S. front line, running east to west, was manned by the Army's 96th Division, joined by the 7th, the 77th on the left flank of the 1st Marine Division, and then the 6th Marines struggling to exploit the capture of Sugar Loaf for the occupation of Naha. Beyond, lay Shuri and its castle, the anchor of the entire Japanese defense.

In the center of the American offense, the 77th Division stood alongside the 1st Marine Division. While other Army units frequently expressed resentment towards the leathernecks, the troops of the Statue of Liberty Division believed they were respected by the Marines. Buckner Creel, of the 77th, notes that on Guam, they served operationally under the III Marine Amphibious Corps. "We had no unforseen problems and, unlike the fiasco on Saipan, things went easily. The III Phib Corps commander, Maj. Gen. Roy Geiger [the 1st and 6th Marine Divisions on Okinawa fell under his command], was a much smoother commander than Howling Mad Smith. Furthermore, our General, A. D. Bruce was respected in all circles. After Guam, we were known as the only division that could get along with the Marines.

"We did not always agree with their tactics. They seemed to use more 'frontal' assaults than we. We preferred fire and maneuver. In their defense, in many situations in the Pacific, frontal assault was the only possible thing to do."

Henry Lopez, with C Company of the 307th, remarks, "During patrols or missions or when attached to the Marines, even seeing a live Jap prisoner being escorted to headquarters for interrogation, we passed Marines. We admired them and had great respect for the way they handled themselves so professionally. We were more than glad to have had them on Guam. On the other hand, they equally respected us for the support and cooperation they received from us.

"There was an age difference between us. We averaged twenty-eight, while they were eighteen to twenty. When the Marines would see us move, some of them yelled, 'Look at those old bastards go.' They bestowed upon us the highest honor the Marines could give an Army outfit, calling us 'the 77th Marines.' Gen. Holland M. Smith in his book in 1949 wrote, 'I was greatly impressed by the 77th Division and felt they would give an excellent account of themselves. When the 77th did move, it moved fast. . . . it showed combat efficiency to a degree one would expect only of veteran troops.' "

There were some naysayers. Ed Fitzgerald, the 1st sergeant of Ser-

Troops from the 306th Infantry Regiment, 77th Division take cover from enemy fire. (*Signal Corps, U.S. National Archives*)

vice Company in the 307th, insists many of his buddies translated the Marine salutation "Semper Fi" as meaning "Fuck you."

Alanson Sturgis, with the 292nd JASCO, recalls a day when the 77th was headed out for a few days of reserve status and some Marines moved past. "They were a lot of young kids and some of them said things like 'the Army can't do it; dogfaces aren't up to it.' A gunnery sergeant stopped me when he saw the 77th Division insignia on my helmet. He said, 'Don't pay any attention to these guys. They're full of piss and vinegar but don't know anything. They'll learn.' "

While the Marines approached Shuri via the Wanna Draw to the west, the 306th and 307th Regiments of the 77th slammed into it head-on and to the east. Their major topographical landmarks were Chocolate Drop, Wart and Flattop Hills, buttressed by some lesser slopes. Buckner Creel's G Company, with the 306th's 2nd Battalion, confronted these obstacles to progress. "I believe I named it Wart Hill," he says, "when told to attack it, because the shape obviously resembled a wart. Chocolate Drop looked just like a Hershey chocolate kiss without the wrapping."

The enemy occupied not only the high ground, but also soldiers protected by a deep trench pumped bullets at the oncoming infantrymen. The GIs fell back more than once. Buckner Creel attempted to rally and direct his men. "While running across an open area, I would be chased by a Nambu machine gun, which failed to 'lead' me correctly. The third time I crossed, he managed to shoot the heel off my combat boot."

Along with Creel's G Company, E and F Companies from the 2nd Battalion had also absorbed horrendous punishment. "In spite of the heroics of the soldiers in G Company," says Creel, "we were now down to two officers and forty men. They formed the battalion into a 'provisional company' by consolidating E, F, and G. We had a total of only seventy-nine effectives. The World War II strength of a rifle company was six officers and 196 men ordinarily, more than 200 total. There should have been 600 troops. I was designated the company commander, although the COs of E and F were senior to me in rank. [The 3rd Battalion of the 306th, in no better condition than the 2nd, also formed into a provisional unit and, with Creel's group, composed a single makeshift battalion.]

"They would come over the hill, push us out of the reverse slope defenses we were in. Then we'd grenade and mortar them. Back over the hill they would go." During a nighttime foray by the Japanese, the GIs were driven out of their foxholes. Afraid to fire weapons for fear of striking buddies, the Americans wielded bayonets and entrenching tools to stave off the enemy.

During one night, a startled Creel saw an Imperial Japanese Marine break through and run at him across an open space. "I was in a hole in the company command post, probably fifty yards behind the front lines. Out of the rain and dark, and illuminated by star shells, came what looked like a giant, with a chrome-plated bayonet that looked about ten feet long. This is the moment when I personally found out about the stopping power of the Colt .45. I put two rounds into his chest when he was about fifteen feet away—stopped him literally dead in his tracks."

The ordeal reduced the effective fighting force even below the number seemingly available to fight. "I don't recall any men who broke and ran," says Creel. "But it is an axiom of combat that it is probably better to wound your enemy than kill him. Because it will take two or more people off the battlefield removing the injured soldier. We did have some problems then getting back people who had assisted the wounded to the rear. They would be gone for a day or so, sometimes because they could not physically return, but sometimes because they dawdled."

Earl Miller, a machine gunner in Creel's G Company, recalls, "When we were relieved on May 15 for a three-day rest, there were only seventy-nine of us left in the battalion of about 400. You remember odd things that happen sometimes. As our truck pulled into the rest camp, there at the gate stood a black soldier and he was playing the song 'Blues in the Night' on his horn. I don't know why that has stuck with me all these years. Perhaps it was that the sound differed from the cries of wounded men, the explosions of artillery shells or the snapping of bullets that I had been listening to for so many days!

"By this time there were just two of us in the machine gun squad. We had gotten fifteen replacements three days before we were relieved, and twelve never made it back to the front lines again. After a few days of rest we were ordered back to the front lines again. That was the quietest truck ride you ever heard. This time up front was also a BITCH, not only because of the fierce fighting, but because of the weather. It rained for the next thirty days, night and day! The mud was so deep and sticky that nothing on wheels could move. The engineers had two big bull-dozers pushing each other, trying to keep some kind of road open up to the front to get us supplies, and pulling jeeps with litters on them to the rear. The water in our foxholes was well up over our combat boots. We had nothing dry to wear and our feet swelled and turned deadly white.

"I can't remember who we replaced that second time, but there were several dead American boys still on the hill, three right in front of our foxhole. We covered them with our ponchos as best we could. It was three days before they could move them. After the bodies were gone, we had a mess of maggots to live with for several days. They crawled up our sleeves, under your shirt and pants and even under your helmet. Pressley and I named it 'Maggot Hill.' "

Somewhat behind the main body of 77th Division GIs, Ernest Schichler, with the division signal company, took part in patrols to roust interlopers or enemy who tried to operate behind U.S. lines. In contrast to Mike Moroz's experience in which civilians committed suicide, Schichler saw a different side of the local people. "A civilian came up to me and bowed, then took out a Japanese flag and handed it to me. He couldn't speak English, but by his actions, I knew he was giving me something that he revered. I looked in his eyes and he looked in mine. I didn't see hate or fear, maybe a slight doubt at first. Then his eyes turned in a loving manner. I think he wanted to convey a message to me by giving me the Japanese war flag and telling me with his eyes that the villagers would submit themselves to us and wanted us not to hurt them, to leave them in peace.

"I gave him back the flag with a respectful gesture of a short bow and looked in his eyes again, as if to tell him thanks and that we respect you and your people with love. I knew he got the message and we both smiled. He then insisted on giving me the flag, putting it in my hands, bowing, and then he walked away as if he was happy."

Such tranquil moments and exchanges were few, however. Frank Barron, A Company CO, with his outfit, attacked across the wide open ground to seize the last hill before the valley below Shuri Castle. The 1st Battalion CO, Maj. Gene Cook, had left for treatment of appendicitis, and Lieutenant Colonel Landrum, who'd been promoted to division headquarters, agreed to replace Cook temporarily.

With his men on the top of the ridge, Barron became aware that it extended about a 100 yards directly towards the enemy. "I ordered a platoon sergeant to get his men out along the ridge, and the sergeant said, 'I can't tell my men to go out there, they'll be killed.' I don't recall my exact words but he got the message and very quickly took over the ridge as I had ordered. I believe that was the only time I encountered any hesitancy in carrying out an order.

"A few minutes later, Colonel Landrum joined me. As he raised his arm to point something out, a Jap bullet knocked him down. I yelled for an aidman. He had been shot through the upper left thigh. The battalion radio operator said regiment was calling, so I left the medic treating

Landrum and reported what had happened. I was asked who was commanding the battalion and I answered, I was now in command.

"I took stock of my command after Landrum was wounded. I realized A and C Companies only had one officer each left. Since B had four, I decided that before we dug in for the night, I'd move one from B to A and another to C. It was a good idea, but before we could set up our foxholes, a single Jap bullet passed through one B Company officer and wounded another.

"Lt. Charles Milo, who'd been a platoon sergeant on Leyte until his battlefield commission, was seriously wounded just before night. The injury looked like it might have taken a kidney. Darkness was quickly settling in, after which we would not be able to evacuate him. When the medics had bandaged him and placed him on a litter, the bearers picked him up to leave. He told them to put him down for a minute. He said, 'Take this watch off my arm and give it to——,' naming one of his men. He directed them then to get his cigarette lighter out of his pocket and give it to another one of his soldiers. Only then was he ready to go.

"I believe fighting for your country in the infantry in battle is the most purifying experience known to man. These men who trained hard together and fought for extended periods together became so completely unselfish, so absorbed with the welfare of the group that you could believe that their principal concern was for the 'other guy.' I've never wished to die before or since, nor did I wish to die in battle then. But I thought there was a good chance that I would, and I thought then there was no better way to die, and no better men to be buried with.

"We consolidated our position and made contact with a Marine battalion to our right. A short while later, regiment called back on the radio and said someone wanted to speak to me. I heard a familiar voice; it was Colonel Kimbrell [the officer who earlier had arranged the transfer of an incompetent leader]. He asked, 'Frank, how the hell are you?' I answered, 'All right, Colonel.' He said, 'Well sound like it, then!' 'Everything's going great, Colonel!' I replied. Later, I learned he would take command of the 305th."

Another steep bump in the landscape, Hill 140, also known as 'Flattop,' became the objective for Larry Gerevas and Company K in the 307th Regiment. His hearing, damaged by a muzzle blast close to his ear, had largely been restored. "After several hours of marching toward the front lines, we started to receive harassing sniper fire. Our squad leader decided it was time to take a break. We stopped by a small, mound-shaped hill and he told us to take cover in a deep, bowl-like recess on the side. I decided to stand under a large rock that protruded from the hillside, thinking it would be good protection against falling mortar rounds. The rest of the squad found cover around the hill or climbed up into the bowl area with the squad leader.

"Mortar rounds started to fall, each one coming closer. From my position I could see the squad leader and I was listening to his instructions. Suddenly, he seemed to explode. The upper part of his torso was gone. A moment later his helmet fell from above and rolled down the hill. A mortar round had made a direct hit on him. We were all sickened to see what was left of him. Others were wounded and taken back to aid stations. The rest of us resumed the march toward Flattop."

Within sight of the objective, Gerevas and his buddies heard the good news that Company K would be in reserve. Other units in the battalion were committed to the assault. "Our location," says Gerevas, "100 yards in front of Flattop, gave us a ringside view of the action. We could clearly see the Japs on the hill, throwing grenades and explosives down on our men. Everyone, including the old timers, was watching this horrible carnage and doing nothing. I began firing at the Japs on the ridge and yelled at the others to do the same. They came out of their stupor and joined me in the shooting. This concentrated fire forced the Japs to withdraw behind the ridge and out of sight. They continued to throw grenades and explosives, but at least they couldn't see their targets. Our rifle fire also killed or wounded a few."

In the face of the strong opposition, the first waves of GIs could not conquer Flattop. Company K moved up. "The face of Flattop was so steep that it was impossible to dig in. The one advantage was that many of the grenades and explosives, thrown at us from above, slid down the steep slope to the bottom before going off. A grenade did land on a shelflike rock projection directly behind me and exploded. The shrapnel stung my legs but I wasn't injured. I concluded, Japs' grenades were not nearly as powerful as ours.

"We were only on the face a short time when the officers began ordering small groups of men to go over the top of the ridge. Those that tried were killed or wounded as soon as they got over. Our company lost a great number of officers and men. The only officer left was Lt. Charles Kunze. He had received a battlefield commission earlier in another company. He was highly respected and circumstances now made him our company commander.

"He organized those of us who were left for one last attempt to go over the ridge and he was killed immediately. He fell back with a bullet hole in his forehead. All of us, ready to follow the lieutenant, now moved down from the ridge, knowing this was an impossible mission.

Seen from the air, U.S. tanks and troops swarm forward.
(*Signal Corps, U.S. National Archives*)

Company K at that moment consisted of only a dozen men. An officer from another unit came up the hill to us, and ordered us to go over the top.

"The officer was unknown to us, and he looked like he had just come from some rear area because he was so clean and neatly dressed. We had lost nearly our whole company in this suicidal, frontal attack and weren't about to go to a certain death for this guy. We all refused. He became very angry and demanded that we follow his orders or we would all face a court-martial. We told him to go to hell. The threat of being court-martialled didn't sound very frightening to any of us at this point. As he stood there, looking at this motley group of weary, unshaven, determined, armed men, he must have realized how hollow his threats were. He turned away, went down to the base of the hill and left the area. A short time later, we were pulled off the hill and sent to the rear. It was May 17, in two days we had lost nearly 85 percent of our company."

Bangalore torpedoes by the ton, according to Gerevas, cleared an adjoining road of mines. That enabled access to tanks and self-propelled guns, which outflanked Flattop and then poured ordnance into the caves and trenches of the reverse slope. By May 20, the struggle for Flattop had ended. Just about simultaneously, other outfits from the 77th, against similarly deadly resistance, knocked the Japanese off Chocolate Drop.

Bill Siegel, now executive officer for the 706th Tank Battalion, labels Chocolate Drop "the worst experience for our battalion. The area was very heavily mined and our vehicle casualties were very high. Fortunately, because of the skill and training of our men, we were able to rescue most of our people with minimum personnel losses. But it was while on an effort to recover some disabled units that M.Sgt. Frederic Hensel stepped on a land mine and became a quadraplegic."

Siegel himself, while taking a foot recon to find a way around the Shuri escarpment via an adjoining Marine sector, was wounded by mortar fire, ending his participation in the Okinawa campaign.

C Company, of the 77th Division's 307th Regiment, from which Henry Lopez had been evacuated for his wounds earlier, and other units now concentrated their attentions on Ishimmi Ridge, an elevation that guarded access to Shuri. Carl Stanick, the company 1st sergeant and career soldier, had reported back for duty, his arm still bandaged from a wound. A few days earlier, ninety-four replacements boosted the unit strength up to 176. Many of these newcomers were fresh out of basic training and there was no time for the indoctrination and training policy, noted Buckner Creel.

The 1st Platoon from C Company, reinforced to fifty-eight soldiers, including thirty riflemen replacements still virgin to combat, joined E Company for a predawn attack on Ishimmi Ridge. Silently, in single file, they climbed the rocky, battle-scarred ground. Bayonets were fixed, but rifles not loaded to prevent an accidental shot that might give them away. Several times they froze as flares lit up the scene. But at 4:45 A.M., May 17, less than an hour after they jumped off, they occupied the site.

The surprise strike using the Japanese technique of nocturnal infiltration enabled the GIs to dig in on the narrow crest of the ridge, at most ten yards wide, without firing a shot. But their presence was discovered at dawn and the enemy directed devastating fire of all types at the 77th Division soldiers. A shell killed platoon leader, Lt. Joseph Lusk. Sgt. Alfred Junkin assumed command of the outfit.

"Junkin," says his friend Henry Lopez, "graduated from Washington and Lee, getting a bachelor's and then a law degree. He volunteered for service and when I asked him how come, with his education, he was not an officer, he explained he could not pass the eye test. He was totally dependent upon his eyeglasses and the only way he got through the induction physical was that he memorized the chart while standing in line.

"When I was wounded just below the escarpment, and evacuation was impossible as the area was completely covered by fire from above, Junkin volunteered to take me to battalion headquarters and the cave where they were located. We had to creep and sometimes crawl along the wall of that ridge until we reached the cave. Then he returned to the position, braving fire again."

Junkin's forces desperately fought off attacks but continued to be depleted along Ishimmi Ridge. "The wounded," notes Lopez, "were crazed for lack of medical care and water. The day had been unusually hot and sunny. Morphine Syrettes and medical supplies soon ran out, as well as water. The wounded went untreated. [No medic accompanied the platoon, and handkerchiefs substituted for bandages.] There was hardly a man on the ridge who was not covered with blood—his own or his buddy's."

By the morning of May 18, the platoon of fifty-eight numbered only about ten still able to fight. Still artillery, mortars, machine gun bullets chopped away at the survivors. Not until midday could reinforcements from the rest of Company C come to the aid of the beleaguered remnants of the 1st Platoon. Junkins, himself bloodied by shrapnel, was ordered to lead the other walking wounded to an aid station.

Those who came to relieve the embattled also were pounded by enemy fire. C Company's commander, Lt. Ivan F. Campbell, died from a bullet wound to the head. And 1st Sergeant Stanick, who could have sat out the battle because of his wound, was killed when a mortar exploded in his foxhole. By May 20, the 77th held all of Ishimmi, opening a path into Shuri. The price paid was extreme. A total of 204 soldiers [1st Platoon Company C, Company E and a heavy weapons group from Company H] had composed the original assault team. Only forty-eight escaped unscathed.

A distraught Alfred Junkin bypassed channels and wrote an impassioned letter to the division commander, Gen. Andrew Bruce. "I believe it is proper to report to you directly on my actions as 1st Platoon, C Company leader from 6:00 A.M. May 17, until 12 noon May 18, due to the fact that Lieutenant Lusk was KIA shortly after our objective was taken. Also, I understand Lieutenant Campbell and Sergeant Stanick since have both been KIA so I am not aware as to who is in command of C Company"

Junkin recounted some of the fight. "The Japs began to pop up on our right flank and we shot them down like ducks. Then all hell broke loose with intense mortar and MG fire punctuated by accurate sniper fire. Sergeant Chambers spotted a Nip AA gun on a knoll seventy-five yards away and blasted the crew. Sergeant Kelly was superb in encouraging thirty replacements to dig in deep and pick off Nip targets.

"I was one of the first to be hit, a mortar fragment punctured my cheek. . . . During the next half hour [Private first class] McCauley and Sergeant Kelly were KIA. We were getting no effective supporting artillery or mortar fire on our right flank and I dropped back to the platoon CP twenty-five yards to report to Lieutenant Lusk. I found him dead in his foxhole from a direct mortar hit."

Junkin described the slight shifts in position he directed in order to protect his diminishing forces. While he praised the mortar work of nearby E Company, he remarked that "our own artillery dropped several shells in our area," but then praised the work of some other big guns and the tanks.

"I was up and down the line, trying to encourage our new men to hold fast, by pointing out troops far below who were trying to pass through us and telling them that water and ammo would be brought in at night and the wounded taken out.

"As night came, H Company withdrew their heavy machine guns, leaving our left flank exposed. By now there was no one left on the ridge except twenty men of C Company . . . We drew a tight line, shifted the wounded so there was not more than one in each hole. Sgt. [Victor] Winschuh set up his light machine gun in the center facing the crest of the ridge. There was nothing we could do except crack down on targets as they came up within twenty or thirty yards, and pray. We did plenty of both.

"A grenade fell into the foxhole next to the CP that Del Rosso and I shared. I pulled out [Pvt. Andrew] Mezines but could not save [Pvt. Arlo] Mellberg. Our thirty replacements showed great courage but were too new to the job. One of them saw two Japs who got Mellberg thirty feet away. His finger froze on the trigger. Another saw a Nip standing on the horizon and shouted wildly at others to shoot the man but he had his own rifle in his hand. Another sees Nips a few yards from his hole, aims and fires an empty rifle. In the excitement he had emptied his magazine and forgotten to reload.

". . . I ask nothing for myself but I would like to see every one of my men on the line that night receive a citation. When twenty men stave off a Jap regiment, it is certainly beyond the call of duty." Junkin seized

the opportunity to call for promotions for several whom he felt deserved recognition, denied because of turnovers in commanders.

The sergeant then expressed his deep misgivings over the exigencies
of the war. "The record speaks for itself . . . [the victory] belongs to
the 77th and especially C Company but I deplore the necessity for
taking green recruits who hardly know how to load a rifle into combat
. . . I know you have the interest of the men in our battalion at heart
and believe you will agree that these teenage youngsters fight with great
courage but are just too green and inexperienced to do the job."

Eventually, Junkin himself received the nation's second highest
award, the Distinguished Service Cross. Several men earned Silver and
Bronze Stars, and the entire platoon was given a Presidential Unit
Citation.

Dick Forse and his M–8 self-propelled 75 mm cannon crew were on
call, available but not out front during the attempts to break into Shuri.
"They wouldn't allow any vehicles in the front line because the Japs
knew every inch of the area and would blast away with artillery if they
saw any targets. The infantry objected to any vehicles because they
drew fire.

"We would pull back five miles every night, then come up close
behind the lines in the early morning and stay there. Waiting drove me
crazy. I spent the day whittling on the slats from ammunition boxes.
The good part was, we had a hot meal in the morning before we left and
another one when we went back at night.

"They did call on us to evacuate wounded from the floor of the valley
to the aid station with litters tied to the deck of the tank. One time I
rode on the outside to make sure the litter didn't shift. We were exposed to firing but weren't hit. There was another occasion when the
wounded guy kept moaning and groaning over every bump. I had been
griping while inside and I realized that was no way to feel. I swore that
the next one we carried out, I wouldn't complain. We did another run
and when we got back to the aid station, the man was dead. I had been
risking my life for a dead man."

After their attempts upon Wart Hill and Chocolate Drop, Buckner
Creel's unit enjoyed a brief rest before returning to the sectors previously manned by the 305th Regiment. "Torrential rains," he remembers, "so bad that when some of our men took shelter in an Okinawan
tomb, it collapsed in a mud slide and we had a terrible time digging
them out. Shortly after, still in the rain, we occupied a very difficult
position. We were on one side of a steep ridge, the Japanese on the
other, within hand grenade range, and under constant exchanges of

mortars. We were so close that when our 60 mm mortars fired, we watched them ascend and then listened to them descend, to make sure they went over the ridge line. There was always a chance they would fall back on us because the range was so short. Most of it was retaliatory. Whoever started it up got an immediate return.

"During one mortar exchange I was sitting in my slit trench/foxhole in the company CP about twenty or so yards to the rear. I was sitting with my back to the 'front,' with my knees spread, my legs drawn out. We heard the incoming rounds. Most landed harmlessly and exploded. But one landed base down between my legs. I sat there looking at it. Since it hadn't exploded, I carefully grasped it with both hands, figuring it was a dud. I flung it out of the hole, and when it landed, it exploded. It was not a dud!"

Creel heartily endorsed the work of self-propelled guns like those in which Dick Forse crewed. "M–18 tank destroyers protected our flanks, firing high velocity 76 mm antitank weapons. They actually were used as 'snipers' during daylight hours and were very effective. But it was disconcerting when they fired directly overhead."

The 7th Division, relieved earlier by the 96th along the eastern side of Okinawa, now returned to the campaign, assuming responsibility for the extreme left flank of the U.S. lines. Ed Smith, promoted to the division staff, says he was unaware of problems caused by the heavy rains. But Bob MacArthur, the engineer officer at division headquarters, recalls a daily grind of trying to scrape away the surface and get down to the rock.

The 96th held positions between the 77th and the 7th. The Deadeyes continued to encounter Japanese forces with no inclination to quit. Even with the neutralization of such strategic redoubts as Conical Hill, there always seemed to be one more heavily defended height to attack. Some were only designated by numbers, others by the likes of Charlie, Dorothy, Oboe, Hector or Hen, but all traded large amounts of Japanese and GI blood.

George Brooks, with the 3rd Battalion of the 382nd Regiment, wounded in the shoulder during the Leyte operation, participated in his outfit's operations at Hector and Hen Hills. "There were an awful lot of replacements in K Company because our casualties had been so high. Many of them would be killed or wounded before we even knew their names. They were put in platoons with veterans but that didn't seem to keep them from getting hit. They had to be lucky to live through the first few weeks before they developed that sixth sense to know when to duck.

"The Japanese were superb soldiers. They gave their all and fought to the death. Some of our guys really hated the Japanese and wanted to kill as many as they could. But I think most of us were not so filled with hatred. It speaks very well of the American soldiers that we were able to defeat the Japanese, who had all the advantages of defensive positions, while we had to be exposed on the offensive. When they did come out of their caves and bunkers and took the offensive, the American GIs mowed them down."

But as Brooks and the rest of the 382nd approached the crest of Hector and Hen, the Japanese did take the advantage of their cover. For nine days, the 2nd and 3rd Battalions of the 382nd struggled to overcome the defenders of Hector and Hen. Repeated attempts to eliminate the enemy met with defeat and a hemorrhage of manpower. "We had one of the best medics in the Army," says Brooks. "His name was Vaughn C. Leubbe, and many wounded owed their lives to his bravery and skill. He had hauled out one of my closest buddies, horribly wounded in the leg on Leyte by the same mortar that got me. On Okinawa, one of our guys was shot through the throat and the bullet sliced his windpipe. Luebbe cut the bladder out of his fountain pen and performed a tracheotomy so the guy could breathe. Later, this man returned to the company; he was healed but his voice was different. Leubbe would go anywhere under fire to save one of our men. He was killed near Hen Hill. He was put in for a DSC several times but received only a Bronze Star; the same medal was given to the officer who kept breaking his glasses until sent to rear echelon."

The Hector and Hen grind chewed up enlisted men and officers at a frightening rate. "When officers were hit," says Brooks, "sergeants took over. When sergeants were wounded or killed, the Pfc.s took charge. More than half the time we operated without platoon leader officers who would replace company commanders right away. There weren't enough replacements for all the platoon officers who were killed or wounded."

But new graduates of OCS or junior-grade commissioned ranks previously laboring at noncombat tasks trickled in to fill the empty slots. Donald Seibert, already a 1st lieutenant with a background in chemical warfare, traveled by ship convoy from the States to Hawaii, from where he and other replacement officers flew to Saipan. They boarded an LST for a ten-days sail to their final destination.

"During our voyage," says Si Seibert, "the conversation inevitably turned to the combat situation we were going to face. I had some serious doubts about my own performance in combat. Perhaps everyone who faces battle has these same doubts. A major concern was how the troops would react to me, 'a stateside' lieutenant with no combat experience, joining a unit that had already been bloodied. Would the men accept my leadership; would I have a problem getting to them? There were reservations about my preparation for duty as a leader in combat. Although I thought I knew my tactics, my weapons, my leadership, did I know enough?" Seibert leafed through field manuals during the trip, fully aware he says, "This was not like cramming for an exam in physics."

After a night at the beach installation on Okinawa, he moved up to the replacement quarters for the 96th Division. Dispatched to the 382nd Regiment, Seibert protested assignment as a headquarters staff officer, arguing he wanted to fight with a rifle company. He convinced the regimental adjutant to change his orders.

Heavy rains continued to render roads into quagmires. Weasels, tracked cargo vehicles which Seibert describes as looking like a large bathtub on treads, carried the fledgling platoon leader to his new command, the 2nd Battalion at the foot of Hector. "We passed all kinds of vehicles stuck in the mud; ammunition and supplies were stacked on the way, ready for weasel transport forward. We saw piles of body bags containing dead soldiers awaiting return to the rear. Each weasel that went forward with supplies would stop to pick up the dead on the way back."

On arrival at the command post, Seibert was startled to hear a radio call ask for "Dean," the battalion CO, Lt. Col. Cyril Dean Sterner. But Seibert quickly learned that it was standard operating procedure to address even officers by nicknames rather than their grades or last names. The informality was intended to baffle enemy intelligence and also prevent severe hostile reactions that greeted the presence of leaders. At an orientation session, he was more shocked to hear the low foxhole strength of the rifle companies. Again, when the battalion staff tried to place Seibert with an antitank platoon, he balked, requesting a rifle platoon, even though, as a 1st lieutenant, he was somewhat senior for that slot. Since the shortages in platoon leaders were acute, Seibert was accommodated with assignment to F Company, along with Lt. Paul McGrath.

Sterner personally escorted Seibert and McGrath forward to an observation post bunker where he could point out the disposition of the companies in the battalion. Sterner located the 77th Division on the right flank abutting the 96th. After perhaps thirty minutes of information and advice, Sterner matter-of-factly ordered the replacements to move out.

"Thinking he meant us to take off down the hill to the F Company, CP," recalls Seibert, "I jumped over the revetment and started to slog through the mud down the slope. There were some shouts, but I did not relate them to my action. Without realizing it, I was completely exposed to Japanese observation and fire. The Japanese, who were extremely accurate marksmen, had been sniping at the OP; in fact, they had wounded a man there the day before. But luck was with me. If I was shot at, I was too green to know it.

"The exec of F Company, 1st Lt. Ed Foley, had been alerted to go to the OP by a covered route to pick up McGrath and me and lead us to the company so we would not be exposed to fire. When I jumped over the parapet before anyone could stop me, everyone held their breath until I reached cover. Foley gave me hell, saying next time I should wait for an escort." [McGrath became the leader of the 1st Platoon. On Seibert's second night at the front, he met T.Sgt. Arnold Dempewolf, McGrath's platoon sergeant. "He told me," says Seibert, "McGrath went out front up on a big rock to observe. I yelled, 'Get your ass down!' But it was too late and he was hit in the throat.' Subsequently, Seibert received a letter from McGrath, written from a hospital bed. He told Seibert he had worried whether the wound would prevent him from resuming his career as a trumpet and trombone player in a dance band. A doctor had reassured McGrath he would fully recover. Seibert never saw him again.]

The company CO, Capt. Cledith Bourneau, "a tall, husky, handsome darkheaded officer with a dazzling smile," interviewed Seibert and then filled him in on what F Company had been through and was now expected to accomplish.

Seibert drew the 2nd Platoon, where he was told he would have the advantage of an excellent platoon sergeant, William Schroeder, who, although wounded on Leyte, was an experienced, steady noncom. However, a dismayed Seibert learned his platoon numbered only twenty, including him, instead of the close to fifty on a table of organization. However, the unit was expected to cover a normal front—100 yards.

Even before the chat with Bourneau ended, battalion headquarters telephoned to alert the company to a pending attack. Other officers and noncoms joined the meeting. The 2nd Battalion had been ordered to assault the Hector-Hen Hill ridge line for the fourth time. F Company would move out in a column of platoons with Seibert's in the lead. When Bourdeau asked if there were any questions, Seibert says, "There were none from the other platoon leaders and I was too dumb or green to think of any. I hadn't even met my platoon yet. Sergeant Schroeder said, 'Let's go, sir.' "

Schroeder led Seibert to his platoon area. "While we proceeded, I was formulating my plan for the attack. As I looked up at Hector Hill, I reviewed the accounts Bourneau and Foley gave about the three previous attacks, how and why they failed. It became clear to me how I was going to attack."

When the two men reached the platoon CP, Seibert met his runner, Robert Laird, and a medic, assigned to them. There was less than half an hour before they jumped off, and Seibert decided the first order of business was for him to greet his troops. Schroeder guided him to the GIs in their two-man foxholes and introduced the new leader.

"They were strange faces; dirty, drawn, tired, and yet the men appeared to have high morale and to be intelligent and professional soldiers. That is a strange sense one develops in the service. One can enter a unit area and know immediately what kind of outfit it is. A quick evaluation, based on appearance, condition or feel, but correct 90 percent of the time. I knew this was a good outfit, though I could not have told you how I knew it. It was impossible to connect all of the names and faces, but I took particular note of the three squad leaders, Roy Rylant, Jay Waxman and Franklin Rose.

"I decided on a formation of two BAR teams, a demolition man (rifleman armed with satchel charges) and the command group—platoon leader, sergeant, runner and medic, a total of eleven men. Everyone would carry as many satchel charges and hand grenades as possible. When we reached the Jap positions, we would blow them up with the satchel charges. Eleven of the twenty in the platoon would make the attack, supported by fire from the remainder. Sergeant Rylant, senior squad leader, would command the fire base.

"When I issued my orders, the platoon sergeant and the three squad leaders looked at me strangely. They had made three determined attacks in force on this position without taking it. Now a lieutenant, new to combat, had decided a very small force could take it. Noting their skepticism, I explained my plan. Hector was a narrow, conical hill. It appeared to me that more than two BAR teams, more than four or six men abreast, would be ineffective. The fire of any additional soldiers would be masked. They would have to be single file behind the leading BAR teams. I was even more sure of my approach because we were to have thorough preparation by artillery.

"My NCOs shrugged and moved out, unconvinced, I am sure. I

wanted to establish liaison with G Company on our right flank and I double-timed over to their CP. The commander gave me his plan; he had to take Hen Hill, a little nipple next to Hector, and part of the ridge to the right. I arranged signals with the platoon leader who would be on my immediate flank. He looked at me oddly when I explained my plan but said nothing.

"Back at my platoon CP just before H-hour, I managed to recognize Staff Sergeant Schroeder and Pfc. Bob Laird, a wiry individual who wore glasses. Although he was a little older than most of us, he had lots of energy. He would tag along behind me in case I had messages to send and carried the Signal Corps Radio (SCR-536), the handie-talkie that operated on the F Company net.

"The artillery preparation was every bit as intense as had been promised. Promptly at 12:30 we moved out, the two BAR teams first, followed immediately by me and the others. The preparatory fire lifted off the hill as we ascended. The BAR men had been told to lay down a steady fire and move as fast as they could. They took me at my word and made those BARs sing. The riflemen were firing also, as was the base of fire at the line of departure. We moved steadily without opposition until two-thirds of the way to the objective.

"Suddenly, the top of the hill erupted with rifle fire, grenades and knee-mortar rounds. Our attack, which had been going so well, halted. We all hit the ground, seeking some fold or cover for protection from the fire. Faintly, I heard Sergeant Rylant below me, 'Put all your fire on the top of the hill and shoot like hell!'

"Japanese bullets zipped over our heads, doing little damage. Their grenades, lobbed blindly over the entrenchments, fell without accuracy and were ineffective. But several mortars dropped in the middle of our formation. Fortunately, the BAR teams were beyond the bursting radius. Not so, Staff Sergeant Schroeder and myself. I felt several pinpricks in the back as tiny shrapnel, almost like bits of wire, cut through my fatigue jacket. But I was not hurt. The shells impacted closer to Sergeant Schroeder, who was riddled with bits of steel. He shouted, 'I've been hit!' I glanced at him. He was bleeding from several wounds but did not appear to be in serious danger as he began to slide back down the hill. Even as I watched, the medic reached him. I was sure he'd be okay.

"I turned my attention back to the firefight, shouting to the BAR men, 'Fire automatic! The rest of you, throw grenades.' We were close enough to the top of the hill, so the natural American ability to throw a baseball carried the grenades over the edge of the trenches atop the hill.

"A few more mortar rounds came in but they landed down the hill, between the assault group and the base of fire. Apparently, the Japs were searching the hill, trying to prevent our ascent. They weren't putting observed fire on us. Scrambling forward, I urged the men up toward the top; hand-grenade range became easier. We threw them as fast as we could. Laird went back for more and, with another man, lugged up an entire case.

"I called forward the demolition man, Sgt. Don Pauley. He armed his satchel charges and threw them into the trenches. When they went off, we jumped up, ran to the top of the hill firing at anything moving in the trenches or beyond. Some Japs tried to escape to the rear, but we killed most of them. None volunteered to surrender.

"Once at the top of Hector, I glanced to my right at the George Company attack. A single soldier was standing astride the trenches on the ridge, firing into them. The thought crossed my mind that he was a courageous soldier, braving enemy fire to do his job. Certainly, he deserved some sort of award, a Silver Star at least. We were able to bring the fire of our BARs to the rear of the ridge and Hen Hill to cut down some of the Japs, preventing them from firing up at this man. But he apparently needed little help from us."

Seibert, on this first day of combat, had glimpsed a moment in one of the most celebrated exploits of a GI on Okinawa. Clarence Craft, a mustachioed former truck driver and replacement in G Company, on his first day in battle, had been among those bent upon shoving the enemy from its Hen Hill dugouts on the flank of Seibert's platoon. Instead of starting with another blind charge, the tacticians of G Company directed a six-man patrol to explore the enemy deployment.

The group provoked a shower of grenades from the residents of a deep trench just behind the crest. Three of the GIs went down, two stopped in their tracks, but Craft continued forward, tossing grenades over the hilltop. The foe threw their own versions back at him but these sailed well over his head and back down the slope. Some of Craft's companions and men farther back down Hen Hill hurriedly passed from hand to hand more grenades. Craft expended at least two full cases of these.

With the enemy stunned by the rain of explosives and showers of shrapnel, Craft leaped over the top and, while straddling the trench, just as Seibert witnessed, sprayed the dazed enemy at point-blank range. Waving to the other GIs to rush up, Craft reloaded and continued to fire into the emplacements. He blasted the crew of a machine gun, then hurled a satchel charge into a cave where a number of Japanese had retreated. When the device failed to explode, Craft retrieved it, reset the charge, threw the dynamite into the opening and was rewarded with a conclusive blast.

George Brooks, with K Company on the other side of Craft from Seibert, also witnessed part of the scene. "He was much higher up than we were, so we could only see him when he came back to get more ammunition and hand grenades. We thought he was crazy."

What Seibert thought at least worthy of a Silver Star, and Brooks believed crazy, brought Craft the nation's highest military award, a Congressional Medal of Honor.

The new platoon leader in Company F had little time to savor his triumph as his troops examined the bunkers and trenches to make certain all of the Japanese were dead. "We searched the bodies for intelligence material. My men looked at the waist of the Japs, where they carried flags, which were highly prized souvenirs. Weapons and swords were also valued. Sergeant Rose amassed five swords, which he carried with him since we had no rear area to store them."

From Hector, the 2nd Battalion plunged forward. Shuri Castle, off to their left, was a shambles from artillery fire, and Seibert never saw the famous landmark. But the enemy continued to fight. "At one point a small group of Japs dashed at us with hand grenades and bayonets, firing as they came. One by one these were cut down. I fired at one, hitting him again and again, but he came on. Japanese soldiers reportedly took drugs and refused to give up, but I could not understand why he was not stopped by my bullets. I was sure I was hitting him. Others were knocked down by a single shot from an M–1.

"When he finally dropped and the action ended, I walked over to make sure I had hit him. I had. The holes made by a round from a carbine are distinct from the gouging and tearing action of an M–1 bullet. There were at least three carbine hits in vital areas readily apparent—and some hits in less critical places. This convinced me that the carbine had little or no shock action. If I wanted to stop a man in his tracks, I had better get an M–1. Despite the additional weight of both the rifle and its ammunition, it was worth it. When I mentioned this to Laird, he eagerly offered to exchange his M–1 for my carbine. The radio made it difficult to carry the M–1, which he rarely got to fire."

As dusk approached, Seibert arranged for the usual perimeter defense. Once satisfied with the deployment of the GIs, he helped dig the four-man hole for his platoon command post. "It was hard work, the ground was rocky, so it was unfair to let only two people do all the work. It was standard procedure to go into a defensive position before dark. One of the weaknesses of the American Army in combat was night operations. We did little fighting at night, almost no movement. Although all service schools taught the principles of night fighting and it was included in all training directives, we were never comfortable with it. On the other hand, the Japs used the darkness; they fought, moved and resupplied in it."

After accepting compliments from company commander Capt. Cledith Bourneau for the successful action, Seibert says he felt relieved of the fears that gripped him while en route to Okinawa. "My first day with this unit, as well as my first firefight, had gone better than I dared hope. It appeared that I had been accepted by the troops. In fact, I got the impression that the men were hungry for leadership, they willingly gave their loyalty and confidence to each officer placed over them until such time as he might prove himself inept, or for some other reason unacceptable. As a result, the men had accepted me with far less reserve than I had anticipated."

That first night in the Hector sector, Seibert survived a wallop from nature. A bolt of lightning struck the ground some yards from his foxhole, and he watched as the arc traveled along the sound-powered telephone line towards his hole, jolting him as it reached the instrument that rested on his thigh. The shock contracted all of his muscles, causing him to leap to attention in the foxhole, exposing himself to enemy fire. The Japanese, however, did not fire and after some minutes, Seibert recovered his poise and control of his body.

Much of the euphoria that gripped him earlier disappeared the following day. "Just as we were looking for a night position, there was a flurry of shots to our front. I watched in horror as one of my soldiers fell to the ground. It was obvious from the way he fell that he was dead.

"It was a traumatic thing for me. He was the first of my men to be killed, and it was the first time that I felt responsible for the death of someone. I didn't even know his name. Suddenly, I was aware of a strange dichotomy in my thinking in combat. Killing the enemy did not bother me, though I took no pleasure or pride in it. There was no sense of responsibility for the enemy's death; it was simply the job to be done. On the other hand, the death of one of my men, although I was not directly responsible for it, placed a heavy burden on me; I could never, and have never, gotten over that feeling. I actually cried a little when that first man was killed, but soon got myself in hand. Nobody noticed.

"It is a feeling I have never ceased to have in combat [Seibert served in Korea and Vietnam]. Where had I erred that this individual was killed? Was my plan or my leadership lacking? This is probably healthy if you do not let it overwhelm you. As a result, you analyze plans, orders or leadership more carefully in order to make the best possible decision. I did not go into a deep depression or permit it to disturb me to the point that I couldn't think of anything else, but it was a difficult thing to accept."

CHAPTER XXVII

LAST WHIFFS OF FADING BLOSSOMS

However awful the losses inflicted on their enemy, the military resources of the Japanese eroded with each attack. The mighty waves of chrysanthemums peaked during April, declined in early May, then erupted in a pair of deadly outbursts the final week before Operation Iceberg entered its third month.

On May 27, the destroyers assigned to Picket Station #5, some forty-five miles due east of Okinawa's midsection, were the *Braine* and the *Anthony*. Clyde Van Arsdall, the *Anthony* skipper, grew up in a small Mississippi delta town, where his father had worked as a bank teller, insurance company employee and ultimately cotton-seed buyer. Van Arsdall attended a tiny high school with only thirteen students in his graduating class.

An athletic, outgoing boy, the young Van Arsdall received an appointment to the Naval Academy and arrived on his seventeenth birthday in 1930. "I was very green, very afraid of this brand-new environment, but it was like throwing a rabbit in a briar patch. I loved it from the beginning."

Too small at 5' 7" to make even the football B team, Van Arsdall played for the varsity baseball squad. He graduated in the upper third of his class and reported to the cruiser *Indianapolis* based at Long Beach, California. "They had some of the smartest officers I ever served under," says Van Arsdall. "They took it upon themselves to see that the youngest officers like myself were trained properly. Because of the way they helped me, it was not difficult for me to associate with the enlisted men, to assist them in the same way."

Not interested in naval aviation and with submarine duty requiring at least an eighteen-month wait for an opening, Van Arsdall, when he finished his tour on the cruiser, requested and received assignment as a deck officer on a destroyer. After three years aboard an old-style four stacker, Van Arsdall returned to cruisers on the *Vincennes.*

With the country at war, the Navy dispatched Van Arsdall to the *Barnett.* The orders didn't say what type of vessel it was, and he was disconcerted to find it a former cruise ship, the *Santa Maria,* in the process of conversion to a Marine Attack Transport. "These were crazy times," says Van Arsdall. "This ship was not ready to take its duty, yet it was being loaded with Marines, all their equipment and munitions alongside the pier in Norfolk. The skipper and exec took a fairly dim view of Marines toting live munitions on their shoulders, and the stuff being channeled down to what were labeled 'magazines,' in effect, were banana holds that had not yet been converted. Her sister ship, the *McCauley,* was in the same shape, and the two skippers got on the telephone and said that, if necessary, they would refuse to get these ships underway until either the munitions were off or somebody who knows safety precautions is assigned and explains what we should do."

The *Barnett* finally was ready to sail with that problem solved. But the ship, built in England, with oversize Swiss-made diesels, mystified Naval engineers, nor could they recruit a knowing hand from the merchant marine. Van Arsdall had reported for duty as gunnery officer but one day the exec greeted him, "Good morning, Chief," and Van Arsdall realized he'd been named the chief engineer. The *Barnett* worked with Marines for a period before embarking on voyages that carried U.S. troops to Northern Ireland, as the buildup began for the invasion of North Africa and the eventual landings at Normandy.

"We could make thirteen or fourteen knots, so we became part of a fast convoy, which meant we were not escorted except during departure and at a point where the British came out and brought us into Belfast. All the way over we would see burning ships. It was not a good feeling, particularly, to see those fires at night."

Van Arsdall left the the transport after it shifted operations to the Pacific. The whim of assignment posted him to the University of Oklahoma Naval ROTC program. For a full eighteen months, he enjoyed a happy life on campus. In June 1944, new orders flew him to the Pacific, where he took command of the *Anthony.*

"The ship had almost its entire commissioning crew. It was a well-knit group that knew how to work together. Their gunnery was good; they had a good record in the squadron and, even before I took over, I realized I was taking over a ship that was fine in all respects." Blooded off Bougainville, the *Anthony*, in fact, had engaged in a number of landing operations, gone through surface battles, shot down attacking aircraft and even survived a strafing run from an errant B–24 that mistook it for an enemy vessel.

Van Arsdall assumed command in time to provide gunfire support for the Guam landing. "We went around the island, looking for things to shoot at," says Van Arsdall. "They said if you see a cave, shoot at it and, sure enough, some Japanese would come out, once in a while."

Anthony's participation in the Iwo Jima campaign was very short. Escorting reserve forces, the destroyer arrived on the second day. "There wasn't room enough for all the fire support ships to get in there," recalls Van Arsdall. "Most people were so close, they used reduced charges. Our 40 mm guns could be put on the main battery fire director with gyro controls, and we could zero in on particular areas, then go to rapid fire with the 40 mms. It was hard to tell how effective the fire was because of the caves. Beach spotters told us whether we were shooting at the right place.

"The water there was shallow enough to reach with an anchor. We came in at 8:00 A.M., dropped anchor underfoot and spent the whole day shooting, with questionable results. This was a twenty-four-hour deal and I was to be relieved the next day. I told the fellow that would be coming in that I would relinquish that spot, which seemed to hold pretty good. I got underway about 7:30 and was leaving when our replacement came in. He dropped his anchor and a shore battery opened up, put a round right by his forward torpedo tube, killing four or five people. The Lord was looking after us." The next assignment for Van Arsdall and his crew took the *Anthony* to Okinawa.

Commissioned in 1943, the *Anthony*, one of 119 Fletcher-class destroyers, was built at Bath, Maine. One of the early crew was Gordon "Pete" Boyd, a native of Philadelphia. His realtor father had an elaborately equipped home workshop that stimulated Boyd's mechanical interests. Boyd graduated from Penn State as a mechanical engineer and two professors influenced him to enter the Naval Reserve. "I had gone to sea on tankers during summer vacations and picked up shipboard experience."

Boyd accepted a job with the New York Ship Building Corporation, whose entire business centered on vessels for the service, including very large tenders, battleships, cruisers and even light carriers. "When I started working for the company in 1939, there were 3,000 employees, and by the time I left three years later, with the war on, we had 30,000 people there. That gives some idea of the industrial power this country could muster.

"I did become acquainted with everything in the way of machinery in a Navy ship and was up to half-speed already by the time I actually joined the *Anthony*. I insisted on going to V–7 school when I went on active duty so I would get duty on a ship, rather than winding up as an inspector."

The V–7 program entailed four months, the first as an apprentice seaman and the last three as a reserve midshipman. "My schooling was at Annapolis," says Boyd, "which gave me a chance to see how Naval officers were formed. I was amazed anyone could stick it out, but we were like senior classman and didn't have to put up with the kind of crap handed out to plebes.

"On graduation I was assigned to a destroyer being built at Bath. I was really pleased because I knew the best ones were constructed there. I had an opportunity to stay and teach Naval machinery but I said, no way. I wanted a combatant ship." With his ensign's commission in hand, Boyd reported to Bath for precommission work on the new ship listed by the Bureau of Ships as DD 515, the *Anthony*.

"We went on a ten-hour cruise and, until you've been on a destroyer at full power, you've no idea what power on a ship means. It was 60,000 horsepower. You could put three destroyers like the *Anthony* up on the deck of one of those big tankers I worked on during my lifetime. A big tanker had 24,000 horsepower. On a destroyer like *Anthony* you could have burned up all the fuel aboard at full power in about twenty-four hours. Normally you'd only run at 1,500 to 2,000 horsepower."

The full crew came aboard when the *Anthony* officially entered the Navy at Boston in February 1943. Boyd's original assignment was as assistant engineering officer, and he served in that capacity as the destroyer participated in its first combat operations off Bougainville. After some nine months he succeeded his immediate superior in the role of chief engineer. His predecessor became the executive officer of the *Anthony*. Still an ensign, Boyd was the lowest rank to hold that responsibility. Nominally, the job called for a lieutenant senior grade or even lieutenant commander.

Boyd contends that, by the time of the Fletcher class, the Navy had taken all of the best features and designed them into the finest destroyers they could have. He marveled at the twenty-two- and twenty-three-year-olds who stood watch over the huge power plant with such competence.

The engineering chief had been on the *Anthony* for more than a year when Van Arsdall surfaced as the new commander. According to Boyd, "There was no one in the Pacific half as good as Van Arsdall. Every fourth day at Okinawa, we'd go in and spend the night at Kerama Retto among the hospital ships, ammunition ships, tankers, and combat ships. It was like a floating naval base and they'd lay down a smoke screen produced by fog generators to cover the entire area. But I used to climb the highest mast and look around, and at the top of the fog blanket all the goddamn masts were sticking up, so I don't know who they thought they were fooling. The only thing was that in a nighttime plane attack, the pilot would have to try and figure out, from the masts sticking up through the fog, what was underneath. Most of the cans [destroyers] that went in there overnight, their commanding officers kept the crew at full General Quarters—all five guns manned, all the magazines manned, all the doors and hatches battened down, same as when out on station.

"Captain Van Arsdall figured, 'The men need some relaxation. They're all keyed up from being out on the firing line with kamikazes.' So we had movies, two showings, way down in the guts of the ship in one of the berthing areas for the crew, and one up in the wardroom for the officers, the chief petty officers and mess boys. We had movies every time we went in there. Many of the other cans were at general quarters the whole time, and then when they went out the next four days, they were at general quarters the whole time.

"He seemed to have some sixth sense about problems. I went up to talk to Van on the bridge about some trouble with a feed pump while we were at anchor there. There were about six radios going in the wheel house at the time. I was talking to him and he was listening and he says, 'Wait a minute, Pete.' He called the officer of the deck, 'Jim, you better sound the gong (General Alarm).' I'm wondering, 'Holy smokes! What did he hear?'

"The alarm went off and I hightailed it down to my battle station in the forward engine room. By the time I got to the hatch, our five-inch guns started to fire. When I came up later, I found out there had been a kamikaze attack, and, I think, the battleship *Maryland* was hit." [Boyd demonstrates the tendency to mythologize the intuitive powers of a favored commander. The chief engineer believes Van Arsdall backed out of his spot off Iwo Jima because, he reports, "Van said, 'I don't like it here. We're too close.' " But as Van Arsdall testifies, he moved the

Anthony in accord with a system to rotate ships at limited firing stations.]

"The design of the *Anthony* had a bridge wing that came out of a door on each side of the pilot house. Van would tell everybody, 'If I want to get from one side to the other, I'm coming through. If you're in the way, I'm going to knock you on your ass. Everybody on the ships were bundled up in these kapok life jackets, which made them about twice as big, topside, as normal. When you got a crowd of people standing around, they took up a lot of room. If Van Arsdall was on one side and wanted to get to the other, he'd get down like a football player and go right through the gang. He'd be over on the other side real quick, but a couple of guys would be picking themselves up."

The fleet disposition for Love Day ticketed the *Anthony* to Fire Station # 1, a spot directly in line with the airport runway at Naha. Van Arsdall says he had "a prize seat to watch all the amphib craft come right by us, using our ship as a right-hand edge for the landing. We received a message to interdict any traffic on the runway. We set up a fire control deal as if we wanted our shot to fall right down the runway at a speed of advance of about forty knots. Intermittently we did that at night and managed to score hits that looked like they walked down the runway."

After the landings had proceeded smoothly with no opposition, the *Anthony* drew ammunition from LSTs and fuel at Kerama Retto. The destroyer fulfilled occasional fire support missions and then received orders to support the establishment of the radar station up north. For about ten days the *Anthony* steamed up and down, doing nothing while the men ashore erected the radar installation. Aircraft passed far overhead, so high that their identity could not be discerned.

The ship now moved to the east coast, part of a force responsible for destroying the barges used by the Japanese to transport supplies and men from the south to the north, including probably the effort to land behind the GIs of the 7th Division. "There were many of them at first," says Van Arsdall. "They were very low in the water, coming right along the beach. But when you started shooting, you frequently could tell that the men were going over the side. We didn't like using spotlights but, instead, saw where they were with star shells."

The Japanese abandoned the tactic and *Anthony* put in at Kerama Retto for resupply. "That's where we got our introduction to what a kamikaze could do," recalls Van Arsdall. "There were destroyers there with all kinds of damages, really an awesome sight. To see where a plane hit the fo'c'sle, split the whole forward end of a ship, opening it up like a cracker box, or where a smoke pipe had come up, there was nothing, or gaping holes in the sides of ships. The sights made Christians out of us in a hurry, wondering how we could stop someone from doing this.

"It was not a feeling of fear but a sense of reality. When you talked to people who had been under the attacks, they said, you don't have time to be afraid. You realize in a hurry it's either that fellow or you.

"We had had our first opportunity to talk to people who had actually been under kamikaze attack right before Iwo Jima," says Van Arsdall. "There was no consensus as to what to do under these attacks. Everybody seemed to have their own ideas." The protocol developed and clandestinely distributed by Ellery Sedgwick and Tom Hamilton had not been created at the time of Iwo Jima, and even later, it was not necessarily an accepted drill.

"Most of the attacks were single planes on single ships. It was not like having a whole bunch come in, although a lot of the picket stations said there'd be four or five flying around, and then suddenly they'd break up, and it would be like a bunch of bees going every which way. You'd just have to see if there were one there for me and try to shoot him down.

"There was a bit of an argument," says Van Arsdall, "whether you should go at high speeds or lower ones, where you had better control of the battery [antiaircraft guns]. I was one who joined the 'speed demons.' If there was an attack imminent, we were at twenty-five knots or better. We tried to keep incoming planes on our beam to allow the maximum number of guns clear shooting. Once a fellow started in, we would then maneuver hard right or hard left to get into a turn. The idea was that when a guy made his decision to come at us in a certain way and we got into a turn, he couldn't keep up with it, so we received some extra shooting time while he maneuvered either astern or on the quarter." Van Arsdall concluded the basic stance was "Keep the guns ready and shoot like hell."

The tactics described by Van Arsdall translated into the need for quick responses from the engine room. Pete Boyd's gang carefully monitored boiler pressure, jacking up the steam to a point where a sudden demand for horsepower could be accommodated.

Van Arsdall recalls some conversations about the mind-set of the kamikaze pilots. "It was agreed that they had been trained for this, this was a part of their life, their career, what they ought to do for the emperor and the country. Whether this was crazy or what the Japanese mentality accepted, I'll never know.

"The statistics that brought this tactic are quite clear. It was to their advantage to use their planes this way. If they sent down fifty planes on a conventional-type raid, they would lose over half to U.S. forces either from gunfire or our aircraft, and the damage was minimal. If they used the same number of planes and zero returned but inflicted maybe 30 percent damage, serious damage on the target, they were winning statistically by the kamikaze tactics, because they were going to lose their planes anyway."

Pete Boyd attributes the dedication of the pilots to the patriotism of youth. "I think they were very, very young. On our destroyer, a lot of real young guys had rushed down to the recruiting stations at the time of Pearl Harbor. I also believe the Japanese knew they were going to be smothered by allied bombing. By the time of Okinawa, our bombers had set most of Tokyo on fire. I believe they figured that if they sat at home, it was going to happen again, and if they got on an airplane, perhaps they could do something about it."

The *Anthony* now started a tour as part of the picket station screen. From May 23 to May 29, she and another destroyer manned Station #5. *Anthony,* maintaining a distance of 1,500 to 2,000 yards from the other vessel, steamed up and down a boxy area. The destroyers were accompanied by four LCI gunboats, which could add firepower and also were well schooled and equipped for fighting fires.

During the hours near midnight of May 25, four pips sprouted on the *Anthony* radar. "They were flying low, rather erratic paths and tracking at very slow speeds, seventy or eighty knots." remembers Van Arsdall. "They seemed to be milling around but not interested in us, although they were well within range of our guns, as close as 5,000 yards. The gunnery officer said, 'Let's shoot 'em down.' They reported they had a solution [target position with appropriate information for gunners].

"I gave them 'Commence Firing,' and within a few minutes they had two fires out there, planes crashing. Later there was another two fires about 5,000–8,000 yards from our picket station. We never found out what they were, but we guessed these were simply some old planes out on a heckling mission and got caught. The other side knew where the picket station was, but perhaps got a fine position from the incident."

That night, the *Braine* relieved the other destroyer and became *Anthony's* partner. About daylight of the following day, radar now picked up four planes coming from the north. "It was accepted," says Van Arsdall, "that if the picket station was attacked, it was every man for himself, with number one, don't have a collision with anybody. We immediately ordered General Quarters. There was a solid overcast, my guess is, 2,000–3,000 yards. Horizontal visibility was very good, there was no sea. *Braine* was clear, the LCI gunboats were out maybe 4,000 yards, and we began to open up a bit on *Braine* and build up some speed.

"Combat kept reporting, 'They're coming straight in toward the picket station,' followed shortly by, 'It looks like they're breaking into two groups.'" The enemy aircraft followed a course to take them directly over the pair of destroyers as the distance between the ships spread to 2,500 to 3,000 yards, as they traveled roughly in the same direction. *Anthony*'s combat now advised two planes were headed for it, while the others would be on the starboard. Fire-control radar began tracking the nearest ones.

The planes passed over the picket station and then Van Arsdall received word they had turned and fire control had a solution. "I couldn't see them through the overcast," says Van Arsdall, "but I immediately gave the 'Commence Firing.' *Anthony* began firing its forward guns, the main battery. I started turning to get our after guns cleared. Things started to happen very fast.

"I heard a report, 'We're on target,' and wanting to get the planes on our broadside, turned left. About that time, a plane, on fire, smoking and out of control, came through the overcast. It went on down and splashed. A second plane headed directly towards us. I tried to keep him on the starboard beam. There was so little time left, the maneuvers of the ship didn't mean anything. Our 40 mms and 20 mms opened up and there was really a blanket of fire going out.

"This joker came right on in. I couldn't do any more maneuvering, he was so close. But he was right where we wanted him, all the guns could bear on him. Some chips flew off but he kept coming. He actually passed over the ship by the stacks, not many feet above the Number One stack. All of us thought he would crash into us, but he did not nose over that much. As he passed, I went to the wing of the bridge so I could watch him there. He had pulled up, just a bit to climb and turn to his left. He did a beautiful job, because pieces were coming off his aircraft.

"It looked like he was in control, because he did a nice climbing left and never came out except to then put his nose down in a loop, crashing into *Braine*, probably 2,500 yards from us. There was a lot of yelling and shouting around me, but from it I got the idea that *Braine* had been hit probably thirty seconds before this plane came down. Two kamikazes had crashed her in succession.

"Those who were watching said the Number Two stack on *Braine* just disappeared. I don't know whether that was the one that came over us or the other. She was hit twice. One struck a little to the starboard of the center at the bridge, demolished the bridge and went down into the wardroom country. A tremendous mess of the ship there caused everyone forward of amidships on the bridge level to abandon ship.

"The second hit destroyed a fireroom, did serious damage in the engine room and, from my vantage point, the whole topside, from the bridge to the after stack, was a mess. The two ships were on almost opposite courses, well clear of one another. *Braine* still was underway.

"What happened to the fourth plane is conjecture, so far as I am concerned. I never saw it. Some on our bridge told me it had gone into the water between the two ships."

Some members of *Anthony*'s crew claim, unbeknownst to Van Arsdall, one of the two kamikazes that splashed down in the vicinity of the *Anthony* struck so close to the ship that the impact, and perhaps the detonation of the plane's bomb, hurled the dead pilot up among the forward torpedo tubes. Sailors reported they paused only long enough to marvel at the dead flier's jacket, decorated with rag dolls and charms, before heaving the corpse overboard. Van Arsdall says he never saw the body, and over the years, during talk with former shipmates, says that some men say it never happened, that this occured on some other vessel. Just as stoutly, other *Anthony* veterans insist the body did tumble onto the ship. Van Arsdall agrees, a wall of water washed over the destroyer, some of which entered the intake pipes of Boyd's machinery and eventually required minor repairs.

With radar indicating all-clear, *Anthony* and the LCIs set about aiding the stricken *Braine*. Van Arsdall instructed one of the 'little fellows' to pick up survivors while the others tied up alongside *Braine* and began spouting fire.

"We could see people from the bridge level of *Braine* jumping over the side into the water, and we saw people on the ship rolling wounded off the deck, which was on fire, into the water. Many of the crew ended up in the water. Gunboats picked up some and so did we."

With the arrival of a relief destroyer, *Porter*, the *Anthony* took the crippled *Braine* in tow and steamed towards Kerama Retto. Machinist Joe McNamara, a thirty-four-year-old original crewman, was appalled. In his diary he scribbled, "Our ship has all compartments full of badly wounded men. Some have already died, others will soon go, under morphine shots they look yellow and half-dead already. The injuries are beyond belief—eyes burned; both legs; both arms broken—all clothes burned off. The ship itself is almost a total wreck . . . I feel sick and my mind is dazed. These Japanese men in planes *cannot be stopped by destroyer fire.*" (Underlining by McNamara.)

At Kerama Retto, McNamara noted, "The #638 under tow by two tugs goes by. She is almost blown in two at gun #4. The other side of [a] repair ship is #458, with only seventy-five survivors, blown apart from fantail to bridge. Twenty-nine damaged ships are in harbor." He records a call to General Quarters on average every six hours. The only satisfaction is to paint six more Japanese kills, making a total of seventeen recorded by the *Anthony.*

The *Braine*'s dead mounted to sixty-six, with another seventy-eight injured. For all of the death and destruction achieved, fewer and fewer Japanese planes made the one-way trips. The chart keepers recorded 275 aircraft in a pair of *kikusui* the final week of May. Only two more mass attacks occurred in June, and the Japanese mustered a relatively puny fifty airships for the first of these and forty-five for the final one. However, well into July, individual or groups of two and three suicide bombers continued to sting the U.S. fleet. Among those sunk would be the *Braine*'s relief, *Porter.*

On June 7, *Anthony,* roaming Picket Station #1, again battled kamikazes. A pair of Vals streaked toward the destroyer, coming in low enough to the water that they escaped interception by a combat air patrol.

Pete Boyd recalls, "When the bridge detected bogeys and sounded the GQ alarm, they also immediately rang up Flank Speed on the engine room telegraph. This was our signal down below to bring up engine revolutions to maximum speed." Boyd notes that in the superheated din of the engine room, in order to converse, one couldn't just shout or yell. "You put your mouth close to the other guy's ear and scream. He may answer with sign language, and lip reading is almost a necessity."

Those down below could see nothing of what was happening on the surface. "In the engine control room," says Boyd, "there were two 'talkers,' ratings who wore sound-powered telephones. The first talker was on the circuit that included the topside stations. This was our only contact with the outside world. The second talker was on the circuit with all of the machinery spaces. He would repeat for them the information from the first talker.

"We'd get the word, 'Bogeys sighted, bearing 200 degrees, 8,000 yards.' We'd wait. Then BAM! BAM! BAM! Our main battery, the five-inch guns, would be firing. Then the report, 'He's coming our way!' and the 40s would start, FWUMP! FWUMP! FWUMP! FWUMP!. Then we'd hear the 20s—tatatatatatat. By this time the first talker usually had frozen. All we could learn from him was through reading his facial expressions. The other talker would then report, 'I think he's gonna hit us,' or 'He missed us.' " Only after securing from General Quarters could the machinery-space personnel emerge and learn from topside observers what actually happened.

Boyd recalls on June 7 hearing the five five-inch main battery firing and then "a good report that the first plane had been splashed at about 2,000 yards. The news on the second wasn't as good. As the ship's speed rapidly increased, the bridge was maneuvering erratically, hard left, hard right, hard left. By now the five-inchers, the 40s and 20s were firing everything they could. The entire ship pitched greatly as the helmsman steered an evasive pattern.

"The FWUMP FWUMP FWUMP of our 40s and the tatatatat of our 20s told us down below that the number two Bogey was almost on us. The ship was turning hard right, then a tremendous WHAM! A very strong smell of gasoline and some smoke followed in about two seconds. The forward repair party hollered that the bow was on fire and they couldn't get pressure on the forward firemain.

"The vessel at very high speed turned in the other direction. As it lurched, a large shower of water came down from the hatch above the chief machinist and me, dousing us completely. My immediate reaction was, the firemain had been hit. I started to discuss it with the chief—screaming at him—the location of the firemain and what to relay to the repair party. Then I saw his lips and hands. He screamed back, 'Does that taste like saltwater to you?'" "We both screamed 'Soap'!"

For the second time in two weeks a kamikaze had plunged into the sea very close to the *Anthony*. The subsequent explosion enveloped the destroyer in sheets of flaming gasoline and other debris, including a boot from the foot of the pilot. Van Arsdall, ordering an abrupt turn by the helmsman, drove the bow beneath the surface, causing a huge wall of water to wash out the fires. The soapy water that soaked Boyd came from the ship's laundry, where the sailor in charge, on hearing the alarm, had rushed to his battle station without turning off the water.

All seemed well, until it was discovered five men, including the ship's doctor, were missing, some knocked into the sea by the rapid traversing of a five-inch gun, and others swept overboard by water sloshing over the deck because of the maneuvers. Darkness enveloped the area and the *Anthony* hunted for its lost crewmen in vain before returning to the proper position in the radar screen. The next morning one of the "Little Boys" in the sector notified *Anthony*, "We were able to find five of your guys! Did we get all of them?" The answer was a joyful affirmative.

CHAPTER XXVIII

LAST LINES OF DEFENSE

The last week of May, Gen. Lemuel Shepherd ordered Tony Walker's Recon Company to sneak into Naha, the city on the western end of the Shuri Line. Walker set up a base camp on the banks of the Asato Gawa River, and a quartet of four-man teams crossed the stream to appraise the enemy strength. The interlopers bumped into Japanese patrols, exchanged a few rounds, but all of the GIs returned safely, with the information that the city was not heavily defended.

On May 28, Recon Company spearheaded an attack into Naha. "A Jap machine gun was firing through a break in one of the concrete walls surrounding most of the houses," recalls Walker. "Fuller Curtis, with his squad, had worked their way next to the wall. On order, each man pulled out a grenade and threw it. Then the squad all together went over the wall. When I got there, they proudly gave me a samurai sword, covered with bits and pieces of a Jap officer."

While the outskirts of Naha appeared lightly defended, the Marines from the 6th Division battled troops in the southern sector and drew intense fire from the heights to the east and from the Oroku Peninsula, an area south of the Kokuba Estuary that marked the southern border of the city. Most of the fighting men holding Oroku came from Imperial Navy forces, whose on-site commander was Rear Adm. Minoru Ota.

Recon settled in for what Harry Manion, one of Walker's sergeants, calls "fun and a nightmare" amid the ruins. "After we cleaned out the university, bank and other smaller buildings, we found millions of yen and Japanese war bonds. Night brought in heavy artillery fire from large caves on the Oroku side of the Naha River. One time, one of our men was waving to a Marine fighter pilot coming in. The pilot shot at our man and killed him with a .50 caliber round. This was the second time Marine pilots fired at Marines on the ground. After that incident I always had a little suspicion about our air close-support Marines. We fired at him, but to no avail. Gone back to the carrier and a hot bath.

"About this time, dead of night, raining like only war can produce, we received a group of replacement Marines. Wet and miserable as Marines should be on their first night. We started switching older men with new men. The new Marines were fresh out of boot camp. Ten-day home leave and over they came. Training started in our platoon. Lessons: Don't go anywhere alone. Don't go into caves. No souvenir hunting. The next day I saw two of these Marines coming back from a souvenir search. A group of us were on a roof and I grabbed an M-1 and fired three or four rounds at the feet of the Marines. They stopped, then came forward into the platoon position. Chew-out time. I believe one later shot off one of his toes." The following day, Manion spied two more recent arrivals investigating a cave. He raced after them, badly cut his head on the cave ceiling while ordering them out. "It was chew-out time again."

Chick D'Angelo, with Headquarters Company of the 4th Marine Regiment, also found the latest replacements occasionally spooked by their first exposure to combat. "I picked up one in a jeep to take him forward. The first time some artillery fire came in, he jumped out of the jeep and ran. Later, I heard that he was killed."

Shepherd now outwitted the defenders on the Oroku Peninsula with a seaborne assault that brought tanks and leathernecks ashore on the western point of the coast, rather than striking at the base of Oroku as the Japanese commander expected. The 4th and 29th Marine Regiments began to push the foe backward. Walker's forces participated, first by seizing the island of Ono-Yama, in the Kokuba Estuary, and then later, wading out 600 yards to capture an offshore patch, Senaga Shima, disposing of a few enemy soldiers and finding many deep caves with some large artillery pieces. Meanwhile, the 22nd Regiment, hitherto in reserve, entered the fray, applying pressure from the east, squeezing a dwindling pocket of resistance.

D'Angelo recalls the shortage of supplies. "For some reason I could go without eating, and at the end of three days, when everyone was out of food, I still had my rations. On the fourth day they finally parachuted supplies in. But I developed jungle rot on my feet. And in some places we took a shellacking."

Stormy Sexton believes the shore-to-shore amphibious assault of Oroku Peninsula never received the appreciation it deserved. "The assault landing on June 4 was a complete surprise to the Japanese. The ten-day fight was difficult, but seizure of the Peninsula outflanked the enemy. The Marine losses were 1,608 killed and wounded, but the enemy suffered 5,000 casualties."

With his position hopeless, his men being cut to pieces and, for the first time on Okinawa, surrendering in large numbers (159), Admiral Ota committed suicide. By June 15, nothing remained of the Oroku defense. Also, about this time, Tony Walker received a promotion, leaving his beloved Recon Company to become a battalion commander in the 29th Regiment.

For almost two months, the focus of the American drive had been the Shuri Line. Solomon Berger, as a machine gunner assigned to the 7th Division artillery's headquarters battery, operated some distance behind the front lines, out of reach of enemy infiltrators or infantry counterattacks. "Our greatest danger came from the counter battery fire and several of our men were killed as a result. The Japanese had more artillery on Okinawa than anywhere else, and the heaviest concentration came during the battle for Shuri Castle.

"Our worst experience during this battle was enemy artillery fire that in spite of heroic efforts by our medics, killed several men laying wire. [Some troops drew the dangerous assignment of stringing lines that maintained communications between forward observers and the batteries.] The constant pounding by the Japanese artillery got on our nerves, but this was our fourth campaign and no one panicked."

Even though the artillerymen were somewhat removed from the worst of the killing grounds, Berger describes their living conditions as "horrendous. There was constant rain and mud. We ate K rations for three months. Dysentery sent many soldiers on sick call all the time. There was no such thing as sanitation—just a hole or slit trench. The mosquitoes almost drove us nuts. But our medical help was superb and we never lacked for ammunition."

To George Brooks, with Company K of the 382nd Regiment in the 96th Division, the Japanese artillery did more than kill and wound. "It gave us fits. It came in very accurate and very often. They were particularly active at night. At night the sound is different, and it seems like each shell is coming right into your foxhole. I believe this caused more mental breakdown—combat fatigue—than anything else. We lost a lot of men this way.

"In one area, we were undergoing our usual artillery bombardment from the Japs. They were firing some large shells. They may have been coastal artillery. One big one hit about ten feet from our foxhole and gouged out a huge opening. The dirt that flew out buried three men in the next foxhole. They dug themselves out, but the next day they broke down and were taken back with combat fatigue. We never saw them again."

Don Dencker, with the 3rd Battalion of the 382nd, says, "I was always amazed how the dogfaces of Co. L did their job in spite of certain death or serious wounding. We had no discipline problems in battle that I heard of. I saw a sergeant from the mortar section space out and go to the hospital after heavy artillery pounding. The only other combat fatigue victim was a platoon leader who had been with us on Leyte, but on Okinawa he became disoriented and was sent back to battalion headquarters for evacuation."

The stubbornness of the enemy, holed up in the Shuri Line's thousands of well-constructed fortifications, produced discouraging statistics. For the Army and the Marines, the losses during April and May totaled 26,044 killed, wounded or missing. Never mind that the experts figured ten Japanese had died for every single American, the casualties for the U.S. added up to the heaviest incurred during war in the Pacific. And to go with those felled by direct enemy action, nonbattle losses also jolted the commanders. Under this heading, the Marines counted 6,315 and the Army 7,762 men unfit for duty, a large percentage of them "neuropsychiatric," or combat fatigue cases.

In his headquarters hundreds of feet below the surface of Shuri, General Ushijima, preoccupied with his own difficulties, had already held conferences on the future of his badly hammered and depleted forces. The staff from the 32nd Army and the various units debated their alternatives; a last-ditch stand on the remnants of the Shuri Line, a retreat to the southeastern Chinen Peninsula or a pull back to another series of hill masses due south. The one option unconsidered was surrender.

Ushijima chose to fall back towards the extreme southern ridge lines and hills. He undoubtedly did not expect a victory through his strategy, but he continued to seek the best means to prolong the struggle and exact the highest cost from the enemy. As early as May 22, the Japanese began to shift wounded and supplies south. Troops, traveling as daylight waned, started to head for their fall-back line several days later. Aerial reconnaissance by U.S. fliers detected movement, but poor visibility, because of rains and low ceilings, prevented accurate description of what was happening. Intelligence specialists at first wrote off the migration as civilians fleeing the battles. In fact, the Japanese executed their maneuvers so skillfully that the American high command became convinced the enemy intended to make his last stand on the battlements of Shuri. Not until May 31, did General Buckner and his people realize Ushijima's plan, and even then the U.S. generals badly underestimated the scope and the effectiveness of their quarry's escape.

In fact, Marines had occupied the site of the now-shattered Shuri Castle on May 29, two days before Buckner's strategists became persuaded the enemy was in retreat. However, the taking of the ancient citadel so early was something of a fluke, being the one case where the Japanese left a gap in their thin line covering the pullback.

The 96th Division followed the footsteps of the Japanese from Oboe, Hector and Hen Hills. When the enemy turned to face the Deadeyes, they operated again from well-prepared caves and burial tombs embedded in the Yaeju Dake-Uza Dake Hills. Death continued to strike veter-

A machine gun from the 7th Infantry Division sprays enemy positions. (*Signal Corps, U.S. National Archives*)

ans and those new to combat. Col. Edwin T. May, in command of the 383rd Regiment since activation, moved into a forward observation post near the Iwa road junction. Bob Muehrcke, with the 1st Platoon of Company F of the 383rd, engaged in a firefight there, says, "Heavy rains, bullets and knee mortars saturated the ground. In spite of a warning, Colonel May remained up front. A Japanese machine gun bullet pierced his heart, killing him instantly." May received a posthumous Distinguished Service Cross.

"A recently arrived captain assigned as company commander of a heavy weapons unit came alongside me," says Muehrcke. "Without introducing himself, he asked, 'Where are the Japs?'

"The captain wore an Army poncho, which protected him from the torrential rain. His battle fatigues were clean and free of mud. He was freshly shaved. The entire 1st Platoon was soaked and filthy. A single shot by a sniper killed him. We never knew his name."

Muehrcke had gained a highly favorable image of the Marines while on Guadalcanal. "They performed with valor and daring; they were outstanding. We relieved Marines around the Torokina River area, and they were not superior to the Army infantry but were our equals. We cooperated with each other.

"On June 16, at a small village in southern Okinawa, we were joined with the Marines for combined tank-infantry operations. I was ordered not to attack unless the tank support was with us for this coordinated Marine-Army-tank venture. We waited for the tanks, as told, but the Marines jumped off and were massacred in the very narrow streets of this small southern Okinawan town. The next day the tanks arrived and the Army troops jumped out in attack and killed every Japanese soldier present. On searching their bodies, we found four to six watches on each Japanese soldier's forearm, all taken from the Marines' bodies by the Japanese the previous day."

On the other hand, Chick D'Angelo tells of a situation where Marines alongside Army troops spotted some Japanese in a vulnerable site. "The Army insisted on waiting for their lieutenant to give them the word to move out. We didn't wait and we routed the Japs."

Marines held the right flank of Don Dencker's 96th Division unit in June. Dencker compares the two branches. "For one thing, they had more tommy guns, which we would like to have had. But they were in the same boat as us doggies, and the only differences I saw on a small scale was a night attack that used war dogs. It sounded like utter confusion and I don't know if it was a success."

Dick Thom, as S–3 [Plans and Operations] for the 381st Regiment's

1st Battalion, held a much less benign view of the Marines on his right flank. "We were held up by a little hill, where we could not get enough weapons firing on it. I went to the lieutenant colonel of the Marines next to us and asked him to put fire on the area. He told me to go to hell. There's a boundary and I was not in control of their weapons.

"Later on we had three companies down to about two platoons of fifty men each, and that's by using clerks, medics, antitank crewmen. Damn if we don't get an order to maintain contact with the Marines, 1,000 yards away. We couldn't even cover the 1,000 yards assigned to us. We had six or eight lightly wounded medics; they were all armed and didn't wear brassards showing a red cross either. I sent them out on the flank with a light machine gun to make contact.

"Suddenly a soldier runs up to me, 'Captain, there's three stars coming.' I saluted the general and he says, 'Now don't give me any bullshit. What have you got in contact with the Marines?' When I told him, he got mad. 'You've got medics out there?' He threw his helmet down and reamed my ass. But then he walked off and never ordered me to change the set-up.

"We had problems with them about supplies. They didn't have trucks; we had to give them one of ours. Every afternoon we'd send for grenades, which would come up in jeep trailers. The Marines beat up one of our drivers, killed him and stole our hand grenades. There was a lot of ill feeling.

"I did them a dirty turn. In a long field, a rice paddy, we were in reserve. Eight or ten Marines came up while I was talking to another officer. They asked where the front line was. We pointed and they went off. The Japs let them get in place but not out. The Marines had to send up tanks to pick up their guys."

Vernon Corbin, a former student under the ASTP and messenger in the 383rd Regiment of the 96th, recalls an unhappy experience alongside Marine artillery designated to support the 7th and 96th Divisions. "The Marine artillery forward observers were very aloof and seemed to resent being associated with our operations. We suggested they find an empty foxhole or start digging in. They ignored our advice, but when we started to receive incoming fire, one of them tried to take over my foxhole. Our relations did not improve."

Jim Moll, of the 1st Marine Division, while reluctant to comment on any specific Army units, says, "There were some real good ones on Okinawa, but I was displeased when I saw some soldiers sitting in a deep hole playing cards early in the morning when we had to make a push on the next ridge. I pointed my tommy gun at them, told them to drop the cards, grab their weapons and get up on the ridge to give us some covering fire."

During the Okinawa campaign, the different branches often worked side by side rather than together, when the situation demanded it. Overt hostility, such as Thom describes, seldom surfaced, but most Marines regarded Army units as less than their equals, even if some GIs individually displayed the qualities admired by leathernecks. For their part, the Army men considered themselves as capable as the Marines, whom they felt benefited from hype pumped out by a massive publicity apparatus.

Another area of some discussion was the forward presence of the top brass. Thom says he never saw his division commander at one of his forward observation posts, but the Tenth Army chief, Simon Bolivar Bucker, occasionally put in an appearance. Herman Buffington, with K Company of the 383rd, had advanced beyond Shuri to a position where he and his buddies occupied the ledge overlooking a large ravine. Perhaps a mile away they could see enemy soldiers on their own knoll, somewhat lower in elevation. "We were shooting at some of them who were cooking rice. We used binoculars to see how well we were shooting and used tracer bullets, which left a red streak. An old fellow, maybe in his fifties, came up and said to me and some nearby soldiers, 'Are you doing any good?'

"We said, 'Yes, sir.' We didn't recognize him but knew he was some kind of top brass. He asked me if he could use my gun and shoot some. He lay there on the ground shooting for ten or fifteen minutes. The soldier with the binoculars let me borrow them and I could see that the 'old fellow' was shooting real well. The enemy would drag one off occasionally. The general then wanted to look through the binoculars and watch me shoot. He said he thought it was 'great.'

"After a while he left, and someone came up and told us that it was General Buckner, head of the Tenth Army, and real 'top brass.' I had also seen Gen. Claude Easley, the 96th Division general and assistant commander, at the front quite often, doing some sniping."

Buckner's sniping occurred as the Japanese doggedly backed up towards the end of the island. Si Seibert, one of the 382nd Regiment's latest replacement officers, whose baptism of fire had come with the cracking of the Shuri Line, after a few days with his company in reserve, started the steady grind toward the southern tip of Okinawa. "Some evenings it was extremely difficult to dig in, especially when we stopped on volcanic rock. Other days we were in the middle of old rice paddies or fields of soft dirt, where digging was easy. But always we kept moving south. There was no letup in the routine. We were tired all the time. The rain gave way to bright sunshine. which baked us as we toiled across the terrain.

"The tension of combat was present always. It was often broken by some inane remark by an unintentional wit—'Wonder what's for chow tonight?' which relieved the strain as we howled insanely.

"We neared a formidable escarpment made of the Uza-Dake and Yaeju-Dake hills. The north side was steep, about 150 feet in height. The 383rd fought for Uza-Dake and was so badly mauled that our 382nd was ordered to relieve two of its battalions. Our 2nd Battalion took over for their 2nd [Muehrke's organization] and, initially attached to the 383rd, was to attack in a narrow zone to gain a foothold on the escarpment. Leading the assault was F Company, with my platoon providing the point."

Told they were at the maximum range beyond their own artillery and mortar support then on the move, and could count on only minimal help from those elements, Seibert says his previous combat experience taught him he was better off in the lead, rather than coming in second or as reserves committed to the battle. "If attacking platoons were in file, it seemed to me that the initial punch-through was easier. After getting beyond the enemy's prearranged defensive area, the platoon would be in comparative safety. Reserves and following units seemed to get more artillery and mortar fire than lead elements."

At first, the advance went well and Seibert's unit gained the top of the escarpment. But as they slipped to one side to permit the remainder of the company to join them, intensive small-arms fire cracked down on them. With one soldier killed and another wounded, the platoon scrunched down behind the ridge line. Seibert peeked over the top to see a completely open field to the front, one pockmarked with bunkers, foxholes and spider holes, undoubtedly occupied by enemy soldiers prepared to spray the area with deadly results.

He consulted with his company commander, Cledith Bourneau, who said, because of other exigencies, no artillery could be brought to bear. The infantrymen would have to charge forward with only the minor aid of 60 mm mortars.

"The machine gun positions," says Seibert, "seemed poorly constructed. I called for rifle grenades, but there were only three and one grenade launcher. It had been so long since the men had used them, they had gradually stopped carrying the weapon. I had failed to check this out since I assumed command, and now my neglect was to be costly. None of the men left had even fired rifle grenades, so I became the grenadier. Because there were no launcher sights, I used the field experience of putting my foot in the rifle sling and measuring the angle with my eye. Surprisingly, I did pretty well. The first round fell short and did no damage but the second and third destroyed two positions.

"As I was sighting the second round, however, the platoon medic came up behind me and looked over my helmet. There was an instant report from a sniper rifle and the medic fell. He had been shot squarely between the eyes and lived only a few minutes, dying before he could be evacuated.

"It was obvious what the platoon was up against. I called again for supporting fire. Bourneau told me none was available, but we had to keep moving to permit the remainder of the company and battalion to get into position. I told him it was suicide to take the platoon into that fire. I asked if there were any tanks. He said no. Finally, Bourneau came up and looked over the situation. As I pointed out the enemy positions which permitted the Japs to cover the area in a crossfire, his radio operator looked over his shoulder. There was a characteristic report and the man fell dead. A sniper round had struck him too, squarely between the eyes.

"Bourneau agreed it was suicidal to continue. He went back to talk to Lieutenant Colonel Sterner, the battalion CO. Bourneau called shortly, ordering me to move out, regardless of the odds. I argued, telling him that I would not feel right if I took my platoon into certain death. Finally, he said, 'I'm giving you a direct order, Si.'

" 'I know you are, Cledith, but I can't obey it. We have to have some support.' There was silence on the radio. Suddenly, Bourneau appeared. 'Dammit, Si, move out! That's a direct order. You know what it means if you fail to follow orders in the face of enemy fire.' "

Seibert says he acknowledged his responsibility but refused to order his platoon to advance without support. Colonel Sterner arrived and inquired of Bourneau why the delay. The company commander explained his subordinate's reluctance.

Seibert says he pleaded his case. "Look at those positions, Colonel. They have us in a crossfire. We have already lost three men. It is suicide to move out there until we knock out some of those positions. We need artillery or tanks." And as Seibert pointed out the foe's emplacements, hostile rounds whizzed overhead.

Sterner responded, "I see what you mean, but we have to get this hill and move on. Move out!" Seibert yelled to his platoon sergeant to get the GIs going and personally started to lead the advance, as some of his men followed. But no sooner did they poke their heads over the ridge than the enemy drove them to cover with a withering slash of bullets.

Seibert told Sterner, "I can't take this platoon out there. You have to get us some support."

Grim-faced, Sterner, as Seibert remembers it, said, "You have violated a lawful order in the face of the enemy. You will have to face the consequences after this campaign is over."

"I realize that," answered Seibert. "Am I relieved of my platoon?"

"No, you will continue to command. Now let's see what can be done."

As they discussed their limited options, a single tank suddenly clanked into view. Sterner and Bourneau immediately informed the platoon leader that the tank now was attached to his platoon. Seibert explained his predicament to the tank commander, who maneuvered into a position where he could hit the enemy machine gun positions, while foot soldiers hugged his sides for protection and added their fire power.

"After he had destroyed several bunkers, he stopped. I got up on the tank deck, while drawing small-arms fire, to communicate with him. He opened a pistol port while the tank remained buttoned up. There were two more bunkers I wanted him to destroy. If they were neutralized, my platoon could take care of the foxholes and the rest of the resistance. As I was talking to him, the tank gunner spotted something and fired. My ear was about an inch from the barrel of the weapon. The concussion knocked me off the tank deck, and it was five days before the ringing stopped in my ears and I could hear again. In fact, my hearing was permanently damaged, resulting in partial deafness.

"Otherwise, however, I was not hurt. The tank knocked out the two targets I had indicated. My platoon moved out, passed ahead of the tank and swept over the area. A quick survey of the Jap defensive positions revealed it was a nest of tunnels and pillboxes completely covered by machine gun fire on the reverse slope of the small ridge behind which we had taken cover. Had we charged over without the tank, we would have been taken in the back by those machine guns. I was glad I had stood fast to protect my platoon. They would have been wiped out if I had not refused to move out without support. But I also knew the seriousness of having disobeyed an order in combat. For the next month I lived with the dread of what would happen when the campaign ended."

The 7th Infantry Division, traveling down the extreme eastern flank of the U.S. front, pushed swiftly into the Chinen Peninsula and then towards the southwest, where it faced a portion of the Japanese along the eastern end of the Yaeju Dake escarpment. Lt. Jack Fitzgerald, a replacement platoon leader with G Company of the 17th Regiment, brought with him thirty-two months of experience in the Pacific theater as well as his sixteen-week tour at OCS. "My greater age, twenty-three at the time, as well as my experience, helped me survive and provide leadership to a platoon of nine men. Most of the losses had been battle casualties, and most of the remaining nine were rather new replacements."

In the area near the line of hills, Fitzgerald put into practice his education while in the Guadalcanal jungles. He explains he learned there the value of cover and concealment, the ability to observe without being seen, how to patrol at great distance over some open ground.

"I led a patrol 1,500 yards across open ground toward the escarpment to determine the strength and position of the enemy. Private first class Perez, a scout of exceptional stealth ability and with superb eyesight, contributed much to the success of the patrol. We crossed the open ground without being discovered, saw and avoided several enemy patrols, found and observed evidence of a large force preparing for attack.

"With that information, we returned to Regimental S–2 [intelligence], reported our observations and prepared for a possible preplanned severe night attack. Because of our dug-in positions and prepared weapons emplacements, we received relatively few casualties, while inflicting severe losses upon a battalion force enemy. Perez, a fine soldier, also played a significant role in the defense."

According to Fitzgerald, that single experience also changed his future life. "I realized I was leading a patrol into unsecured territory while the officers at S–2 Regiment, all college graduates, 'pinned' my progress on a map from headquarters. I vowed then and there that college was my first priority on returning to the U.S."

Roland Lea, as a BAR man with Company B in the 17th Regiment, dug in with the other GIs on high ground overlooking a flat valley with no concealment. Beyond, loomed the Yaeju Dake ridge. "The valley floor extended some 1,000-plus yards to the base of this formidible cliff with only a small, four-foot-high volcanic outcrop ridge a short distance from its base. My casualty-depleted platoon was ordered to cross this valley and occupy the outcrop. We did it with limited opposition from the Japanese in their defensive positions atop the escarpment. But no sooner were we dug in than the small-arms fire and mortar rounds rained upon us from the heights above. The intense fire until darkness left us with sixteen killed and wounded.

"My squad of seven was ordered to advance to the base of the bluff and, if possible, work our way upwards. Fire from above caught us in the waist-high grass and two men were hit immediately. We were fortunate to withdraw under the cover of smoke and return to the outcrop.

"During the hours of darkness, my company and others crossed the valley, and with them we made our only night attack of the Okinawa campaign. The escarpment was scaled with such stealth that not a single shot was fired. The Japs awakened with dawn's light and we had a field day killing a surprised enemy. A real turkey shoot."

The pressure by the Americans squeezed the remaining defenders into ever smaller parcels of land and forced them out of their protected enclaves. George Brooks remembers a terrible scene as the last of the enemy yielded their places on the Yaeju-Dake Escarpment. "There was no escape for them. We had blocked them off. The heavy weapons company had set up their water-cooled machine guns, and it seemed like they would never stop shooting. Some of them were laughing and chortling all the while they were killing anything that moved within their field of fire. I was disgusted with their glee. It turned me off."

CHAPTER XXIX

KUNISHI RIDGE
AND BEYOND

Knocked off the Yaeju-Dake and Uza-Dake series of hills, the main body of the surviving Japanese soldiers made their final stand at Kunishi Ridge. A 2,000-yard-long, steep and smooth-sided elevation, Kunishi Ridge, like the previous defensive positions, boasted an elaborate system of caves, tunnels and protected gun emplacements. Similarly, a low flat expanse in front of the ridge created a killing field.

The task of securing this last rampart fell to the 1st Marine Division. The armor designated to work with the infantry came from the 1st Tank Battalion. Bob Neiman served as executive officer of the organization. A 1940 University of Maryland graduate, Neiman, with a precollege background of boys' summer camps, military and prep schools, on the advice of a mentor, volunteered for a Marine Corps officers training program before the draft could envelop him. Astigmatism threatened to bring rejection, but he corrected the problem with two hours of daily eye exercises under supervision of an ophthalmologist, and by downing a quart of carrot juice every day. Neiman, after completing boot camp and then the course for officer candidates, received assignment to Camp Lejeune, North Carolina. While there, he discovered tanks.

Meanwhile, the relationship between Japan and the U.S. continued to deteriorate until, one Sunday in Raleigh, North Carolina, Neiman, a fellow officer and two dates attended a movie packed with Marines from the nearby installation at New River. "When the showing finished," remembers Neiman, "the lights went on and the manager came

413

on stage and announced, 'My friends, I must announce that the United States and Japan are now at war.' There was dead silence for a moment and then, as though rehearsed, all of the Marines burst into 'From the halls of Montezuma . . .' snaked danced through the aisles and threw their hats in the air. I thought to myself, 'My God, do the Japs know what they've started—if they could see the reactions of the Marines?' "

Neiman and his friend dropped their dates off at the railroad station and returned to the base. He remembers the company commander addressed the men when they fell out the following morning with the official declaration of war. The CO finished his statement, "I guess there's nobody we'd rather fight than those little yellow bastards."

As a tanker, Neiman served with C Company of the 4th Marine Tank Battalion, first on Guadalcanal in 1943, and then participated in island campaigns, such as Kwajalein, Saipan, Tinian and Iwo Jima. The armor people benefited from on-the-job training in tactics and the tricks of survival. "We learned it was important for tanks to support one another and get help from the infantry whom we were working with. On Guadalcanal, the Japanese took advantage of the very dense vegetation to suddenly jump out with explosives. We found that if the tanks operated so they could see each other, it was very easy to dispose of these Japs by firing a machine gun right onto the other tanks. Likewise, if we were really overwhelmed by a large number of enemy soldiers, we wanted the infantry around, where they could support us with their fire.

"I learned on Guadalcanal, even though I did not fight there in a tank, that the Japanese used themselves as kind of human bombs. They would infiltrate through heavy jungle underbrush and try to place explosives on tanks, climb on top or the side of a tank while setting off an explosive charge. Their antitank gun was powerful enough to pierce even the side of a Sherman tank, depending upon the angle and distance of the fire. We decided we had to increase the protection on the sides of our tanks. My tank company modified our tanks in a number of ways. To make ineffective the magnetic mines the Japs liked to slap on the sides of the tanks, with the help of the Seabees, we welded two-inch U-channels to the tanks and bolted lumber to them. If a magnetic mine was pushed against one of our tanks, it wouldn't stick against the wood. The wood also added a two-inch air space between any explosive charges and the armor plate of the tank, dissipating the effect of the blast." [Bill Siegel, with the 706th Tank Battalion, says the Army never adopted this technique. In Siegel's experience, the Japanese usually tried to place a satchel charge underneath a tank, where the steel was not as thick or a tread could be blown off.]

After dealing with Japanese antitank guns at Kwajalein, and before embarking for the Saipan and Tinian operations, Neiman's tank company poured reinforced concrete into spaces between the lumber strips to help stop projectiles from piercing the armor plate. Again, this was a technique unique to Neiman's unit; other tanks did not add a concrete blanket.

According to Neiman, his outfit further protected their vehicles with extra track draped around the turret or over the front slope plate. The surplus tread provided shielding as well as a replacement part. Sandbags were fastened over the top of the critical engine compartment.

"The Japanese recognized we were vulnerable around the hatches, which needed to open easily. You could not put concrete around them. We had two in front and two on top for the turret. The Seabees used welding wire to make four-inch bird cages, which they welded over each hatch. If a Jap jumped on a tank and lay over the hatch with his explosive charge under his belly, there would still be four inches of space to dissipate the force on the hatch." With the bird cages in place, Neiman's tankers incurred no injuries from satchel charges applied to hatches, but other outfits lost men when the blast blew the hatch down upon them.

"During a period while I was at tank school, we had received twenty diesel tanks, originally destined for the Soviet Union but, somehow, they wound up with us. The Red Army had requested each tank have a self-sealing fuel tank welded to a bracket on the bustle at the rear of the tank. No fuel had ever been put in these [auxiliary] tanks, and I commandeered all of them for my company. I had them welded on our own tanks, put on little spigots and filled them with about twenty-five gallons of water. We carried plenty of water for the crews in a five-gallon can inside the tank, but whenever there was a lull in the fighting, the nearby infantry could fill up their canteens from these containers, originally designed for the Soviet-ordered armor. The infantry loved this item. Water was a crucial item in the South and Central Pacific fighting.

"Usually, all of my tanks were connected by a radio frequency with the infantry battalion companies that we supported. But below battalion level it was frequently difficult to communicate, especially when we came under fire. A foot soldier often had to bang on the side of a tank to get the attention of those inside, and then, when the tanker stuck his head outside to talk, there was a good possibility both would be shot.

"We placed telephones on the bottom right rear of our tanks. They had a long wire that, by means of a spring, retracted itself. An infantryman could crawl over, just reach up a few feet, grab the phone and get back into a foxhole while he had an instant dialog with the tank commander inside. The infantry could then point out the targets,—'200 yards at two o'clock are machine guns playing hell with us'; 'right at the base of those three trees over there . . .' We put the phone in a little steel box and ultimately all tanks became manufactured with telephones installed. But we started it."

"The Japanese soldiers were well trained, well disciplined, with little regard for their own lives. They were, however, pretty rigid in the thinking. When confronted with a new situation, they were often at a loss on how to cope. But they were tenacious, among the finest fighters in the world, next to the Marine Corps. We believed the Marines were superior in training, determination and the ability to innovate.

"The Jap tanks were no match for our Shermans. They had smaller guns, thinner armor plate and, in general, were inferior. And Jap tank tactics were not bright. They frequently attacked at night. You can't see well from a tank during the day. You're really at a loss in the dark. They should have known or learned, but they persisted in such tactics. They were usually destroyed by infantry or U.S. tanks.

"On Iwo they came up with one terrifically effective antitank weapon, the use of aerial bombs as antitank mines. With their airplanes all destroyed there, they had lots of 500–1000-pound bombs and they hit on the tactic of placing these vertically, nose up, just an inch or so below the surface in areas where tanks operated easily. They put a five-pound antitank mine on top, and when a tank ran over one that normally just blew off a section of track, now it would detonate the bomb below and blow up the tank. We lost a dozen tanks on Iwo to these, and one on Okinawa. There were usually no survivors.

"I was on Maui, after having been at Iwo, when word came that the commander of the 1st Tank Battalion, Lt. Col. Jeb Stuart, had been wounded and evacuated. I flew to Okinawa on a four-engine Navy transport," recalls Neiman. "The pilot announced that if we looked out the window, we would see Okinawa. I saw a rather large island, with lots of smoke, the sort of thing one sees from the air of a battlefield where people are fighting and dying.

"Just about the moment we started to look at Okinawa, our plane took some violent twists, up and down, sideways. I could see the black smoke of ack-ack all around us as the pilot took evasive action. He got word to the trigger-happy gunners down below that we were friendly.

"When calm was restored and we went in for the landing at Yontan, I was greeted by the unexpected sight of smashed-up Japanese planes all over the place, what looked like dead Jap paratroopers in the trees, lots of dead bodies and pretty heavily pockmarked runways. We were the first friendly plane to arrive after the Japanese airborne troops had launched their assault on Yontan, and the gunners were, therefore, jumpy."

Neiman hitched a ride with a long line of trucks headed south. When he reached the headquarters of the 1st Tank Battalion, he was surprised to find its commander, Jeb Stuart, still in place. Rather than wounded, Stuart suffered from amoebic dysentery. But he informed his supposed replacement, "I am not leaving until the fighting is over." Neiman agreed then to become Stuart's exec.

He learned that the 1st Tank Battalion suffered its highest loss in tanks while moving south through the Wanna Draw. "Kunishi Ridge," says Neiman, "was a very tough nut to crack. Jeb Stuart had developed a tactic called 'processing.' Tanks would go through the rice paddies towards the 200–300-foot-high ridges in Okinawa, almost up to the ridge line itself. Then the tank commander, using field glasses and the periscope, would scan for cave openings, which would be processed with 75 mm flat-trajectory fire until these caves could no longer serve as defensive positions. Together with artillery, naval gunfire and air support, that would make it possible for infantry to get across the rice paddies.

"But at Kunishi Ridge, the Japanese had a German 88 mm antitank gun. I don't know where or how they obtained it, but they had a few of them toward the end of the war. The one 88 at Kunishi Ridge moved from cave to cave very effectively, and as long as it was operating, there was no way to process the place. Everytime one of our tanks poked its nose over the ridge line we had taken earlier, that 88 would hit it.

"We had one platoon leader, a big lieutenant who always wore red socks. They saved his life. His tank was one of those that the 88 struck while it was going over the ridge and down the forward slope towards Kunishi. The 88 destroyed the tank, blowing the lieutenant clear out of it. He was lying there and given up for dead, while we tried to figure out how to get that 88. Somebody saw the red socks move and we realized he was wounded, still alive. A couple of guys volunteered to go out and get him. They crawled down the slope and dragged him back. In a hospital, he recovered completely.

"But we still had to find out the location of the 88. When I was on Saipan, I had encountered a somewhat similar problem. Going through the sugar cane fields, which were eight feet high, you couldn't see what was ahead. I carried a sawed-off shotgun I would fire into the cane ahead whenever I got out of the tank. After the campaign was over, I decided airplanes could help us. I got hold of the skipper of an observa-

tion squadron in the 4th Marine Regiment, and we practiced on Saipan
with an O–1 plane. We had a tank officer ride in the O–1 with a radio on
my frequency. They flew above us and would tell me what lay ahead.
The system worked and was used to good advantage on Tinian, where
there were even more sugar cane fields.

"I passed on the idea to Jeb Stuart, although the 1st Marine Tank
Battalion had never used the technique. Jeb agreed we ought to try, and
I drove by jeep to the O–1 squadron, taking with me a radio adjusted to
the tank frequency and a box of smoke grenades. However, Jeb had
insisted a young lieutenant, an intelligence officer, would go up in the
plane. I had protested but to no avail.

"The squadron commander agreed to our plan, and they took off with
the lieutenant as the observer. They flew over Kunishi Ridge and
radioed they were in good position. We sent one whole platoon of tanks
over the ridge and the balance of the company right behind them. Sure
enough, the 88 opened up but the observer quickly spotted him. He
described its location to the tanks and then dropped smoke grenades
over the position. He advised us where the gun was in relation to the
smoke. Acting as a forward observer, he guided the fire from an entire
tank company, which succeeded in destroying the 88. Unfortunately,
the plane came a little too close to some Japanese positions. Our lieutenant received a burst of machine gun fire in his knee, ultimately
costing him his leg. But the battle for Kunishi Ridge could now begin in
earnest, and the tanks would play a major role. That would have been
impossible if the 88 wasn't knocked out.

"Our battalion, now that the tanks were safe, moved down into the
rice paddies between the two ridges and began to process Kunishi
Ridge with direct fire into any caves we could see. But so many of them
were honeycombed, interconnected, with entrances and exits on the
reverse slope, that the Marine infantry still was hit very hard every time
it tried to cross the 1,500 yards separating the two ridges. Though we no
longer had the 88 to contend with, the Japanese had so many mortar,
light artillery and machine gun positions, there were too many for our
tanks to destroy or quickly neutralize. The infantry suffered very heavy
casualties trying to reach Kunishi Ridge."

The 1st Division's 7th Marine Regiment was a pitiful semblance of its
once robust fighting force. Jim Moll, in A Company, recalls, "As we
moved farther and farther south toward Kunishi Ridge, we were losing
more and more men, until finally we had to consolidate the rifle platoons from the entire company into a single platoon, with Lt. Tom Cook
as the leader and myself as platoon sergeant.

"It was about a month since I had the concussion, and each day since, my physical condition was going downhill fast. I was just about run out of gas, losing my equalibrium and falling down a lot. Every bone in my body ached. I was becoming short of breath and had no more energy or endurance left. I told Cook that I thought I should turn myself in to sick bay for a few days. Maybe with some medication and a shot of something that would knock me out for a few days, it would do the trick. Cook asked me to hang on a little longer and I agreed."

Don Farquahar, as a platoon leader during the march south beyond the Shuri Line, says, "There were no major battles, only small firefights along the way. The rains were over and we moved fast. The most interesting thing was, almost all our supply had to come by air. The landscape was dotted with parachutes of different colors. But at Kunishi Ridge, as we had found earlier on Okinawa, was one more ridge line with no room to maneuver by means of an end run."

Although his 1st Battalion of the 7th Marine Division had absorbed 125 dead and wounded in a single day at Dakeshi Ridge, Charles Owens, the kid who joined the Marines at age fourteen, says, "The battle for Kunishi Ridge was the hardest fighting I saw. The regiment took heavy casualties because of fire coming from the front and flanks while trying to go over a long open area. Col. Edward Snedeker, the regimental commander, knew he had to do something desperate and he did. On the night of June 12, he had two companies, C and F, jump off at night. This had never never been done before. We thought someone had gone nuts."

Snedeker actually had personally flown at low level over the site in an observation plane before crafting his daring tactic. Then-1st Lt. Winston Huff, the CO of F Company, says, "From my jarhead worm's-eye view, it was a terrible idea." Huff was unhappy at the prospect because his troops already had been through a rough time during the afternoon. Furthermore, he remembered "the general snafu that always accompanied our night training on Pavuvu. In retrospect," says Huff, "the night attack was a bright idea because it succeeded. Heaven only knows what would have transpired if the Japs were awake at night, like they were during the previous afternoon. That's why Pedro del Valle, commanding general, the 1st Marine Division, was a general, Snedeker a colonel, and I was a first lieutenant."

"The two companies got on Kunishi Ridge okay," says Charles Owens. "However, at daylight, the shit hit the fan. The remaining rifle companies tried to cross the open area three times to join those already on the ridge. Because of heavy losses we had to stop, although C and F needed water, ammo and medical help."

Jim Moll remembers, "The first troops that pushed out on the low, flat terrain in front of the objective received all kinds of shelling from a Jap artillery, so they decided to take us in in tanks."

The 1st Tank Battalion made arrangements to bring reinforcements, carry supplies and remove wounded. Bob Neiman explains, "The men up on Kunishi Ridge were surrounded by thousands of enemy soldiers and the Japs were mortaring, machine gunning and grenading them. They had to have reinforcements. In the past, Marine tanks occasionally carried men into battle, but this was more significant in the outcome of the fighting than at any previous time.

"Each Sherman normally carries a crew of five, but needs only one man to drive it and a tank commander to guide it. If we removed the gunner, loader and assistant loader, there was room for at least three men, and if the ammo was removed, that made room for a fourth man. On a short trip, you could squeeze in a fifth Marine.

"Our tanks went to the designated infantry battalion, where the Marine riflemen climbed in with the two-man crews and the reduced loads of ammo. The supplies for the infantry were strapped on the backs of the tanks. We began crossing the rice paddies and climbing up Kunishi Ridge, single file, like a line of ants.

"When the tanks reached the Marine positions on Kunishi, they opened the escape hatches and the riflemen crawled out through the bottom of the tank. Someone would scrape off all the ammo and other supplies from the top of the engine compartment. Marine wounded then got inside the tank or, if too badly hurt, they were strapped on the back along with the dead. The tanks then backed down through the valley until they could disgorge their cargo in safety. Another group of riflemen then boarded the tanks for the trip. This continued for two days."

Neiman's description fits that of the foot-soldier passengers except in one respect. From their accounts, it appears that the tank commanders initially expected the riflemen to exit through the top of the tank. Jim Moll, the platoon sergeant in Company A of the 7th Regiment, says, "I think there were only four of us with the driver and commander. We went like hell through the shellfire, and as we neared our destination, we heard small-arms fire hitting the tank. Finally, the tank stopped and the officer said that was where we got out.

"He opened the door on the turret, and as I started to climb out, machine gun bullets were hitting the door. One ricocheted off my helmet. I dropped down and asked if there were another exit. He told us about the trap door in the floor. Also, earlier, when I stuck my head out the turret opening, I noticed the tank was still out in the open and we'd have no kind of cover. I asked him to move in closer to the base of a vertical ridge. Reluctantly, he moved a little closer to it. One by one we stripped off our packs, canteens, etc., so we could squeeze out the trap door. Soon as our bodies were out of the tank, they pushed out our gear. Then we crawled out from under the tank and ran like hell to the base of this high, vertical ridge.

"As I was crawling out from under our tank, I saw another one nearby, and the first Marine who got halfway out the turret was killed by machine gun fire. After that, they also began to leave from the bottom."

Earl Rice endured the privilege of one of these tank rides to the battlefield. "Lieutenant Cook, the other guys and I had never been in a tank before. I could hear the bullets bouncing off the sides. I was standing beside the ladder when the tank commander ordered me to go up out the hatch. I realized the odds were against me getting out alive. Lieutenant Cook asked if there were a way out below, and the tank commander said yes. Cook said that's the way we would go.

"Even then, on the way out, one of our guys got shot in the leg by a sniper. Later, I saw a Marine come out the top of a tank with a smoke bomb. The Japanese kept firing into the smoke. I also saw some of the casualties tied to the tanks get hit by sniper bullets as they left.

"After we left the tank, we tried to take the pinnacle of our hill. My good buddy and former squad leader, Pop Wilson, was hit in the throat by a dumdum bullet. Others were either hit or scattered back down the hill. The corpsman stayed with Pop until he passed away. I was upset, stood on the top of the hill and yelled, 'You yellow bastards! Get up here!' There was a surprised look on Lieutenant Cook's face and they all came back up.

"There was a Marine there, a replacement about my age, who'd cracked up. Lieutenant Cook told me, 'You two take Pop back and stay there.' I protested that there wasn't anything wrong with me. I just got angry. He said, 'The less people we got up here, the more chance we'll be relieved.' We carried Wilson back and put him on a pile. The pile was over five feet, at least up to my shoulders, if not higher. It was a helluva feeling to put that guy on there.

"Two Marines there told me to give them Wilson's wallet, watch and ring. They'd see that these did not arrive before the family got the telegram about him. I found out what slimeballs they were when, a year later, someone wrote me that Wilson's family had taken out an ad in a Marine magazine asking if anyone might know where Wilson's belongings were. I did send them the rifle he took off a Jap whom he killed.

"There was a sergeant there when we brought in Wilson, a guy who looked like a poster for the Marines, but I never saw him in any bit of combat. He was giving out supplies. He says to me, 'Get back up there.' I says, Lieutenant Cook told me to stay here. He says, 'You get back up there; that's an order.' He made me take the kid back with me. Cook was very angry when we came back but he couldn't do anything about it at the time."

Charles Owens rode up onto Kunishi Ridge in the belly of a tank like the others. "The only way off was to be killed or wounded. Myself and a buddy, Jim Wolff, were put on a working party, to load the dead on trailers pulled by tanks. The bodies were wrapped in ponchos and the pile covered with a parachute. Before we finished, most of the working party had left. Wolff and I got all of the dead on the trailers. The smell was on us for a month.

"It was like being on an outpost. Our supplies were dropped by parachutes from planes. We could get hit in the head because the containers would come open and cases of ammo and food fall to the ground. We just knew we were going to die on this ridge. There was no sleep. The replacements who reached us were either old or very young and not very well trained. Before you got to know them, they were dead."

Like Owens, Earl Rice depended upon airborne supply. "They dropped things like cases of donuts, one of which hit a guy and left him in terrible condition. But we had two donuts apiece; that was the greatest meal I ever had, two donuts and coffee."

Jim Moll spent nearly a week on Kunishi Ridge in something of a daze. "We had very little protective coverage and many casualties from grenades dropped down on us. We finally found what we thought was a way to the top, and I took a squad up one morning, climbed the cliff, which I never thought I'd make in my condition. Up there, we received lots of sniper fire and our squad leader, kneeling next to me, had his whole jaw shot off. I guess they were using dumdum bullets.

"I cannot remember how the hell we got back to our platoon that night, but I know that Earl Rice carried the squad leader back to where we had climbed up that cliff. A few days later, I woke up in the field hospital. Our company was taken off the lines. I missed about two days of the whole damn battle and it bothers me even today."

Earl Rice stuck it out. "I think I became a man on Kunishi Ridge because Lieutenant Cook treated me like one. He made me a squad leader with a corporal under me. I had been the biggest shitbird in the company and he talked of me being a sergeant. I felt like I was thirty-five. I learned what discipline and responsibility were all about. When they wanted to organize petitions to leave the hill and asked me to sign, I refused.

"Later, a fellow named Birch, thirty-eight, thirty-nine years old, a replacement who had something like nine kids, because of his family, was supposed to leave the ridge. But a damn knee mortar landed in his hole. He cried for his wife and kids. There's no way an old man should have died that way.

"On the 16th it was our turn for another push. I had a squad with me, and as we moved up I knew there were Japs there. It had gotten to the point where I could smell them. I ran to Cook and told him there was Japs there, lots of them. He said to me, 'I know it's getting near the end and you're all excited.' I said, 'Lieutenant, I'm not excited; I'm out of breath from running.' Then the Japs opened up and Cook was hit in the head. The corpsman told me to hold his hand while he worked on him. Cook looked like that actor Dick Foran; he was a strong guy, a football player. I held his hands and I didn't think he would pass away. I thought he'd just been creased but he died right there.

"At this point, with all the people killed and wounded, I am only two or three men away from being platoon leader. Lieutenant Farquahar took over the company. The corporal in my squad said for us to move to the rear. As I turned around, Lieutenant Farquahar put a tommy gun in my face and said, get back. That really upset me. I may have been a screwup, but I was not a coward and I thought the order to move back was his order. Subsequently, Farquahar sent me out on a few skirmishes.

"Then June 18, Lieutenant Farquahar told us we would be relieved the next morning. That night we were pretty high up on the pinnacle, with Burns and me on the flank in a hole. Arky and a new guy were in the nearest hole. I knew that during the night, the Japs would make their move. I had sixteen hand grenades around my hole, plus my weapon and Burns's. After an hour or so into my watch during the night, I called over to Arky and got no answer. I called a second time. Still no answer; they were both napping. I rolled a hand grenade over, seven or eight feet from their hole, and when it went off, that woke them up. 'Man alive,' I yelled, 'didn't you see them?'

"I didn't have to worry any more about them being awake during the night. Then the Japs started moving down on us. I threw about a dozen grenades all over the area. I heard some hollering and knew I hit somebody. The rest of the night there was very little sleep. The booming of the grenades kept everyone up.

"At the crack of dawn, I looked out the front for Japs but didn't see anybody. All at once I hear someone coming over the top. It was a bunch of 2nd Division Marines, in fresh uniforms. I started to prowl around, seeing what I got during the night—always the souvenir hunter. One of the 2nd Marine Division guys, just coming in, got shot. I went back to my hole quick."

The relieving troops belonged to the reinforced 8th Regimental Combat Team of the 2nd Marine Division, in reserve from the time of a Love Day feint at the Minatoga Beaches until finally capturing two small nearby islands against minimal opposition. Rice recalls his departure from Kunishi. "I wasn't moving too fast but when I reached the place where that Marine had been hit, I did a 100-yard dash. We came off the Ridge of Death to hot food, showers—we hadn't showered from May 8 to June 18. I didn't realize until we were off the line for a few days that I had been hit, that I had shrapnel in my face. I knew I had a hole in my hand and in back; both had turned green. They put Merthiolate on my back, hand and face. But the wounds stayed green."

The night before the 2nd Division forces actually appeared on the ridge, Bob Neiman and his commander, Jeb Stuart, met with their opposite numbers from the tank battalion that would supplant them. "We renewed old friendships," says Neiman, "and filled them in on what to expect in the way of Japanese tactics and resistance. Jeb Stuart and I climbed way out on the south end of the ridge and watched 2nd Marine Division fire teams with tanks move out. The Japanese positions were quickly overcome; the casualties were light. The Japanese opposition was not as strong as earlier, but nevertheless, it strengthened my conviction that relief by a complete fresh unit is better than bringing up individual replacements. The fire teams knew what they were doing, they knew each other's capabilities and how to work together. They went through the Japs like the proverbial hot knife in butter."

On June 18, as the defenders of Kunishi Ridge fell back in disarray, the Americans on the left flank of the 1st Marine leathernecks completed their mission. Bob Muehrcke and another platoon leader, Lt. Bill Frothinger, the two surviving officers of Company F, walked off the Uza-Dake escarpment, leading the handful of twenty-one GIs still on their feet. Says Muehrcke, "The men hadn't washed or shaved for the past thirty-nine days. They were exhausted, filthy dirty, their combat fatigues were coated with blood, either from their buddies or from their own bodies. All but one were wounded at least once. They were a pitiful sight, but they were alive and very proud men as they walked off the Okinawa escarpment to the reserve area. The sun was shining brightly but they still received heavy enemy fire."

The imminent demise of the Japanese resistance and the presence of a strong new element under his command brought Tenth Army commander General Buckner to the scene. In the early afternoon of June 18, he stopped at an 8th Marine Regiment forward observation post to watch the progress of the leathernecks. A shell struck the sheltered area and the blast drove a piece of coral into the general's chest, a fatal injury. Until Gen. Joseph Stilwell arrived, Marine Gen. Roy Geiger commanded the Tenth Army.

Chick D'Angelo, as a runner at Headquarters Company of the 3rd Marine Regiment, wonders about the official version of Buckner's death. "Buckner was on the back side of a ridge facing our position on a higher ridge. The Japs were either committing suicide or surrendering. I don't think they had any artillery left. There's no doubt in my mind that friendly fire killed him."

Buckner had already become a controversial figure by the time of his

A monument marks the spot where an artillery shell fatally wounded Gen. Buckner. (*Signal Corps, U.S. National Archives*)

death. The slow progress and the high number of casualties on Okinawa attracted notice in the States, now that the main focus of attention, the war in Europe, was over. On June 4, columnist David Lawrence wrote, "Why is the truth about the military fiasco at Okinawa being hushed up . . . mistakes that appear to have made the Okinawa affair a worse example of military incompetence than Pearl Harbor." He continued on to describe the severe losses in the services engaged in Operation Iceberg.

Lawrence, another strategist observing from his Washington D.C., base, drew on the account of New York *Herald-Tribune* war correspondent Homer Bigart, who described the Tenth Army's approach in football terms. "Instead of an end run, we went down the middle of the line." Bigart suggested that, without fear of a southern invasion, the Japanese could concentrate all of their troops at the Shuri Line. The correspondent was in error because, as later interrogations and captured documents indicated, General Ushijima worried about a thrust from behind him as late as June 14. Not until the abortive offensive of May 4–5 did the Japanese shift a substantial number of troops from the south coast to the Shuri Line. And by that time, both Marine Divisions were already plugged into the American front and unavailable for a landing.

The author of "Today in Washington" lambasted Buckner. "The Army general in command got bogged down with his troops in the south end of the island while the Marines quickly cleared the northern end and instead of using the Marines for amphibious landings to the rear of the Japanese lines by coming up from the south coast, the Marines were thrust into the middle of the line to pound away as if time were not of the essence."

He declared that amphibious warfare tactics would have achieved aerial supremacy, had the Navy not had to contend with kamikazes. The columnist declared, "An island battle cannot be fought by massing artillery or deploying troops as would be done on a vast terrain in Europe."

Lawrence implied that the Army did not understand the dynamics of island warfare and decisions should have been left with those most experienced in those kinds of operations, Marine officers. Subsequently, an Army historian, Roy Appleman, noted that the Marines, as determined and valorous as they were, performed no better against the enemy than the Army units.

Gen. Andrew Bruce, who had volunteered his 77th Division for such an expedition immediately after taking Ie Shima, remained convinced that it would have shortened the conflict, privately noted, "My division was virtually chewed up in costly, frontal attacks."

However, most military chieftains publicly rallied around Buckner while he was still alive. Secretary of the Navy James Forrestal, Admirals Turner and Mitscher rebutted the arguments against the Tenth Army strategy. Admiral Nimitz held a press conference on Guam on June 17, one day before Buckner was killed, and defended the decisions made.

Following the conquest of the island, Gen. John Hodge, commander of the XXIV Corps, which included Buckner and his Tenth Army, said that any seaborne adventure in the south before May 4–5 "might have resulted in a debacle, in a catastrophe." The Marine generals, however, kept a discreet quiet.

One day after Buckner fell, Gen. Claudius Easley, the assistant commander of the 96th, known for his predilection to hang about the front lines, while pointing out the site of an enemy machine gun that had wounded his aide, took two bullets from that weapon in the forehead. Within twenty-four hours, and victory only a few days off, death in combat had claimed two general officers.

Easley's conduct also provoked some controversy, although it was confined to official quarters. After hostilities were over, the upper echelons reviewed strategy and tactics. Dick Thom, as a participant at Kakazu Ridge, was summoned to the inquiry. "Easley of course was dead, my colonel was gone," says Thom, "and I was the only guy left. I did all I could to hang the vast number of casualties on Easley, who, I thought, was going to get us all killed."

Si Seibert, however, like most of the Deadeyes, admired the general as "an aggressive assistant division commander, the type of individual who was always up with the troops. They had a great deal of respect for him, hence his death was a blow to all of us."

Seibert had little time to mourn; his unit continued to plug south steadily, alert to the possibility of a final banzai charge, and with sporadic rifle fire still coming from the enemy. On June 20 his outfit swept through the small town of Aragachi, a site of several days of hard fighting. Six soldiers from one of Seibert's squads were wounded when a band of eight Japanese soldiers tried to blow up an American tank. All of the enemy died. That night Seibert saw shadowy figures moving along a slope opposite his position. Quick conferences with his company commander, and then the forward artillery observer, arranged for an artillery barrage on what appeared to be one of the anticipated last-ditch banzai ventures. "Fortunately," recalls Seibert, "only one or two rounds were fired before somebody called a cease-fire. We almost put a Corps Time-on-Target on the 305th Regiment from the 77th Division. No one was hurt." Later, however, Deadeyes killed five Japanese soldiers sneaking up to a nearby watering hole. Infiltrators appeared; one of Seibert's men broke the stock of his rifle over the head of a foe who entered his foxhole.

A week before his death, Buckner approved a serious effort to persuade the Japanese to surrender. He authorized a message to General Ushijima that read, "The forces under your command have fought bravely and well, and your infantry tactics have merited the respect of your opponent . . . Like myself, you are an infantry general long schooled and practiced in infantry warfare . . . I believe therefore that you understand as clearly as I that the destruction of all Japanese resistance on the island is merely a matter of days."

Buckner's staff arranged for the note to be dropped by air and it took a week for the surrender proposal to reach the final headquarters on the southwestern coast. No one seriously expected Ushijima to quit but, having made that offer, the Americans felt free to paper the area still harboring enemy soldiers with surrender leaflets that emphasized their leader's refusal to save their lives.

Rather than negotiate with the enemy, Ushijima sent off a series of messages to Japan including one that said, "I have no adequate words of apology . . . It has come to the point where we are about to deploy all surviving soldiers for a final battle—in which I will apologize to the emperor with my own death. Yet the regret for not having accomplished my enormous responsibility will torment my soul for thousands of years to come."

Ushijima did not, however, intend to tender his apology through death in a "final battle." In the early morning of June 22, he and General Cho dined ceremoniously, toasting guests with sake and swallowing draughts of Scotch whiskey. Ushijima wore his white dress uniform, while Cho dressed in a white kimono. The pair then walked to a designated site where, supposedly in the rite of *seppuku,* they disemboweled themselves with knives while aides simultaneously struck them on their necks with sabers. Some accounts allege that, in fact, the two died of gunshot wounds. In any event, their deaths coincided with the date that the U.S. declared the island secured.

As their final redoubts crumbled, and their leader readied himself for suicide, a substantial number of weary, wounded and hungry Japanese soldiers forsook their obligation to die for the emperor and began to surrender. Others still continued to strike at the invaders. Herman Buffington, with K Company of the 383rd Regiment, pushed half a mile farther to a ridge line that overlooked the coastline. "From the escarpment we could see the enemy down on the end of the island. They were going in circles and surrendering in droves. They weren't being killed but they were being stripped down to their shorts."

The Deadeyes pressed ahead half a mile. Relates Buffington, "We could see a village between us and the end of the island. Miles of Japanese soldiers were milling around there. We dug in and planned to take the village. I really dreaded it. The Japs were throwing small mortars up on us. They weren't too far away. Two or three of our boys were hit during the night. The next morning I was picking up their packs and things when the mortars started dropping again, thirty or forty feet away. You weren't safe, even in foxholes.

"Suddenly, one dropped down among three of us, wounded all. One boy got shrapnel up and down his back, one got it in his face, and I was hit in my right leg. I was, the luckiest of the three. Yes, it hurt. The shell had lodged against the bone. The most I remember about it was that the meat on my leg kept frying and burning.

"Strenski was a medic was there, and I told him, 'Give me your belt.' I wanted to make a tourniquet. He said he'd give me a shot of morphine but I said, 'No, I'd be out and just bleed to death. I don't want anything.'" The medic obliged and Buffington walked four or five miles, periodically releasing the tourniquet, before a jeep carried him to an aid station. He continued to refuse morphine, even there, for fear he would doze off while his life oozed away.

He arrived at a hospital after a trip by stretcher, landing boat and ambulance. "The hospital was just three rows of tents connected end to end. In the first, you got the shots. In the second, they operated. And in the third, they bandaged the wound. They said they wouldn't put me to sleep to operate, so they put a few shots around the wound and gave me something to hold in my hand. The surgery hurt. Boy, did it hurt! The day I got hit was the last before the official ending of the Battle of Okinawa."

Frank Barron, made executive officer of the 1st Battalion of the 305th Infantry, with the return of Maj. Gene Cook, the battalion CO, after his appendicitis flare-up, and his outfit, relaxed in a rear area in preparation for leaving Okinawa. "We had tents to sleep in, cots to sleep on. Unexpectedly, we received orders to move up behind the 96th

Division in case of a banzai attack. Barron thought he might be excused in order to make arrangements for leaving Okinawa, but Cook insisted Barron accompany him to the front.

After a long, rough ride marked by reports of a dozen casualties absorbed by a brother battalion cleaning out bypassed caves, Barron selected a well-protected command post amid huge boulders and surrounded by GIs. He and Cook went to sleep in a tent with cots, hauled from the rear area. During the night Barron was awakened by nearby rifle fire and several grenades exploded. "I heard a couple of 'blip-blips' as fragments passed through the wall of the tent. I looked over at Gene when it happened, but he was still asleep on his cot. Later, when it happened again, I was ready to look for an improvised foxhole, but Cook was still there, so I went back to sleep. The next morning he told me that each time he woke up, he looked to see if I was still on my cot before deciding to stay on his. What comfort we find in one another's foolishness."

Early in the morning, two battalions of the 305th, with Frank Barron on the scene and elements of the 96th Division, attacked Hills 79 and 85. The skirmishes lasted almost two days but with another 600 enemy dead, the final defenses collapsed. The date was June 22; Ushijima and Cho were now dead and there was no more organized resistance.

Joe Budge, the mortar sergeant in the 305th Infantry Regiment, remembers, "We closed in on the final place of resistance of the Japanese. There was a high, brooding, dark ridge which ended in a steep cliff over the southern beach. Inland for several hundred yards was a flattish plain, broken by rock piles and earthen banks. Nips could be seen from time to time, scuttling about out there. Parallel with the shoreside ridge was another, lesser one with several knolls wooded with pine trees. We were to attack, our mortars and machine guns set up behind us on the rise so they could fire over our heads. We were to advance in World War I-style, open order, firing from the hip. We did not expect the Nips would be heavily fortified. Nor were they."

The troops with Budge achieved their immediate objectives and settled in to watch some tanks trundle ahead. Budge reports, "All of a sudden a Nip appeared out of a spider hole near a tank, threw a burlap sack on the flat back of the tank, jumped up and lay on top of the sack. Then it blew and the man disintegrated. The tank stopped and presently another came alongside it. The crew got out of the escape hatch and into the second tank. Three or four other Nips popped up in the next half-hour but we were ready for them. The moment they were hit

The huge cemetery on Okinawa testifies to the heavy casualties suffered by the Americans. *(National Archives)*

and went down, if they were still alive, they blew themselves up with grenades.

"Japanese interpreters with loudspeakers in tanks were making speeches trying to get more to surrender, and several civilians did. Some Nip rifle fire came at them, presumably to save them from a fate worse than death." More and more Okinawan natives, risking bullets from Americans and the holdouts, filtered into the U.S. lines. After another day or so of dealing with small groups of Japanese, Budge's outfit returned to a rest area.

Ed Fitzgerald, the 1st sergeant with Service Company of the 307th Regiment, said, "The last night of the war wasn't the worst one, but it was the loudest. It was the night of June 21, and it was almost over now and the ground rolling under our stomachs and the persistent screams of shells over our heads was mostly our artillery going out, not much of theirs coming in. Naha and Shuri Castle had finally been taken, and all the Japanese had left was a few miles of mostly flat ground.

"The next night we were still on the same hill, right in the same place but it was a whole lot different. We went out of our holes and we were heating our C rations on Coleman stoves for the first time in four months. I mixed water and a can of meat-and-vegetable stew in my canteen cup and it was delicious, especially with some of the Medical Detachment's whole-grain alcohol mixed with grapefruit juice on the side. Nobody was shooting at us and we guessed nobody was likely to, because the word was that the Japanese commander, General Ushijima, had leaned on his dagger and was no more. We would be going down to the beaches in a few days, they said, to load on a ship, for a rest before Japan."

Okinawan civilians wash their clothes following the American conquest of their homeland. *(Jack Lewis)*

CHAPTER XXX

FINAL STROKES

While, officially, Okinawa was in American hands, the killing continued. Si Seibert and F Company of the 382nd Regiment reversed direction and trekked north. "We had a multiple mission; to locate, flush out, capture or kill any enemy bypassed during the fighting south; to seal all caves and tunnels; to recover all Japanese and usable American equipment; and to bury the enemy dead.

"So many Japanese soldiers had been killed in the last ten days of the fighting that it had been impossible to remove the bodies for identification and burial. Now these bodies were blackened and bloated, swarming with huge bluebottle flies. Maggots were eating the flesh away. It is difficult to estimate the number of unidentified bodies we placed in massed or isolated, but unmarked, graves. Distasteful as this burial task was, it had to be done.

"About ten days were spent in this final sweep. There were occasional firefights as fanatic Nipponese sought 'honorable death' rather than surrender. Many bodies and equipment were booby trapped. A continual toll was taken of American soldiers, all the more difficult to accept, now that the island was 'secure.'"

Seibert and the troops now set up a bivouac area, a garrison-style life, even though the hills and caves still harbored soldiers who refused to surrender. Seibert and other officers wrote letters of condolence to the families of the dead and also responded to complaints from those who thought their sons ill-treated. It was also a time for drafting award recommendations. Seibert contributed a statement that bolstered the case for Clarence Craft's Medal of Honor, wrote up the efforts of Cledith Bourneau, who received a Distinguished Service Cross. Seibert also sought Silver and Bronze Stars for members of his own unit and he himself received one of the former.

"The matter of awards became quite an undertaking. Col. Macey Dill [the Regimental CO] had been at division headquarters when several of the rear-echelon troops, including the division information and education officer, had been awarded the Bronze Star for meritorious service. Upon his return from that ceremony, he held an Officers' Call at which he told us that if division headquarters troops earned Bronze Stars, then every man in the regiment deserved one. He directed a major effort to see that his men were recognized. We started cranking out recommendations for awards. There had to be a specific action or service to justify a reommendation, but many of them were 'stretched' to meet the criteria."

Early in July, the 77th Division sailed to Cebu, in the Philippines, to take on replacements and replace gear in preparation for the invasion of the Japanese home islands. While in camp there, the job of writing up candidates for medals fell to Joe Budge. "Nobody wanted any medals," claims Budge, "until the point system for discharge was revised to give points for medals and combat time. As originally drafted by some moron, the system proposed demobilization on a simple seniority system, so that a recruiting sergeant, serving in his hometown, would have been discharged before some wretch who had been in combat for three years, wounded and decorated.

"I got the jargon down right and I cranked these things out with no problem, in longhand. Sometimes one from another regiment would come to me with the general's [Andrew Bruce] huge scrawl, 'Send it to the guy from the 305th for revision.' He was tough on medals, compared to most divisional commanders, who had the authority to award all but the top two, the DSC and the Medal of Honor, which had to have Washington's approval. I wrote one MH and revised one successfully for another battalion. Quite often in talking to witnesses, I found that the proposed recommendation was too high or too low or not deserving of anything, according to the rules I had been given.

"One factor bureaucrats insisted upon was that one had to have done something above and beyond one's normal duty. A machine gunner could kill a large number of the enemy with his gun. That was his job. But if he picked up an entrenching tool and did some execution with that, why, this was 'above and beyond.' For top medals, there had to be an element of leadership—individual heroics were most commendable, but leadership was better.

"In our division, the general had once run an army school for tanks and tank destroyers and was a nut on intelligent use of these weapons. So where it could be honestly done, I was careful to make mention of any such laudable behavior. Reference to 'General Bruce's crack 77th Division' did no harm either in the accompanying press releases."

Somewhat abashed, Ed Fitzgerald, the 1st sergeant with the 307th Regiment's Service Company, notes his Bronze Star order credited him for "aggressive, tireless organization"—the effort to feed ammunition to the troops doing the fighting. Buckner Creel, with the 306th Infantry, expressed outrage when he learned that a man being treated for a self-inflicted wound had been nominated for a Purple Heart by the hospital staff in Hawaii. Creel filed a protest. The Marine Corps could be stingy in its distribution of honors, but Earl Rice, with the 1st Division, remembers a leatherneck given a Bronze Star for shooting up a pillbox that had already been destroyed by an amphtrac. The extravagance of some commanders in passing out awards cheapened the value for the many who truly performed "above and beyond."

While Seibert, with the 96th Division, engaged in the art of award recommendations, he paused to visit Bob Nims, a doctor who had sailed with him on the LST from Saipan to Okinawa, and was attached to a field artillery outfit. Nims proposed a trip to the site of some of Seibert's combat experiences and arranged for a jeep and driver.

"Bob directed the driver to the location, using my map. Without difficulty, we found the path to the top of the hill mass and stopped the jeep. Just as I was about to jump from the vehicle, two Japs popped up and ran around a small knoll. Without a second thought, I leaped out of the jeep, grabbed my rifle and went after them.

"Fortunately, Bob Nims, although a medic, was an expert rifleman and had a carbine with him, which he grabbed, and followed me. The fugitives disappeared for a moment. There was a small ditch directly in front of me. As I jumped over it, I looked down and saw them. Aware that I had spotted them, they immediately jumped up, cocking their arms to throw grenades. Both Bob and I fired, killing them before they could lob the grenades.

"The jeep driver was upset about the incident. As a medic, he had not volunteered to get into this sort of combat. But Bob was elated that he had been in on the kill of two of the enemy."

For about eight weeks after Okinawa was pronounced secure, this kind of activity continued. But on August 6, the first nuclear bomb detonated over Hiroshima. Three days later, the second atomic explosion devastated Nagasaki. On August 15, Emperor Hirohito broadcast to his 100 million subjects the acceptance of unconditional surrender terms, whose only exception provided he should retain his position.

One serious stumble marked the steps to the surrender ceremonies. Radio operator Joe Di Stanislao, radio shack supervisor aboard the cruiser *Columbia,* received a message on August 11, while they were anchored at Buckner Bay [named for the dead commander] on the east coast of Okinawa. The Americans were advised to be alert for a Japanese Betty [two-engine plane], which was to be painted white with green crosses on the tail rudder, fuselage and wings. "We were instructed not to shoot down this plane. However, instead of a white plane with green crosses, we got a torpedo plane which flew right over us and dropped a torpedo that hit the battleship *Pennsylvania,* anchored 1,000 yards away. The direct hit caused many casualties."

Not until August 19 did two properly decorated airplanes loaded with top Japanese officers touch down at the air base set up on Ie Shima. From there they transferred to U.S. aircraft for the flight to Manila and arrangement of the formal surrender ceremonies aboard the *Missouri* on September 2.

On Okinawa, where news of what happened at Hiroshima and Nagasaki received the unmitigated approval of the GIs and leathernecks now facing another invasion, the capitulation, announced by the emperor on August 15, triggered a wild celebration of drinking and rounds fired into the air.

In his hideout on a mountain peak on the island of Tokashiki, in the Keramas, Yoshihiro Minamoto, commander of a company, realized that peace had arrived. "Surrender and disarmament for us came on August 23. We had sent a representative of the unit before as a military envoy to contact the regimental commander and an agreement had been reached. The reception was extremely cordial, and there was no threat of any executions. This was after the country had surrendered, so there was no reason to be ashamed."

In spite of all that had occurred, a considerable number of Japanese soldiers had not yielded to the entreaties or demands issued by loudspeakers in their native tongue. Among these unwilling to give up was Koichi Itoh, the battalion commander who achieved some success in the May 4–5 counterattack but had then been driven back. The Americans now filled the air with quotes from the emperor's rescript that advised soldiers they could now surrender without dishonor.

"Between August 22 and September 3," says Itoh, "I negotiated our disarmament with 1st Lt. [actually a captain, according to U.S. records] Howard Moss [7th Division], Major Train, Captain Torawa and another captain from the XXIV Corps artillery. These men were gentlemen and I had a good feeling about them."

According to *Typhoon of Steel* by James and William Belote, Moss, accompanied by a Japanese prisoner, had persuaded Itoh to leave his cave and talk. Subsequently, with permission to negotiate from his colonel, Itoh traveled to Kadena Airfield to listen to a recording of the Imperial rescript. At a POW camp, Itoh also met Colonel Yahara, who assured the captain this was not an American trick. The war, indeed, was over. Itoh was now persuaded.

He reports the regimental force that he arranged to turn over numbered 350, including stragglers from other units. The group, although sizable, posed little threat to the Americans. Many were wounded, half-starved, afflicted with dysentery—from which Itoh suffered. Soon afterwards, Itoh helped convince Capt. Tsuneo Shimura, who had slipped through the enemy lines to set up a possible guerrilla camp in Okinawa's northern wilderness, to surrender.

In July, elements of the 6th Marine Division sailed from Okinawa to Guam for refitting. But like the 1st Marine Division, the end of hostili-

With the fighting almost over, a captured Japanese soldier leads GIs to one of the defensive caves. *(Signal Corps, U.S. National Archives)*

ties transformed their mission from one of preparing for assault to occupation and disarmament of Japanese forces in the home islands and northern China. The Army's 7th Division followed a similar route, which brought it to Korea.

After V-J Day, the Liberty Division boarded ships to sail for Japan proper and serve as one of the initial occupation forces. By mid-August, Ellis Moore, of the Headquarters Company in the 383rd Infantry, like the other Deadeyes, was in an encampment on Mindoro, a Philippine Island. Promoted to a T/5 in the weeks that followed, Moore wrote home expressing the typical citizen-soldier gripes about the slow pace of demobilization now that peace had come. "It seems to me that our 96th Division should qualify as the forgotten division of the Pacific, and I can't see why. Here the war has been over for a month and a half and we are still sitting around doing nothing, while every other outfit is either being used for occupation or is going stateside." Shortly after he sent this glum message, Moore was on a ship bound for San Francisco and an honorable discharge.

On Mindoro, Si Seibert finally faced the consequences for having refused the order to move his troops out in the waning days of the campaign. Summoned to a meeting with Colonel Sterner in his tent, Seibert reported with a sense of "foreboding." The battalion commander reviewed various events before turning to the main matter. "He told me I was absolutely wrong. I admitted that I was. He said that he had considered what action to take against me. He felt that my refusal of an order in combat warranted some action, but after wrestling with his conscience and in view of my subsequent conduct and performance in combat, he concluded this was an isolated case. He admitted I had probably saved a number of lives as a result of my stubbornness. On balance, he had decided to take no action. I heaved a sigh of relief, saluted and left."

CHAPTER XXXI

ICEBERG AND ITS AFTERMATH

In the euphoria that inevitably surrounded the end of World War II, the awful toll of Okinawa and its meaning evaded the consciousness of much of the world. General Ushijima, in his final apologies to Tokyo, did not do himself justice. He and his troops may not have deterred the Americans from continuing the war but, against overwhelming odds, they extracted a fearful price.

From April 1 through June 30, the U.S. dead added up to 12,520, composed of 4,582 GIs [93 missing], 2,938 leathernecks dead or missing, and 4,907 killed and missing from the Navy. American wounded from the three services were 36,631. Nonbattle casualties totaled more than 26,000. The Japanese military dead amounted to 110,071, with 7,401 captured. Figures for the Okinawan civilian dead range from 75,000 to 140,000. Destroyed American aircraft numbered 763, compared to the Japanese 7,700 planes. The Imperial forces sank thirty-six U.S. ships, damaged another 368, while the Japanese Navy, whose surface action was limited, had sixteen sunk, four damaged.

The dead and maimed from Japan far outnumbered those of their attackers. But to U.S. policy makers and strategists, the figures for their countrymen approached the unacceptable. Even though the cessation of hostilities in Europe had released hundreds of thousands of soldiers for the invasion of the enemy's home islands, the mortality rate, coupled with the criticisms of the likes of David Lawrence, must have reverberated through the halls of the Pentagon and in the offices at the White House.

Certainly, the events on Okinawa influenced the decision to use the first atomic bomb. If the Japanese would defend Okinawa so fiercely, literally to the death, how desperately would the several million soldiers still under arms resist on their native soil? If the indigenous Okinawans would support, and even fight with, the troops, how much would the population of the home islands add to the defense? Just as those on Okinawa had organized a bunker-to-bunker war, so were the home islands being prepared. For example, George Fifer in *Tennozan* notes that occupation forces later marveled at the awesome concrete and firepower that protected Tokyo Bay. Sea walls bristled with great cannons. There were even reports of huge amounts of spears for a primitive, last-ditch fight, although Koichi Itoh, for one, discounts this as a serious possibility.

For the Navy that would convoy the invasion forces and then stand offshore to provide fire and supply support, there would be no picket line of destroyers whose radar would detect the approach of kamikazes. Japan still had thousands of planes available for suicide crashes and men able to carry out the missions.

Soldiers and Marines interviewed for this book voiced their dread of participating in an assault on Japan proper. They speak of the projections of dead and wounded, even fifty years later. There are no doubts in their minds that the casualties would have been horrific.

From the 77th Infantry Division, Earl Miller says, "Without a doubt it was God's work that Uncle Sam was the only one to have such a weapon at that time."

Alanson Sturgis, the artillery coordinator, says, "My attitude about those weapons is that it was a painful necessity."

Andy Anderson, the gunnery officer who served on the sunken destroyer *Little*, says, "I felt strongly then, as I do now, that President Truman's decision to use the A-bomb was justified."

Infantry sergeant of the 96th Division, Don Dencker speaks for most when he declares, "God Bless the atomic bomb. It probably saved my life."

One argument against the use of the A-bombs revolves around the numbers of killed and wounded predicted, when compared with the statistics for Hiroshima and Nagasaki. In those two cities, the initial blasts killed 210,000, and another 130,000 died from their injuries or radiation within five years. The quoted estimates for U.S. casualties in an invasion of Japan have run from 46,000 to 1,000,000. The low figure hardly seems credible, in light of the losses sustained against an army of about 100,000 on Okinawa rather than the several million that could be mobilized in the home-island defense. In any case, guesses are generally just about that; the expectations for Normandy fell well below projections, while on islands like Iwo Jima, Tarawa and Okinawa, the losses ran considerably higher than expected. Furthermore, the extrapolations on killed and wounded for an invasion of the home islands do not include the Japanese military and civilian losses, which, if one uses Okinawa as a base marker, would have been staggering.

Comparing body counts for the A-bombs and the invasion is a fruitless exercise. When the figures rise into the hundreds of thousands, debates about which act is more or less moral seem absurd. Certainly the A-bombs largely killed civilians, women, old people and children, although there were military installations or industrial plants in both cities. However, twentieth-century war makes little distinction between combatants and civilians, not even with the advent of the so-called smart bomb.

The criticism of the A-bomb use seems connected to the horror of death through the enormous fireball and shock wave. The literature drawn from survivors paints frightful pictures of the blast effects. But those incinerated or suffocated by a flame thrower or disemboweled by shrapnel, had huge pieces of their faces shot away, suffered ragged amputations from mines, died no less terribly than the hapless citizens of Hiroshima. Don Dencker comments, "Thank God, World War II was fought before television. No bleeding hearts would have derided our use of great enemy killers such as white phosphorus shells and flamethrowing tanks, which roasted Japs into good [dead] Japs." And many who did come home, like Gage Rodman and Leonard Schweitzer have endured a lifetime of pain and disability, as surely as some victims of the A-bomb.

The revulsion toward the nuclear bomb may also come from its effectiveness, a device capable of wiping out so many in a single gigantic explosion. It is possible to focus on the only two atomic bombs used upon humans. They even had names—Little Boy and Fat Man. There were no individual titles for the thousands of incendiaries and other explosives dumped on Tokyo March 9–10, 1945, in which an estimated 85,000 to 100,000 Japanese died. There have not been nearly as many letters to the editor or op-ed columns about the inhumanity of these raids. While indignation greeted the first aerial attacks on cities—Guernica, Addis Ababa, Coventry and London—that outcry became muted once it was seen that urban centers, with their war goods potential and workers, were a strategic target, and it was the Allies doing the bombing. Hamburg, Berlin, Dresden—some without even much war material responsibilities—all were blanketed with explosives. Reduction of the labor force and the willingness of the people to support the war were justifications.

Considering Japanese military actions in subjugated countries, one would not expect them to have shown restraint had they decided to build long-range bombers. And absent the nuclear bomb, it is probable that cities like Hiroshima, Nagasaki, as well as others, would have been deluged with incendiary and big bomb attacks until surrender or as a prelude to a seaborne invasion. More planes, more bombs, eventually would mean a comparable number of victims as suffered in Hiroshima and Nagasaki.

Some researchers and ideologues condemn the use of the A-Bomb as unnecessary. They argue that peace feelers from the Japanese indicated surrender was imminent. There is a welter of evidence that suggests powerful elements in Japan wanted to reach peace with the Allies, possibly on the winner's terms. On the other hand there was strong opposition to any treaty based on a deal remotely approaching unconditional surrender. There were talks between Japanese and Soviet officials. However, the alleged word from Stalin to his allies was that the enemy refused to accept the unconditional surrender demanded by the West, a condition designed to insure there could be no resurgence of an only partially demolished Imperial Empire.

That his country was willing to accept defeat explains the viewpoint of Kerama Island defender Yoshihiro Minamoto. "I do not believe that the atomic bomb was necessary to encourage our surrender. I believe that in using it, the United States committed an act of treachery against twentieth century civilization."

Bob Jackson is one of the few sources for this book to agree, at least with the first part of the statement. "I felt then, and still feel now, that a bomb in the mountains would have had the same effect. They were beaten!" Hardly anyone else voiced similar sentiments.

There was controversy among the top American strategists about whether nuclear weapons should be employed. Gen. Dwight D. Eisenhower, fresh from victory in Europe, believed the Japanese about to give up. He says he told Secretary of War Henry Stimson ". . . it wasn't necessary to hit them with that awful thing . . . I hated to see our country be the first to use such a weapon." Stimson furiously rejected Eisenhower's point of view, as did President Harry Truman and Chief of Staff George C. Marshall and Secretary of State James Byrnes, who brought to the argument an agenda aimed at cutting short the war before the Soviet Union could become a major player. Other U.S. military leaders took opposing sides.

The decision was Truman's to make. Truman, a political realist, must also have taken into account the reaction of Americans at the ballot box if he did not use the ultimate weapon and the foe did not quit. A number of men interviewed for this work praised him specifically. Considering the vicious attacks by his opponents in the 1950s, with the nonsensical charge that he was responsible for "losing China," one can sympathize with Truman if, indeed, he took politics into account. What is more difficult to accept perhaps is his callous remark that, once he decided to use the A-bombs, he never lost a night's sleep about it. To be the single person in a position to sign the death warrant for hundreds of thousands or extend them mercy, at a potential cost, and not agonize over one's choice during those hours of dark solitude does not bespeak a feeling soul.

On July 28, the Japanese had appeared to reject the Potsdam Declaration as a basis for surrender. That set in motion the events that brought the nuclear age to Hiroshima on August 6. In the few days following the Hiroshima holocaust, the Imperial Empire was wracked by plots and counterplots that did not stop short of assassinations. While the military and civilian leaders of Japan argued about what should now be done, the second bomb had obliterated much of Nagasaki. One might wonder what the rush was to hit a second city, without waiting for the full import of Hiroshima to influence the Japanese decision makers. In any event, the emperor himself now overrode objections of those who wanted to continue the war, and he publicly accepted the terms of the Potsdam Declaration in a radio address to his people on August 15. In the absence of conclusive proof, whether the Japanese would have given up without at least the first strike at Hiroshima remains a matter of conjecture.

Ian Buruma in his book *The Wages of Guilt* says most Japanese mistakenly appear to feel that the use of A-bombs was something outside of the war, an act of inhumanity on a par with the Holocaust at Auschwitz. Buruma notes, the use of nuclear devices on cities could be described as part of the war, an effective means to pursue ends. The extermination camps of Nazi Germany, however, had nothing to do with successful prosecution of a war. It would seem thus unjustified to make the extermination camps an equivalent of the events at Hiroshima and Nagasaki.

Koichi Itoh, the battalion commander who held out for two weeks after the surrender, says, "The dropping of the atomic bombs did hasten the end of the war, but I believe these were inhumane acts. Wouldn't it have been possible to cause us to surrender by first warning of the power of the atomic bomb, and then showing what would happen by dropping it in an uninhabited area—one with few people in it?" (In fact, according to Richard Rhodes in *The Making of the Atomic Bomb,* a committee of atomic scientists had been asked to design a demonstration that could convince the enemy, but concluded they could not create a show that would be persuasive.)

The campaign on Okinawa unfortunately links directly to the use of the atomic bombs on a largely civilian target. While the action of Operation Iceberg was directed at the Japanese military, as many as 75,000 to 160,000 Okinawan civilians may have perished. In a modern war the combatants do not easily separate out from the rest of the population. The person behind the individual with a gun is a target and so is the will of a nation to fight on.

And on Okinawa, as the war ground into its fourth year, the nature of the beast was to become ever more terrible in its appetite for blood. Little Boy and Fat Man were logical extensions of the firepower that made Operation Iceberg, itself the end of a long series of similar actions in the Pacific theater, a success. From the accounts of the men who fought there and the cold statistics, the savagery of combat on Okinawa over a period of three months epitomized war at its worst. A combination of factors reduced human behavior to killing machines. The defenders could not back up; they had no escape. They could not be rescued, as were beleaguered soldiers on Guadalcanal or Kiska.

They so internalized their sense of duty to the emperor and their obligations as soldiers that they sacrificed the urge for self-preservation. The rescripts and the literature to which they were exposed conditioned them to resist to their deaths. That held from the top commands down to the lowliest of privates. Japanese society was based on a hierarchy with the emperor, at least spiritually, at the top. Obedience, acceptance of orders was instilled in the soldier. And that submission was required even when those in charge might be in error. This also explains why the Japanese soldier was so superbly disciplined but, at the same time, so lacking in an ability to act on his own.

Understandably, Japanese soldiers had shown great resolve early in the war, when to many of them it appeared they might be victorious. On Okinawa they were just as determined, even though they were losing, if not already defeated. In contrast, the German soldiers, once they realized they could not halt the Allied advance, surrendered by the tens of thousands in the final months. Nor did their generals commit suicide; instead, they frequently gave the orders for their men to put down their arms.

Furthermore, years of anti-Western propaganda endowed the fight against the U.S. with the quality of a spiritual struggle. John Dower examined the conflict in the Pacific [*War Without Mercy*] on the basis of the attitudes of the two parties. Studying the images both sides published of their enemies, Dower says the propaganda offered mirror images of people who were "brutal, imperialistic and contemptuous of other races." Dower suggests that the Japanese derived much of their image of Americans from U.S. movies, ones that featured gangsters, lawless behavior, subjugation of non-Caucasians in the cowboy and Indian genre. The disdain for Americans was fueled by the Japanese leadership that harped on the racial superiority of their own people. Crude cartoons, particularly once the war began, depicted Americans as thuggish and animal-like. And as both Yoshihiro Minamoto and Koichi Itoh indicate, the Japanese felt themselves threatened by the unwillingness of the West to accept their country's needs if it were to preserve their way of life in the twentieth century.

U.S. troops were imbued with a different form of patriotism. Americans volunteered for military service or honored the call of the draft because they felt their country threatened and they accepted the laws that governed it. They did not, however, have the same reverence for superiors as their Japanese counterparts, nor did they attach an otherworldly quality to the nation's head of state. They followed orders to a point, but as several examples, notably those of Si Seibert and Larry Gerevas indicate, the men would not go blindly into certain death. Says Bob Jackson, "After I was evacuated I learned later some of 'my boys' those I'd trained back when, and others refused to leave their foxholes before Naha, and the commander had to threaten to shoot them to get an attack going."

Americans responded to the requirement to serve because their way of life was in jeopardy and not to preserve a spiritual idea, regardless of propaganda blather about democracy or "The Four Freedoms." According to Jackson, "I think the reason we kept going was that we had no choice. Or we didn't think we had a choice. This is a function of good training and the desire to 'get it over with.' I never heard discussions 'why are we here?' I suspect we were like prisoners, there was no hope for a change, so we moved along."

Gordon Larkins succinctly declares, "We saw [the fighting] as a way to get home."

Bob Craig, the Marine platoon leader, thinks much of the impetus behind the response of Americans lies in the state of the nation prior to the war. "We were the children of the Depression, and although there were different degrees of deprivation among us, because all of us suffered, we knew we were all in the same boat. People helped their friends and coworkers, most of whom were jobless. The immediate needs were taken care of on a local basis, because it was quite a while before the big government aid programs became effective.

"There is no doubt in my mind this cooperative spirit became ingrained and, together with the spirit of patriotism that in those days was always there, were the grass roots of a winning team that so quickly overcame the disaster of December 7, 1941. Individuals accepted the responsibility of becoming good soldiers and to adjust to the rigors of military training in order to get the job done."

Fellow Marine Stormy Sexton believes the Great Depression's influence was less a factor than "the basic values as taught and practiced in the average American home, which provided the 'hard core' principles by which men and women lived."

Herman Buffington, wounded the day before Okinawa was declared secure, says, "Patriotism was still a big factor, but when you are in battle, you don't have much time to think of that—you're thinking of how to stay alive."

As Buffington suggests, while the initial impetus to serve may have been patriotism, other forces came into play while under the guns. It can be readily understood the Japanese had no choice but to fight to the death on Okinawa. With the mind-set instilled in them from birth through their military careers, with no place to escape or seek refuge, they had no choice. But Okinawa was 8,500 miles from the U.S. homeland, and while, initially, men may have entered the service to protect their way of life, it does not follow that they would feel it necessary to participate in the blood bath with the constancy that most demonstrated.

Eugene Prather, a line captain early with the 7th Division and later a staff officer, suggests that feeling of omnipotence that some people maintain. "We were trained to fight and expect casualties and were pumped full of propaganda against the Japanese and a 'do or die' to save the U.S. and Allies from Japan, Germany and their associates. But one also had to have an inherent belief and faith that he would not be the one who would be wounded or killed. For if you believed you were the doomed person, you lost rationality and effectiveness." Obviously, as in the case of Paul Westman's buddy, Shelby Allen, individuals did perceive their mortality. The wonder is that they nevertheless carried on.

Because they stuck it out, Len Lazarick celebrates in particular the foot soldiers, whom he feels never received the honor due them. "If higher echelon headquarters erred in judgment or planning, the combat troops suffered. If the combat troops erred, again, they suffered. There is a great deal of confusion and chaos during battle. Events occur quickly, plans fall apart and the unexpected is a certainty. The best foot soldiers do not always survive because of this uncertainty. Who decides a sniper's choice in his sights, where a mine is planted, where the short round will fall? Lady luck plays a big part in whether or not you go home. This used to disturb me, but I've finally come to the conclusion that it was God's will that I am alive today. I used a powerful drug during combat. It was called adrenalin and it probably saved many lives besides mine. I wouldn't give up my 96th Inf. Div. combat experience for a million dollars. I wouldn't take a million to try it again. Some of my 96th Inf. Div. buddies are my best friends. They are the residue of what was best in the U.S. in the 1940s."

Joe Budge, from the 77th Division, echoes Lazarick. "One learned a profound and lasting respect for the infantryman and his company officers, whether called Marines, airborne, paratroops or whatever, not so much the teenage kids but the older men, often married, who had left behind a career and children. They were sarcastic, irreverent, patriotic, tired, always with some humor close to the surface, always supportive of mates but never unnecessarily cruel, even to an enemy who could be as bestial as the Japanese."

Frank Barron, on the crest of a hill, not knowing whether the next hour would be his last, noted, "These men who trained so hard together and fought for extended periods together became so completely unselfish, so absorbed with the welfare of the group that you could believe that their principal concern was for the 'other guy.' "

The residue of that period and the bonding that Lazarick mentions exists even fifty years later. Many friendships made in U.S. camps continue today or are renewed through attendence at reunions. There is still pride in having been a Deadeye, a 77th Division foot soldier, a rifleman with the 17th Infantry Regiment.

The Marines elevated that spirit which began in the first days of service to a new high with the techniques that distinguish boot camp. Few GIs boast of having been a member of the U.S. Army. Instead they speak of the squad, platoon or, perhaps, company, with occasional obeisance to the biggest organization to gain their loyalty, the division. But the Marine system, partly because it was almost entirely volunteer, created an esprit, where its alumni speak with pride of having been a Marine, as well as their own particular organization.

Don Farquahar, the Marine platoon leader, says, "The attitude of the average Marine was one of pride in the Corps, instilled at boot camp but honed by his NCOs in the field. The Marine Corps got all the stuff the Navy didn't want or had worn out. The weapons, BARs and machine guns we used on Okinawa were the same ones that had come across the Pacific for the Guadalcanal invasion. We just took care of our stuff. The Marines were the 'Raggedy Ass Marines' and proud of it. The fight was for the guy on your left and right. You knew they wouldn't let you down, and you felt the same way about them."

Squad leader Jim Moll says, "If a fellow Marine was wounded, we usually had somebody stay with him until help arrived. If a Marine was killed, I never knew of a case where his body disappeared. I never knew any Marines who were taken prisoner in either of my two campaigns."

The loyalty that helped men continue, of course, also fuels the less admirable sniping over who did more to win the battle of Okinawa. Some old soldiers still grouse about what they perceive as undue credit for the achievements of the Marines. The irritation is not helped by hearing Marines claim to have conquered seventy-five percent of the island, when the top half of Okinawa saw only a tiny fraction of enemy resistance. Still, there are survivors who disdain the controversy, content to note there was blood enough spilled by all concerned.

The feeling of belonging to a group, and of special emotions about those in closest proximity, also, of course, affected Japanese soldiers. They too benefitted from the sense of comradeship that comes from prolonged association within a group. Koichi Itoh, in the years since Okinawa, has made a strenuous effort to preserve the memory of some with whom he served, writing newspaper and magazine articles about the long dead and forgotten. Sakae Kogono, the naval officer, continued to pay homage to his shipmates many years after their demise.

The fact that they were not imbued with a controlling ideological *raison d'être* did not make U.S. soldiers any less willing to kill an enemy bent on their destruction. The desire to live, for GIs and leathernecks, made them just as fiercely dedicated to their purposes as the Japanese so determined to honor *bushido.*

"I never had a problem getting men to volunteer for a patrol," says, former Marine sergeant Jim Moll. "Some just liked to kill Japs. Some collected ears; some gold teeth. We had one guy who was collecting skulls, which didn't go over too well with the brass. But if I ever had it to do over again, I would want to be with the same guys."

To the war in the Pacific, Americans also brought racist feelings. Prior to Pearl Harbor, the U.S. image of Japan was that of an imperialist country bent on subjugating far off lands and whose contribution to civilization consisted of cheap copies of goods better designed and manufactured by Western nations. As the war deepened, the image of them as buck-toothed, bespectacled predators who raped and murdered civilians, tortured and killed prisoners, pervaded the media. The *Why We Fight* films, designed to innoculate troops with a large dose of pro-American, antienemy attitudes, if not stereotyping the Japanese, gave no consideration to their perceptions, which led to the outbreak of war. While many survivors of the Okinawa fighting today insist they respected the Japanese as soldiers and as human beings, "those little yellow bastards" was a popular way to refer to the enemy.

Tony Walker, who commanded the 6th Marine Recon Company for much of the Okinawa campaign, remarks, "The Marine attitude toward the Japanese was 'kill the bastards!' The only good word I ever heard about the Japs was that they were willing to die for the emperor. We figured on helping them do just that."

The extraordinarily high ratio of dead to captured on Okinawa is, however, only partly ascribable to racism. By their actions at Nanking and in Manila, through the U.S. perception of a sneak attack at Pearl Harbor, with the treatment of Americans taken prisoner from Bataan and Corregidor, the oppression of subjugated peoples, the forced labor that killed thousands building the infamous bridge over the River Kwai, the execution of downed pilots in Tokyo and other events, the Japanese military created an enormous amount of hatred. The percentage of Allied prisoners who died while in Japanese captivity was seven times as high as that for those held by the Germans. After the few experiences of surrender, Allied forces became unwilling to put themselves in the hands of the Japanese even when hurt. In Europe, wounded were sometimes left behind in the usually justified belief the Germans would give them medical treatment. On Okinawa, as elsewhere in the Pacific, men risked their lives, sometimes losing them, retrieving fallen comrades because they were certain the Japanese would show no mercy.

Dower points out a difference in the animosity towards the European enemy. Aside from the fact that they were Caucasians with ethnic connections in the U.S., the Germans, and to a lesser extent the Italians, offered leaders upon whom one could focus. The Nazis provided a string of targets, beginning with dictator Adolf Hitler, who strutted in triumph, whose bellicose statements appeared regularly in print or were heard on radio. Obese air force chief Hermann Goering, the oily statements of propaganda chief Josef Goebbels, the sinister looks of SS leader Heinrich Himmler, represented the foe. Americans had seen these people before the war began and would continue to see them through the access of neutral press sources. They were the figures upon whom Americans could readily vent their hate, instead of the average German. (To be sure, once a GI became engaged in a shooting war with the faceless German, he could develop a fierce antagonism toward him.)

In contrast, the ostensible head of Japan, Emperor Hirohito, did not make angry statements carried by the media. His physical appearance belied his position as the head of a huge, aggressive war machine. And General Tojo, the man running the country, was largely invisible to the average American. There were no cameras, reporters or radios to demonize the Japanese leaders to the U.S. once the war started. Absent specimens like Hitler, Goering and Goebbels, it was easier to hate all Japanese.

In Europe it was sometimes possible to distinguish between the avowed Nazis, members of the more fanatical elite SS forces, and the ordinary, *Wehrmacht* common soldier. On Okinawa, the U.S. troops had no means, nor desire, to distinguish between the "good" and the "bad" Japanese.

The urge to kill infected even a man trained to save lives, like the doctor who accompanied Si Seibert on a tour after the island was officially conquered. Granted, he acted in self-defense, his exultation over shooting a human being indicates how deeply the hostility towards the Japanese bit.

The orgy of killing also owed something to the duration of the war and to the nature of it on the Pacific islands. Most of those who first assaulted Okinawa had already seen combat, had served for a considerable time in service. Not only were they veterans, but undoubtedly the accumulation of experiences had drained their sense of humanity. For both sides, the ongoing murderous confrontations with the enemy and the miserable living conditions eroded pity and replaced it with hate for those who refused to give up.

Furthermore, the war in the Pacific, much more so than in Europe, became personal. During much of the combat against the Axis powers in North Africa, Italy, France and Germany, the enemy was, at best, barely visible. Long-range artillery duels, large-scale armor operations over big areas, distant pillboxes with machine guns frequently marked the fighting. Soldiers in the European theater often caught only a fleeting glimpse of an adversary. Of course there was house-to-house close-in combat and short-range confrontations. Still, there were periods of time when the distances between the front lines were enough to limit sight and sound of the individual enemy.

On Okinawa, once the invaders approached the first outposts of the Shuri line, those up front were always within shouting, if not whispering, distance of the foe. The Japanese style of infiltration or banzai charges at night meant hand-to-hand combat was commonplace, rather than duels from a distance. Pistol, club, bayonet and knife work, the weapons of intimate contact, were much more common on Okinawa. That kind of warfare could only add to the stress and the animosity.

Speaking of his own experience as a member of the Japanese Army, Koichi Itoh claims, "There were no directives whatever concerning prisoners. I never had an opportunity to take one. I had not heard that Americans refused to take prisoners. When we retreated from Tanabaru Highlands on May 7, we left behind our seriously wounded and I heard that five of those were taken prisoner."

While Itoh heard no instructions on handling prisoners, there is no record of a single American having been found alive in Japanese hands at the conclusion of the Okinawa fighting. And the Americans, unless pushed, showed little inclination to take prisoners. Don Dencker expresses what was a common sentiment and its consequences. "Hell, the only good Jap is a dead Jap. We didn't take any prisoners until about the 18th of June, when they started to surrender."

Dick Thom, an operations officer for the 96th Infantry Division, says, "My regiment took only one prisoner. We never turned any others in. We had another exit for them, particularly since quite a few of them held up their hands to surrender while carrying a grenade. We thought of the Japs as just monkeys. You could sit on a dead Jap and eat your lunch."

As Thom says, an apparent surrender frequently served only as a ruse to cover a grenade or other attack. The prevailing malevolence undercut even occasions when a dollop of mercy could have profited both sides. Joe Budge, during a respite in the battle around Shuri, was with a group who saw an apparently unarmed Japanese soldier, probably preparing to give himself up. "When he got within fifty yards, he fumbled with a grenade at his belt, probably to throw it away. But even if he tried to throw it at us, there was no need to worry. He couldn't pitch it that far. We could kill him before he armed it, dodge it and so on. But

Junior [an ineffective soldier in the platoon] killed him with a carbine bullet between the eyes. He was a kid, probably not more than eighteen. This was a criminally foolish thing to do, even if it had not been plain murder. It took place in full view of any Nips defending this part of the Shuri fortress, undoubtedly reinforcing their determination to fight to the death. Each cave we attacked cost lives and we grumbled that Junior, that stupid little blank blank, was going to get us all killed."

Bob Muehrcke reports, "No one informed us on how to treat Japanese prisoners should we take them. At times our division general officers offered a case of either beer or hard liquor or both to us in exchange for a Japanese prisoner. In addition, they gave us time to drink it. This was for intelligence purposes. Prisoners gave us valuable information. In general we would take prisoners, especially as the war was drawing to a close. We treated them with respect. We did not push them around, beat or abuse them. However, we made absolutely certain they had no hidden weapons, such as hand grenades, in their loincloths."

Jim Moll says of his 7th Marine Regiment company, "I never witnessed our outfit taking a prisoner. Maybe that was because I never saw any surrender with their hands in the air. I saw guys trying to be overly helpful to civilians. They gave them food, cigarettes, candy, and the guys showed a lot of compassion. However, none could be trusted, so we didn't allow any fraternizing."

The willingness to carry on, to leave the sanctuary of a foxhole and expose the limb and life to enemy fire, is perhaps inexplicable. Gene Prather comments on a paradox. "How strange it is to see a person do something in combat that he would probably never do otherwise. However, the people who shoot, stab or blow up others and then risk or give their lives to save someone else are the soldiers in combat who do 'insane' things."

Great stress in common, as in time of natural disasters as well as war, does bring people together. The formation of military units, where the young—males during World War II—come together to live under a common discipline, eat, sleep, train and pursue together the pleasures considered appropriate to their age, forges very strong attachments. For the duration of their service, even though in civilian life their backgrounds and interests might be hugely different, they have a kinship. And when in combat, that connection seems almost to prove the existence of the elusive altruistic gene sought in humans. For they will act for one another in ways that place themselves at mortal risk. It is more than just wanting not to look bad in front of the other guys; it is a statement of brotherhood. It is an irony of war that the most awful things one human can do to another cause others to perform heroic, even noble acts.

ROLL CALL

Anderson, Ed (Andy). Gunnery Officer, *USS Little*. Upon leaving the Navy in 1946, he embarked on a career in petroleum geology and now lives in Seattle.

Axtell, George. Commander, Marine Fighter Squadron 323. He made the Marines his life. "During World War II, I met and served with a fascinating group of men who called themselves Marines. They set high goals of integrity and excellent professional standards. The Corps tolerated and encouraged the frank exchange of ideas between all levels of rank. New and controversial concepts were openly and professionally discussed. Despite my being forthright in expressing my opinions and advocating different solutions to a few challenges, I was encouraged by several high ranking officers to make a career of the Corps." After serving in Korea and in Vietnam, Axtell retired as a lieutenant general to Weaverville, North Carolina.

Bak, Michael. Quartermaster, *USS Franks*. He was employed in the telephone industry before his retirement to the New Jersey shore at Surf City.

Barron, Frank, Jr. Company Commander, Co. A, 305th Infantry, 77th Division. Barron used his education at Auburn as a springboard for executive positions in the textile industry and now lives in Columbia, South Carolina.

Behil, Steve. Forward Observer, 294th FA Battalion, 27th Division. He became Secretary/Treasurer of the division association, working from his home in Endwell, NY.

Berger, Solomon. Machine Gunner, 7th Infantry Division. He tried college after his honorable discharge but found it difficult to settle down. "I feel that I saw too much killing and horrendous conditions." He joined the Merchant

Marine, rising from ordinary seaman to 3rd mate. His home is in San Francisco.

Bergtholdt, Henry S. Supply Officer, *USS Bache*. He stayed with the Navy until retiring in 1964 to teach and then serve as a docent at the Empire Mine State Historical Park near his home at Penn Valley, CA.

Boyd, Gordon (Pete). Chief Engineer, *USS Athony*. Boyd returned to the ship building industry and now resides in Huntingdon Valley, PA.

Brooks, George B. Rifleman, Co. K, 382nd Regiment, 96th Division. He pursued the education begun as a member of the ASTP, earning first a Bachelor of Science engineering degree and then an MBA. He lives in Kalamazoo, MI.

Bruce, Gen. Andrew. Commanding General, 77th Division. Retired after thirty-seven years in uniform in 1953. He died in 1965.

Budge, Joseph. Mortar Section Sergeant, 305th Regiment, 77th Division. Budge came back to Hawaii when the war ended. "Truthfully, my readjustment and that of chaps that I knew was not traumatic. For a year of so, I tended to hit the floor at any suggestive noise. I awoke once during a thunderstorm, dreaming of a rifle whose trigger had broken off at the wrong moment, and there I was under my bed. There was a craving for excitement. I had difficulty sleeping. I backed my bed up so I could sleep with my back against the wall. That was a little better. Then I went out and bought myself a small handgun. That did it. I slept like a baby ever after and very soon locked up the gun." Budge resumed his farm management for a time but then switched to personnel and transferred to the continental U.S., where he makes his home in Moraga, CA.

Buffington, Herman. Rifleman, Co. K, 383rd Regiment, 96th Division. Buffington attended business school and college after the war and with his wife eventually became the owner of three weekly newspapers and a commercial printing plant. He lives in Jefferson, GA.

Coobs, Melvin. Rifleman, Co. I, 383rd Regiment, 96th Division. He lives in Boise, ID.

Craig, Robert F. Platoon Leader, Co. G, 1st Marine Regiment, 1st Marine Division. "I didn't stay in the Marines, partly because of the nature of my wounds but primarily because I wanted to complete my education and get on in my civilian life." Craig chose law school at the University of Virginia and after graduation he and his wife headed for Florida. He signed up with a land title company and for forty years practiced in that business. His home is in Winter Haven, FL.

Creel, Buckner, III. Company Commander, Co. G, 306th Regiment, 77th Division. Creel followed the family tradition with a military career. "If the war had not come on, it was my intention to enter the U.S. Military Academy. Having survived the war, and having done very well in it, having been modestly 'gonged' [decorated], and with pretty good efficiency ratings, I had discovered that I was a good combat leader and commander and the troops would willingly follow me."

Creel commanded a company during the Korean War, was wounded twice and says of his men, "They took a lot more leading, cajoling and persuading than my World War II Company." As a colonel he led the Support Command for the 1st Infantry Division in Vietnam, logging more than 800 hours in helicopters during a single year. He retired as a colonel to a home in Arlington, VA.

Cypher, Bob. Clerk, Headquarters Co., 27th Division. Like many of his Orion Division comrades, Cypher still resents the stigma placed on his organization. He points out, "For those who questioned the courage of the men of the 27th, Lt. Col. O'Brien and Sgt. Baker of the 105th Infantry were both awarded the Medal of Honor for their heroism in the last banzai attack [on Saipan]. Both were KIA." After separation from the Army and further education, Cypher worked in advertising sales for *Civil Engineering Magazine.* He retired in 1984 and lives in White Plains, NY.

D'Angelo, Louis (Chick). Runner, Headquarters Company, 3rd Battalion, 4th Marine Regiment, 6th Division. He operated a plastics factory for many years, did construction and served as a union rep. He lives in Mount Vernon, NY.

DeMatteis, Lou. 304th Field Artillery Battalion, 77th Division. DeMatteis was in a machinery business and now lives in Yonkers, NY.

Dencker, Don. Squad Leader, Co. L, 382nd Regiment, 96th Division. "I came home on points ahead of the 96th Division. The actress Marjorie Main [chiefly known for the role of Ma Kettle] who won a pin-up girl contest in the 96th Division under the slogan a 'Rough Tough Girl for a Rough Tough Outfit,' greeted the troops when they arrived. I went back to the University of Minnesota to get my degree and master's degree in civil engineering." He resides in Sun Prairie, WI.

DiStanislao, Joe. Radio Operator, *USS Columbia.* His home is Newport Beach, CA.

Farquahar, Don. Platoon Leader, Co. A, 7th Marine Regiment, 1st Marine Division. Farquahar entered the family tire business and lives in Redlands, CA.

Fitzgerald, Ed. 1st Sergeant, Service Co., 307th Infantry Regiment, 77th Division. Fitzgerald left his reporter job first for editing slots on magazines before becoming the editor-in-chief of the Book of the Month Club. Retired, his home is in Eastchester, NY.

Fitzgerald, Jack. Platoon Leader, 17th Infantry Regiment, 7th Division. He followed his vow to get an education, enrolling at the University of Illinois. A member of the reserves, he was called up in 1950 and rejoined the 17th Infantry Regiment. "Korea was a terrible experience. It was a cold, brutal war with mountains, artillery and bitter fighting. Our troops were ill trained and lacking in the same World War II ethic. Support at home was usually from the family only. Equipment was substandard, batteries did not work. The ammunition was faulty." When discharged again, Fitzgerald went to work for an insurance investment company. He resides in Devon. PA.

Forse, Richard. Gunner, Cannon Co., 305th Infantry Regiment, 77th Division. He was employed in accounting for a road and bridge building company until retirement. He lives in West Caldwell, NJ.

Foss, Eugene. Commanding Officer, *USS Emmons.* Foss needed sixteen months in a Navy hospital before he recovered sufficiently from his injuries to receive his discharge and enter the family business. He winters in Florida and summers in Franconia, NH.

Gerevas, Larry. Rifleman, Co. K, 307th Infantry Regiment, 77th Division. He worked as a machinist at the Mare Island Naval Shipyard, instructed in drafting and blueprint reading to apprentices there while attending night school. With a Bachelor's and then a Master's degree in hand, he chose to teach drafting technology at colleges and authored two books on the subject. His home is in Napa, CA.

Guaraglia, Dante. 304th Field Artillery Battalion, 77th Division. He resides in Passaic, NJ.

Gunther, Harry. Deck Officer, *USS Bache.* Annapolis grad Gunther went through flight training and then guided missile school for the Navy. He resigned his commission after deciding the life was not conducive to marriage and a family. He lives in Memphis.

Hall, Kitt. Seaman, *USS Bache.* "I was fortunate enough to be home in Keene, NH on V-J Day, having dinner with my parents, brother and sister, when the announcement came over the radio. The following day, a crowd of some 100,000 people gathered for a fantastic parade. About eighteen to twenty servicemen who were home on leave, instead of riding, elected to march. It was really something special." Hall then pursued the trade of carpenter for forty-five years in St. Louis.

Hallden, Charles. Staff Officer, 106th Infantry Regiment, 27th Division. He makes his home in Madiera Beach, FL.

Hamilton, Thomas. Flag Secretary, Task Group 51.1. Hamilton practiced law, specializing in probate matters. He travels frequently from his base in Santa Barbara, CA.

Haynes, J.G. 132nd Combat Engineers, 77th Division. Haynes became a minister and now lives in Mesa, AZ.

Itoh, Koichi. Battalion Commander, 24th Division, Imperial Japanese Army. His "good feeling" about those who negotiated his surrender was not always replicated with the U.S. Army of Occupation. "I often felt they were arrogant, but I think they were magnanimous compared to the Soviet army." He became an electronics manufacturer and lives in Yokohama.

Jackson, Bob. Platoon Leader, Co. A, 382nd Infantry Regiment, 96th Division. "Army, a career? You gotta be kidding! Got out and got away from those supercilious hierarchies as soon as possible." He opted for the securities business and makes his home in Anacortes, WA.

Johnson, Elmer. Platoon Sergeant, Co. C, 1st Marine Regiment, 1st Marine Division. "From the hospital on Guam where my wound was treated, I was sent to a huge transit center. It was like a family reunion. Some were going back to the States, others on their way to Okinawa. There we were able to find out what happened and where and when, who got killed, wounded and earned medals. I found out that one of my machine gun squad leaders, who was in the same hole I crawled to when I got hit, was killed that same day and recommended for the Congressional Medal of Honor (Cpl. Louis Hauge, Jr.)." Johnson abandoned plans to make the Marines his life and after a couple of jobs was accepted at the post office in Tyrone, PA, where he rose to superintendent before he retired to his home in Tyrone.

Kishiue, Nobuo (Dick). Intelligence Specialist, 27th Division. "During the mop up campaign in Northern Okinawa, we witnessed one kamikaze ram a destroyer and another kamikaze pilot ditch his aircraft between two ships. I interrogated him, why he did this, and he answered that as he left the base in Japan, he thought about getting fuel for one way and carrying a 500 pound bomb into combat. The more he thought about it, the dumber he thought it was to fight. So he ditched the aircraft. I told him it would be up to him and others of his generation to rebuild Japan, and he did the right thing by surviving."

Americans with no Japanese antecedents, and taught rudimentary Japanese, had received commissions, but the Army refused to make Nisei officers until the time of the occupation of Japan. Then noncoms like Kishiue were told that if they would agree to serve another year, they might be awarded commissions. Kishiue responded, "Shove it." He farmed in California for thirty years after the war and now lives in Hanford, CA.

Kogono, Sakae. Deck Officer, *Yamato*, Japanese Imperial Navy. He became a principal in a municipal school.

Kriegsman, John. Pilot, 304th Field Artillery Battalion, 77th Division. He makes his home in Pekin, Il.

Larkins, Gordon. Machine Gunner, 106th Regiment, 27th Division. Larkins worked on an assembly line, owned a party store and then found work in building maintenance for the city of Troy, MI, where he still lives.

Lazarick, Len. Squad Leader, Co. K, 382nd Regiment, 96th Division. He attended evening college at Drexel University while working as a draftsman during the day. After receiving a degree he was hired by RCA as an engineer at the missile and surface radar plant in New Jersey. He resides in Croydon, PA.

Lea, Roland. BAR Man, Co. B, 17th Regiment, 7th Division. He took advantage of the GI Bill of rights to further his education. He had a career in hospital administration in his hometown of St. Louis.

Lopez, Henry D. Squad Leader, Co. C, 307th Infantry, 77th Division. Lopez held various positions in building services. For forty-six years he acted as secretary and chief historian of the 307th Infantry Veterans Society and wrote a book, *From Jackson to Japan: The History of Company C.* He lives in Daytona Beach, FL.

MacArthur, Bob. Engineering Officer, 7th Division. He tried the trade of sales engineer before setting up his own business as a manufacturer's rep. His home is Hamden, CT.

McCormack, Clement R. Sonar and Radar Officer, *USS Bache.* He spent fifteen years in the investment securities business and then another twenty-one dealing with life insurance. He makes his home in Bridgton, ME.

McLane, Merrill. Platoon Leader, Co. F, 4th Marine Regiment, 6th Marine Division. McLane left the Corps for cultural anthropology and a residence in Bethesda, MD.

Manion, Harry. Reconnaissance Company, 6th Marine Division. Manion stayed with the Corps to retire as a Sergeant Major. He lives in Comstock Park, MI.

Marbrey, Nolen (Bama). Fire Team Leader, Co. K, 5th Marine Regiment, 1st Marine Division. Marbrey worked at an Alabama facility making rockets and space vehicles. His home is in Brooksville, FL.

Miller, Earl. Machine Gunner, Co. G, 306th Regiment, 77th Division. He dons his complete WW II uniform every Memorial Day in Hiram, Ohio where he operated a farm.

Minamoto, Yoshihiro. Commander, 3rd Company, 3rd Marine Advance Squadron, Japanese Imperial Army. Minamoto continued to wear his country's uniform. "I served in the Land Self-Defense Forces from 1951-1977, becoming a major general. In 1958-59 I attended the U.S. Army Corps of Engineers School at Fort Belvoir. Since 1977 I have been an executive of an environment-related company." His home is in Saitama-ken.

Moll, Jim. Squad Leader, Co. A, 7th Marine Regiment, 1st Marine Division. "After V-J Day, the Regiment traveled to North China to guard railroad bridges while the Nationalist and Communist forces confronted one another. My intentions were to make a career of the Marine Corps. However, the first leave after the war I met my present wife; her husband had been killed at Normandy and she had two little girls." Moll worked during the day while taking classes at Stevens Institute of Technology in New Jersey. He acquired a professional engineer's license, which enabled him to have a career in that field. He retired to Tequesta, FL.

Moore, Ellis. Communications Specialist, 1st Battalion Headquarters, 383rd Regiment 96th Division. Moore worked on newspapers in Arkansas and Tennessee before switching to radio and TV, becoming a vice president of ABC. He continues to live in Pelham, NY.

Moroz, Mike. Squad Leader, Co. L, 382nd Regiment, 96th Division. He helped build nuclear power plants and now lives in Mt. Laurel, NJ.

Muehrcke, Robert. Platoon Leader, Co. F, 383rd Regiment, 96th Division.

Influenced by the bloody carnage he witnessed, Muehrcke decided to become a doctor. He specializes in kidney and related diseases, practicing in Oak Park, IL.

Neiman, Bob. Executive Officer, 1st.Tank Battalion, USMC. With a former fellow Marine, Neiman established a lumber business. His home is in Indian Wells, CA.

Owens, Charles. Rifleman, Co. A, 7th Marine Regiment, 1st Marine Division. After a year in North China, Owens came home. "All the jobs had been taken, so I stayed in the Marine Corps." He retired as a Master Sergeant and resides in Lafayette, GA.

Parsons, Lloyd. Pilot, Marine Fighter Squadron VMF (N) 542. He continued to fly, as a civilian pilot for private companies and in connection with an aviation training organization. He lived in Duluth, GA.

Powers, James. Communications Specialist, Marine 8th Defense & Antiaircraft Artillery Battalion. Powers became a Massachusetts government official and has served on the Town of Needham council from 1951 to the present.

Prather, Eugene. Commanding Officer, Headquarters Company, and Adjutant, 1st Battalion, 32nd Regiment, 7th Infantry Division. As a reserve officer, Prather was recalled for Korea and then went Regular Army for more than twenty-three years, retiring as a colonel. His home is in Oceanside, CA.

Reeves, Maurice. 1st Sgt., Co. C, 13th Combat Engineer Battalion, 7th Division. Finding the right employment was difficult, he almost returned to the Army, but marriage and a job with the Postal Service intervened. Called to active duty during Korea, he served for one year. President of the 7th Division Association, he lives in Little Rock.

Replogle, Art. Supply Officer, *USS Luce.* His uncle, the founder of the world's largest geographical globe manufacturer, brought him into the company. After twenty-five years in that line, he accepted a position with a not-for-profit, community development organization in his hometown of Oak Park, IL.

Rice, Earl. Rifleman, Co. A, 7th Marine Regiment, 1st Marine Division. Rice indulged his wanderlust for several years, seeing the U.S.A. and looking up other leathernecks. He then entered the restaurant trade, holding down a variety of positions culminating in management. He lives in Fort Lauderdale, FL.

Riddel, Bob. Radio Operator, 594th Joint Signal Assault Co., 27th Division. Riddel became a life insurance agent and now resides in Des Plaines. Il.

Roddy, Joe. Deck Officer, *USS Cepheus,* U.S. Coast Guard. Originally supportive of the decision to use the A-bomb, his mind changed after a sermon by a priest a few months later convinced him that the use of such weapons against civilians could never be justified. He worked for such magazines as *Look* and *Life* while free lancing mostly in the area of music reviews and critiques. He lives in Croton-on-Hudson, NY.

Rodman, Gage. Platoon Leader, Co. G, 17th Infantry Regiment, 7th Division. The wounds suffered on Okinawa led to a series of painful brain abcesses and operations that invalided him for life. He lives with his brother Walt, a veteran of the European Theater, in Hurricane, Utah.

Rose, Albert. Radio Technician, Marine Night Fighter Squadron VMF 533. Rose maintains strong ties to other survivors of the squadron and makes his home in Wilmington, DE.

Schlichter, Ernest. Communications Specialist, 77th Signal Company, 77th Division. Schlichter went back to the optical factory in Rochester, NY, but found himself relegated to unpleasant tasks with no regard for his four years of military service. He relocated to Columbia, SC, and held positions with an insurance company and then the Veterans Administration before chronic illness forced him to accept a pension. He lives in Columbia.

Schweitzer, Leonard. Rifleman, Co. K, 306th Regiment, 77th Division. To treat the wounds from the volley of machine gun bullets that knocked him down, surgeons performed a series of operations and fitted him with a full-body cast. After a year in hospitals he worked for a period of time at a munitions plant, then under the GI Bill, studied farm management. With his wife he acquired seven farms and other real estate in the area near his home at New London, IA.

Seibert, Donald (Si). Platoon Leader, Co. F, 382nd Regiment, 96th Division. Seibert discovered he wanted to make the service a career. "My opinion of the troops I served with on Okinawa, in Korea and in Vietnam is essentially the same. The men in general were good soldiers, responded to positive leadership and tried to accomplish their mission while remaining alive. Combat, it seems to me, at the small unit level is very personal, and survival and approval of one's buddies are the primary motivating factors. Charismatic leadership can be a factor, as when someone starts to move out in the face of great odds, but it, again, is a function of the small unit. In that context, I thought the soldiers in the three wars I participated in were very much alike. In each, of course, the men reflected the current values of the community from which they came. Obviously, the use of drugs, the racial tensions which were building during the sixties, and disenchantment with the war affected the men in Vietnam. But most of the men were typical young Americans." His home is in Fort Belvoir, VA.

Sexton, Martin (Stormy). Company Commander, Co. K, 4th Marine Regiment, 6th Marine Division. Rotated home and teaching tactics after Okinawa, he accepted a regular commission. "By that time I had five years of active duty, and my wife and I both met some wonderful families who were also assigned to Marine Corps Schools. The troops that I landed with at Inchon, Korea, were every bit as professional as the ones I had served with on Okinawa. And the same was true in Vietnam, when I commanded the 4th Marine Regiment." Retired as a colonel, he lives in Fallbrook, CA.

Siegel, William. Executive Officer, 706th Tank Battalion. Siegel helped organize a reserve tank battalion (813) while first running a parking and service center and mangaging a bank facility. He lives in Philadelphia.

Smith, Ed. Deputy Commander, 17th Regiment, 7th Division. As a West Point grad, Smith made the Army his career, commanding the 7th Division in Korea and eventually retiring as a Major General. He lives in Hilton Head, SC.

Spencer, Richard. Plans and Operations Officer, 1st Battalion, 307th Regiment, 77th Division. Awarded a Bronze Star and Purple Heart for actions in Okinawa, he died in 1991.

Staley, Ken. Rifleman, Co. K, 383rd Regiment, 96th Division. He practices commercial art and lives in Florida.

Sturgis, Alanson, Jr. Forward Observer, 292nd Joint Assault Signal Company, 77th Division. Sturgis became a high school teacher and makes his home in Portsmouth, NH.

Thom, Charles R. (Dick). Plans and Operations Officer, 381st Regiment, 96th Division. Thom organized a county-wide police force and then accepted an appointment as a judge. He lives in Port Washington, NY.

Van Arsdall, C.J. Commanding Officer, *USS Anthony.* Annapolis grad Van Arsdall continued his Navy career, achieving the rank of Rear Admiral before retirement. He lives in Gulfport, MS.

Walker, Anthony. Commanding Officer, Reconnaissance Company, 6th Marine Division. Walker remained in the Corps until retirement as a colonel. "I suppose I decided to stay on because I liked the life, was reasonably successful in the War and had nothing else to do, not being qualified or interested in other professions or business. The Marine Corps provided us with a challenging, adventurous life, which was appealing. Even proved to be a good environment for raising a family. All three sons joined the Marines. The Marines in Korea and Vietnam were the same breed as those in World War II at Okinawa, but the circumstances were different. In Vietnam, for instance, every officer and Marine rotated each year, went home. Thus we could never really produce the kind of veteran, battle-wise units we had in WW II." His home is Middletown, RI.

Westman, Paul. Rifleman, Co. K, 382nd Regiment, 96th Division. "My wife's first husband, Austin Hatcher, was in my basic training company and we shipped out together. He went to the 77th Division, saw combat on Leyte, Ie and Shima and was killed on Okinawa. I was a pall bearer for his funeral in Stillwater, Oklahoma, in 1949." Westman's wounds required a long period of convalescence in hospitals before he could leave the Army and go back to ranching and mining near Hudson, Wyoming, where he now lives.

BIBLIOGRAPHY

Appleman, Roy E., Burns, James M., Gugeler, Russell A. and Stevens, John. *Okinawa: The Last Battle* (Washington, D.C.: Center of Military History, United States Army, 1991).

Bak, Michael, Jr. Oral History Project, United States Naval Institute. (Annapolis, 1984).

Belote, James and William. *Typhoon of Steel, the Battle for Okinawa* (New York: Harper & Row, 1970).

——— Papers of (Carlisle, PA: United States Army Military History Institute).

Billingsley, Edward B. *The Emmons Saga* (Privately Published, 1989).

Bruce, Gen. Andrew D. Personal Papers (Carlisle, PA: United States Military History Institute).

Budge, Joseph. Unpublished Memoir (Moraga, CA).

Buffington, Herman. Unpublished Memoir (Jefferson, GA).

Cass, Bevan G. *History of the Sixth Marine Division* (Washington, D.C.: Infantry Journal Press, 1948).

Cook, Haruko Taya and Theodore. *Japan at War* (New York: The New Press, 1992).

Craig, Berry. *The Deadeyes* (Paducah, KY: Turner Publishing Company, 1991).

Craig, Robert. Unpublished Memoir (Winter Haven, FL).

Davidson, Orlando R., Willems, J. Carl, and Kahl, Joseph A. *The Deadeyes: The Story of the 96th Infantry Division* (Washington, D.C.: Infantry Journal Press, 1947).

Deyo, Vice Adm. M.L. *Kamikaze* (Washington, D.C.: Unpublished Memoir, United States Naval Historical Center).

Dower, John W. *War Without Mercy* (New York: Pantheon, 1986).

Fahey, James C. *The Ships and Aircraft of the United States Fleet*(New York, Ships and Aircraft, 1945).

Feifer, George. *Tennozan* (New York: Ticknor & Fields, 1992).

Fitzgerald, Ed., *A Penny An Inch,* (New York, Atheneum, 1985).

504th Field Artillery Newsletter, *The Pirate Piece* (New York).

Gerevas, Larry. Unpublished Memoir (Napa, CA).

Hallden, Col. Charles. Unpublished Memoir (Madiera Beach, FL).

Hamilton, Robert. *Reflections of an Amphibious Force Staff Officer in the Second World War.* Privately published manuscript (Sunnyvale, CA 1993).

Harries, Meirion and Susie. *Soldiers of the Sun* (New York: Random House, 1991).

Haynes, Rev. J.G. *The Last Battle.* Unpublished Memoir (Mesa, AZ).

Huber, Thomas. *Japan's Battle of Okinawa-Leavenworth Papers #18* (Fort Leavenworth, KS: U.S. Combat Studies Institute, 1990).

Inoguchi, Captain Rikihei, Tadashi, Commander Nakajima with Roger Pineau. *The Divine Wind* (Annapolis: United States Naval Institute, 1958).

Jackson, Robert. *War Stories.* Unpublished Memoir (Anacortes, WA).

Leckie, Robert. *Strong Men Armed: The United States Marines Against Japan* (New York: Random House, 1962).

Lopez, Henry D. *From Jackson to Japan* (New York: Privately Printed, 1977).

Manchester William. *Goodbye Darkness* (Boston: Little, Brown and Company, 1979).

McLane, Col. Merrill F. *Guadalcanal to Japan.* Collected letters home to Mr. & Mrs. Jesse B. McLane (Rockport and Bethesda, MD 1993).

Marbrey, Nolen. Unpublished Memoir (Brooksville, FL).

Moore, Ellis O. *Notes On Leaving Okinawa* (Pelham, NY: Privately Published, 1988).

Morison, Samuel Eliot. *New Guinea and the Marianas, Vol. VIII, History of the U.S. Naval Operations in World War II* (Boston: Little, Brown and Company, 1953).

———. *Aleutians, Gilberts and Marshalls, Vol. VII, History of U.S. Naval Operations in World War II* (Boston: Little, Brown and Company, 1951).

———. *Victory in the Pacific, 1945, Vol. XIV, History of U.S. Naval Operations in World War II* (Boston: Little, Brown and Company, 1960).

Mountcastle, John. *Trial by Fire: Incendiary Weapons 1918-1945*(Durham, NC: Duke University Doctoral Thesis, 1979).

Muehrcke, Robert (editor). *Orchids in the Mud* (Chicago: Privately Published, 1985).

Porter, Bruce (with Eric Hammel). *Ace!* (Pacifica Press, 1985).

Pyle, Ernie. *Last Chapter* (New York: Henry Holt and Company, 1946).

Rhodes, Richard. *The Making of the Atomic Bomb* (New York: Simon and Schuster, 1986).

Rodman, Gage. Unpublished Memoir (Hurricane, UT).

Roscoe, Theodore. *United States Destroyer Operations in World War II* (Annapolis: United States Naval Institute, 1953).

Schlichter, Ernest. Unpublished Copyrighted Memoir (Columbia, SC).

Seibert, Col. Donald A. Unpublished Memoir (Fort Belvoir, VA).

77th Infantry Division Association. *Ours to Hold High* (Washington, D.C.: Infantry Journal Press, 1947).

Spencer, Richard E. Unpublished Memoir (Springfield, PA).

VMF (N) 542 (Marine Night Fighter Squadron) Newsletters.

Walker, Col. Anthony (editor). *Memorial to the Men of C/P Company, 4th Marine Raider Battalion* (Middletown, RI: Privately Published, 1992).

——— (editor). *Memorial to the Men of Reconnaissance Company, 6th Marine Division* (Middletown, RI: Privately Published, 1994).

INDEX